Caribbean Trade and Integration

Caribbean Trade and Integration

ROGER HOSEIN, JEETENDRA KHADAN
AND RANITA SEECHARAN

THE UNIVERSITY OF THE WEST INDIES PRESS
Jamaica • Barbados • Trinidad and Tobago
UWI PRESS

The University of the West Indies Press
7A Gibraltar Hall Road, Mona
Kingston 7, Jamaica
www.uwipress.com

A catalogue record of this book is available from the National Library of Jamaica.

ISBN: 978-976-640-557-1 (print)
978-976-640-566-3 (Kindle)
978-976-640-575-5 (ePub)

Cover design by Robert Harris
Typesetting by The Beget, India
Printed in the United States of America

Contents

Figures

Tables

Preface

The quest for Caribbean regional integration is well documented and its success, though limited, has formed an unavoidable element in the policymaking process within many Caribbean states. While its packaging has changed from the Federation of the West Indies to CARICOM Single Market and Economy, the main motives for deeper regional economic integration remain the same: cost sharing for common services and functional cooperation, the amalgamation of bargaining power in the international market, and the affirmation of a shared West Indian identity. Certainly, few issues in Caribbean affairs have generated such heated controversy as the Caribbean's approach to regional economic integration. The long-running debate on the subject has not only played a major part in the region's trading practices but has also exposed major fault lines within many Caribbean states, particularly, weaknesses in production capacity, institutional capacity and capability, debt, among others.

This book provides a comprehensive and perceptive examination of Caribbean regional integration since the 1950s. It combines an historical account with sound economic and policy analysis to illustrate the changing and multifaceted nature of the region's integration process and the attendant implications for the region's internal and external trading relationships. The book is engaging in its discourse as it transitions from a historical overview of the roots of Caribbean regional integration to a rich assessment of the economic landscape of CARICOM economies. This is followed by a theoretical interlude of key concepts and models of economic integration, juxtaposed by attendant empirical applications for the Caribbean. Moreover, the implications of emerging economies on the Caribbean are assessed followed by an evaluation of the region's limitations to market access. Penultimately, the book reviews a survey of several key historical studies that have identified the urgent need for a change in policy action among CARICOM member states over time and that have outlined many pointed policy suggestions to effect the same. The book culminates by addressing the need to unpause the CSME and proposes a number of initiatives to generate this outcome.

Acknowledgements

I would like to acknowledge my wife, Denise Hosein, and my children, Amartya, Daniel, Jayelle, Ava and Desiree. This book would not have been completed without the assistance of Rebecca Gookool and Rishi Singh.

—Roger Hosein

I would like to acknowledge my parents, colleagues and friends for their support in writing this book. Special thanks to Ashley Bobb, Amelia Katwaroo, Satish Maharaj and Varin Edwards for their research assistance.

—Jeetendra Khadan

I would like to express sincerest gratitude to my parents, Ramnarace and Dhanpathy Seecharan, and my sister, Aneisha, for their encouragement and support in this endeavour.

—Ranita Seecharan

Abbreviations

ACP	African Caribbean and Pacific bloc
ACS	Association of Caribbean States
AfT	Aid for Trade
AFTA	ASEAN Free Trade Area
AIC	Akaike information criterion
ALBA	Alianza Bolivariana para los Pueblos de Nuestra América (Bolivarian Alliance for the Peoples of Our America)
APTA	Asia Pacific Trade Agreement
ASEAN	Association of Southeast Asian Nations
BRICS	Brazil, Russia, India, China and South Africa
CIF	cost, insurance and freight
CACM	Central American Common Market
CaFAN	Caribbean Farmers Network
CAFTA-DR	Dominican Republic–Central America–United States Free Trade Agreement
CAIC	Caribbean Association of Industry and Commerce
CAL	Caribbean Airlines
CARIBCAN	Caribbean-Canada Trade Agreement
CARICOM	Caribbean Community and Common Market
CARIFTA	Caribbean Free Trade Association
CARTfund	Caribbean Aid for Trade and Regional Integration Trust Fund
CBI	Caribbean Basin Initiative
CDB	Caribbean Development Bank
CEFTA	Central European Free Trade Agreement
CEMAC	Economic and Monetary Community of Central Africa
CEZ	common economic zone
CFNI	Caribbean Food and Nutrition Institute
CGCED	Caribbean Group for Cooperation in Economic Development Report
CGCED	Steering Committee of the Caribbean Group for Cooperation in Economic Development
CIS	Commonwealth of Independent States
CMO	common market organization
COMESA	Common Market for Eastern and Southern Africa

COTED	Council on Trade and Economic Development
CSME	CARICOM Single Market and Economy
CTAG	Caribbean Trade and Adjustment Group
CXC	Caribbean Examination Council
DLP	Democratic Labour Party
EAC	East African Community
EAEC	Eurasian Economic Community
EBA	Everything But Arms
ECLAC	Economic Commission for Latin America and the Caribbean
ECO	economic cooperation organization
ECOWAS	Economic Community of West African States
EEA	European Economic Area
EFTA	European Free Trade Association
EITI	Extractive Industries Transparency Initiative
EPA	economic partnership agreement
EU	European Union
FNS	food and nutrition security
FPE	final prediction error
FTA	free trade area
GATT	General Agreement on Tariffs and Trade
GCC	Gulf Cooperation Council
GDP	gross domestic product
GSP	generalized system of preferences
HDI	human development indicators
H-O-S	Heckscher-Ohlin-Samuelson
HQ	Hannan-Quinn information criterion
IICA	Inter-American Institute for Cooperation on Agriculture
IIT	intra-industry trade
IMF	International Monetary Fund
ISI	import substituting industrialization
LAC	Latin America and the Caribbean
LAIA	Latin American Integration Association
LDC	least developed countries
MDC	most developed countries
MERCOSUR	Mercado Común del Sur (Common Market of the South)
MFN	most favoured nation
MIIT	marginal intra-industry trade
MSG	Melanesian Spearhead Group
NAFTA	North American Free Trade Agreement
NBTs	non-tariff barriers
OAS	Organization of American States
OCT	Overseas Countries and Territories
ODA	Overseas Development Assistance
OECD	Organisation for Economic Co-operation and Development

OECS	Organization of Eastern Caribbean States
PAFTA	Pan-Arab Free Trade Area
PICTA	Pacific Island Countries Trade Agreement
PNM	People's National Movement
PNP	People's National Party
PSH	Prebisch-Singer Hypothesis
PTA	Preferential Trading Agreement
RFNSP	Regional Food and Nutrition Security Policy
RTA	regional trade agreement
RTTF	regional transformation task force
SACU	Southern African Customs Union
SADC	Southern African Development Community
SAFTA	South Asian Free Trade Agreement
SAPTA	South Asian Preferential Trade Arrangement
SC	Schwarz information criterion
SDT	special and deferential treatments
SEM	single economic market
SEZ	special economic zone
SITC	standard international trade classification
SPARTECA	South Pacific Regional Trade and Economic Cooperation Agreement
TRIMS	trade-related investment measures
TRIPS	trade-related intellectual property rights
TRTA	trade-related technical assistance
UMCIT	unmatched changes in trade index
UNCTAD	United Nations Conference on Trade and Development
UNECE	United Nations Economic Commission for Europe
VAR	vector autoregressive
VER	voluntary export restraint
WAEMU	West African Economic and Monetary Union
WDI	World Development Indicators
WIFLP	West Indies Federal Labour Party
WITS	World Integrated Trade Solution
WTO	World Trade Organization

1 | From Federation to the CARICOM Single Market and Economy

1.1 Introduction

Economic integration is probably one of the most pervasive issues of the postcolonial era in the Caribbean region. Sir Arthur Lewis was perhaps foremost among West Indian intellectuals in recognizing the need for West Indian integration. He explicitly argued in his 1950 article "The Industrialisation of the British West Indies" that before the islands of the Caribbean area engaged in any form of industrialization, they should form a customs union. He proposed the establishment of a regional customs union and a united political federation to allow the islands to benefit from harmonized customs arrangements and policies. According to Lewis, a regionalist at heart, a federation was the only solution to the problems of the islands of the region. Indeed, Lewis noted that economic and political integration has been a perennial and neuralgic issue in the Caribbean. Moreover, "the recognition of seminal truth that only a unified Caribbean politically and economically can save the region from fatal particularism is at least a century old" (Lewis 1968, 363).

1.2 West Indian Federation

Integration efforts formally began in 1958 through the formation of the West Indies Federation by the British Federal Act of 1956. This first attempt at Caribbean integration was political in nature as Caribbean countries aimed to obtain political independence from Britain as a single federal state. The federation was made up of ten members: Antigua and Barbuda, Barbados, Dominica, Grenada, Jamaica, Montserrat, St Kitts–Nevis–Anguilla, St Lucia, St Vincent and the Grenadines, and Trinidad and Tobago. Even though its aim was political independence from Britain, its head of state was in fact the crown, which had some legislative authority over certain matters such as financing the federation. Its appointed governor general was Lord Hailes of Britain and the elected prime minister was Sir Grantley Adams of Barbados with the capital of the federation being located in Trinidad and Tobago. Some commentators, such as Mordecai (1968), noted that "the Federation was designed rather to help limit the costs of the empire to an almost bankrupt post-war Britain by rendering its Caribbean territories 'viable' to sustain self-government as a single sovereign unit" (Bishop and Payne 2010, 5).

An important example of the cooperation of the federation is the University of the West Indies, which was established as the University College of the West Indies in 1948 with one campus located at Mona in Jamaica. A campus in St Augustine, Trinidad, was opened in 1960. Indeed, Mordecai (1968, 454) noted that with reference to the West Indies Federation,

> the most important accomplishment was that the regional structure of the University was saved. Moves at the Common Services meeting, suggesting that Trinidad (where the Agriculture and the new Engineering Faculties were based) would cease to support the University, were suddenly reversed on receipt of the text of a speech made by Dr. [Eric] Williams to West Indian students in London. Williams[1] had denounced anyone who wanted to break up the University and has maintained that position ever since.

In fact, Eric Williams was among the first to propose the establishment of a British West Indian university that would reflect and "take into account the social and economic needs of the islands" and documented this view in *Education in the British West Indies* (1946). He further argued that "an independent university will give to the people of the British West Indies a confidence in themselves, their roots, and their potentialities" (Palmer 2011, 6).

However, the West Indies Federation collapsed in 1962 as the two largest members Jamaica and Trinidad and Tobago withdrew seeking national autonomy. Indeed, Williams (1966, 13) noted that "the independence of Trinidad and Tobago cannot be developed on the basis of intellectual concepts and attitudes worked out by metropolitan scholars in the age of colonialism". Following the departure of Jamaica from the federation in 1961, it was up to Trinidad and Tobago to finance the majority of the budget.[2] At this point, Williams made the famous statement, "one from ten leaves nought" (Palmer 2011, 8) as it indicated that without Jamaica, the federation was nothing. It also indicated Williams's intention for Trinidad and Tobago to leave the federation and gain independence.

Tension arose in the federation (1958–62) as disagreements occurred in relation to certain proposals such as an oil refinery in Jamaica. Norman Manley's[3] proposal included a consumption tax which would in fact seek to protect Jamaica's production from Trinidad's competition. It also meant that imports from Trinidad would be reduced. Williams was against this view as he saw it as a contradiction of the ideas on which the federation was based. Therefore, Trinidad proposed a more centralized federation with authority at its centre to assist in the development of the region. Jamaica was opposed to this view and argued for a less centralized federation with limited central authority and that the region needed a design that would fit its unique circumstances. There was also contention on the free movement of people with some territories supporting this move and others against (Mordecai 1968). Trinidad and Tobago was adamant that there should be no freedom of movement and demanded that restrictions should be implemented while smaller islands in the eastern Caribbean lobbied for the federation to facilitate freedom of movement. Jamaica was Trinidad's only ally in this issue ("Trinidad and the Freedom of Movement", *Gleaner*, 5 December 2013).

In fact, Chernick (1978) argued that the West Indian federation languished mainly because federalism progressed much more slowly than the advancement of national independence, thus rendering the federation as an inferior instrument to achieve political reform. Specifically, Chernick (1978, 5) noted that "during the 1950s, the movement towards local autonomy advanced faster than that of federalism among the larger British possessions in the Caribbean. By the time of its establishment in 1958, the West Indian Federation was no longer viewed as a necessary instrument of reform. Indeed, the Federation had in the views of some commentators, built-in 'self-destruct' features, the most important of which was its lack of power to tax."

It is argued that the inability of political leaders to conduct negotiations on issues created a hindrance to successful achievement of the purpose and objectives of the federation. For instance, "the Federation fell victim to a combination of the muddled thinking of British political leaders, civil servants, the political immaturity of local Caribbean leaders, and the inadequate support and understanding of the Caribbean people it was designed to satisfy" (Bishop and Payne 2010, 5).

This point is further emphasized as Sir Arthur Lewis argued that "the leadership of the Federation was awful given that Sir Grantley Adams, Norman Manley and Dr. Eric Williams, men of immaculate integrity, were unable to understand the very nature of the Federation" (Mordecai 1968, 457). Indeed, Lewis seemed to be of the view that all three leaders were negligent in understanding the qualities required for development and success of the federation: concentration and cooperation on regional needs, the spirit of compromise, and the principles of social intercourse between equals (ibid.).

According to Lewis, the personal relationship between these men deteriorated because of the "open diplomacy" practised at that time, which meant that they rarely communicated "quietly" but instead utilized the media as the form of communication. Lewis noted that if Manley had quietly communicated his plans to Williams to protect the Jamaican oil refinery, it might have led to an understanding and saved their relationship (Mordecai 1968, 455).

Not all economists agreed with Arthur Lewis's perspective on the structure of a regional trade agreement, and Brewster and Thomas (1967) provided their variant. Specifically, they noted that "the West Indies reference is often made to federation, free trade, customs union and so on as forms of integration which either failed or, regrettably, failed to materialize. This is a natural consequence of considering integration as a purely mechanistic device. In our conception, it is possible to see these forms of association as processes of disintegration rather than integration" (Brewster and Thomas 1967, 3).

They further argued that the Caribbean region already had the relevant raw materials necessary for economic development and that a pooling of resources in the context of a well laid out regional integration plan could lead to a broadening of the productive base. In particular, even though free trade may increase trade in the region, it may be limited by the structure of demand and the limited capacity for production by the economies. Therefore, trade creation is itself limited and a custom union will not be effective unless certain conditions were established. "Integration in the West Indies should not be limited to those conditions which govern the exchange of goods, but should also include in its perspective, the integrated production of goods" (Brewster and Thomas 1967, 19). This strategy they classified as both functional and sectoral as it allowed for complete economic cooperation of sectors and involved integration from resource inputs to the sale of the final product (Brewster and Thomas 1967, 25).

Demas (1965), Brewster and Thomas (1967), and McIntyre (1971) argued against the regional economies undertaking Lewis's export-oriented industrialization. Girvan (2010, 6) explained that this was because "it focused unduly on the static efficiency gains of trade creation, which, given the small size and lack of structural diversification of regional economies, would be limited in quantum and skewed in their distribution towards the more industrially advanced countries". Instead, they proposed "development through structural transformation" to satisfy regional and incremental demand in the regional market by pooling natural resources of the economies in vertically integrated complexes. In this way, the production possibility frontier of the region would exceed that of any one economy.

1.3 Caribbean Free Trade Association

The dissolution of the federation left some members still wanting to be part of an economic union. These smaller islands, known as the West Indies Associated States (Antigua-Barbuda, St Kitts–Nevis–Anguilla, Dominica, Grenada, St Lucia and St Vincent), were viewed as being unable to act as fully independent states. Additionally, the newly independent members were at different stages of development and viewed cooperation as a way to smoothly develop their economies both individually and regionally. It was not long after Caribbean countries reconsidered regional integration, but this time through the formation of the Caribbean Free Trade Association (CARIFTA) in 1965, with the signing of the Dickenson Bay Agreement in Antigua. The founding members were Antigua and Barbuda, Barbados, Guyana, and Trinidad and Tobago. These members had recently gained independence and it became obvious that a form of union or integration would be a benefit to all instead of standing individually against the wider markets. According to Warner (2012, 3),

> Despite the failure of federation, an interest in economic integration persisted. Local economists and political thinkers, including the Caribbean's Nobel laureate in Economics, Arthur Lewis, had long argued in favour of regional integration and cooperation to address the constraints of small size on development, to share the costs of common services and to pool bargaining power in international fora. In the early 1960s Caribbean states embarked on a series of integration initiatives of expanding ambition and varying geographic coverage. These initiatives started with the establishment of the Caribbean Free Trade Association (CARIFTA) in 1965.

During that post-federation period, larger islands such as Jamaica and Trinidad and Tobago gained independence and experienced sustained economic growth which made it highly possible for these countries to be successfully independent.

By 1968, Dominica, Grenada, St Kitts–Nevis–Anguilla, St Lucia, St Vincent and the Grenadines, Montserrat, and Jamaica joined the association followed by Belize in 1971. The underlying principles of the CARIFTA agreement sought to improve the economic conditions for members of the Caribbean region. The objectives of the association as noted in article 2 of the Dickenson Bay Agreement are to

1. promote the expansion and diversification of trade in the area of the association;
2. secure that trade between member territories takes place in conditions of fair competition;
3. encourage the progressive development of the economies of the area;
4. foster the harmonious development of Caribbean trade and its liberalization by the removal of barriers to it.[4]

CARIFTA also promoted the development of the smaller islands through various initiatives, such as providing special treatment in terms of liberalizing trade barriers on sensitive sectors at a slower rate and promoting the development of their industries. CARIFTA was different in the sense that it recognized member states that were at different levels of development and it made a distinction between most developed countries (MDCs) and least developed countries (LDCs), and integration should follow along these distinctions.

In essence, the innate objectives of CARIFTA were to ensure the equitable distribution of free trade benefits among its members, promote industrial development in the LDCs and the development of the coconut industry through an "oils and fats agreement", which was significant in many of the LDCs.[5] In addition, CARIFTA sought to rationalize agricultural production in the long run, but in the interim, it desired to facilitate the marketing of selected agricultural products of particular interest to the LDCs. This was to be done through the agricultural marketing protocol. Furthermore, CARIFTA aimed to provide a longer period to phase out customs duties on certain products that were more important for the revenue of the LDCs.

CARIFTA was later replaced by the Caribbean Community (CARICOM) in 1973. CARIFTA had no significant developmental effect on the export performance of the twelve countries and as such, the larger countries, especially Jamaica and Trinidad and Tobago called for a deepening of the process. In particular, the available data showed that the free trade area experienced increases in the trade of manufactured goods, but this was mostly benefit to the MDCs (Chernick 1978, 22). According to Chernick (1978), intra-regional trade increased during the CARIFTA period; however, the MDCs accounted for 96 per cent of exports and 90 per cent of imports in 1974 with Jamaica, Trinidad and Tobago dominating intra-regional exports. Jamaica and Guyana had the largest levels of imports. The LDCs experienced decreasing exports and imports simultaneously. Another important point to note is that during the CARIFTA period, all members except Trinidad and Tobago, experienced deterioration in trade balances with Jamaica having the largest decline (see table 1.1). In particular, at the beginning of the agreement, Trinidad and Tobago recorded the largest share of regional exports with 51.6 per cent, followed by Guyana with 23 per cent. Trinidad and Tobago's dominant export position improved by 1974 and accounted for 61.9 per cent of regional exports, while Jamaica was the second largest regional exporter with 14.2 per cent, surpassing Guyana. The increase in the production of alumina in Jamaica after the mid-1960s contributed to this occurrence.[6] There was a decline in the share of imports in the LDCs as well as the MDCs, with the exception of Barbados. All LDCs and MDCs with the exception of Trinidad and Tobago sustained an unfavourable trade balance over the indicated period.

The trade matrices for the CARIFTA economies for the years 1967, 1971 and 1973 are shown in table 1.2. The matrices for 1967 and 1973 show that notwithstanding trade between Trinidad and Tobago and Guyana demonstrating the largest flows, the most noteworthy development with

Table 1.1 Intra-CARIFTA trade by category, 000s of EC\$, 1967–1974

Category	1967 Amount	%	1972 Amount	%	1973 Amount	%	1974 Amount	%
			Domestic exports (f.o.b.)					
MDCs								
Barbados	5,593	6.5	17,709	8.0	21,847	8.2	30,141	6.7
Guyana	19,903	23.0	34,722	15.6	39,128	14.7	60,909	13.5
Jamaica	10,598	12.3	41,179	18.6	47,241	17.7	64,002	14.2
Trinidad & Tobago	44,631	51.6	114,356	51.5	143,384	53.8	279,147	61.9
Subtotal	80,725	93.4	207,966	93.7	251,600	94.4	434,199	96.3
LDCs	5,755	6.6	14,022	6.3	14,691	5.5	16,608	3.7
Total	86,480	100.0	221,988	100.0	266,291	100.0	450,807	100.0
			Imports (c.i.f)					
MDCs								
Barbados	13,414	14.0	36,501	15.1	42,863	15.0	72,292	15.6
Guyana	25,741	26.9	47,337	19.6	75,987	26.5	138,013	29.7
Jamaica	8,895	9.3	63,864	26.4	68,943	24.1	145,861	31.4
Trinidad & Tobago	15,982	16.7	41,167	17.0	41,153	14.4	61,261	13.2
Subtotal	64,032	66.9	188,869	78.1	228,946	80.0	417,427	89.9
LDCs	31,652	33.1	52,953	21.9	57,457	20.0	46,863	10.1
Total	95,684	100.0	241,822	100.0	286,403	100.0	464,290	100.0
			Trade balance					
MDCs								
Barbados	−7,821		−18,792		−21,016		−42,151	
Guyana	−5,838		−12,615		−36,859		−77,104	
Jamaica	1,703		−22,685		−21,700		−81,859	
Trinidad & Tobago	28,649		73,189		102,231		217,886	
Subtotal	16,693		19,097		22,656		16,772	
LDCs	−25,897		−38,931		−42,766		−30,255	
Total	−9,204		−19,834		−20,110		−13,483	

Source: Chernick (1978) and Caribbean Community Secretariat (various years).

the inception of CARIFTA has been an improvement in trade between Trinidad and Tobago and Jamaica, particularly an expansion in exports from Trinidad and Tobago, which increased from 3.5 per cent in 1967 to 7.1 per cent by 1973. At the same time, the share of MDCs exports going to LDCs also decreased over the period 1967–73 (Chernick 1978, 29–35).

The data on exports from the MDCs reflected that there was an increase in manufactured products (SITC 5, 6, 7 and 8) which were seen by some as an indication of structural changes during the period (see table 1.3).

Table 1.2 CARIFTA matrix of trade by importers and exporters, t.o.b. values (%), 1967–1973

	Exporters						
	Barbados	Guyana	Jamaica	Trinidad & Tobago	Subtotal	LDCs	Total
1967							
Importers	–	–	–	–	–	–	–
MDCs	–	–	–	–	–	–	–
Barbados	–	0.6	–	1.5	2.1	4.4	6.5
Guyana	5.8	–	4.4	9.7	19.9	3.1	23.0
Jamaica	1.3	2.6	–	3.5	7.4	4.9	12.3
Trinidad & Tobago	8.4	21.3	3.0	–	32.7	18.9	51.6
Subtotal	15.5	24.5	7.4	14.7	62.1	31.3	93.4
LDCs	1.6	0.7	0.9	2.2	5.4	1.2	6.6
Total	17.1	25.2	8.3	16.9	67.5	32.5	100.0
1971							
MDCs	–	–	–	–	–	–	–
Barbados	–	0.5	0.5	2.0	3.0	4.1	7.1
Guyana	4.3	–	3.5	6.6	14.4	2.8	17.2
Jamaica	2.3	2.3	–	6.9	11.5	5.3	16.8
Trinidad & Tobago	9.7	17.5	10.4	–	37.6	16.5	54.1
Subtotal	16.3	20.3	14.4	15.5	66.5	28.7	95.2
LDCs	1.3	0.5	1.3	1.1	4.2	0.6	4.8
Total	17.6	20.8	15.7	16.6	70.7	29.3	100.0
1973							
MDCs	–	–	–	–	–	–	–
Barbados	–	0.7	1.4	2.8	4.9	3.4	8.3
Guyana	2.3	–	5.8	4.7	12.8	2.1	14.9
Jamaica	2.8	4.2	–	7.1	14.1	3.9	18.0
Trinidad & Tobago	8.8	17.8	15.3	–	41.9	12.8	54.7
Subtotal	13.9	22.7	22.5	14.6	73.7	22.2	95.9
LDCs	0.6	0.5	0.6	0.9	2.5	1.5	4.1
Total	14.5	23.2	23.1	15.5	76.2	23.7	100.0

Source: Chernick (1978).

1.4 The Caribbean Community

The Treaty of Chaguaramas established the Caribbean Community (CARICOM), originally referred to as the Caribbean Community and Common Market, on 4 July 1973 for the purpose of facilitating the economic and social development of its member states, and as a movement towards greater integration in the Caribbean. The initial signatories were Barbados, Guyana, Jamaica, and

Table 1.3 Composition of intra-CARIFTA exports of the MDCs by commodity group (%), 1967–1973

SITC	Commodity Group	1967	1971	1973	1967–1973 Average Annual Growth Rate (%)
0	Food	30.8	25.4	22.9	15.0
1	Beverages and tobacco	2.8	2.9	3.4	25.4
	Subtotal	33.6	28.3	26.3	16.0
2	Crude materials	1.7	2.9	0.8	7.5
3	Fuels	28.2	23.1	24.7	18.2
4	Oils and fats	0.4	0.2	0.2	11.0
	Subtotal	30.3	26.2	25.7	17.6
5	Chemicals	17.2	14.7	15.3	18.5
6	Wood, textiles, metals	12.1	13.5	13.1	22.5
7	Machinery, transport equipment	0.3	1.2	2.7	74.4
8	Clothing, footwear, similar items	6.4	16.0	16.8	42.0
	Subtotal	36.0	45.4	47.9	26.8
9	Miscellaneous	0.1	0.1	0.1	7.9
	Total	100.0	100.0	100.0	20.9

Source: Chenick (1978).

Trinidad and Tobago. The treaty entered into force on 1 August 1973. Belize, Dominica, Grenada, Montserrat, St Lucia and St Vincent became members of the community and common market in April 1974, and Antigua and St Kitts and Nevis, and Anguilla in July 1974. On 4 July 1983, the Bahamas became the thirteenth member state of the Caribbean Community. The British Virgin Islands and the Turks and Caicos Islands became associated members of CARICOM in July 1991. Several other members of the Commonwealth Caribbean and some Latin American countries now enjoy observer status in CARICOM. On 14 July 1995, Suriname became the fourteenth member of CARICOM. Haiti was granted full membership in CARICOM in July 1999.

Within the definitions of article 4 of the Treaty of Chaguaramas, the Bahamas, Barbados, Guyana, Jamaica, Suriname, and Trinidad and Tobago are referred to as MDCs, while the remaining member countries are referred to as LDCs. Provision of assistance to the LDCs came in the form of the Caribbean Development Bank (CDB), which was established in 1969. The CDB is a regional financial institution which was established by an agreement signed on 18 October 1969 in Kingston, Jamaica, and entered into force on 26 January 1970. In chapter 1, article 1 of the agreement establishing the CDB (as amended August 2007), it is stated that the "purpose of the Bank shall be to contribute to the harmonious economic growth and development of the member countries in the Caribbean (hereinafter called the 'region') and to promote economic cooperation and integration among them, having special and urgent regard to the needs of the least developed members of the region".

The CARICOM agreement has the following objectives:

1. improved standards of living and work;
2. full employment of labour and other factors of production;

3. accelerated, coordinated and sustained economic development and convergence;
4. expansion of trade and economic relations with third states;
5. enhanced levels of international competitiveness;
6. organization for increased production and productivity;
7. the achievement of a greater measure of economic leverage and effectiveness of member states in dealing with third states and group of states;
8. enhancing coordination of member states and foreign economic policies;
9. enhanced functional cooperation, including:
    a. more efficient operation of common services and activities for the benefit of its peoples;
    b. accelerated promotion of greater understanding among its peoples and the advancement of their social, cultural and technological development;
    c. intensified activities in areas such as health, education, transportation and telecommunications.

CARICOM's basic trading rule allows for the complete unrestricted flow of goods that originate from within the body of members to other members within the body. According to article 15 of the annex to the agreement, application of import duties by member states on goods that are of common market origin is prohibited. Article 21 prohibits the application of quantitative restrictions on such goods. However, these general provisions are subject to a number of exceptions, which are set down in the annex in articles 28, 29 and 56. Article 14 defines "common market origin", and the detailed rules regarding the application of that article are set out in Schedule II to the annex. It is the drive towards closer economic integration that has created the need for the development of a common market. Article 3 of the annex to the Treaty of Chaguaramas identifies the following objectives of the common market:

1. The strengthening, coordination and regulation of the economic and trade relations among member states to promote their accelerated harmonious and balanced development;
2. The sustained expansion and continuing integration of economic activities, the benefits of which shall be equally shared; and
3. The achievement of a greater measure of economic independence and effectiveness of its member states.[7]

The Common Market Council was given the responsibility, under the common market annex to the treaty, for the efficient operation and development of the common market. The council may make changes to the system in furtherance of the objectives of the common market. The detailed provisions of the system and any changes to the system agreed by the council are given effect in the member states through the enactment of domestic legislation or the adoption of other appropriate national-implementing measures.

Owing to both internal and external factors during the 1970s and the 1980s, CARICOM faced a number of challenges in their goal of deeper trade integration. Hornbeck (2008) noted that the extreme economic environment of these two eras, that is, swinging from oil price shocks and high interest rates to slow growth and rising debt discouraged the islands from further integration. In terms of trade, he further noted that from 1970 to 2003 intra-regional trade grew faster than extra-regional trade, with the former dominated by Trinidad and Tobago's oil exports. Moreover, the limited advancement in intra-regional trade after the formation of CARICOM was due to the slow progress of implementing CARICOM policies. Hornbeck added that the limited intra-regional trade could also be the result of structural factors such as the similarity of the economies of the islands and the high concentration of exports.

1.5 CARICOM Single Market and Economy

Regional integration in the Caribbean further deepened as CARICOM members in 1989 agreed to establish the CARICOM Single Market and Economy (CSME). Regional leaders urged progression to the CSME to move from a common market to a more in-depth single market and economy as the benefits of the CSME included not only the free movement of goods and services but also provisions to ensure deeper economic cooperation and integration. According to Brewster, Dolan and Stewart (2002, 4), "the CSME is an attempt to create a larger, unified economic space within which greater productive efficiency and competitiveness could be achieved and regional economic growth accelerated, particularly through the expansion of exports to increasingly liberalized hemispheric and world markets". The CSME continued to build on the foundation principles of CARICOM and expanded the scope and depth of regionalism in the Caribbean (Girvan 2010, 7). The key elements of the CSME as proposed in the Revised Treaty of Chaguaramas as noted by Kendall (2008a, 4) are as follows:

1. Free movement of goods and services (Common Market);
2. Rights of establishment (Protocol II);
3. Free movement of capital (Protocol II);
4. Free movement of labour (Protocol II);
5. Common trade policy (Protocol IV);
6. Economic, fiscal and monetary policy harmonisation (Protocols III to V);
7. Harmonisation of policy with respect to competition, consumer protection including sanitary and phyto-sanitary measures, dumping and subsidies (Protocol VIII);
8. Support to disadvantaged countries, regions and sectors (Protocol VII);
9. Other policy harmonisation (transportation policy (Protocol VI), company policy, intellectual property, technology, banking and securities, standards and technical regulations, commercial arbitration).

Table 1.4 provides the objectives of each integration arrangement for the Caribbean region.

The main areas of coverage under the CSME included (1) the removal of all barriers to intra-regional trade, (2) elimination of restrictions on the expansion of CARICOM businesses in the regional market, (3) establishment of a common external tariff, (4) coordination of internal and external trade policy and (5) facilitation of labour and capital mobility among CARICOM countries (CARICOM Secretariat 2013).

The purpose of the removal of all barriers to intra-regional trade is to allow for the free movement of goods and services within the region which will create wider market access for regional

Table 1.4 Objectives of West Indies Federation and CARIFTA

WI Federation	CARIFTA	CARICOM	CSME
Proposed political union	**Free trade area**	**Customs union/ economic union**	**Economic union**
• To create a common identity or nationalism after a period of colonization. • To create a self-governing political union to become independent from Britain.	• To promote free trade of goods among members. • To encourage product diversification to increase variety. • To liberalize trade among members by removal of tariffs and quotas on goods produced within the association. • To assist the development of LDCs. • To create a regional community.	• To deepen economic integration via a common market (free movement of goods and services). • To enhance the relationship between member states by the coordination of foreign policies and deepening functional cooperation. • To assist and expand trade relations with LDCs.	• To promote a single market and progress to a single economy. • To further deepen integration by encouraging the free movement of capital and labour. • To promote common trade policies. • To engage in economic, fiscal and monetary policy harmonization in order to strengthen regional integration within the union. • To sustain a regional development to assist LDCs.

Source: Caribbean Community Secretariat (various years).

producers and encourage competition. It will improve quality standards, increase efficiency and result in more competitive prices, on a regional and international scale.

The elimination of restrictions on the expansion of CARICOM businesses in the regional market allows nationals to move to any member country to establish businesses. It relates to the rights of establishment or protocol II. The purpose is to create competition regionally and internationally.

> Again, the intention is essentially the same – to enhance the performance of regional service providers through the promotion of competition. As in the case of the producers of goods, however, the ability to survive depends not only on the ability to be competitive regionally, but also internationally. Of course, the Rights of Establishment apply not only to service providers but to all producers, who now have the right to establish production anywhere within the Region. (Kendall 2008a, 5)

The establishment of a common external tariff (CET) is intended to encourage trade between members of the CSME and discourage trade with countries that do not belong to the union. The purpose of the coordination of internal and external trade policies is to create common trade policies as this will improve bargaining power in a global context. The facilitation of labour and capital mobility among CARICOM countries is intended to generate a cohesive Caribbean labour

Table 1.5 Economic integration initiatives from CARIFTA to the CSME

	CARIFTA	CARICOM	CARICOM Revised/CSME	Single Development Vision
Duration	1968–1973	1973–1989	Post-1989	2008–2015
Membership	12 anglophone Caribbean countries	13 anglophone Caribbean countries	CARICOM: 15 countries CSME: 12 countries	12 CSME member countries
Form	Free trade area	Customs union	Economic union	Economic union
Scope	Merchandize trade	1. Merchandize trade 2. Minimal provision for services and capital 3. Incentives policy harmonization 4. Industrial allocation 5. Joint development of agriculture and natural resources	1. Merchandize trade 2. Services 3. Capital 4. Skilled labour 5. Macroeconomic policy harmonization 6. Monetary union 7. Sectoral policy harmonization	1. CSME completion road-map 2. Multi-dimensional development framework 3. Coordinated policies for economic drivers 4. Coordinated policies for enabling an economic environment

Source: Girvan (2010).

market by removing restrictions to intra-regional movement of skills and establishing common equivalency and accreditation standards. The purpose of capital mobility is to integrate capital markets, encourage a common currency and remove foreign exchange controls.

Regional integration agreements in the Caribbean have focused largely on setting a framework to enhance trade and economic relations among CARICOM members (see table 1.5).

1.6 Organization of Eastern Caribbean States

The Organization of Eastern Caribbean States (OECS) was signed on 18 June 1981 under the Treaty of Basseterre. Its members include Antigua and Barbuda, Dominica, Grenada, Montserrat, St Kitts and Nevis, St Lucia, St Vincent and the Grenadines, Anguilla, and the British Virgin Islands. The treaty was signed with the intention that the countries agree to cooperate with each other and promote unity. The OECS grew out from the perspective that small islands were disadvantaged in the sense that they are unable to survive and cope with competition independently. The idea was to encourage cooperation and common representation. The organization's objectives as set out in the Treaty of Basseterre were:

1. to promote cooperation among the member states and the regional and international level;
2. to promote unity and solidarity among the member states and to defend their sovereignty, territorial integrity and independence;

3. to assist the member states in the realization of their obligations and responsibilities to the international community with due regard to the role of international law as a standard of conduct in their relationships;

4. to seek to achieve the fullest possible level of harmonization of foreign policy among the member states; to seek to adopt, as far as possible, common positions on international issues and to establish and to maintain wherever possible, arrangements for joint overseas representation and/or common services;

5. to promote economic integration among the member states;

6. to pursue these purposes through its respective institutions by discussion of questions of common concern and by agreement and common action.

The OECS was originally viewed as a monetary union.

In June 2010 the Revised Treaty of Basseterre was signed to establish the OECS Economic Union and subsequently came into force in January 2011. It makes provision for the pooling of national sovereignty at the supranational level, with the OECS gaining legislative competence in five areas: the common market and customs union, monetary policy, trade policy, civil aviation, and maritime jurisdiction and boundaries. Over time, it is conceivable that further areas of competence will become the purview of the subregion, rather than national governments. Issues which CARICOM has struggled to resolve have been resolved within the OECS; for example, all people of the subregion will be able to move and work freely in other member states by August 2011. In addition, it is expected that a regional Assembly of Parliamentarians (with, initially, national politicians operating at the OECS level) will also become influential in the organization's policymaking. (Bishop et al. 2011, 25)

The Protocol of Eastern Caribbean Economic Union under the Revised Treaty of Basseterre is geared towards creating closer economic relations among the members (article 2) to contribute towards the growth of each member state and the community at large. Article 3 of the Protocol of Eastern Caribbean Economic Union states the following:

1. The prohibition, as between Protocol member states, of customs duties and of quantitative restrictions on the importation and exportation of goods, as well as of all other measures with equivalent effect;

2. Subject to article 35, the establishment of common customs tariffs and common commercial policies towards countries and territories not parties to this Protocol;

3. The abolition, as between Protocol member states, of the obstacles to the free movement of persons, services and capital;

4. The progressive harmonization of investment and development policies;

5. The coordination of monetary and financial policies;

6. The progressive harmonization of taxation policies and incentive legislation;

7. A cooperative approach to infrastructural development especially in the fields of transport and communications, utilities, education, health, social protection, and public administration;

8. A common policy toward development in agriculture, manufacturing, tourism, information and communications technology, and other services;

9. The facilitation by the appropriate authorities, institutions and instruments of cross-border economic and financial activities between Protocol member states;
10. Joint negotiating stances and arrangements for negotiations between Protocol member states and third countries or groups of countries;
11. A common social policy framework for national and regional development; and
12. A common competition policy.

ECLAC (2007) recognized the impact of special and deferential treatments (SDT) on the economic asymmetries within the Association of Caribbean States (ACS). In terms of the Caribbean region, the report noted that SDT were incorporated into the defined objectives of CARICOM to achieve a number of goals, namely,

1. to increase the flow of resources to LDCs;
2. to aid in the ascension of the OECS into a trade regime;
3. to remove the common market initial point of CARICOM;
4. to recognize the difference in economic conditions among the Caribbean countries; and
5. to reduce the polarization among the member states of CARICOM.

The signed CARICOM treaty articles 56 and 59 dealt with SDT, where article 56 focused on facilitating production in the LDC and article 59 allowed for the flow of capital into LDCs. The report noted that overall SDT in CARICOM was dealt with in a three pronged approach based on trade facilitation and regulation, capital movements facilitation and finance flow facilitation to LDCs. According to the report, overall the SDT inclusion into the CARICOM treaty did protect the food and beverage sector of the OECS countries; however, over time the OECS lost market share both regionally and internationally.

The report also noted that in the late 1980s and early 1990s, there was some economic convergence between the OECS and CARICOM; however, this was followed by increased divergence in the later part of the 1990s and onwards. This divergence, the report went on to note, can be partly blamed on the partial implementation of some of the SDT goals but it also occurred when there were wide economic imbalances between CARICOM and the rest of the world. These imbalances took the form of fiscal imbalances, constraints of balance of payments and high levels of foreign debt. Owing to all of these factors, the OECS islands became more polarized, even within CARICOM.

Despite the many challenges and hiccups faced by the region with regard to integration, the fact that some level of integration has survived since the 1960s, according to Hall and Sang (2012), is due to the similar historical evolution of the islands. Hall and Sang (2012) noted that the region's common history of slavery, indentureship, religious beliefs and a common language has led to a common identity among the islands. This in turn has forged a bond of unity among the islands based on similar values and shared beliefs and despite the many issues that arise, some level of integration remains.

1.7 Conclusion

This chapter provided a review on the regional integration initiatives in the Caribbean from the establishment of the Federation of the West Indies in 1956 to the CSME. The history and evolution of Caribbean integration was discussed and it is noted that these efforts have expanded from a focus largely on improving intra-regional trade under CARIFTA to one that encompasses the free movement of factors of production and engendering a greater level of functional cooperation under CARICOM and the CSME.

2 | Macroeconomic Overview of CARICOM Economies

2.1 Introduction

A major constraint to the development of small poor nations is their inability to finance the development process. An important aspect of this process is the expansion of infrastructural, human and physical capital, which is critical to the growth of output and the creation of employment. In the absence of adequate domestic financial resources, countries tend to look abroad. Given the increasing competition for foreign capital, CARICOM countries need to pay greater attention not only to resource mobilization but also to resource use.[8]

Standard Keynesian economics relates that the level of savings determines the level of investment in any country. Aggregate savings comprise three main components: government savings, private savings and corporate savings. Government savings in most LDCs are customarily low, particularly as the revenue base of the government is usually narrow and the growth of the main taxable items is either low or negative. In contrast, the pressure on governments to spend is great, given the need not only to provide current goods and services to their populations, but also to increase the capital stock. With respect to personal savings, low levels of income means that the marginal propensity to consume is high, so that the amount of savings that would be available from the private sector, at least from individuals, may be quite low. Low savings in turn tend to hamper the capital formation process and so create a vicious cycle by inhibiting income growth.

Foreign savings can be used to help finance the developmental process in LDCs. Foreign direct investment (FDI), loans and gifts can increase foreign exchange availability to developing countries and can play a critical role in financing consumption and investment. In the absence of adequate foreign exchange earnings from exports, countries tend to become increasingly dependent on foreign borrowing to the extent they can do so. Borrowing itself, however, can become a problem when servicing capacity is adversely affected for one reason or another, including the poor use of resources. When a high proportion of foreign exchange earnings and public revenues are diverted to debt servicing, not only can serious social problems emerge creating an unstable environment, but the development effort itself can be compromised, in terms of expanding and diversifying output and trade capacity. As far as CARICOM countries are concerned, trade has a deep influence on their welfare and development prospects.

This chapter assesses aspects of the economic landscape in CARICOM. In particular, it assesses the macroeconomic performance of CARICOM countries in the 1990s. It examines the debt dilemma of CARICOM states including the fiscal burden of interest payments, some important characteristics of CARICOM's trade including their external competitiveness, terms of trade and the relationship between the composition of trade and public revenues growth, as well as examines of the implications of free trade for future public revenue flows in the region.

2.2 Economic Overview of CARICOM Countries

2.2.1 Gross Domestic Product: Growth and Structure

The level and growth of economic activity has a major effect on the magnitude of the public revenues of any country as it conditions the size of individual and corporate incomes (of course, there are other factors that determine the relationship between the two aggregates). A decline in total production often has a negative impact on the government purse, and any reduction in revenue can have a ripple effect in the society, impacting on the basic social and economic conditions which in turn can have a negative feedback on productive capacity. As open economies, trade plays a major role in the economic performance of Caribbean states. Prices and production levels are affected by a wide array of internal and external factors making volatility a major feature of these societies. In 2000, real gross domestic product (GDP) of CARICOM member states were higher than in 1990 for the most part, but there were wide differences in the growth rates in this period and the subsequent years (see table 2.1). In particular, Grenada's growth fell dramatically from 17.5 per cent to −0.8 per cent between 2000 and 2012. Similar observations can be made for Trinidad and Tobago, Belize between 1990 and 2009 and St Kitts and Nevis between 1995 and 2009. Guyana and Suriname were the only two countries to record consistent growth after 2008. The fastest growing economies overall on average from 1990 to 2012 were Belize and Trinidad and Tobago (over 4.5 per cent on average), followed by St Kitts and Nevis (3.9 per cent), Guyana (3.5 per cent), and St Vincent and the Grenadines (3 per cent). Three other countries had rates exceeding 2.5 per cent, while Jamaica which has the largest population in CARICOM (excluding Haiti) experienced an average growth rate of less than 1 per cent.

Owing to an expanding tourism industry, foreign investment inflows and increased earnings from banana exports, the LDCs of CARICOM performed favourably in the 1980s growing by more than 5 per cent per year on average (see table 2.2). In the 1990s, the growth rate fell in the LDCs as a result of the confluence of several factors, an important one being the decline of the banana industry. Economic activity, however, picked up in the MDCs, with real income increasing by 37 per cent between 1990 and 2000 in Trinidad and Tobago, although it was not

Table 2.1 Real GDP growth rates in CARICOM member states (%), 1990–2012

Country	1990	1995	2000	2005	2006	2007	2008	2009	2010	2011	2012	Average (1990–2012)
Antigua & Barbuda	2.5	−4.2	1.5	6.1	13.4	9.5	0.1	−12.0	−7.1	−2.8	2.3	2.4
Bahamas	−1.6	4.4	4.1	3.4	2.5	1.4	−2.3	−4.2	1.0	1.7	1.8	1.5
Barbados	−3.3	2.0	2.3	4.0	5.7	1.7	0.3	−4.1	0.2	0.6	0.2	0.8
Belize	11.4	0.3	12.3	3.0	4.7	1.2	3.9	0.3	3.9	2.3	5.3	4.7
Dominica	6.4	3.4	0.6	−0.3	4.6	6.0	7.8	−1.1	1.2	1.0	−1.5	2.5
Grenada	5.2	3.1	17.5	13.3	−4.0	6.1	0.9	−6.7	−0.4	1.0	−0.8	2.9
Guyana	−3.0	4.6	−0.7	−2.0	5.1	7.0	2.0	3.3	4.4	5.4	4.8	3.5
Jamaica	6.3	2.5	0.7	0.9	2.9	1.4	−0.8	−3.5	−1.5	1.3	−0.3	0.9
St Kitts & Nevis	3.1	22.1	4.3	8.9	6.0	2.8	4.6	−6.0	0.2	1.7	−1.1	3.9
St Vincent & the Grenadines	6.7	8.9	1.8	2.5	7.7	3.3	1.6	−2.3	−3.4	−0.7	1.5	3.0
St Lucia	4.4	1.7	−0.2	−1.2	8.9	1.6	5.1	0.4	0.2	1.4	−3.0	2.3
Suriname	−4.6	2.8	1.9	7.2	11.4	4.0	3.1	7.7	7.3	4.7	4.4	2.8
Trinidad & Tobago	1.5	4.0	6.9	5.4	14.4	4.5	3.4	−4.4	0.2	−2.6	1.2	4.5

Source: United Nations Economic Commission for Latin America and the Caribbean (ECLAC) (2014).

until 1999 that this country retained the level of GDP it carried in 1983. Throughout the 1990s, however, the Jamaican economy stagnated with growth averaging just above 1 per cent per year. Between 2001 and 2009, some reversion in countries' growth rates occurred, with Trinidad and Tobago and Suriname boasting of strong growth performances above 4 per cent. For the individual years, 2010, 2011 and 2012, Guyana and Suriname stood out as consistent real economic growth trends were reported above 4 per cent, for each economy.

Of course, the pattern of growth in total production tends to be reflected in trends in per capita income, which can also fluctuate correspondingly. As seen in table 2.3, real per capita income has grown, although the performances of the 1970s and 1980s have never been replicated. Steady growth since the 1990s has been realized by most of the countries, however, for the period 2001–9 per capita growth trends have deteriorated. In particular, the Bahamas, Barbados, Belize, Grenada, Guyana, Jamaica, St Kitts and Nevis, and St Vincent and the Grenadines have all posted reductions in growth relative to the period 1991–2000. Again, Trinidad and Tobago and Suriname outperformed their regional partners, reporting percentages above 3.5 for the period 2001–9. As was the case demonstrated in table 2.2, Guyana and Suriname recorded strong, consistent per capita growth performances for the individual years 2010, 2011 and 2012.

In the 1960s, heavy dependence on a few primary exports for foreign exchange earnings, government revenue, income and employment was seen as a major weakness in the functioning of Caribbean economies, and diversification was a major objective of the development plans of the various territories. Economic integration was also pursued as a means of developing a larger

Table 2.2 Average growth rates of real GDP (%), 1961–2012

	1961–1970	1971–1980	1981–1990	1991–2000	2001–2009	2010	2011	2012	1961–2012
Antigua & Barbuda	–	6.71	6.14	3.63	3.09	–7.14	–2.82	2.33	3.94
Bahamas	8.30	3.53	3.23	2.21	0.65	0.99	1.66	1.83	3.52
Barbados	6.67	2.87	1.28	1.58	–0.11	–	–	–	0.46
Belize	5.16	7.37	5.07	6.01	4.06	2.90	1.93	–	3.41
Dominica	–	2.53	5.38	1.19	3.28	1.20	1.01	–1.45	2.96
Grenada	–	3.66	5.57	3.33	2.15	–0.35	0.97	–0.82	3.40
Guyana	3.72	1.42	–3.28	4.95	1.16	4.37	5.44	4.82	1.79
Jamaica	12.06	–0.56	2.72	1.83	–0.39	–1.50	1.30	–0.30	1.59
St Kitts & Nevis	–	8.26	5.47	3.84	3.02	0.23	1.69	–1.07	4.17
St Lucia	–	–	7.62	3.28	2.44	0.23	1.39	–3.04	4.05
St Vincent & the Grenadines	1.71	3.18	6.07	3.00	3.60	–3.35	–0.67	1.52	3.26
Suriname	–	0.58	–0.90	0.73	4.98	4.14	4.67	4.48	1.60
Trinidad & Tobago	4.83	5.33	–2.15	3.20	6.41	0.21	–2.58	1.24	3.24

Source: World Development Indicators (2014).

Table 2.3 Average growth rates of real GDP per capita (%), 1971–2012

	1971–1980	1981–1990	1991–2000	2001–2009	2010	2011	2012	1971–2012
Antigua & Barbuda	3.36	7.42	1.20	1.79	−8.85	−6.00	−0.10	2.88
Bahamas	1.29	1.23	1.01	−0.85	−1.14	0.37	1.30	0.67
Barbados	2.09	0.57	0.81	0.79	−0.01	0.38	0.68	1.02
Belize	2.36	2.24	2.36	1.81	0.69	0.34	2.16	2.12
Dominica	4.44	6.03	2.12	3.18	2.33	0.66	2.02	3.80
Grenada	6.56	4.18	4.14	0.72	0.05	−0.38	0.01	3.69
Guyana	1.08	−2.61	4.84	1.86	3.43	4.37	3.58	1.46
Jamaica	−1.96	1.47	0.60	0.29	−1.81	1.13	−0.56	0.06
St Kitts & Nevis	5.52	6.42	3.33	1.48	−3.65	−1.27	−1.99	3.79
St Lucia	3.89	5.26	1.28	1.55	−0.64	0.25	−0.09	2.80
St Vincent & the Grenadines	1.98	5.75	3.23	3.00	−2.82	0.11	1.50	3.22
Suriname	3.01	0.05	−0.42	3.55	3.15	3.56	2.68	1.61
Trinidad & Tobago	4.19	−3.45	3.86	5.99	2.12	−1.73	0.65	2.40

Source: United Nations Conference on Trade and Development (UNCTAD) (2014).

manufacturing sector. As a result of the policies adopted in the post-independence period, a perverse kind of development has taken place, which in essential ways has weakened rather than strengthened the economic structure. Some CARICOM economies were basically agricultural in nature, but the labour-intensive agricultural sector with one or two exceptions has been declining, leading to greater dependence on food imports, and loss of employment opportunities and foreign exchange earnings. Continued efforts at trade liberalization were also expected to impact on the agricultural sector negatively in the absence of policies to revitalize this sector. The diversion of agricultural land to non-agricultural uses did not help to improve this situation.

The structure of a nation's economic activity is always an important matter as it has implications for the nature of its employment pattern and the extent of foreign technological diffusion, and so on. In particular, it is widely understood that a country with a large manufacturing sector can benefit from favourable price and income elasticities of demand, technological spillovers and greater learning by doing. Some authors, such as Hirschman (1958), have also identified the greater backward and forward linkages between manufacturing and the rest of the economy. Hirschman (1958, 109–10) argued

> the lack of interdependencies and linkages is of course one of the most typical characteristics of underdeveloped economies . . . agriculture in general and subsistence agriculture in particular, are of course characterized by the scarcity of linkages effects. By definition, all primary production should exclude any substantial degree of backward linkage . . . the case for inferiority of agriculture to manufacturing has most frequently been argued on grounds of comparative productivity. While this case has been shown not to be entirely convincing, agriculture certainly stands convicted on the count of

its lack of direct stimulus to setting up new activities through linkage effects: the superiority of manufacture in this respect is crushing. This may yet be the most important reason militating against any complete specialisation of underdeveloped countries in primary production.

In the early 1980s, the agriculture sector accounted for a large share of GDP, with Dominica, Grenada and Guyana being the only member states of CARICOM in which the agricultural sector accounted for more than 21 per cent of GDP (see table 2.4). As concerns Guyana, the rice and sugar industries have benefited from measures aimed at increasing production through reorganization and the adoption of more up-to-date and relevant technologies.[9] The success of these measures is partially reflected in an increase in the contribution of the sugar cane industry to Guyana's GDP from 9 per cent to 17 per cent between 1990 and 2000 (ECLAC 2002).

It may be argued that for CARICOM as a whole, the relative decline in the output share of the agricultural sector is as a result of its weakening competitiveness. This is the consequence of higher production costs, external shocks and, in particular, dependence on margins of preference which has helped to stimulate X-inefficiency in intra-regional production functions (in this context, X-inefficiency refers to the managerial slack offered by safe extra-regional markets such as the European Union). With high costs of production, profit margins are seriously affected and this in turn retards the reinvestment capability of firms and hence their dynamic competitiveness.

The share of the mining sector in GDP in countries such as Jamaica, Suriname, Guyana, and Trinidad and Tobago fluctuates from year to year within what appears to be a long-term increasing trend (with the exception of Jamaica). Trinidad and Tobago has, in fact, moved from an oil-based to a gas-based economy producing a range of energy intensive products for exports. While the mining sector is still important in terms of foreign exchange earnings, it is less so for employment and has few linkages with the rest of the economy. Excluding the refining and processing of traditional primary products, manufacturing accounts for less than 10 per cent of GDP in most cases and production is largely for the local and regional market. In its present form, the employment potential is small despite being one of the largest sources of foreign exchange, particularly for Trinidad and Tobago in the last decade. Leaving aside traditional refining activities, the manufacturing sector of CARICOM caters mainly to the protected intra-regional market, the Canadian (under the Caribbean-Canada Trade Agreement [CARIBCAN] and the Canada-CARICOM Free Trade Area [FTA] presently under negotiation) and the United States (through the Caribbean Basin Initiative [CBI]) markets. In many regards though, this manufacturing sector has not adequately blossomed to achieve the level of efficiency necessary to break into extra-regional markets, which do not offer CARICOM member states margins of preference.

In most Caribbean economies, services account for more than 60 per cent of GDP (see table 2.4). Tourism is the dominant activity in the smaller islands and has emerged as the single most important foreign exchange earner in most of them. Experience has shown that tourism is a competitive and volatile industry easily affected by a range of forces outside the control of national governments. The activity itself has a high import content and little linkage with the rest of the economy.

CARICOM provides a market for certain lines of production, while the bulk of the region's trade is with the outside world. If integration, however, is confined to simple market integration, this will have limited impact on employment and growth, since the small market by itself cannot provide the stimulus for trade creation and growth.

Table 2.4 Structural composition of GDP in CARICOM countries (%)

	Year	Agriculture	Mining and Quarrying	Manufacturing	Services
Antigua & Barbuda	1981	6.6	0.4	4.6	88.4
	2012	1.8	0.7	2.2	85.8
Barbados	1981	8.7	0.5	11.6	79.2
	2011	2.1	0.4	3.7	78.8
Dominica	1993	23.8	0.8	7.6	67.8
	2012	12.9	1.4	2.6	76.1
Grenada	1981	21.7	0.4	5.4	72.6
	2012	4.7	0.2	3.2	80.3
Guyana	1981	24.9	16.1	18.1	40.7
	2012	16.4	18.7	5.6	53.9
Jamaica	1982	6.6	10.7	17.4	65.4
	2012	5.6	1.1	7.8	78.4
St Kitts & Nevis	1981	16.7	0.2	14.5	68.6
	2012	1.4	0.1	9.0	77.0
St Vincent & the Grenadines	1981	19.3	0.3	10.4	70.0
	2012	6.2	0.2	5.6	75.9
St Lucia	1985	12.6	0.5	8.6	78.3
	2012	3.5	0.2	3.4	83.4
Suriname	1981	9.6	7.1	17.6	65.8
	2012	9.7	9.2	23.3	51.1
Trinidad & Tobago	1980	1.9	23.5	9.8	64.8
	2012	0.6	43.1	6.0	50.3

Note: Values for 2011/2012 do not sum to 100 due to changes in the classification of industries.

Source: United Nations Economic Commission for Latin America and the Caribbean (ECLAC) (2014).

2.2.2 The Balance of Payments and Foreign Direct Investment Flows

Commercial service exports (the main commercial export of CARICOM countries is tourism) of CARICOM countries increased from US$4.15 billion in 1990 to US$7.06 billion in 2011, an increase of 70 per cent at current prices. For all individual member states, the trend has been for the exports of commercial services to increase between 1990 and 2011. The range of commercial service exports for 1990 was from US$0.03 billion in Dominica and Suriname to US$1.47 billion in the Bahamas. In 2011, the range of commercial service exports was from US$0.13 billion in Dominica to US$2.59 billion in Jamaica (see table 2.5). The rapid growth in commercial service exports for Jamaica can be attributed to increase in personal travel by tourists (table 2.6).

Tourism export revenues have become an important part of the export earnings of some CARICOM economies. In terms of tourist arrivals, the number of tourists visiting each CARICOM member state expanded between 1990 and 2011, and correspondingly, the amount of

Table 2.5 Commercial service exports of CARICOM member states, US$ billion, 1990–2011

	1990	1995	2000	2005	2006	2007	2008	2009	2010	2011
Antigua & Barbuda	0.31	0.35	0.41	0.45	0.46	0.51	0.55	0.5	0.47	0.48
Bahamas	1.47	1.52	2.00	2.46	2.40	2.57	2.49	2.31	2.46	2.56
Barbados	0.63	0.84	1.06	1.43	1.58	1.67	1.79	1.46	1.60	–
Belize	0.08	0.12	0.15	0.29	0.34	0.37	0.36	0.32	0.33	0.31
Dominica	0.03	0.06	0.09	0.09	0.10	0.11	0.12	0.11	0.12	0.13
Grenada	0.06	0.10	0.15	0.11	0.13	0.15	0.15	0.14	0.14	0.15
Guyana	–	0.13	–	0.15	0.15	0.17	0.21	0.17	0.25	–
Jamaica	0.98	1.57	1.99	2.30	2.61	2.67	2.76	2.62	2.60	2.59
St Kitts & Nevis	0.05	0.08	0.09	0.16	0.17	0.17	0.16	0.13	0.13	0.14
St Lucia	0.15	0.26	0.31	0.43	0.34	0.35	0.36	0.35	0.39	0.38
St Vincent & the Grenadines	0.04	0.07	0.12	0.16	0.17	0.16	0.15	0.14	0.14	0.14
Suriname	0.03	0.10	0.09	0.18	0.21	0.22	0.23	0.26	0.21	0.19
Trinidad & Tobago	0.32	0.33	–	0.88	0.80	0.91	0.92	0.76	0.87	–

Source: World Development Indicators (2014).

tourist receipts earned by each member state also increased. Jamaica remains the largest recipient of tourists among all the member states with numbers increasing by 132 per cent since 1990. It also receives the second largest amount of tourism receipts (US$2.06 billion in 2011) in relation to its CARICOM counterparts. Note though that between 1990 and 2011, the relative share of total export earnings accounted for by the tourism sector declined in Antigua and Barbuda, Bahamas, Barbados, Guyana, and St Kitts and Nevis (table 2.6).

With respect to current account balances as a percentage of GDP, the following trends are observed for the period 1990–2012. In 1990, the average current account balance as a percentage of GDP for CARICOM as a whole was –8.03 per cent, worsening to –9.69 per cent in 2012 (table 2.7). According to table 2.7, it can be noted that with the exception of Trinidad and Tobago and Suriname, all countries showed an average negative current account balance for the period 1990–2012. Grenada and St Vincent averaged current account balances as a percentage of GDP are –26.16 per cent and –22.39 per cent, respectively. St Kitts and Nevis, Dominica, and St Lucia were listed as –19.72 per cent, –18.79 per cent and –18.2 per cent, respectively. Trinidad and Tobago had the highest current account balance of 16.82 per cent followed by Suriname which attained a balance of 6.85 per cent of GDP.

Tables 2.8 and 2.9 provide data on the position of CARICOM member states with respect to net FDI inflows. The CARICOM region received a total of US$410.1 million in net FDI inflows in 1990 as compared to US$5,303.9 million in 2012, an increase of 1,193 per cent (at current prices). In 1990, the biggest recipient of FDI was Jamaica that received US$174.9 million, with Suriname experiencing a net outflow of FDI amounting US$76.8 million. By 2012, however, the largest recipient of net FDI in the CARICOM region was Trinidad and Tobago which received US$2,527.1 million as compared to the paltry US$19.7 million received by Dominica and US$70.1 million received by Suriname. The growth in Trinidad and Tobago's receipt of net FDI

Table 2.6 Tourist arrivals and tourism receipts in selected Caribbean countries, 1990 and 2011

	Number of Tourist Arrivals (000)		Tourism Receipts (US$ Million)		Tourism Earnings as % of Total Export Earnings	
	1990	2011	1990	2011	1990	2011
Antigua & Barbuda	197	241	298	312	86.4	58.1
Bahamas	1,562	1,346	1,324	2,269	87.9	66.0
Barbados	432	568	494	1,074[a]	59.1	51.9[a]
Belize	88	250	51	253	19.0	26.8
Dominica	45	76	20	98	19.4	58.9
Grenada	76	118	38	105	36.0	57.0
Guyana	6	157	27	80[a]	10.7	7.1[a]
Jamaica	841	1,952	740	2,060	30.1	48.1
St Kitts & Nevis	73	92[a]	63	93	61.2	40.8
St Lucia	141	312	154	317	51.1	56.7
St Vincent & the Grenadines	54	74	56	90	37.7	48.3
Suriname	28	220	1	69	0.2	2.6
Trinidad & Tobago	195	386[a]	95	630[a]	4.1	5.2[a]

[a] Refers to 2010 data.

Source: World Development Indicators (2014).

Table 2.7 Current account balance as a % of GDP in CARICOM countries, 1990–2012

	1990	1995	2000	2005	2006	2007	2008	2009	2010	2011	2012
Antigua & Barbuda	−8.0	−0.1	−11.9	−17.1	−25.7	−29.9	−25.9	−14.0	−14.3	−11.1	−6.9
Bahamas	−3.1	−4.2	−14.8	−9.1	−17.6	−15.8	−14.8	−10.3	−10.3	−14.4	−17.5
Barbados	−1.0	2.3	−6.0	−15.5	−11.1	−8.1	−13.0	−7.2	−5.3	−8.5	−5.7
Belize	3.9	−2.9	−10.6	−13.6	−2.1	−4.1	−10.6	−6.1	−3.3	−2.9	−1.6
Dominica	−25.6	−18.5	−15.3	−21.0	−13.0	−21.1	−27.5	−21.2	−17.3	−14.7	−11.5
Grenada	−20.9	−14.8	−17.9	−27.6	−32.4	−34.8	−33.2	−24.4	−28.7	−25.1	−28.0
Guyana	–	−21.7	−11.0	−11.7	−12.4	−6.5	−10.0	−8.2	−7.1	−14.4	−13.9
Jamaica	−8.2	−1.8	−3.0	−9.7	−9.9	−15.9	−20.4	−9.3	−7.1	−14.3	12.9
St Kitts & Nevis	−29.4	−19.8	−27.7	−12.1	−13.4	−16.2	−23.8	−24.2	−18.1	−15.2	−17.0
St Lucia	−11.4	−5.9	−11.8	−14.3	−30.6	−30.6	−29.2	−12.0	−15.2	−15.8	−23.4
St Vincent & the Grenadines	−13.5	−5.8	−8.1	−18.5	−19.5	−28.0	−33.1	−29.3	−31.3	−28.9	−30.3
Suriname	11.7	17.9	−3.3	−8.0	8.4	11.1	9.2	2.9	14.9	5.8	4.8
Trinidad & Tobago	9.1	5.5	0.5	24.1	38.6	23.8	30.3	8.5	20.2	12.3	12.1

Sources: United Nations Conference on Trade and Development (UNCTAD) (2014) and World Development Indicators (2014) and Country Reports (various years).

Table 2.8 Net foreign direct investment inflows in CARICOM member states, US$ million, 1990–2012

	1990	1995	2000	2005	2006	2007	2008	2009	2010	2011	2012
Antigua & Barbuda	58.8	31.5	66.6	237.5	361.0	340.5	160.8	84.6	101.3	68.3	74.0
Bahamas	−17.3	106.8	609.1	1,054.3	1,492.1	1,622.8	1,512.3	873.1	1,147.6	1,533.3	1,093.9
Barbados	11.2	11.8	54.7	240.0	342.3	476.4	464.1	247.1	289.7	532.3	356.4
Belize	19.0	20.8	29.6	155.1	116.6	150.3	180.1	113.1	99.8	98.5	197.9
Dominica	7.6	54.1	20.3	32.2	28.9	47.9	56.8	43.0	24.9	14.2	19.7
Grenada	13.1	20.0	39.4	73.3	95.6	172.4	140.7	104.0	63.6	45.2	32.6
Guyana	7.9	74.4	67.1	76.8	102.4	152.4	168.0	208.0	269.6	215.2	230.9
Jamaica	174.9	147.4	468.8	682.5	882.2	866.5	1,436.6	540.9	227.7	218.2	362.2
St Kitts & Nevis	48.8	20.5	99.0	104.3	114.6	140.8	183.9	136.0	118.8	111.6	100.8
St Lucia	45.9	32.8	58.2	82.0	237.7	277.5	166.2	151.9	126.6	116.3	112.8
St Vincent & the Grenadines	7.7	30.6	37.8	40.7	109.8	121.0	159.3	111.0	97.4	85.8	125.5
Suriname	−76.8	−20.6	−148.0	27.9	−163.4	−246.7	−231.4	−93.4	−247.7	69.8	70.1
Trinidad & Tobago	109.4	295.7	679.5	939.7	882.7	830.0	2,800.8	709.1	549.4	1,831.0	2,527.1

Table 2.9 Net inflows of foreign direct investment as a % of gross capital formation, 1990–2012

	1990	1995	2000	2005	2006	2007	2008	2009	2010	2011	2012
Antigua & Barbuda	40.2	14.6	28.8	80.9	77.3	67.4	30.5	17.1	24.2	20.7	20.8
Bahamas	−2.3	13.4	37.2	56.6	64.0	71.9	71.6	45.9	63.0	75.7	47.6
Barbados	3.7	4.5	9.9	32.6	41.3	51.4	62.4	37.9	48.9	84.6	48.8
Belize	18.0	15.3	12.4	75.2	50.6	61.0	52.1	38.1	39.6	35.2	66.2
Dominica	13.0	89.5	30.6	44.0	38.6	58.5	59.2	44.7	23.9	12.8	21.2
Grenada	15.3	22.5	20.0	22.8	38.4	64.2	54.9	56.4	38.4	27.0	22.3
Guyana	4.7	26.4	24.5	28.8	24.8	35.5	36.5	38.5	47.0	38.7	37.1
Jamaica	15.1	9.0	22.4	22.7	26.3	25.9	43.7	20.9	8.6	7.2	11.8
St Kitts & Nevis	38.5	13.3	42.2	42.1	39.1	42.0	56.4	43.5	45.4	44.5	39.3
St Lucia	44.8	24.1	27.9	30.4	61.3	87.1	45.6	46.1	31.6	26.2	25.2
St Vincent & the Grenadines	12.8	37.9	40.7	27.8	63.2	64.9	77.9	68.3	55.7	49.2	66.5
Suriname	−68.1	−7.4	−29.7	2.8	−16.4	−19.9	−14.4	−5.1	−15.1	3.8	3.5
Trinidad & Tobago	15.7	29.3	53.5	20.5	31.7	32.3	103.1	23.7	17.7	54.8	70.6

Source: World Development Indicators (2014).

flows between 1990 and 2012 was 2,209 per cent, attributable mainly to a significant amount of resource-based (petrochemical, natural gas) industrialization activities. Significantly, the net FDI flows to some CARICOM countries, including Bahamas and Suriname, decreased between 1990 and 2012. Cumulative net FDI inflows for the twenty-three-year period to the CARICOM bloc of countries amounted to US$80,314 million, of which Trinidad and Tobago alone, received US$40,157 million, or approximately 50 per cent. These are by no means insignificant numbers.

One of the more important contributions made by FDI to the overall process of economic development in CARICOM has been its role in financing domestic investment. In general, CARICOM economies have tended to depend on FDI flows to reduce their two main financing gaps, the foreign exchange and the savings/investment gaps. FDI as a percentage of gross capital formation in the various member countries is also shown in table 2.9. In 1990, only St Lucia had a net FDI inflow, which as a percentage of gross capital formation, exceeded 44 per cent. In 2012, the percentage representation of net FDI in gross capital formation increased for all the listed CARICOM countries except Antigua and Barbuda, Jamaica and St Lucia.

For CARICOM as a whole, the average share of FDI in gross capital formation increased by 25.3 percentage points between 1990 and 2012 (that is, from 11.7 per cent in 1990 to 37 per cent in 2012) with one member state alone, Trinidad and Tobago, realizing a 29.4 percentage point increase. On average for CARICOM as a whole, the ratio of FDI to gross capital formation was almost three times the international average for all developing countries (ECLAC 2002). Part of the reason for this has to do with the fact that foreign investment projects in CARICOM tend to be expensive and capital intensive. In contrast, most projects in which domestic capital is involved are labour intensive (ECLAC 2012).

However, the least developed countries of the OECS region did not have the same type of access to foreign capital as enjoyed by Trinidad and Tobago, for instance, and as a consequence have had to place a greater degree of reliance on official and multilateral financial flows.

Other forms of private capital flows, however, have not been important as FDI inflows have been for CARICOM countries. Importantly though, some member states, especially Trinidad and Tobago, Jamaica, and Barbados, have utilized bonds on the international market place to raise financial resources (Pemberton et al. 2005). In part, this was made possible because these particular countries were given improved credit ratings by the international investment agencies such as Standard and Poor and Moody's investor services.

In summary, it can be discerned that although CARICOM countries have managed to achieve a moderate (unweighted) real growth rate of 2.6 per cent between 1990 and 2012, the manufacturing sector remains relatively underdeveloped. Also, import growth continues to outstrip export growth so that the current account balances in the region have continued to be in deficit. The overall macroeconomic position of a region is important to its trade sector, as it influences its ability to borrow from abroad. Macroeconomic strength at home also influences the growth of the domestic price level and so impacts on the country's external competitiveness. These factors would affect the country's export capability which in turn would influence the magnitude of public revenues and hence the fiscal balance of the country.

2.3 The Debt Dilemma

In the absence of sufficient savings, governments tend to borrow both locally and abroad. Borrowed resources are sometimes wasted, but even when they are used to expand the country's infrastructure, the returns are not immediately forthcoming. Complementary investments by private investors are also sometimes necessary to make full use of infrastructural developments. In the absence of proper debt management, debt servicing can become a major problem by worsening fiscal deficits. Current fiscal deficits are a notable feature of most CARICOM economies. In 1990, the deficit as a per cent of GDP ranged from −25 per cent for Guyana to a surplus of 4.8 per cent in Jamaica. By 2010, all Caribbean countries (with the exception of Dominica) recorded fiscal deficits as a percentage of GDP with Barbados having the largest deficit of 8.7 per cent (see table 2.10). By 2012, fiscal deficits worsened for some countries, namely, Antigua and Barbuda, the Bahamas, Dominica, Grenada, Guyana and St Lucia. St Kitts and Nevis was the only country to record a fiscal surplus as a per cent of GDP for 2012.

2.3.1 Fiscal Burden of Interest Payments

For small states, interest payments on debt can have a serious impact on the growth potential of their economies. As a proportion of current expenditures, interest payments for CARICOM as a whole averaged 15.31 per cent in 1990 with a range of 4.91 per cent in St Vincent and the Grenadines to 39.17 per cent in Jamaica. In 2011, the average value of this ratio increased marginally to 17.06 per cent with a range of 3.19 per cent in St Vincent and the Grenadines to 28.96 per cent in Jamaica. Note that the interest payments as a per cent of current expenditures had increased to as

Table 2.10 Fiscal balance as a % of GDP in CARICOM member states, 1990–2012

	1990	1995	2000	2005	2006	2007	2008	2009	2010	2011	2012
Antigua & Barbuda	1.2	−2.9	−2.2	18.0	−7.8	−5.6	−5.9	−10.6	−1.1	−1.3	−1.4
Bahamas	–	−1.2	0.4	−2.6	1.7	−1.2	−2.9	−3.1	−3.2	−2.4	−6.2
Barbados	−8.4	−0.9	−1.5	−4.3	−2.0	−1.6	−5.1	−7.9	−8.7	−7.0	−5.3
Belize	0.3	−4.3	−9.0	−3.4	−1.9	−1.2	1.5	−2.8	−1.9	−0.9	−0.5
Dominica	−10.0	−5.7	−5.5	2.6	1.4	−0.9	−2.6	−2.1	1.4	0.1	−1.2
Grenada	−15.0	0.3	−3.4	3.7	−6.4	−5.3	−5.0	−5.0	−1.7	−2.8	−3.8
Guyana	−25.0	0.1	−6.6	−12.6	−13.1	−4.5	−3.8	−3.7	−2.9	−3.0	−4.7
Jamaica	4.8	−5.4	−0.3	−3.5	−5.4	−4.2	−7.2	−5.8	−6.3	−5.1	−5.1
St Kitts & Nevis	−0.3	−6.6	−14.2	−4.1	−2.4	−1.9	−0.3	−0.6	−4.2	1.5	7.2
St Lucia	1.0	−1.2	–	−6.5	−6.2	−2.0	0.0	−2.2	−0.6	−3.9	−7.2
St Vincent & the Grenadines	−0.8	−2.4	−5.8	−4.2	−3.9	−2.5	−0.6	−2.6	−3.5	−2.7	−1.8
Suriname	–	4.3	–	−0.8	1.7	8.0	0.0	−2.4	−2.8	−2.2	−2.6
Trinidad & Tobago	−1.2	0.2	1.6	5.0	6.9	1.8	7.8	−5.6	−2.2	−5.5	−1.3

Source: UNELAC Preliminary Overview of the Economies of Latin America and the Caribbean (various years).

much as 45.28 per cent in Jamaica in 2000. For the entire data period, the lowest mean value of this ratio was realized in St Vincent and the Grenadines, with Jamaica having an average value in excess of 38 per cent. Significantly, in every CARICOM member state (with the exception of Trinidad and Tobago) interest payments as a per cent of current expenditures increased (see table 2.11).

In terms of interest payments as a per cent of current revenues, the average value of this ratio for the entire CARICOM body was 15.02 per cent with a range of 4.07 per cent in St Vincent and the Grenadines to 35.16 per cent in Jamaica in 1990. By 2011, the average value of this variable

Table 2.11 Interest payments as a % of current expenditures in CARICOM member states, 1990–2011

	1990	1995	2000	2005	2006	2007	2008	2009	2010	2011
Bahamas	11.75	13.63	11.13	10.85	9.83	10.09	10.64	10.85	12.78	13.80
Barbados	12.60	15.27	14.77	–	–	14.22	13.35	14.18	15.70	–
Grenada	9.11	9.61	10.48	9.22	9.14	9.54	8.43	10.88	10.53	12.27
Jamaica	39.17	40.44	45.28	39.77	38.62	34.62	35.53	43.24	31.38	28.96
St Kitts & Nevis	12.88	9.08	14.50	21.78	22.84	23.17	24.03	22.59	24.72	21.14
St Vincent & the Grenadines	4.91	6.91	10.41	11.11	12.13	11.83	10.98	10.86	10.61	9.13
Trinidad & Tobago	16.74	20.12	22.35	11.14	7.17	8.04	6.40	8.74	–	–

Table 2.12 Interest payments as a % of current revenues in CARICOM member states, 1990–2011

	1990	1995	2000	2005	2006	2007	2008	2009	2010	2011
Bahamas	12.40	12.30	9.84	10.97	9.10	9.52	10.02	11.71	13.82	14.63
Barbados	13.92	16.28	13.04	–	–	15.35	15.06	17.00	20.27	–
Grenada	9.53	8.75	7.20	5.34	5.92	7.36	6.76	10.51	9.24	10.62
Jamaica	35.16	33.37	45.99	39.10	38.54	35.84	38.68	53.97	34.79	31.50
St Kitts & Nevis	12.55	9.29	16.75	20.56	21.06	21.28	22.56	20.39	23.32	17.51
St Vincent & the Grenadines	4.07	6.10	9.01	10.45	10.65	9.66	8.88	9.39	10.67	9.40
Trinidad & Tobago	17.53	18.65	20.77	8.23	6.09	6.47	5.03	8.41	–	–

Sources: Economist Intelligence Unit (various years), Country Reports (various years) and World Development Indicators (2014).

across all CARICOM member states increased to 16.73 per cent with a range from 9.40 per cent in St Vincent and the Grenadines to 31.50 per cent in Jamaica. Between 1990 and 2011, interest payments as a per cent of current revenues increased in all the member states for which consistent data is available except for Trinidad and Tobago (see table 2.12).

Advances in endogenous growth theory have emphasized the importance of human capital formation in the economic growth of nations (Nelson and Phelps 1966; Romer 1986, 1990; Lucas 1988). By expending almost one-fifth of their current revenues on interest payments, CARICOM member states are deprived of resources to finance education (creating human capital) and health (preserving human capital). Resources targeted at interest payments could also have helped to encourage the growth of non-traditional dynamic comparative advantage in export commodities on the upswing of the international product cycle or in the creation of an even better infrastructural base to attract FDI inflow in export oriented sectors.

2.4 Important Characteristics of CARICOM Trade Relations

2.4.1 External Competitiveness of CARICOM Countries

Antigua and Barbuda, Dominica, Grenada, St Kitts and Nevis, St Lucia, and St Vincent and the Grenadines (Montserrat and Anguilla are still territories of the United Kingdom) formed the Eastern Caribbean Central Bank in 1983 after a period of extensive monetary cooperation. These countries have a common currency, the Eastern Caribbean dollar, pegged at the rate EC$2.7 = US$1. The Bahamian, Belizean and Barbadian currencies are also pegged at the rates Bahamian$1 = US$1, Barbadian$2 = US$1 and Belizean$2 = US$1, respectively (table 2.13). Three member states, Guyana, Trinidad and Jamaica, have floating exchange rates, with their respective central banks intervening in the foreign exchange market if necessary. In practice, most CARICOM countries peg their exchange rates, as is reflected in the generally low degree of variability in their nominal exchange rates (see table 2.14).

Table 2.13 Nominal units of national currency for US dollar (annual average) in CARICOM member states, 1990–2012

	1990	1995	2000	2005	2006	2007	2008	2009	2010	2011	2012
Antigua & Barbuda	2.7	2.7	2.7	2.7	2.7	2.7	2.7	2.7	2.7	2.7	2.7
Bahamas	1.0	1.0	1.0	1.0	1.0	1.0	1.0	1.0	1.0	1.0	1.0
Barbados	2.0	2.0	2.0	2.0	2.0	2.0	2.0	2.0	2.0	2.0	2.0
Belize	2.0	2.0	2.0	2.0	2.0	2.0	2.0	2.0	2.0	2.0	2.0
Dominica	2.7	2.7	2.7	2.7	2.7	2.7	2.7	2.7	2.7	2.7	2.7
Grenada	2.7	2.7	2.7	2.7	2.7	2.7	2.7	2.7	2.7	2.7	2.7
Guyana	39.5	142.0	182.4	199.9	200.2	202.3	203.6	204.0	203.6	204.0	204.4
Jamaica	8.0	39.6	43.1	62.3	65.7	69.2	72.8	87.9	87.2	85.9	88.8
St Kitts & Nevis	2.7	2.7	2.7	2.7	2.7	2.7	2.7	2.7	2.7	2.7	2.7
St Lucia	2.7	2.7	2.7	2.7	2.7	2.7	2.7	2.7	2.7	2.7	2.7
St Vincent & the Grenadines	2.7	2.7	2.7	2.7	2.7	2.7	2.7	2.7	2.7	2.7	2.7
Suriname[a]	1.8	442.2	2,178.5	2.7	2.7	2.7	2.7	2.7	2.7	3.3	3.3
Trinidad & Tobago	4.3	5.9	6.3	6.3	6.3	6.3	6.3	6.3	6.4	6.4	6.4

[a] "Effective 20 January 2011, the authorities devalued the currency by 20 per cent vis-à-vis the US dollar in the official market. With the devaluation, the authorities set a band of Surinamese dollars (SRD) 3.25–3.35 per US dollar, within which all official and commercial market transactions are allowed to take place" (IMF 2012).

Source: International Financial Statistics Database (IFS) (2014).

Controversy exists as to the effectiveness of exchange rate policy to correct trade imbalances in small countries with a fledgling manufacturing base and which operate very much in the Dudley Seersian sense of "exporting what they don't need and importing what they need" (the consequence of which are high import bills). If the Marshall-Lerner criteria does not hold, then what may happen is that a devaluation, by increasing the price of imports, can lead (in the tradition of the "J curve") to a worsening current account balance, at least in the short-run. Even more, the rise in imported goods can lead to imported inflation which in turn can spark an increase in demand for higher wages and salaries that can offset any competitive gain the devaluation (or depreciation) of the nominal exchange rate provided in the first instance.

Table 2.14 Nominal exchange rates (national currency per US dollar) in Guyana, Jamaica and Suriname, 1990–2012

	1990	1995	2000	2005	2006	2007	2008	2009	2010	2011	2012
Guyana	39.53	141.99	182.43	199.88	200.19	202.35	203.63	203.95	203.64	204.02	204.36
Jamaica	7.18	35.14	42.99	62.28	65.74	69.19	72.76	87.89	87.20	85.89	88.75
Suriname	–	0.44	1.32	2.73	2.74	2.75	2.75	2.75	2.75	3.27	3.30

Table 2.15 Current account balances of Guyana, Jamaica and Suriname, US$ Million, 1990–2011

	1990	1995	2000	2005	2006	2007	2008	2009	2010	2011
Guyana	–	−134.80	−113.00	−96.30	−180.60	−112.30	−191.60	−165.30	−159.70	–
Jamaica	−312.10	−98.70	−274.60	−1071.30	−1182.90	−2038.10	−2793.30	−1127.50	−934.00	−2063.20
Suriname	37.40	62.80	32.30	−143.60	220.60	324.50	324.70	111.30	650.80	251.10

Source: World Development Indicators (2014).

Devaluations or depreciations of their respective currencies did not apparently lead to any significant improvements in the current account balances of Guyana, Jamaica and Suriname as shown in table 2.15. However, in Suriname there was an improvement, but this was more precipitated by improvements in the prices of its main export goods. Thus, the source of the current account imbalances in the Caribbean is perhaps not to be found in currency misalignment or overvaluation but is perhaps reflective of deeper underlying structural problems relating to the nature of exports, outdated technology and absence of relevant skills. Continuous depreciation of the currencies of the region (especially in Guyana and Jamaica) may also have eroded the confidence economic agents had in their domestic currencies as a store of wealth. In many instances, this may have prompted capital flight as economic agents sought out more stable foreign currencies (for example, the US or Canadian dollar). Note though, even if foreign currency accounts are held in banking accounts located in the domestic economy, these resources can represent a potential leakage from the system if they are not put to use in the interest of the domestic economy.

One aspect of the external competitiveness of CARICOM countries is presented in table 2.16, which provides data on real effective exchange rates. The real effective exchange rate is a trade weighted index (it also considers relative inflation rates) which takes into account the bilateral exchange rates between the home country and its trading partners. A rise in this index reflects a decrease in external competitiveness. In general, what the data suggests is that CARICOM countries are becoming less competitive externally. This is very disturbing as the world economy is becoming increasingly globalized, and CARICOM economies are being asked to enter into trading arrangements with greater "reciprocation", the consequence of which may be an eventual loss of market share for CARICOM member states which do not improve their external competitiveness. As concerns public finances, one would expect that government's current revenues would expand as their external competitiveness is improved. Improving external competitiveness by stimulating exports can have both a direct impact on government revenues and an indirect effect, working through the multiplier effect on other activities.

2.4.2 Terms of Trade

The amount of export revenues that a country collects is not only conditioned by the volume of its exports, but also by their unit prices. If the export prices of a country are increasing more slowly than its import prices, then this country would have to export a greater volume of its produce and deploy more of its scarce productive resources in order to procure the same amount of imported goods as it did previously. The terms of trade index shows the relationship of the export price

Table 2.16 Real effective exchange rate index (2007 = 100) in CARICOM member states, 1990–2011

	1990	1995	2000	2005	2006	2007	2008	2009	2010	2011
Antigua & Barbuda	105.7	103.4	128.2	108.0	106.8	100.0	98.2	101.2	104.0	101.0
Bahamas	103.9	105.5	116.8	104.6	102.9	100.0	100.1	105.3	103.3	99.8
Barbados	97.3	98.2	109.3	98.7	102.4	100.0	102.2	109.6	111.9	112.5
Belize	110.9	105.4	108.5	102.4	103.2	100.0	100.5	105.7	101.7	98.1
Dominica	109.6	108.5	118.7	104.3	103.5	100.0	98.6	102.4	101.1	98.0
Grenada	107.6	106.1	111.9	101.7	102.2	100.0	101.4	103.1	103.3	101.9
Guyana	112.5	93.9	99.1	94.0	96.5	100.0	100.7	106.3	106.7	106.3
Jamaica	83.6	77.1	107.9	102.0	101.7	100.0	109.6	101.3	111.3	116.3
St Kitts & Nevis	90.2	87.9	104.7	96.6	101.2	100.0	99.8	104.1	101.6	100.9
St Lucia	97.7	102.7	113.0	103.3	103.5	100.0	99.5	102.0	102.0	98.6
St Vincent & the Grenadines	100.8	100.4	123.9	101.7	101.3	100.0	102.3	106.6	104.6	99.8
Suriname	304.9	70.2	101.3	93.4	100.4	100.0	106.7	108.6	112.5	104.4
Trinidad & Tobago	97.0	80.7	88.0	93.8	98.1	100.0	106.4	115.8	123.0	128.4

Source: Zsolt (2012).

index to the import price index. A rise in this index above one hundred implies an improvement in the purchasing capabilities of the home country.

The data in table 2.17 suggest that the terms of trade of Antigua and Barbuda, Jamaica, and St Kitts and Nevis worsened during the period 2001–11 in response to a slowing global economy and subsequent global financial crisis in 2008. Indeed, weak external demand and falling bauxite prices led to a terms of trade deterioration (ECLAC 2012). Furthermore, the terms of trade of Dominica, St Lucia and St Vincent and the Grenadines, although still above hundred, has definitely deteriorated. Part of the reason for the deteriorating terms of trade is shown in table 2.18. Specifically, for Dominica, St Lucia and St Vincent, banana accounts for a significant part of their export earnings and although the price offered by the European Union (the main export market for bananas from these countries) remains above the price level in the more competitive US market, it appears to be in a state of decline, certainly after 2009.

For at least one of the member states of CARICOM, Trinidad and Tobago, the time has probably come or is close to arriving when researchers would need to look at the income terms of trade as compared to the commodity terms of trade. The income terms of trade caters for feedback of changes in the output levels of the exporting country on the export prices of its main export commodities. As it stands, "Trinidad and Tobago is the world's largest exporter of ammonia and the second largest exporter of methanol" (Ministry of Energy and Energy Affairs 2014, para 4). Since train 4 of Atlantic Liquefied Natural Gas came on stream in 2005, Trinidad and Tobago has matured into being the seventh largest exporter of liquefied natural gas in the world (Ministry of Planning and Sustainable Development 2012).

Fluctuating export prices have both direct and indirect effects on CARICOM economies. A change in the export prices for any country affects the capacity of the country to import foreign goods, the country's international reserves, the government's fiscal accounts and also the level of

Table 2.17 Net barter terms of trade (2000 = 100) of some CARICOM member states, 2000–2011

	2000	2001	2002	2003	2004	2005	2006	2007	2008	2009	2010	2011
Antigua & Barbuda	100.0	94.9	95.7	91.0	87.0	82.2	83.2	84.1	84.4	82.2	75.4	75.1
Bahamas	100.0	93.1	91.1	94.5	94.6	92.8	94.7	95.1	102.2	93.5	100.3	108.5
Barbados	100.0	97.5	96.2	100.4	107.4	116.9	120.5	118.6	119.6	123.7	115.8	111.0
Belize	100.0	104.5	96.9	86.8	88.4	86.9	92.9	87.1	86.0	93.8	100.6	104.4
Dominica	100.0	111.6	110.4	97.3	104.1	100.7	102.4	98.7	102.6	116.5	110.2	104.2
Grenada	100.0	88.3	89.9	93.3	87.6	79.8	85.0	89.9	94.8	98.6	99.5	101.9
Guyana	100.0	98.8	99.2	97.6	94.7	94.4	107.0	97.0	106.4	122.4	129.8	130.0
Jamaica	100.0	100.2	95.7	94.5	99.1	86.0	89.7	102.5	83.4	65.6	70.7	68.6
St Kitts & Nevis	100.0	102.2	98.3	93.4	86.5	83.7	81.7	79.1	74.2	76.7	72.7	66.8
St Lucia	100.0	115.6	110.7	96.5	105.4	111.6	114.7	110.4	96.6	117.3	103.3	94.8
St Vincent & the Grenadines	100.0	99.9	100.9	93.4	91.9	81.4	84.7	86.1	97.2	118.8	118.3	107.2
Suriname	100.0	96.8	95.0	94.8	100.5	97.4	117.6	115.6	116.8	119.3	137.5	141.8
Trinidad & Tobago	100.0	99.8	93.2	103.5	108.1	123.2	135.6	133.7	160.5	132.5	131.4	152.6

Source: World Development Indicators (2014).

income in the industries concerned. (Adverse movements in the price of key export commodities could be offset by increases in production. But there are limits on the extent to which this can be done, assuming the demand is there.) The reduction in the capacity of a country to import goods can affect its economic development. The indirect effect of price fluctuations occurs through the

Table 2.18 Price of bananas in the EU and US markets, 2000–2012 (nominal US$/mt)

	Banana (Europe)	Banana (United States)
2000	712.43	424.00
2001	777.24	583.25
2002	759.42	528.58
2003	790.40	374.79
2004	891.99	524.58
2005	1,172.58	602.84
2006	897.03	677.24
2007	1,037.01	675.81
2008	1,187.71	844.21
2009	1,144.90	847.14
2010	1,002.24	868.32
2011	1,124.74	967.99
2012	1,099.73	983.98

Source: World Bank (2013).

exchange rate. In floating exchange rate regimes, falling export prices can trigger current account deficits and prompt a worsening of a country's balance of payments, thus encouraging a depreciation of a country's currency. In this context, if the appropriate import and export elasticities are not present, then the country's net exports can decrease and this could lead to a fall in overall tax revenues collected.

2.4.3 Decline of the Banana Industry

After World War II, Europe entered into a banana agreement with several of its Caribbean colonies. This agreement became known as the EU-Caribbean banana agreement. During this time, various specific banana arrangements were being engineered; however, the largest agreement was developed in the 1950s between Britain, Jamaica and the Windward Islands (a bloc of economies within the Caribbean comprising Dominica, Grenada, St Lucia, and St Vincent and the Grenadines). Until then, exports from the Commonwealth Caribbean were comprised mainly of sugar produced on the plantations, but with the increase in global competition, the sugar industry declined significantly, which prompted the colonizers to seek out an export alternative. This alternative came in the form of banana, a fruit that had long been cultivated on the islands primarily for domestic consumption. Britain's choice of banana was conditioned by its populace's growing demand for fruit coupled with its shortage of money domestically. A "restricted, sterling area trading zone" was therefore established, and immediately the promotion of banana exports ensued (Fridell 2010). Not long after, calls for the promotion of "global distributive justice" were voiced by social groups within the United Kingdom. These groups demanded that Britain strengthen ties with its colonies. Ultimately, this gave rise to a preferential trade arrangement (PTA), based on a quota system. This meant that the largest share of the UK market for bananas was reserved for its colonies trading in pounds sterling. In contrast, a small quota was reserved for non-sterling sources, particularly those trading in US dollars such as the Latin American countries. A monopoly position was therefore cemented by Jamaica and the Windward Islands, both of which benefited from banana export booms in the 1950s and 1960s. These desirable conditions inspired the establishment of state-managed marketing boards, namely, the St Vincent Banana Growers' Association in 1954 and the Windward Islands Banana Growers' Association in 1958 (Rittgers and La Gra 1991).

In 1973, the United Kingdom joined the European Community (EC). This meant that the ECs trading rules would also apply for UK trade with its colonies. In particular, the United Kingdom was required to open its market for bananas to all former European colonies, which comprised the forty-five members of the African Caribbean and Pacific (ACP) countries.[10] While the Caribbean faced competition from these export sources, the EC market, however, remained closed to Latin America (Raynolds 2003). Latin America and Ecuador, in particular, was regarded as the most competitive exporter of banana in the world as bananas were grown on plantations spanning over five thousand hectares. Additionally, high capital intensive methods were employed, coupled with an exploited low-wage labour force. In contrast, labour-intensive methods on small family plots of less than five hectares on average predominated on plantations in the Windward Islands. Labourers worked fewer hours on a daily basis and were paid as much as three times the amount paid to unionized banana workers in Latin America. This, notwithstanding, the Latin American banana industry had generally been more productive and less costly than the Windward Islands, mainly due to the latter's location within the hurricane belt that exposed the industry to a constant annual threat (Andreatta 1998; Myers 2004; Frundt 2009).

The Jamaican banana industry underwent a slow decline from the 1970s onward due to a combination of political, economic and environmental issues. However, exports from the Windward Islands continued to grow steadily, from 100,673 tonnes to 274,442 tonnes between 1961 and 1992 (see table 2.19). According to Myers (2004), by this time the banana industry was responsible for "between 50 to 70 per cent of all export earnings and over one-third of all employment in Dominica, Saint Lucia and St Vincent and the Grenadines".

In 1993, the single economic market (SEM) was created when the single economic policy introduced by the EC replaced the separate national banana trade policies of the then eleven EU countries with a common EU banana import regime. This regime included the establishment of a common market organization (CMO) for bananas and also included a complex system of tariff rate quotas and licences which controlled the importation of bananas into the EU market. Each ACP country was allowed duty-free entry into the European Union for a designated quantity of bananas (857,700 metric tonnes in total) under the "C" quota. This duty-free quota was based on each ACP country's annual historical level of banana exports. A tariff of 750 ECU per tonne was charged for exports in excess of the quota. Bananas originating from Latin American, however, were subject to a quota of 2.5 million tonnes. In addition to quotas, licences were needed to import bananas into the European Union. There were three categories of operators designated.

Table 2.19 Banana industry in Latin America and Commonwealth nations compared, 1961–2011

	Export Quantity (Tonnes)			Export Value (1,000 US$)			Price (US$/Tonne)		
	Ecuador	Windward Islands	Jamaica	Ecuador	Windward Islands	Jamaica	Ecuador	Windward Islands	Jamaica
1961	985,300	100,673	124,800	80,900	8,237	13,692	82.1	81.8	109.7
1962	1,100,000	111,355	131,600	88,500	8,441	12,633	80.5	75.8	96.0
1963	1,340,000	125,598	146,300	85,200	9,514	13,563	63.6	75.7	92.7
1964	1,382,700	142,196	159,100	88,080	11,077	16,925	63.7	77.9	106.4
1965	1,200,000	180,514	182,900	95,904	11,888	17,091	79.9	65.9	93.4
1966	1,264,801	169,733	182,900	105,358	12,757	17,747	83.3	75.2	97.0
1967	1,262,800	169,825	175,600	104,651	13,698	18,085	82.9	80.7	103.0
1968	1,251,516	180,460	140,400	93,864	13,784	16,560	75.0	76.4	117.9
1969	1,189,625	172,700	137,700	101,000	15,652	14,964	84.9	90.6	108.7
1970	1,246,332	123,299	136,410	83,299	9,536	14,186	66.8	77.3	104.0
1971	1,350,600	123,525	125,850	101,155	9,696	14,266	74.9	78.5	113.4
1972	1,406,800	122,267	129,084	109,009	10,326	14,896	77.5	84.5	115.4
1973	1,368,223	94,780	109,437	109,418	12,928	18,130	80.0	136.4	165.7
1974	1,356,706	112,517	73,388	113,528	20,771	12,552	83.7	184.6	171.0
1975	1,384,486	84,960	68,099	138,652	18,819	16,141	100.1	221.5	237.0
1976	937,259	121,986	77,840	103,224	23,728	13,113	110.1	194.5	168.5

Table 2.19 Banana industry in Latin America and Commonwealth nations (*continued*)

	Export Quantity (Tonnes)			Export Value (1,000 US$)			Price (US$/Tonne)		
	Ecuador	Windward Islands	Jamaica	Ecuador	Windward Islands	Jamaica	Ecuador	Windward Islands	Jamaica
1977	1,317,733	112,293	76,166	148,260	25,267	16,747	112.5	225.0	219.9
1978	1,223,785	132,594	75,137	150,935	32,082	19,579	123.3	242.0	260.6
1979	1,170,104	101,106	65,517	156,539	27,875	18,228	133.8	275.7	278.2
1980	1,290,621	73,950	33,124	195,591	24,201	10,486	151.5	327.3	316.6
1981	1,229,555	110,543	18,141	207,879	37,715	4,251	169.1	341.2	234.3
1982	1,261,284	103,837	21,226	213,297	38,126	4,671	169.1	367.2	220.1
1983	909,956	119,285	23,037	152,926	44,074	7,047	168.1	369.5	305.9
1984	924,355	136,698	10,902	136,460	49,622	1,625	147.6	363.0	149.1
1985	1,075,027	156,535	12,490	186,341	63,982	4,202	173.3	408.7	336.4
1986	1,364,697	210,249	20,306	257,897	103,548	9,174	189.0	492.5	451.8
1987	1,374,319	191,514	33,324	261,699	101,052	19,113	190.4	527.6	573.6
1988	1,516,700	281,238	27,435	292,189	144,721	156,66	192.6	514.6	571.0
1989	1,725,936	246,568	43,000	369,000	123,189	19,259	213.8	499.6	447.9
1990	2,156,617	281,177	61,073	460,312	153,374	38,182	213.4	545.5	625.2
1991	2,662,750	227,746	73,545	707,617	132,319	48,460	265.7	581.0	658.9
1992	2,682,831	274,442	70,861	667,917	146,123	39,707	249.0	532.4	560.4
1993	2,563,223	259,392	74,322	550,643	110,794	35,469	214.8	427.1	477.2
1994	3,007,925	175,126	75,503	692,170	86,555	46,148	230.1	494.2	611.2
1995	3,665,182	204,791	82,753	818,545	99,046	45,701	223.3	483.6	552.3
1996	3,866,079	196,086	85,724	964,119	92,132	43,616	249.4	469.9	508.8
1997	4,462,099	143,857	76,167	1,311,639	66,130	45,230	294.0	459.7	593.8
1998	3,855,643	125,113	61,938	1,058,729	68,273	36,000	274.6	545.7	581.2
1999	3,966,126	135,227	51,512	945,560	67,995	32,380	238.4	502.8	628.6
2000	3,993,968	124,788	40,900	809,364	53,879	21,200	202.6	431.8	518.3
2001	3,990,427	88,170	43,535	828,573	38,086	18,272	207.6	432.0	419.7
2002	4,199,156	107,546	39,900	936,596	47,252	20,200	223.0	439.4	506.3
2003	4,664,814	75,675	41,869	1,084,169	35,115	22,029	232.4	464.0	526.1
2004	4,521,458	87,402	27,575	972,899	41,267	12,229	215.2	472.2	443.5
2005	4,764,193	70,832	11,713	1,068,659	35,157	4,693	224.3	496.3	400.7
2006	4,908,564	71,830	31,863	1,184,355	36,546	14,783	241.3	508.8	464.0
2007	5,174,565	58,065	17,391	1,282,036	30,251	9,222	247.8	512.2	530.3
2008	5,270,688	32,366	40	1,626,170	14,612	37	310.0	570.9	925.0
2009	5,700,696	25,512	7	1,983,974	14,301	6	348.0	560.6	857.1
2010	5,156,477	16,814	1	2,033,794	10,487	1	394.4	623.7	1,000.0
2011	5,778,170	16,813	1	2,246,351	9,598	1	388.8	570.9	1,000.0

Sources: Food and Agriculture Organization of the United Nations Database (FAO) (2014) and http://faostat.fao.org/site/535/DesktopDefault.aspx?PageID=535#ancor.

The Windward Islands fell under the category of "B" operators, defined as "those which prior to 1992 had marketed community bananas and/or traditional ACP bananas". This category of operators was entitled to 30 per cent of the licences for the importation of 2.5 million tonnes (Williams and Darius 1999).

The SEM faced opposition from both within and outside the European Union. Germany and the Benelux countries had traditionally operated duty-free markets and relied heavily on Latin American bananas. These countries challenged the SEM on several occasions with little success. The strongest challenge was launched by the Latin American banana exporting countries under a series of trade disputes brought first under the GATT (General Agreement on Tariffs and Trade) and subsequently under the World Trade Organization (WTO). Under the GATT, five Latin American countries claimed that the European Union's regime for the import, sale and distribution of bananas which had been established by the SEM was inconsistent with the EC's GATT obligations and although two GATT rulings found aspects of the regime to be inconsistent with the EC's obligations under the GATT, the EC and the ACP were successful in blocking the adoption of these rulings. However, the establishment of the WTO in 1995 brought with it a new system for the adoption of panel rulings, which significantly strengthened the opposition to the regime. Major criticisms to the agreement were launched in 1997 and again in 1999. On both occasions, the WTO ruled against the agreement citing disruption to free trade and the principle of "non-discrimination". Permission was then granted to the United States to apply sanctions against the European Union amounting to US$191 million annually. This resulted in the crumbling of the SEM as the European Union "agreed first to increases in the size of the quota for non-ACP bananas and eventually to removing the tariff quotas entirely by 2006 and replacing them with a tariff-only regime" (Clegg 2005).

The implication of this for the Windward Islands was severe. Specifically, in St Vincent and the Grenadines, there was a decline in banana exports from 79,863 tonnes to 24,765 tonnes between 1992 and 2007 (see table 2.20). Furthermore, there was a substantial decline in the number of active farmers from 7,855 to 1,151 for the same period.

The US and Latin American exporters intensified its pressure on the European Union, this time to reduce or eliminate their different overall tariff rates imposed on ACP and non-ACP producers. The European Union responded and "in December 2009 the EU agreed to lower the import duty on Latin American bananas from 176 euros per tonne to 148 euros per tonne in 2010, followed by a further reduction to 114 euros by 2017". In light of this, the WTO has pushed for formation of new economic partnership agreements (EPAs) between the European Union and ACP countries premised on "reciprocity" rather than on preferential trade (Brewster, Girvan and Lewis 2010) and in October 2008, the European Union and thirteen Caribbean nations concluded negotiations for their own EPA (Brown 2000; Clegg 2005; Orbie 2007).

2.4.4 Composition of Trade

The composition of the export baskets of CARICOM countries also influences their export earnings. According to the Prebisch–Singer hypothesis (PSH), the prices of agricultural commodity are constantly decreasing relative to the prices of manufactures, so that in a global economy

Table 2.20 Declining banana industry in St Vincent and the Grenadines, 1992–2011

	Active Farmers	Export Quantity (Tonnes)	Export Value (1,000 US$)
1992	7,855	79,863	41,540
1993	7,543	64,608	25,696
1994	6,139	34,552	16,704
1995	5,991	54,788	24,463
1996	5,665	48,850	20,490
1997	4,670	32,865	14,397
1998	4,152	40,820	20,891
1999	3,696	40,211	20,523
2000	3,623	43,400	18,300
2001	3,360	33,000	13,500
2002	2,673	39,664	16,727
2003	2,309	28,455	12,582
2004	2,099	30,315	13,972
2005	1,737	27,470	12,815
2006	–	23,783	11,162
2007	1,151	24,765	11,654
2008	–	21,432	8,290
2009	–	18,053	7,770
2010	–	12,103	5,906
2011	–	12,200	6,000

Sources: Fridell (2010) and Food and Agriculture Organization of the United Nations Database (2013).

characterized by low price and income elasticity of demand for agricultural goods, expanding the output of primary commodities may not be the best developmental option (Imani Development Report 2005).

The implications of a low price elasticity of demand for primary agricultural goods for a country exporting such commodities may be expanded as follows. A rise in price would lead to a less than proportional increase in output because of factor input and other constraints. Even more, if enough producers of a commodity which is inelastic in demand, expand output, then its price would fall more than proportional to any increase in its quantity demanded with the consequence that export revenues would fall (this is the familiar "fallacy of composition" argument). Fluctuations in the prices of export commodities for the price-taking small firms in CARICOM also result in greater export earnings instability which adversely affect economic growth (see Gyimah-Brempong 1991; Parimal 2006).

For CARICOM countries, the majority of their export earnings come from the primary sector, represented here by the sum of SITC[11] 0 through SITC 4 (see table 2.21). If we exclude SITC 3 which mainly represents the mineral exports of CARICOM countries, then the non-mineral primary commodity exports of CARICOM countries in 1990 was 16.7 per cent of total merchandise

Table 2.21 Value of CARICOM total exports to the world by single-digit sectors, US$ million, 1990–2012

	0	1	2	3	4	5	6	7	8	9	Total
1990	586.93	82.60	17.44	1,478.11	8.00	1,333.04	281.28	76.20	182.04	6.54	4,149.46
1991	514.79	73.03	123.90	1,370.54	5.90	1,193.54	262.72	43.77	161.59	4.29	3,754.07
1992	563.32	77.64	104.82	1,203.11	3.76	1,054.05	284.08	43.30	243.44	1.33	3,578.85
1993	609.03	90.79	101.23	945.59	5.73	774.32	254.08	89.25	310.00	34.57	3,214.61
1994	691.41	94.13	93.29	976.05	6.55	1,480.60	347.22	76.41	348.02	3.72	4,117.40
1995	889.01	121.36	122.13	1,199.08	7.32	1,631.76	462.59	103.27	396.84	3.07	4,936.43
1996	856.80	129.68	103.29	1,310.94	6.95	1,528.77	414.62	66.94	351.86	14.72	4,784.58
1997	1,156.45	157.60	230.32	1,212.04	9.17	1,683.04	523.38	83.57	348.22	3.13	5,406.94
1998	1,026.60	197.73	448.39	1,038.57	10.41	1,271.21	550.39	123.34	339.50	2.99	5,009.16
1999	950.21	196.66	178.62	1,571.25	7.48	1,613.37	454.19	162.96	377.03	116.47	5,523.73
2000	1,028.81	206.66	178.12	2,813.10	5.70	1,663.43	460.94	154.03	283.91	464.43	7,259.14
2001	897.03	227.04	238.02	2,525.53	6.19	1,826.50	536.66	895.67	219.86	475.95	7,848.45
2002	835.02	239.12	200.00	2,360.35	7.53	1,428.96	556.64	153.90	136.25	532.83	6,450.61
2003	974.41	220.89	187.53	3,215.90	8.07	2,110.03	532.60	83.70	125.81	546.89	8,005.83
2004	1,043.90	232.56	215.75	3,988.53	10.75	2,618.81	730.21	186.74	134.62	725.42	9,887.27
2005	1,010.94	280.95	255.49	6,901.10	12.23	3,021.93	592.72	207.93	154.38	883.81	13,321.50
2006	1,108.77	310.20	387.22	1,110.70	7.81	3,403.14	798.38	247.49	146.63	1,060.04	18,576.70
2007	1,129.13	362.93	873.98	9,363.11	7.74	4,242.16	825.84	375.78	176.88	1,212.98	18,570.50
2008	1,232.23	392.26	940.50	1,3796.7	10.07	5,121.77	976.29	452.70	138.37	1,436.23	24,497.10
2009	1,038.53	316.38	491.95	7,272.25	8.46	1,703.33	500.10	86.20	104.77	1,228.42	12,750.40
2010	1,027.43	291.99	394.58	7,254.46	5.26	3,129.45	731.50	113.84	104.30	1,665.69	14,718.50
2011	977.22	205.73	434.36	752.74	4.72	916.71	89.90	156.85	62.97	2,033.46	5,634.65
2012	538.96	149.99	148.59	513.18	3.52	787.18	37.16	24.98	54.46	4.32	2,262.34

exports. If mineral exports are included, the primary exports of CARICOM countries tallied to 52.4 per cent in 1990. By 2010, primary commodity exports (non-SITC 3) of CARICOM countries amounted to 11.7 per cent or 60.9 per cent when SITC 3 is included (see table 2.22).

In value terms and as a percentage of total exports, intra-regional trade has grown since the 1970s (see table 2.23). In particular, SITC 0, 1 and 5 have grown by 63.8 per cent, 47.5 per cent and 18.1 per cent, respectively, for the period 1973–2012. The main export of the region, however, continues to be SITC 3. Apart from SITC 0 which is a traditional intra-regional export, the only other intra-regional export to exceed 10 per cent on a consistent basis was SITC 6 (although after 2007 it has not crossed this threshold).

Given the differences among CARICOM members in terms of development, size of markets and infrastructure, it was expected that the forces of polarization would be strong and a number of measures were put in place to counter these forces. The original members were also divided into MDCs and LDCs.

Table 2.24 shows that the MDCs account for over 90 per cent of the intra-regional exports and around 75 per cent of intra-regional imports. Because of its oil exports, Trinidad and Tobago dominates the MDCs' position, accounting for 75.4 per cent (on average) of intra-regional exports since 1995, as compared to under 65 per cent in the 1980s. The share of LDCs exports increased in the 1980s to over 9 per cent because of the lower price of oil, but has fallen to under 7 per cent in recent years. Not all member countries are dependent on the regional market to the same extent and some have become less dependent than others. In the case of Trinidad and Tobago, for example, the share of total exports going to CARICOM increased from under 12 per cent in the 1970s and early 1980s, to over 18 per cent in recent years. On the other hand, the proportion for Jamaica has fallen in the 1970s and 1980s to around 4 per cent. In the case of Barbados, CARICOM now accounts for about 20 per cent of its domestic exports as compared to under 10 per cent, in the 1970s. The proportion for St Kitts and Nevis, Dominica, St Lucia and St Vincent, respectively, has fallen as compared to the earlier decades.

The share of Trinidad and Tobago's total imports originating in CARICOM has declined from the 1970s, amounting to under 10 per cent in recent time. The proportion for Jamaica has increased from less than 23 per cent up to the mid-1990s to over 38 per cent in recent years. Generally, the LDCs source more than 15 per cent of their import needs from the region.

2.5 Trade and Growth

There is little evidence to indicate that the formation of CARICOM has had a significant effect on the growth of intra-regional exports (table 2.25). The correlation between the share of intra-regional exports and the growth of GDP also tends to be weak (table 2.26).

2.6 Vulnerability of CARICOM Countries

In regional and international trade discussions, the governments of CARICOM countries have been underscoring the point, that despite middle-income status, their economies remain extremely vulnerable and poverty is a serious concern. They are faced with not only natural

Table 2.22 Percentage distribution of CARICOM's total exports to the world by single-digit sectors, 1990–2012

	0	1	2	3	4	5	6	7	8	9	Total
1990	14.14	1.99	0.42	35.62	0.19	32.13	6.78	1.84	4.39	0.16	100
1991	13.71	1.95	3.30	36.51	0.16	31.79	7.00	1.17	4.30	0.11	100
1992	15.74	2.17	2.93	33.62	0.11	29.45	7.94	1.21	6.80	0.04	100
1993	18.95	2.82	3.15	29.42	0.18	24.09	7.90	2.78	9.64	1.08	100
1994	16.79	2.29	2.27	23.71	0.16	35.96	8.43	1.86	8.45	0.09	100
1995	18.01	2.46	2.47	24.29	0.15	33.06	9.37	2.09	8.04	0.06	100
1996	17.91	2.71	2.16	27.40	0.15	31.95	8.67	1.40	7.35	0.31	100
1997	21.39	2.91	4.26	22.42	0.17	31.13	9.68	1.55	6.44	0.06	100
1998	20.49	3.95	8.95	20.73	0.21	25.38	10.99	2.46	6.78	0.06	100
1999	17.20	3.56	3.23	28.45	0.14	29.21	8.22	2.95	6.83	2.11	100
2000	14.17	2.85	2.45	38.75	0.08	22.91	6.35	2.12	3.91	6.40	100
2001	11.43	2.89	3.03	32.18	0.08	23.27	6.84	11.41	2.80	6.06	100
2002	12.94	3.71	3.10	36.59	0.12	22.15	8.63	2.39	2.11	8.26	100
2003	12.17	2.76	2.34	40.17	0.10	26.36	6.65	1.05	1.57	6.83	100
2004	10.56	2.35	2.18	40.34	0.11	26.49	7.39	1.89	1.36	7.34	100
2005	7.59	2.11	1.92	51.80	0.09	22.68	4.45	1.56	1.16	6.63	100
2006	5.97	1.67	2.08	59.79	0.04	18.32	4.30	1.33	0.79	5.71	100
2007	6.08	1.95	4.71	50.42	0.04	22.84	4.45	2.02	0.95	6.53	100
2008	5.03	1.60	3.84	56.32	0.04	20.91	3.99	1.85	0.56	5.86	100
2009	8.15	2.48	3.86	57.04	0.07	13.36	3.92	0.68	0.82	9.63	100
2010	6.98	1.98	2.68	49.29	0.04	21.26	4.97	0.77	0.71	11.32	100
2011	17.34	3.65	7.71	13.36	0.08	16.27	1.60	2.78	1.12	36.09	100
2012	23.82	6.63	6.57	22.68	0.16	34.79	1.64	1.10	2.41	0.19	100

Source: World Integrated Trade Solution (WITS) (2014).

Table 2.23 CARICOM intra-regional export composition (%), 1973–2012

	0	1	2	3	4	5	6	7	8	9
1973	21.07	3.23	0.83	32.30	1.24	12.67	10.97	3.89	13.69	0.13
1975	20.63	2.49	0.89	42.54	0.89	10.40	9.27	3.27	9.56	0.08
1980	9.35	1.90	0.28	64.64	0.74	7.76	6.54	2.09	6.63	0.07
1985	6.56	2.87	0.39	69.30	0.40	7.65	8.02	1.08	3.39	0.34
1990	13.21	6.49	0.72	32.36	1.57	12.93	19.74	3.68	9.10	0.21
1991	13.71	6.30	0.35	30.49	1.33	15.39	20.83	3.92	7.51	0.18
1992	15.78	6.25	0.57	30.68	0.91	13.78	21.04	3.25	7.69	0.04
1993	18.18	6.37	0.47	28.45	0.77	14.80	20.00	3.46	7.43	0.06
1994	17.54	6.31	0.66	31.13	0.84	13.61	19.96	3.03	6.91	0.00
1995	17.41	6.64	0.38	36.16	0.82	12.37	17.65	2.62	5.95	0.01
1996	16.34	6.04	0.37	38.54	0.81	12.68	17.27	1.98	5.96	0.01
1997	20.49	5.98	0.55	35.47	1.00	12.05	16.47	1.95	6.04	0.01
1998	20.78	7.11	0.73	33.71	1.07	9.25	18.43	2.55	6.33	0.05
1999	18.27	6.48	1.00	38.16	0.64	10.22	17.72	1.79	5.65	0.07
2000	15.62	6.11	1.01	48.84	0.39	8.38	12.67	1.99	4.92	0.08
2001	16.74	6.82	1.00	45.98	0.38	8.03	12.57	3.20	4.64	0.64
2002	19.95	8.07	1.07	37.38	0.61	8.94	15.24	2.24	5.74	0.78
2003	16.69	5.94	0.93	51.47	0.55	7.11	10.74	1.21	5.16	0.21
2004	20.50	7.01	1.44	39.91	0.80	8.58	14.68	1.82	5.10	0.16
2005	11.00	4.49	0.83	65.28	0.45	4.76	8.29	1.54	3.20	0.16
2006	10.21	4.31	0.84	67.91	0.24	4.35	7.51	1.79	2.75	0.10
2007	13.71	5.75	0.97	55.57	0.27	6.28	10.43	1.96	4.94	0.10
2008	9.42	3.86	0.74	72.36	0.24	3.74	6.36	1.19	2.05	0.06
2009	16.10	6.50	1.07	53.30	0.42	5.79	9.76	0.92	3.40	2.74
2010	11.30	3.94	0.63	71.03	0.19	4.29	5.29	0.76	2.24	0.34
2011	35.22	4.16	2.49	31.79	0.65	7.23	6.26	7.24	2.94	2.02
2012	34.51	4.76	0.71	24.35	1.27	14.96	9.81	2.81	6.39	0.42

Source: World Integrated Trade Solution (WITS) (2014).

factors (for example, hurricanes) but also by market developments affecting their major exports. Conditions change quickly, creating unstable social and political situations.

Glewwe and Hall (1998) put forward the notion that, theoretically speaking, economic agents are disadvantaged due to factors such as external shocks, unstable employment opportunities and the fall in demand for lowly paid jobs as technology changes. Table 2.27 gives some indication of the poverty levels in CARICOM countries. The poverty gap ratio, which is a measure of the mean distance separating the population from the poverty line (with the non-poor being given a distance of zero) expressed as a percentage of the poverty line, varies from 0.02 per cent and 1.1 per cent in Jamaica and Trinidad and Tobago to 17.1 per cent in Suriname for the years available.

Table 2.24 Share of intra-CARICOM trade, 1980–2012

Year	Share of Intra-CARICOM Exports				Share of Intra-CARICOM Imports			
	TT/CARICOM	MDC/CARICOM	LDC/CARICOM	OECS/CARICOM	TT/CARICOM	MDC/CARICOM	LDC/CARICOM	OECS/CARICOM
1980	78.13	94.65	5.35	4.42	26.83	69.43	30.57	17.08
1981	66.80	93.93	6.07	4.51	23.39	87.05	12.95	9.19
1982	69.72	94.68	5.32	3.88	42.25	81.33	18.67	8.56
1983	56.60	87.68	12.32	6.38	47.23	83.06	16.94	10.52
1984	69.71	92.12	7.88	1.68	52.71	91.80	8.20	5.41
1985	75.52	89.41	10.59	7.24	32.08	74.65	25.35	17.86
1986	57.80	86.19	13.81	12.48	26.12	67.85	32.15	29.62
1987	59.42	86.70	13.30	9.82	20.42	68.74	31.26	28.80
1988	55.13	86.16	13.84	7.14	21.82	73.65	26.35	23.35
1989	56.45	90.57	9.43	7.75	20.16	76.67	23.33	20.87
1990	63.30	93.06	6.94	7.97	19.43	74.71	25.29	22.37
1991	61.23	94.62	5.38	8.48	18.15	76.89	23.11	23.11
1992	65.70	95.23	4.77	3.27	17.50	83.84	16.16	13.61
1993	65.95	88.20	11.80	10.93	12.08	60.23	39.77	37.46
1994	67.76	88.72	11.28	10.44	8.92	66.90	33.10	31.16
1995	71.71	90.44	9.56	8.83	7.99	69.18	30.82	28.65

Year								
1996	73.52	91.92	8.08	7.52	11.37	76.13	23.87	22.43
1997	68.84	91.54	8.46	7.62	10.23	75.00	25.00	18.90
1998	72.28	94.14	5.86	4.61	11.53	79.45	20.55	18.92
1999	67.91	85.97	14.03	6.67	10.47	64.13	35.87	19.07
2000	76.61	93.47	6.53	5.65	9.73	74.69	25.31	20.23
2001	78.46	94.00	6.00	5.10	9.69	77.67	22.33	19.31
2002	72.58	93.24	6.76	5.73	8.45	75.40	24.60	21.92
2003	75.18	93.46	6.54	5.17	6.41	80.20	19.80	17.82
2004	70.74	92.41	7.59	5.68	6.94	77.55	22.45	20.96
2005	84.07	95.99	4.01	2.99	4.79	79.42	20.58	15.42
2006	84.10	96.25	3.75	2.97	4.19	76.62	23.38	17.86
2007	76.28	95.17	4.83	3.95	4.69	77.48	22.52	19.21
2008	84.64	96.91	3.09	2.66	3.52	83.07	16.93	15.37
2009	74.91	94.72	5.28	2.95	5.28	80.89	19.11	13.74
2010	76.02	97.35	2.65	1.95	5.51	84.83	15.17	9.66
2011	75.16	91.15	8.85	4.90	5.41	86.07	13.93	6.19
2012[a]	74.32	87.09	12.91	3.27	4.53	98.28	1.72	8.32

[a]Preliminary.

Source: World Integrated Trade Solution (WITS) (2014) and CARICOM Secretariat.

Table 2.25 Intra-CARICOM exports as a share of total exports in various member states, 1980–2012

	ATG	BRB	DOM	GRD	GUY	JAM	KNA	LCA	VCT	TTO
1980	–	27.99	58.18	11.30	–	6.21	–	38.66	41.20	11.64
1981	69.12	33.32	43.22	–	19.23	7.16	14.58	48.02	–	11.37
1982	–	31.26	–	–	–	11.12	21.38	47.70	–	12.62
1983	–	21.09	49.42	–	–	14.13	21.40	41.31	–	12.57
1984	–	10.36	–	35.61	–	7.64	–	–	–	12.03
1985	–	2.10	38.61	35.74	–	9.22	–	21.29	–	13.54
1986	–	13.48	26.42	24.62	–	7.88	12.05	15.68	–	10.71
1987	–	23.48	20.77	14.34	–	7.06	7.00	20.41	–	12.89
1988	–	27.38	1.47	16.68	–	7.38	–	18.03	–	13.99
1989	–	32.90	28.52	21.29	–	6.97	–	19.36	–	17.51
1990	–	30.78	25.42	28.09	–	6.54	–	16.22	–	14.85
1991	–	32.84	25.41	34.74	–	6.11	–	15.59	–	13.18
1992	–	39.49	–	–	–	5.96	–	11.44	–	14.36
1993	–	45.37	29.03	32.07	–	5.63	7.36	12.17	46.63	21.58
1994	–	39.67	35.42	24.88	–	4.96	7.90	15.76	54.68	20.08
1995	–	42.94	42.96	25.49	–	4.19	9.58	16.05	46.42	21.93
1996	–	40.53	47.36	27.71	–	3.87	1.78	12.81	49.44	24.75
1997	–	41.80	51.29	31.75	11.49	3.34	2.87	16.03	58.95	25.35
1998	–	49.07	–	23.19	11.26	3.41	–	18.75	50.26	30.17
1999	72.31	49.70	57.07	28.37	11.77	3.39	3.14	21.86	49.29	26.61
2000	66.39	51.42	58.33	14.48	19.45	3.35	6.54	26.15	49.05	23.30
2001	–	50.22	59.99	17.49	18.87	3.99	2.42	29.26	59.74	21.00
2002	–	51.99	57.33	27.65	25.92	4.14	1.45	33.21	51.61	21.26
2003	–	51.83	65.04	37.49	25.46	4.01	1.20	43.16	58.17	19.62
2004	–	52.33	60.91	31.09	24.88	3.28	1.75	42.68	58.64	13.59
2005	58.18	55.18	57.79	44.07	23.11	2.80	2.19	49.56	63.68	21.66
2006	–	51.95	63.12	62.19	23.42	2.45	4.81	47.95	67.37	17.42
2007	63.66	59.89	64.29	37.37	24.93	2.25	5.92	56.80	68.82	13.30
2008	–	51.96	61.34	58.01	19.07	2.42	6.46	43.68	82.70	18.02
2009	44.79	50.71	61.31	–	16.00	4.68	8.97	–	85.68	15.97
2010	46.37	44.47	72.28	–	20.87	4.77	8.49	–	84.94	20.32
2011	27.57	45.31	–	–	22.45	3.96	8.36	–	93.90	–
2012	–	47.66	–	–	–	5.71	–	–	–	–

Note: ATG, Antigua & Barbuda; BRB, Barbados; DOM, Dominica; GRD, Grenada; GUY, Guyana; JAM, Jamaica; KNA,
St Kitts and Nevis; LCA, St Lucia; VCT, St Vincent and the Grenadines; TTO, Trinidad and Tobago.

Economic vulnerability can be defined as the risk of harmful unforeseen events associated with exogenous shocks (Guillaumont 1999). These shocks, which can negatively impact on welfare, growth and development, can be grouped into three categories and are as follows:

Table 2.26 Correlation between growth of GDP and share of intra-regional exports in total exports in CARICOM member states, 1980–2012

ATG	BRB	DMA	GRD	GUY	JAM	KNA	LCA	VCT	TTO
0.69	−0.18	−0.21	−0.27	0.34	−0.02	−0.02	−0.04	−0.52	0.13

Source: World Integrated Trade Solution (WITS) (2014).

(1) environmental shocks, which include natural disasters such as earthquakes, hurricanes, typhoons and drought; (2) external trade and exchange-related shocks such as global interest rate fluctuations, severe decreases in demand, instability of commodity prices; and (3) non-environmental domestic shocks such as political instability as well as uprisings.

Briguglio (1995) derived a composite vulnerability index for small island states and their economic vulnerabilities. Briguglio attempted to show that small states are typified by a special set of disadvantages, which makes them very vulnerable to a number of external forces. Based on three variables, economic exposure, a transport index and a disaster prone index, Briguglio determined that the fifteen most vulnerable economies in the world were as shown in the table 2.28. Note that eight of these fifteen countries are CARICOM member states.

One of the main economic factors that impact upon Caribbean trade and development is the relatively small size of these countries. According to ECLAC (1996), smallness does not inherently result in a negative impact, but it does limit the choices of the policymakers when prescribing developmental plans.

Another factor is domestic macroeconomic and regional trade policies. In particular, for those countries that implemented import substituting policies,[12] they are still attempting to recover as they have not experienced similar levels of economic growth and are still handicapped by recurring shortages of foreign exchange. Further, these countries are characterized by slow export earnings, high vulnerability to the vagaries of export markets and increased dependence on trade preferences. In recent years, efforts have been made to reform these ineffective policies, but

Table 2.27 Poverty gap ratio (%) for CARICOM states

Country	Latest Available Year	Percentage
Antigua & Barbuda	2006	6.60
Belize	2002	11.10
Dominica	2010	0.52
Grenada	2008	10.10
Guyana	2006	11.50
Jamaica	2004	0.02
St Kitts & Nevis	2008	6.40
St Lucia	1995	8.60
St Vincent & the Grenadines	1995	12.60
Suriname	2008	17.10
Trinidad & Tobago	2008	1.10

Source: Millennium Development Goals (2013).

Table 2.28 Highest ranked countries using Briguglio's composite vulnerability index

Rank	Country
1	Antigua & Barbuda
2	Tonga
3	Seychelles
4	Vanuatu
5	St Kitts & Nevis
6	St Lucia
7	Chad
8	Singapore
9	St Vincent & the Grenadines
10	Grenada
11	Bahamas
12	Jamaica
13	Kiribati
14	Mauritius
15	Belize

Source: **Briguglio (1995).**

this also has its own complications as the rate of change has been uneven among the countries. Another complication is the fact that reform of regional policies have occurred at a much slower rate than domestic policies and this has resulted in inconsistency which in turn constrains trade and development within the region as a whole (Garrity and Picard 1996; Powell 2013).

2.7 Prospects for the Caribbean Single Market and Economy

The CSME requires a level of cooperation and interaction which so far has eluded Caribbean governments who continue to hold onto an outdated concept of national sovereignty. The absence of a penalty for non-implementation or breaking the rules will continue to encourage the "agreement without commitment" approach to integration which has failed to deepen the movement without destroying the minimalist type economic interaction from the pre-integration period.

The experience with the common external tariff, the movement of people and capital, the programming of industrial production, the rationalization of agriculture, air and sea transportation, the joint development of natural resources, harmonization of fiscal incentives to industry and the coordination of foreign policies point to the considerable gap between rhetoric and policy. For over three decades, CARICOM governments have ignored critical provisions of the treaty and have failed to pursue action which could realize regional objectives. Agriculture continues to decline, while the food import bill continues to increase. Air and sea transport remain chaotic and inadequate. The competition for foreign investment leaves members vulnerable to manipulation and exploitation. The coordination of foreign policies except for a few instances has not been followed in practice. For a region with differing levels of development, industrial programming is critical, but has largely been ignored.

The CARICOM economies are no longer low cost producers based on cheap wages; however, comparatively speaking, CARICOM countries have relatively high standards of education and quality infrastructure and these can be used to foster the growth of industries (HDR 2001).

In this regard, the strategy of development that CARICOM countries can embrace would have much in common to that proposed by Lewis (1950) in his "industrialization by invitation" thesis. Basically, Lewis recognized that CARICOM countries were deficient in several important areas, but especially as concerned the availability of physical capital, entrepreneurial capital, technology and markets. One CARICOM member state, Trinidad and Tobago, has adopted a particular strain of the IBI strategy as proposed by Lewis. In particular, Trinidad and Tobago embraced a resource-based industrialization strategy, in that they sowed some of the economic rents realized during the oil boom into the formation of a series of natural gas–based plants. Trinidad and Tobago has also attracted a substantial amount of foreign players to help exploit its abundant resource of natural gas. In the same vein therefore, resource rich countries such as Suriname, Guyana and Jamaica can pursue more downstream processing of their bauxite and alumina.

CARICOM member states need to recognize that some types of investments which are cost-based are very positively correlated with exports. These types of investments would flow into an economy in search of lower costs of factors of production. In this sense, therefore, the member states of CARICOM should actively seek to promote their comparative advantage, which would include not only its natural resources but also the quality of its labour force and the infrastructure of the region. For CARICOM countries to encourage greater FDI flows, they would need to become more dynamic and try to identify sunrise industries, that is, commodities at the early stages of the international product cycle. (Market seeking investment will not flow into the CARICOM bloc as the market size of CARICOM, even with the inclusion of Haiti, is too small.) The question which arises is whether CARICOM has the potential to identify and germinate such industries, and if not what measures are being put in place to make this capacity a reality?

One definite option for CARICOM states to improve their productivity rests with overall improvements in its stock of human capital and administrative infrastructure, the occurrence of which would increase the regional chance of attracting FDI inflows in those areas, where FDI flows are likely to experience the most rapid growth: biotechnology, information technology and microelectronics. Improvements in the labour productivity of a country through further training and education can also help to attract FDI flows.

Characteristically, CARICOM member states are small and have undiversified export and production structures which are very vulnerable to changes in the international conditions of trade. Consequently, these countries "cannot afford to isolate themselves from their major markets, because they are unlikely on their own to reap sufficient economies of scale and scope to compete effectively in global markets. For small economies, the issue is not whether to integrate with their hemispheric trading partners, but how" (Schott 2001, 99).

Importantly though, regardless of the extent of trade liberalization practised by CARICOM member states they would still need to administer sound macroeconomic management policies in order to take a meaningful part in the proposed Canada-CARICOM FTA. Regardless of the extent of liberalization practised by member states, they will not be able to overcome the costs of macroeconomic deficiencies if they cannot practise the right amount of macroeconomic reforms domestically. In addition, one may point out that for small economies, the type of adjustment that they may be required to adopt in the context of the pending FTA would not be significantly different from that required by multilateral liberalization. In this regard, therefore, and on the presumption that globalization is not likely to change direction, small economies of the Western Hemisphere are on the correct pathway.

2.8 Conclusion

This chapter examined several key macroeconomic and trade indicators for CARICOM countries. The main findings indicate that while aggregate GDP has increased for all CARICOM members over the period 1990–2012, there were significant differences in the growth rates of these economies over the same period. The data showed that countries such as Grenada, St Kitts and Nevis, and St Vincent and the Grenadines experienced significant contractions in economic activity while Belize and Trinidad and Tobago emerged as two of the fastest growing economies in CARICOM for the period 1990–2012. An examination of the structure of CARICOM economies revealed that most of the economies are becoming more dependent on services and this is associated with a decline in the output share of the agricultural sector. In addition, there has been an increase in the contribution of the mining sector to GDP for countries such as Suriname, Guyana, and Trinidad and Tobago. The analysis shows that all CARICOM countries have negative current account balances and fiscal deficits as a share of their GDP (with the exception of Trinidad and Tobago and Suriname in the case of the former). Indeed, fiscal deficits for Antigua and Barbuda, the Bahamas, Dominica, Grenada, Guyana and St Lucia have worsened in recent times. This situation is further troubling as an evaluation of the real effective exchange rate indicated that the CARICOM economies are becoming less competitive in the external market while engaging in a more competitive global marketplace. The chapter examined the structure and composition of CARICOM trade and noted that issues such as poverty and inequality can aggravate the region's vulnerability.

3 | Regional Economic Partnership Agreements
The European Union–CARIFORUM Agreement

3.1 Introduction

The global economy is currently witnessing a growing wave of regionalism. For example, in 1991, there was the formation of MERCOSUR, a new regional trade agreement (RTA) in South America. Also, in 1994, the North American Free Trade Area, between Mexico, Canada and the United States was formed. The number of regional trade agreements in the world has increased steadily in recent years and according to the World Trade Organization, 583 notifications of regional trade agreements were made by January 2014.[13] The majority of these RTAs are free trade agreements and partial scope agreements (90 per cent) while only 10 per cent are customs unions. Additionally, in Africa several new preferential trading agreements have been founded and old ones have been revitalized. For instance, there was the creation of economic partnership agreements (EPAs) between the European Union and African Caribbean Pacific (ACP) countries, which intended to foster North-South cooperation, through trade development, sustainable growth and poverty reduction. EPAs date back to the signing of the Cotonou Agreement in 2000 and are tailor made to focus on specific regional situations.

Within the realm of the Caribbean, the Canada-CARICOM Free Trade Agreement was established. This agreement intended to strengthen ties with the Americas especially with reference to trade in agricultural foods. The Caribbean region has enjoyed for many years, preferential access to foreign markets for their goods and services. However, especially within recent times, there has been a gradual removal of non-reciprocal trade preferences (one way preferences) in extra-CARICOM markets. As the US and Canadian governments negotiate for bilateral and/or more reciprocal trade agreements with other countries for further liberalization to take effect, the preferences are becoming increasingly eroded. This trend has already started with CARIFORUM signing a new EPA with the European Community (EC) that allows the EC phased duty-free market access for approximately 87 per cent of EC imports coming from CARIFORUM markets (Wharton 2009). This chapter is divided into two parts. The first part discusses some of the background theory to the economic integration process (sections 3.1–3.8), while the second part discusses the application of various aspects of this theory to the regional economic partnership agreement signed between the European Union and the CARIFORUM.

Within the Caribbean, as mentioned earlier, the CARICOM Single Market and Economy was formed among thirteen small Caribbean economies in 2006. Table 3.1 shows various trading agreements and their member countries around the world.

Table 3.1 List of regional trade agreements in the global economy and their membership

Regional Trade Agreement (RTA) Name	Type	Membership
Andean Community (CAN)	CU	Bolivia, Plurinational State of; Colombia; Ecuador; Peru
ASEAN – Australia – New Zealand	FTA & EIA	Australia; Brunei Darussalam; Myanmar; Cambodia; Indonesia; Lao People's Democratic Republic; Malaysia; Philippines; Singapore; Vietnam; Thailand; New Zealand
ASEAN Free Trade Area (AFTA)	FTA	Brunei Darussalam; Cambodia; Indonesia; Lao People's Democratic Republic; Malaysia; Myanmar; Philippines; Singapore; Thailand; Vietnam
Asia Pacific Trade Agreement (APTA)	PSA	Bangladesh; China; India; Korea, Republic of; Lao People's Democratic Republic; Sri Lanka
Caribbean Community and Common Market (CARICOM)	CU & EIA	Antigua & Barbuda; Bahamas; Barbados; Belize; Dominica; Grenada; Guyana; Haiti; Jamaica; Montserrat; St Kitts & Nevis; St Lucia; St Vincent & the Grenadines; Suriname; Trinidad & Tobago
Central American Common Market (CACM)	CU	Costa Rica; El Salvador; Guatemala; Honduras; Nicaragua
Central European Free Trade Agreement (CEFTA) 2006	FTA	Albania; Bosnia and Herzegovina; Moldova, Republic of; Montenegro; Serbia; The former Yugoslav Republic of Macedonia; UNMIK/Kosovo
Colombia – Northern Triangle (El Salvador, Guatemala, Honduras)	FTA & EIA	Colombia; El Salvador; Guatemala; Honduras
Common Economic Zone (CEZ)	FTA	Belarus; Kazakhstan; Russian Federation; Ukraine
Common Market for Eastern and Southern Africa (COMESA)	CU	Burundi; Comoros; DR Congo; Djibouti; Egypt; Eritrea; Ethiopia; Kenya; Libyan Arab Jamahiriya; Madagascar; Malawi; Mauritius; Rwanda; Seychelles; Sudan; Swaziland; Uganda; Zambia; Zimbabwe
Commonwealth of Independent States (CIS)	FTA	Azerbaijan; Georgia; Turkmenistan; Uzbekistan
Dominican Republic – Central America	FTA & EIA	Costa Rica; Dominican Republic; El Salvador; Guatemala; Honduras; Nicaragua

Table 3.1 List of regional trade agreements in the global economy (*continued*)

Regional Trade Agreement (RTA) Name	Type	Membership
Dominican Republic – Central America – United States Free Trade Agreement (CAFTA-DR)	FTA & EIA	Costa Rica; Dominican Republic; El Salvador; Guatemala; Honduras; Nicaragua; United States of America
East African Community (EAC)	CU & EIA	Burundi; Kenya; Rwanda; Tanzania; Uganda
EC Treaty	CU & EIA	Austria; Belgium; Bulgaria; Croatia; Cyprus; Czech Republic; Denmark; Estonia; Finland; France; Germany; Greece; Hungary; Ireland; Italy; Latvia; Lithuania; Luxembourg; Malta; Netherlands; Poland; Portugal; Romania; Slovak Republic; Slovenia; Spain; Sweden; United Kingdom
Economic and Monetary Community of Central Africa (CEMAC)	CU	Cameroon; Central African Republic; Chad; Congo; Equatorial Guinea; Gabon
Economic Community of West African States (ECOWAS)	CU	Benin; Burkina Faso; Cape Verde; Côte d'Ivoire; Ghana; Guinea; Guinea-Bissau; Liberia, Republic of; Mali; Niger; Nigeria; Senegal; Sierra Leone; The Gambia; Togo
Economic Cooperation Organization (ECO)	PSA	Afghanistan; Azerbaijan; Islamic Republic of Iran; Kazakhstan; Kyrgyz Republic; Pakistan; Tajikistan; Turkey; Turkmenistan; Uzbekistan
El Salvador – Honduras – Chinese Taipei	FTA & EIA	Chinese Taipei; El Salvador; Honduras
EU – CARIFORUM States EPA	FTA & EIA	Antigua & Barbuda; Austria; Belgium; Bulgaria; Croatia; Cyprus; Czech Republic; Denmark; Estonia; Finland; France; Germany; Greece; Hungary; Ireland; Italy; Latvia; Lithuania; Luxembourg; Malta; Netherlands; Poland; Portugal; Romania; Slovak Republic; Slovenia; Spain; Sweden; United Kingdom; Bahamas; Barbados; Belize; Dominica; Dominican Republic; Grenada; Guyana; Jamaica; St Kitts & Nevis; St Lucia; St Vincent & the Grenadines; Suriname; Trinidad & Tobago
EU – Central America	FTA & EIA	Austria; Belgium; Bulgaria; Croatia; Cyprus; Czech Republic; Denmark; Estonia; Finland; France; Germany; Greece; Hungary; Ireland; Italy; Latvia; Lithuania; Luxembourg; Malta; Netherlands; Poland; Portugal; Romania; Slovak Republic; Slovenia; Spain; Sweden; United Kingdom; Costa Rica; El Salvador; Guatemala; Honduras; Nicaragua; Panama
EU – Chile	FTA & EIA	Austria; Belgium; Bulgaria; Croatia; Cyprus; Czech Republic; Denmark; Estonia; Finland; France; Germany; Greece; Hungary; Ireland; Italy; Latvia; Lithuania; Luxembourg; Malta; Netherlands; Poland; Portugal; Romania; Slovak Republic; Slovenia; Spain; Sweden; United Kingdom; Colombia; Peru

(*Table 3.1 continues*)

Table 3.1 List of regional trade agreements in the global economy (*continued*)

Regional Trade Agreement (RTA) Name	Type	Membership
EU – Eastern and Southern Africa States Interim EPA	FTA	Austria; Belgium; Bulgaria; Croatia; Cyprus; Czech Republic; Denmark; Estonia; Finland; France; Germany; Greece; Hungary; Ireland; Italy; Latvia; Lithuania; Luxembourg; Malta; Netherlands; Poland; Portugal; Romania; Slovak Republic; Slovenia; Spain; Sweden; United Kingdom; Madagascar; Mauritius; Seychelles; Zimbabwe
EU – Overseas Countries and Territories (OCT)	FTA	Anguilla; Aruba; Austria; Belgium; Bulgaria; Croatia; Cyprus; Czech Republic; Denmark; Estonia; Finland; France; Germany; Greece; Hungary; Ireland; Italy; Latvia; Lithuania; Luxembourg; Malta; Netherlands; Poland; Portugal; Romania; Slovak Republic; Slovenia; Spain; Sweden; United Kingdom; British Indian Ocean Territory; Cayman Islands; Falkland Islands (Islas Malvinas); French Polynesia; French Southern Territories; Greenland; Mayotte; Montserrat; Netherlands Antilles; New Caledonia; Pitcairn; St Helena; St Pierre and Miquelon; South Georgia and the South Sandwich Islands; Turks and Caicos Islands; Virgin Islands, British; Wallis and Futuna Islands
EU – Papua New Guinea / Fiji	FTA	Austria; Belgium; Bulgaria; Croatia; Cyprus; Czech Republic; Denmark; Estonia; Finland; France; Germany; Greece; Hungary; Ireland; Italy; Latvia; Lithuania; Luxembourg; Malta; Netherlands; Poland; Portugal; Romania; Slovak Republic; Slovenia; Spain; Sweden; United Kingdom; Fiji; Papua New Guinea
EU – Switzerland – Liechtenstein	FTA	Austria; Belgium; Bulgaria; Croatia; Cyprus; Czech Republic; Denmark; Estonia; Finland; France; Germany; Greece; Hungary; Ireland; Italy; Latvia; Lithuania; Luxembourg; Malta; Netherlands; Poland; Portugal; Romania; Slovak Republic; Slovenia; Spain; Sweden; United Kingdom; Liechtenstein; Switzerland
Eurasian Economic Community (EAEC)	CU	Belarus; Kazakhstan; Kyrgyz Republic; Russian Federation; Tajikistan
European Economic Area (EEA)	EIA	Austria; Belgium; Bulgaria; Croatia; Cyprus; Czech Republic; Denmark; Estonia; Finland; France; Germany; Greece; Hungary; Ireland; Italy; Latvia; Lithuania; Luxembourg; Malta; Netherlands; Poland; Portugal; Romania; Slovak Republic; Slovenia; Spain; Sweden; United Kingdom; Iceland; Liechtenstein; Norway
European Free Trade Association (EFTA)	FTA & EIA	Iceland; Liechtenstein; Norway; Switzerland
Gulf Cooperation Council (GCC)	CU	Bahrain, Kingdom of; Kuwait, the State of; Oman; Qatar; Saudi Arabia, Kingdom of; United Arab Emirates

Table 3.1 List of regional trade agreements in the global economy (*continued*)

Regional Trade Agreement (RTA) Name	Type	Membership
Latin American Integration Association (LAIA)	PSA	Argentina; Bolivia, Plurinational State of; Brazil; Chile; Colombia; Cuba; Ecuador; Mexico; Paraguay; Peru; Uruguay; Venezuela, Bolivarian Republic of
Melanesian Spearhead Group (MSG)	PSA	Fiji; Papua New Guinea; Solomon Islands; Vanuatu
North American Free Trade Agreement (NAFTA)	FTA & EIA	Canada; Mexico; United States of America
Pacific Island Countries Trade Agreement (PICTA)	FTA	Cook Islands; Fiji; Kiribati; Micronesia, Federated States of; Nauru; Niue; Papua New Guinea; Samoa; Solomon Islands; Tonga; Tuvalu; Vanuatu
Pan-Arab Free Trade Area (PAFTA)	FTA	Algeria; the Palestinian Authority of the West Bank and the Gaza Strip; Bahrain, Kingdom of; Egypt; Iraq; Jordan; Kuwait, the State of; Lebanese Republic; Libya; Morocco; Oman; Qatar; Saudi Arabia, Kingdom of; Sudan; Syrian Arab Republic; Tunisia; United Arab Emirates; Yemen
South Asian Free Trade Agreement (SAFTA)	FTA	Bangladesh; Bhutan; India; Maldives; Nepal; Pakistan; Sri Lanka
South Asian Preferential Trade Arrangement (SAPTA)	PSA	Bangladesh; Bhutan; India; Maldives; Nepal; Pakistan; Sri Lanka
South Pacific Regional Trade and Economic Cooperation Agreement (SPARTECA)	PSA	Australia; Cook Islands; Fiji; Kiribati; Marshall Islands; Micronesia, Federated States of; Nauru; New Zealand; Niue; Papua New Guinea; Samoa; Solomon Islands; Tonga; Tuvalu; Vanuatu
Southern African Customs Union (SACU)	CU	Botswana; Lesotho; Namibia; South Africa; Swaziland
Southern African Development Community (SADC)	FTA	Angola; Botswana; DR Congo; Lesotho; Malawi; Madagascar; Mauritius; Mozambique; Namibia; Seychelles; South Africa; Swaziland; Tanzania; Zambia; Zimbabwe
Southern Common Market (MERCOSUR)	CU & EIA	Argentina; Brazil; Paraguay; Uruguay; the Bolivarian Republic of Venezuela
Trans-Pacific Strategic Economic Partnership	FTA & EIA	Brunei Darussalam; Chile; New Zealand; Singapore
Treaty on a Free Trade Area between members of the Commonwealth of Independent States (CIS)	FTA	Armenia; Belarus; Kazakhstan; Kyrgyz Republic; Moldova, Republic of; Russian Federation; Tajikistan; Ukraine
West African Economic and Monetary Union (WAEMU)	CU	Benin; Burkina Faso; Côte d'Ivoire; Guinea Bissau; Mali; Niger; Senegal; Togo

Note: CU, customs union; FTA, free trade agreement; PSA, partial scope agreement; EIA, economic integration agreement.

Source: World Trade Organization (2014).

Intra-PTA trade represented about 35 per cent of total world merchandise trade in 2008, compared with 18 per cent in 1990. In practice, RTAs are designed to offer reciprocal trading preferences to those within the RTA and discrimination against external parties. However, this drift towards increased RTA in the global economy has sprouted an important concern, that is, RTAs while potentially acting as instruments for trade creation within the membership pact, impose an opportunity cost, especially in small economies, of diverting trade from more efficient extra-regional partners. This and other theoretical attributes of RTAs are detailed in this chapter.

3.2 Categories of Regional Trade Agreements

There are several forms of regional economic integration. These are as follows:

1. Free trade areas (FTA): This is where member states remove all barriers to trade between themselves and their integration partners. However, members of an RTA retain the right to have their own independent commercial policies. Examples include the Latin American free trade area (LAFTA) and European Free Trade Association (EFTA).
2. Customs union: These are similar to FTAs but carry the attachment of a common commercial policy, that is, it includes a common external tariff, for example, the Central American Common Market (CACM) and CARICOM.
3. Common market: This is a customs union which has graduated to the stage of allowing the free intra-regional movement of factors of production. The CARICOM integration agreement graduated to the stage of a single market in January 2006.
4. Complete economic union: This is a common market which carries a common block of fiscal and monetary policies.
5. Complete political union: This is where the member states involved actually become one nation, for example, the political union of East and West Germany in the 1980s to form Germany.

Table 3.2 provides summary information on the various attributes of RTAs.

Table 3.2 Categories of regional trading agreements

Free Trade Area	Customs Union	Common Market	European Union	Political Union
1	1	1	1	1
	2	2	2	2
		3	3	3
			4	4
				5

Source: El Agraa (1999).

where

1 = removal of intra-group tariffs
2 = external tariff

3 = intra-group capital and labour mobility
4 = common economic policy and common currency
5 = one government.

Economic integration schemes occur at various degrees, and once the integration process has started, it can evolve over time.

3.2.1 Dynamic Gains from a Customs Union

Countries embrace RTAs for a number of reasons. This section discusses some of the dynamic gains and losses associated with RTAs.

Greater specialization and economies of scale: When a customs union is formed, there is an expansion in the preferential market base of the home country firm, beyond that of the home country's economy, towards that of the market base represented by the customs union. This greater target market base can encourage domestic firms to specialize and benefit from economies of scale. Thus, within CARICOM, firms from Trinidad and Tobago, for example, would have access to a market size of approximately seventeen million people compared to only 1.3 million which exists in the local economy. In other words, firms in Trinidad and Tobago would have access to a larger market base, under the umbrella of the CARICOM regional integration arrangement (table 3.3).

Table 3.3 Population of CARICOM economies, 2012

CARICOM Country	Population 2012	Population as a % of Total CARICOM Population
Antigua & Barbuda	89,069	0.52
Bahamas	371,960	2.17
Barbados	283,221	1.65
Belize	324,060	1.89
Dominica	71,684	0.42
Grenada	105,483	0.62
Guyana	795,369	4.64
Haiti	10,173,775	59.36
Jamaica	2,707,805	15.80
St Kitts & Nevis	53,584	0.31
St Lucia	180,870	1.06
St Vincent & the Grenadines	109,373	0.64
Suriname	534,541	3.12
Trinidad & Tobago	1,337,439	7.80
Total	17,138,233	100.00

Source: World Development Indicators (2014).

Higher levels of competition: With the larger number of firms that would exist in a regional trade bloc as a whole as compared to any single member of that trade bloc, there is naturally a fiercer amount of rivalry among firms, especially among those in the same industry. Increased competition helps to minimize economic wasting by improving factor allocation.

Higher levels of investment: RTAs by virtue of representing larger markets help to stimulate investment by both domestic and foreign firms. Domestic firms invest more within RTAs as the larger market requires greater volumes of output. Larger markets also potentially offer higher levels of profits. Foreign firms may invest in RTAs so as to escape any tariff barriers that are enacted with the formation of the RTA. Jaumotte (2004) examined the relationship between RTAs and FDI for seventy one developing countries over the period 1980–99 and found that RTAs have a positive impact on inward FDI. Jaumotte (2004) also noted that countries with a larger population (labour supply), educated labour force, and stable financial environment within the RTA tend to command a larger share of inward FDI in the RTA. Te Velde and Bezemer (2006) also found that RTAs with more trade and investments provisions are likely to attract a greater share of FDI inflows. Specifically, RTAs such as ANDEAN, ASEAN, CARICOM and NAFTA have benefited from increased FDI from the United States and the United Kingdom (Liu 2006; te Velde and Nair 2006; Thangavelu and Findlay 2011).

3.2.2 Possible Dynamic Losses

Economic integration often results in some inequitable distribution of benefits. In general, the advanced countries gain, and the less advanced ones tend to lose. In order to avoid the fragmentation of any RTA, as a consequence of an inequitable distribution of the material gains, suitable policy measures should be established to assist disadvantaged economies. Assistance can be provided in the form of financial and technological investments.

3.3 Phrases and Concepts Used in Regional Trade Agreement Discussions

In the literature, there are two key phrases and two key concepts used in the study of economic integration arrangements. The two key phrases are preferential trading agreements (PTAs) and regionalism. The two key concepts are trade creation and trade diversion, as introduced by Viner (1950), and stumbling blocks and building blocks, as introduced by Bhagwati and Panagariya (1996). PTAs refer to trading blocs where special access is given to specific products from certain countries. In this case tariffs are reduced but not removed completely. This is the weakest form of economic integration. One such example is the free trading area formed between the European Union and ACP countries. Viner (1950) outlined the concepts of trade creation and trade diversion as two possibilities that define the second best nature of the static analysis of PTAs. Trade diversion refers to the shift in import source from an efficient to an inefficient source, while trade creation refers to the shift in import source from an inefficient source to an efficient source.

The main aim of Viner's (1950) trade creation and trade diversion concepts was to divide PTAs into those that were bad and those that were good in the static sense. The main objective of Bhagwati's (1991) introduction of the terms building block and stumbling block, was to divide PTAs into those that are good and those that are bad in the dynamic, time path sense. According to Bhagwati (1991, 77), this is done either by progressively adding new members or by prompting the accelerated freeing of trade (building blocs), and those that do the opposite and hence are stumbling blocks to the goal of the multinational freeing up of trade.

3.4 World Trade Organization Provisions for PTAs

The member countries of the WTO, under the GATT, banned member countries from pursuing discriminatory trade policies against one another. This ban was implemented under the MFN clause in article I of the GATT. The 1994 Marrakesh Agreement established that the WTO is quite unequivocal: "With respect to customs duties and charges of any kind . . . any advantage, favour, privilege or immunity granted by any contracting party to any product originating in or destined for any other country shall be accorded immediately and unconditionally to like product originating in or destined for the territories of all other contracting parties" (GATT 1994, 486).

Article XXIV of the GATT, however, provided accommodation for PTAs providing that they remove rather than lower within-union trade barriers, on goods produced outside the union. Under these provisions, FTAs are legalized and the average external tariff remains unchanged.

3.5 Export Performance of Trade Blocs and Member Countries

Table 3.4 shows the export performance of NAFTA and the European Union alongside some trade blocs in Latin America and the Caribbean (LAC) for the period 2001–12. Among the trade blocs listed, the European Union experienced the greatest amount of total intra-regional exports, with

Table 3.4 (a) Exports in US$ million, (b) exports within bloc as % of total exports, (c) total exports by bloc as % of world exports

Year	ACS	ANDEAN	CACM	MERCOSUR	LAIA	OECS	NAFTA	EU	CARICOM
				(a) *Exports in US$ million*					
2001	10,832	2,328	5,066	15,181	44,064	30	603,807	1,623,194	1,377
2002	9,856	2,541	4,464	10,189	37,794	30	591,203	1,737,875	1,137
2003	11,031	2,932	4,725	12,771	43,292	32	614,530	2,092,667	1,350
2004	11,977	3,368	4,968	17,105	59,206	32	679,751	2,499,408	1,268
2005	17,045	4,537	6,073	21,121	75,104	38	759,273	2,666,800	2,488
2006	18,107	5,190	5,246	25,766	93,130	40	830,280	3,040,577	2,933
2007	23,107	5,922	7,820	32,379	107,117	45	876,823	3,540,520	2,380
2008	28,238	7,073	8,940	41,635	136,896	55	932,502	3,850,750	4,020
2009	21,054	5,835	7,737	32,725	99,638	31	694,264	2,962,758	1,900
2010	27,530	7,743	9,264	44,602	129,896	28	861,675	3,249,517	2,695

(*Table 3.4 continues*)

Table 3.4 (a) Exports in US$ million, (b) exports within bloc and (c) total exports by bloc (*continued*)

Year	ACS	ANDEAN	CACM	MERCOSUR	LAIA	OECS	NAFTA	EU	CARICOM
2011	37,595	9,198	15,889	54,244	164,483	23	992,700	3,724,691	693
2012	33,114	10,356	11,880	48,539	158,452	27	1,039,638	3,467,534	481
(b) *Exports within bloc as a % of total exports*									
2001	5.59	9.27	10.82	17.26	13.86	14.71	55.63	67.03	17.33
2002	4.97	9.78	9.74	11.45	11.84	16.35	56.69	67.11	17.35
2003	5.32	9.84	9.42	11.97	12.35	18.96	56.46	68.07	16.67
2004	5.03	8.57	7.04	12.60	13.48	18.03	56.04	67.85	12.69
2005	6.17	8.90	6.39	12.90	14.18	22.50	56.00	67.07	18.57
2006	5.66	7.97	4.90	13.55	14.78	22.34	53.84	67.31	15.72
2007	6.57	7.72	13.69	14.47	16.69	22.85	51.29	67.38	12.71
2008	7.32	7.47	6.10	14.96	16.83	25.02	49.34	66.12	16.27
2009	6.91	7.43	6.82	15.06	15.61	29.45	47.58	65.87	14.58
2010	7.15	7.81	6.78	16.00	15.94	29.88	48.35	64.23	17.89
2011	8.10	6.90	8.32	15.25	16.03	32.40	47.96	62.98	11.61
2012	6.96	7.30	13.34	14.30	17.03	37.48	48.36	61.38	12.97
(c) *Total exports by bloc as a % of world exports*									
2001	0.19	0.04	0.09	0.26	0.76	0.00	10.37	27.88	0.02
2002	0.16	0.04	0.07	0.17	0.62	0.00	9.67	28.42	0.02
2003	0.15	0.04	0.07	0.18	0.61	0.00	8.61	29.33	0.02
2004	0.14	0.04	0.06	0.20	0.69	0.00	7.87	28.95	0.01
2005	0.18	0.05	0.06	0.22	0.77	0.00	7.80	27.39	0.03
2006	0.16	0.05	0.05	0.23	0.82	0.00	7.28	26.66	0.03
2007	0.18	0.05	0.06	0.25	0.82	0.00	6.74	27.20	0.02
2008	0.19	0.05	0.06	0.28	0.91	0.00	6.19	25.56	0.03
2009	0.18	0.05	0.07	0.28	0.85	0.00	5.95	25.41	0.02
2010	0.19	0.05	0.07	0.32	0.92	0.00	6.09	22.98	0.02
2011	0.22	0.05	0.09	0.32	0.97	0.00	5.88	22.06	0.00
2012	0.20	0.06	0.07	0.30	0.97	0.00	6.34	21.16	0.00

Source: United Nations Commodity Trade Database (UNCOMTRADE) (2014).

as much as US$1,623 billion in 2001, which increased to US$3,467 billion in 2012, an increase of 114 per cent. The growth of MERCOSUR's exports was much sharper, increasing from US$15 billion in 2001 to US$48 billion in 2012. None of the trade blocs within the Latin American region experienced export levels that were as significant as those of the European Union and NAFTA. Among the Latin American and Caribbean trade blocs, OECS exports decreased from US$30 million in 2001 to US$27 million in 2012. In the larger trade blocs, NAFTA's exports as a proportion of total world exports experienced a small decline from 10.37 per cent to 6.34 per cent while EU's exports as a percentage of world exports decreased from 27.88 per cent to 21.16 per cent for the same period.

3.6 Welfare Impact of Economic Integration

To assess the net welfare effect of an economic integration arrangement, consider figure 3.1. In this diagram, the following representations hold:

D_H: home country's demand curve
S_H: home country's supply curve
S_W: rest of the world's supply curve
S_P: partner country's supply curve
S_{H+P}:   supply curve of home and partner country.

The analysis presumes the interaction of three regions, W, HC and PC, where:

W: rest of the world
HC: home country
PC: partner country.

In initial conditions of free trade, the HC imports q_5 units from the globally most efficient player in the world (supply curve S_W) at a cost per unit of $A. At this price level, observe that neither the

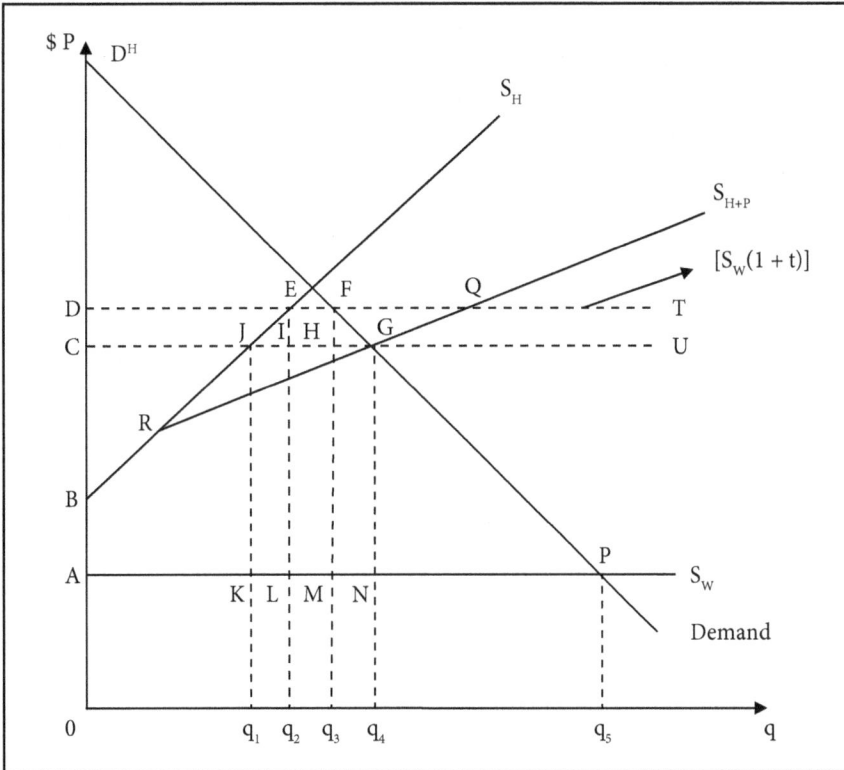

Figure 3.1 Trade creation and trade diversion with a tariff

PC nor HC can supply. Assume now that the HC imposes a non-discriminatory tariff so that the price of imports from W increases to $A(1 + t) = \$D$. With the implementation of this discriminatory tariff, domestic production increases to $0q_2$ and domestic consumption falls from $0q_5$ to $0q_3$, so that imports with a tariff falls to $q_3 - q_2$. Also, with the tariff, consumer surplus in the HC is D^HFD and the associated producer surplus is BDE. The HC collects LEFM in tariff revenues and expends q_2EFq_3 on securing q_2q_3 units of imports.

Let us assume at this stage that the HC and PC form a custom union. This results in a new regional supply curve of S_{H+P}, a new level of domestic production of $0q_1$ and a new level of domestic demand of $0q_4$. With the formation of this customs union, the HC's consumer surplus increases to D^HGC. The change in consumer surplus with the formation of a customs union is given by CDFG.

Let us consider the change in consumer surplus in more detail as shown in figure 3.2.

Observe that this change in consumer surplus can be disaggregated into several parts. The first part shows that part of producer surplus which gets passed onto domestic consumers who benefit from a lower intra-customs union price level. The triangles JEI and HFG represent additions to consumer surplus posted by the fall in the price level. The first triangle JEI represents a cost saving on imports to consumers which extends consumer surplus. The second triangle, HFG, occurs because of the increase in the quantity demanded as price decreases. This brings us to the rectangular area IEFH. Recall that total government revenue with a non-discriminatory tariff was LEFM (figure 3.1). With the formation of a customs union, the government loses this tariff revenue. The sub-rectangular area IEFH is transferred to consumers as consumer surplus. If we assume that consumers and the government value this resource equally (that is, if we assume the principle of equi-marginal valuation holds), then this transfer from government to domestic consumers has no bearing on economic welfare. The sub-rectangular area, LIHM (read from figure 3.3), however, is lost and remains unaccounted.

For a customs union of this nature, the change in welfare (ΔW) is equal to the sum of the change in consumer surplus (ΔCS – this is the gains from trade creation) plus the change in tariff revenues (ΔTR – this is the loss from trade diversion), that is,

$$\Delta W = \Delta CS + \Delta TR$$

A diagrammatic illustration is provided in figure 3.4.

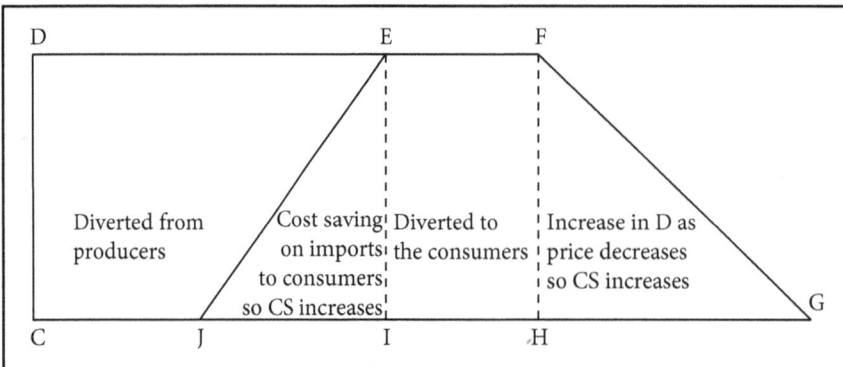

Figure 3.2 Detailed breakdown of change in consumer surplus with a customs union

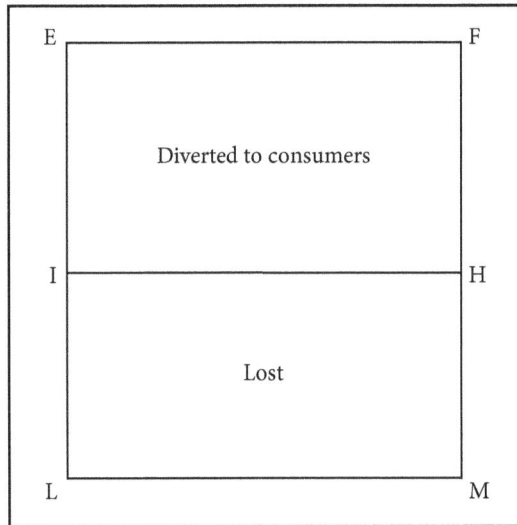

Figure 3.3 Detailed breakdown of government revenues

The reader should ensure an awareness of the following:

If the initial price occurred at the intersection of D_H and S_H in figure 3.1 (this can occur because the initial tariff was set at a higher rate), the formation of a customs union would have been purely trade creating. This is simply because a tariff which posts equilibrium at D_H and S_H is a prohibitive tariff so that no imports result. The formation of the customs union lowers the level of the prohibitive tariff and results in pure trade creation. If the initial price level was OC, then the formation of a customs union would lead to pure trade diversion from the more efficient W to the less efficient PC.

It is then obvious that trade creation is economically desirable while trade diversion is undesirable. It is the relative strength of these two effects which determine whether or not forming a customs union is economically beneficial or harmful.

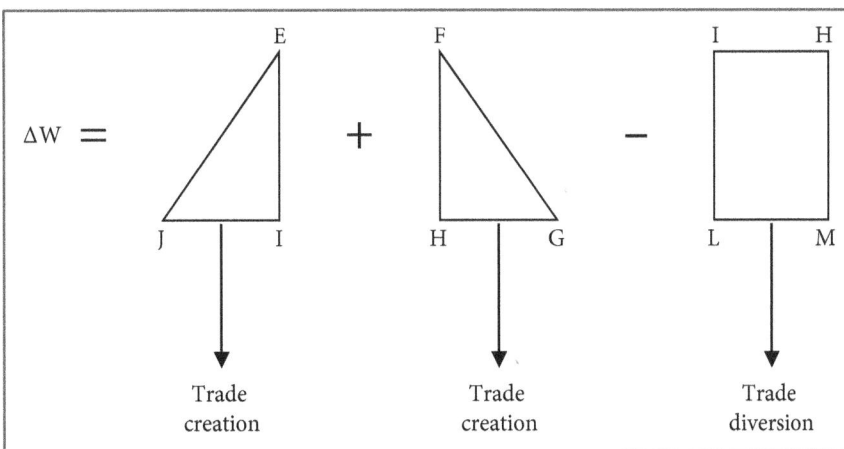

Figure 3.4 Decomposing consumer surplus for a customs union

Table 3.5 Economic effects of a tariff in a small economic integration arrangement

	Before Tariff	With MFN Tariff
Price to consumer	$A	$D
Domestic consumption	q_5	q_3
Domestic production	0	q_2
Imports	q_5	$q_3 - q_2$
Consumer surplus	AD_HP	DD_HF
Producers surplus	NA	BDE
Government revenue	NA	LEFM
Deadweight consumption loss	NA	PFM
Deadweight production efficiency loss	NA	ABEL

3.7 The Cooper-Massell Criticism

The argument of Viner (1950) as outlined in section 3.5 was challenged by Cooper and Massell (1965). Basically, Cooper and Massell argued that the reduction in price from OD to OC should be treated in two phases:

1. Reduce the tariff level for both the PC and W to OC

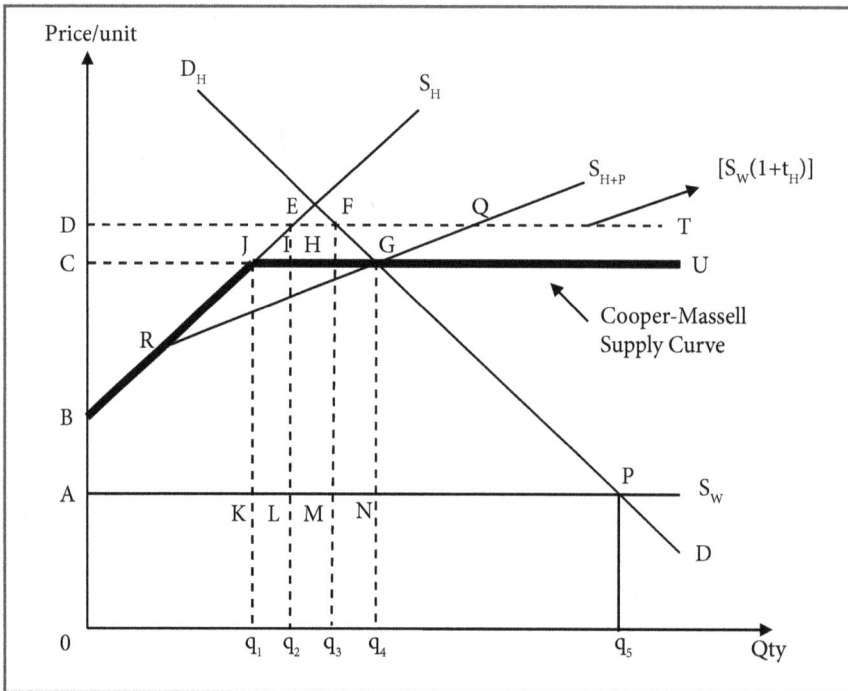

Figure 3.5 Partial equilibrium analysis in a Cooper-Massell setting

Table 3.6 Economic benefits of the Cooper-Massell condition

	Customs Union with PC	**Cooper-Massell Condition**
Price to consumer	OC	OC
Domestic consumption	q_4	q_1
Domestic production	q_1	q_4
Imports	$q_4 - q_1$	$q_4 - q_1$
Consumer surplus	$CD_H G$	$CD_H G$
Producers surplus	BCJ	BCJ
Government revenue	None	KJGN
Deadweight consumption loss	HGPM	GPN
Deadweight production efficiency loss	ABJIL	ABJK

2. Form the customs union at the price OC (figure 3.5).

Under the Cooper-Massell condition, the union price as well as the same levels of production, consumption and imports exists as in the Vinerian model. With the second step, the gains from trade creation, JEI and HFG will continue to result, but the losses from trade diversion (LIHM) no longer accrue as the new supply curve of the home country is BJGU and implies that imports originate from the W at $q_2 LMq_3$, so that the government does not lose the area LIHM as tariff revenues. In this context, Cooper and Massell indicated that a policy of unilateral tariff reduction is superior to a customs union (El Agraa 2002).

3.8 Natural Trading Partner Hypothesis

There are a number of studies in the literature which review the notion that some economies may have natural trading partners. The substantive statements by some of these studies are presented in table 3.7.

Wonnacott and Lutz (1989) introduced the natural trading partner hypothesis and the notion that FTAs among natural trading partners is more likely to improve their economic welfare. The literature identifies several measures for determining a country's natural trading partner. Prominent among them are the initial volume of trade, geographic proximity and trade complementarity.

3.8.1 Volume of Trade

Lipsey (1960) introduced the notion that a high initial volume of trade between prospective members of an FTA will increase welfare. Lipsey (1960, 507–8) asserted that "the larger are purchases of domestic commodities and the smaller are purchases from the outside world, the more likely it is that the union will bring gain". Wonnacott and Lutz (1989, 69) argued that if the prospective members of an FTA are initially important trading partners, then the formation of an FTA among them "will be reinforcing natural trading partners, not artificially diverting them".

Table 3.7 Empirical evidence on natural trading partners

Study	Substantive Statement Supporting the Natural Trading Partner Hypothesis
Lipsey (1960)	A customs union is more likely to raise welfare the higher is the proportion of trade with the country's union partner and the lower the proportion with the outside world.
Summers (1991)	If the prospective members are already major trading partners, integration will be reinforcing natural trading patterns, not artificially diverting them.
Wonnacott and Lutz (1989)	Since proximity between PTA members increases trade between them (due to lower transport costs), it reduces the extent of trade diversion and increases the benefits of PTA.
Krugman (1993)	Due to transportation and communication costs there is a strong tendency for countries to trade with their neighbours. And if free trade agreements are formed with neighbours, the gains from freeing intra-regional trade will be larger and the losses of reducing intra-regional trade will be smaller than if these costs are ignored.
Krugman (1991)	If a disproportionate share of world trade would take place within trading blocs even in the absence of any PTA, then the gains from TC within blocs are likely to outweigh any possible losses from external trade diversion.

Source: Schiff (1997).

Summers (1991, 3) supporting the initial volume of trade criterion, argued that if "blocs are created between countries that already trade disproportionately; the risk of large amounts of trade diversion is reduced". Park (1995) also suggested that the likelihood that trade blocs would result in trade diversion increases when the share of intra-regional trade in total trade is small.

3.8.2 Geography

Wonnacott and Lutz (1989) identified geographic proximity as another important criterion for identifying a natural trading partner. Krugman (1993) noted that there is a strong tendency for countries within geographic proximity to trade more with each other because of the benefits from low transportation and communication costs. Indeed, Deardorff and Stern (1994) asserted that if countries are located close to each other, then the formation of an FTA could increase their economic welfare, as there are benefits to be derived from lower transaction costs. Krugman (1991, 1993) considered economic geography, transportation cost in particular, to show that the success of FTAs depend on the geographic proximity of trading partners. The underlying principle of Krugman's notion is that in the case where inter-continental transport cost is zero, the creation of continental FTAs is likely to reduce economic welfare. On the other hand, when inter-continental transport cost is infinite, continental FTAs are likely to be welfare improving (see also Frankel et al. 1996). This notion was strongly refuted by Panagariya (1999, 16) using the following example:

Suppose the world consists of two continents, two countries per continent, and two goods produced at constant but different labour costs *à la* Ricardo. Suppose further that the countries located on the same continent are identical in all respects but differ across continents. Despite positive transport costs across continents, but none within a continent, there are no gains from forming continental blocs whereas, with sufficiently large comparative cost differences across continents, gains are available to blocs between countries across continents.

Lawrence (1996) and Krueger (1999) have also argued that FTAs between countries that are geographically close may not necessarily lead to trade creation as they are likely to be characterized by similar factor endowments. In particular, Krueger (1999, 116–17) argued that "when neighbors can be similar, it is hard to conclude that trade between neighbors will necessarily be 'natural' in some way . . . (as) neighbors by definition have closer proximity, but their factor endowments and production structures may be quite similar".

Moreover, it is more likely that countries in geographic proximity may share similar factor endowments, technological and production functions (Nadav and Kleiman 2008) implying that FTAs among distant countries can be welfare improving, based on comparative cost differential.

Bhagwati (1993) and Bhagwati and Panagariya (1996) strongly criticized both criteria (initial volume of trade and geographic proximity) for defining a natural trading partner.[14] Specifically, Bhagwati and Panagariya (1996) noted that while a high initial volume of trade among prospective members of an FTA may reduce the scope of trade diversion, it is "actual trade diversion" that is more important. Panagariya (1999) suggested that actual trade diversion is dependent upon the response of the partner country's export to the tariff preference at the margin, while the scope for trade diversion may depend on the extent of intra-union trade. For example, consider a three-country model, inclusive of country A, country B and country C. The higher the volume of trade between country A and country B, implies the lower the level of trade between these two countries and country C, therefore, if countries A and B form an FTA then their scope for diverting trade is likely to be small.

In addition, Bhagwati and Panagariya (1996, 17) argued that an FTA which consists of members that have "asymmetric levels of protection" will tend to result in losses despite net trade creation. Asymmetric levels of protection among prospective members of an FTA occur when some members have a higher level of protection (tariff rate) relative to other countries joining the FTA. This situation can lead to losses to the country with the higher level of tariff protection because of the "tariff-revenue-redistribution effect". The country with a higher tariff rate will forgo tariff revenues previously collected in the pre-FTA environment when it forms an FTA with the other members that have a lower tariff rate. Thus, the loss in tariff revenues to the country with the higher tariff rates can be so much as to offset any gains from trade creation. Bhagwati and Panagariya (1996, 19) demonstrated that trade diversion can still occur even with a high initial volume of trade between two countries in the pre-FTA environment since other countries (outside the FTA) may develop a comparative advantage and greater efficiency in their production function. Bhagwati and Panagariya (1996, 62) argued that "the proponents of the complacent high volume of imports thesis are trapped in a static view of comparative advantage that is particularly at odds with today's volatile, 'kaleidoscopic' comparative advantage in the global economy".

Schiff (2001) also added to the critique of the initial volume of trade criterion by noting that a high initial volume of trade may also occur due to discriminatory trade policy. In particular Schiff

(2001, 4) noted that "the volume of trade is itself affected by trade policy. Ideally, we would like to have a 'natural trading partners' criterion that is independent of trade policy."

Empirical evidence refuting the natural trading partner hypothesis on the basis of a high initial volume of trade and geographic proximity was first provided by Krishna (2003) and then Magee (2004). The shortcomings associated with the natural trading partner hypothesis formulated in reference to geographic proximity and volume of trade paved the way for Schiff (2001) to redefine the hypothesis in terms of trade complementarity. Schiff (2001, 22) asserted that trading partners are natural if their trading structure is "characterized by complementarity in trade".[15] The rest of this section introduces a formal critique for the initial volume of trade criterion and outlines the natural trading partner hypothesis based on trade complementarity.

3.8.3 Testing the Initial Volume of Trade Criterion in a Partial Equilibrium Model

This section introduces a formal theoretical critique of the "initial volume of trade" criterion.[16] The model consists of a home country (HC), a partner country (PC) and the rest of the world (ROW).[17] The partial equilibrium model examines the welfare effect of forming an FTA between the HC and the PC at two different levels of their "initial volume of trade". In figure 3.6, D_A represents the HC's import demand function while the supply curves for the PC and the ROW are represented by S_B^0 and S_W^0, respectively. In a free trade environment, the HC's total imports are given by OM_4 at the world price of P_W. The welfare for the HC in free trade is therefore equal to its consumer surplus (HLE), that is, $W_{FT} = HLE$.

Assume that the HC imposes a most favoured nation (MFN) tariff on imports, then the supply curves for the PC and the ROW shift left to S_B^1 and S_W^1, respectively. In the MFN tariff scenario, the HC's total imports fall to OM_3, of which OM_1 is sourced from the PC and M_1M_3 originates from the ROW. The HC's welfare in the MFN environment is now made up of tariff revenues and consumer surplus. In particular, the HC's welfare is given by the area HKVE. HKVE is further decomposed into the consumer surplus (HKF) and tariff revenues (FKVE). The tariff revenues accruing to the HC can be separated into tariff revenues on imports from the PC (FQJE) and from the ROW (QKVJ). However, the HC will experience a welfare loss associated with the area KVL after it imposes an MFN tariff on imports. Therefore, welfare for the HC in the MFN environment is given as: $W_{MFN} = HKVE$, where $W_{FT} > W_{MFN}$.

Next, assume that the HC proceeds to form an FTA with the PC. The formation of this FTA will result in the removal of tariffs on imports from the PC, while tariffs on imports from the ROW are maintained. In this FTA environment, the PC's supply curve shifts to S_B^0 while the ROW supply curve is unchanged. The HC's total imports in the FTA environment remain the same, but its imports of M_1M_2 are diverted from the ROW to the PC. The HC's welfare in this FTA (hereafter W_{FTA}) environment changes to HKF + GKVI, where consumer surplus remains the same as in the MFN scenario. However, since the HC remove tariffs on imports from the PC, they lose tariff revenues of the amount FGIE (that is, tariff revenues on imports OM_2). Thus, welfare for the HC in the FTA environment is given as: $W_{FTA} = HKF + GKVI$, where $W_{FT} > W_{MFN} > W_{FTA}$. In addition, since the PC's producer surplus is defined by the area FGJE, the welfare loss to the FTA as a whole is GIJ.

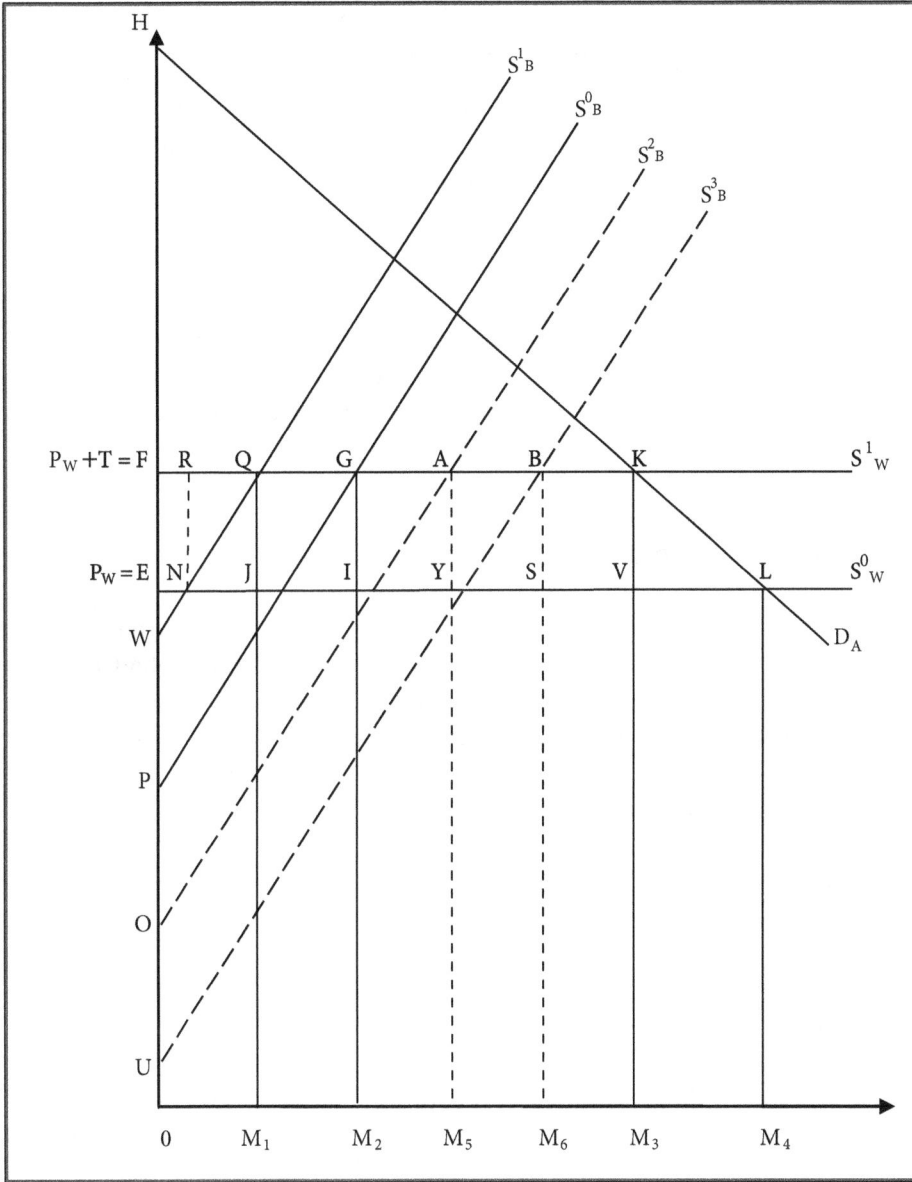

Figure 3.6 Testing the initial volume of trade criterion

The natural trading partner hypothesis based on the initial volume of trade criterion asserts that if there is a high initial intensity of bilateral trade between the HC and the PC in pre-FTA, then the formation of an FTA between the HC and the PC will improve economic welfare. Therefore, by introducing a new supply curve for the PC in a pre-FTA environment, such as S_B^2 at a higher level of trade (M_5), would provide some insights into the welfare impact of forming the FTA at a higher level of trade (M_5). Assume that the HC and the PC form an FTA at a higher volume of trade such as M_5 (as compared to M_1), then its supply curve will shift to S_B^3. In this new FTA environment, the welfare for the HC is now defined as HKF + BKVS and is less than welfare

Table 3.8 The impact of the volume of trade (at different import levels) in the FTA environment

The effects of forming a FTA between the HC and the PC	Pre-FTA imports at M_1 FTA imports at M_2	Pre-FTA imports at M_5 FTA imports at M_6
HC losses in tariff revenues	FGIE	FBSE (an increase by GBSI)
PC gains in producer surplus	FGJE	FBYE
Loss to the FTA as a whole	GIJ	BSY (GIJ = BSY)

at a lower level of trade (M_2) as the HC loses tariff revenues FBSE. Furthermore, assuming that the slope of the supply curve for the PC is constant, then PC's producer surplus is now FBYE. This assumption implies that GIJ is equal to BYS and the welfare loss to the FTA as a whole does not fall as asserted by the initial volume of trade argument for determining a real natural trading partner (see table 3.8 for a summary).

3.8.4 Trade Complementarity

A major limitation associated with the previous standard analysis is that it ignores the trading relationship between the PC and the ROW (rest of the world). To address this shortcoming, Schiff (2001) introduced a new trading relationship to the model, that is, between the PC and the ROW and showed that the welfare outcomes for prospective members of an FTA depend largely on trade complementarity as compared to other factors. The same three countries are considered in Schiff's model for two scenarios:

1. PC exports to the ROW
2. PC imports from the ROW[18]

3.8.4.1 Partner Country Exports to the Rest of the World

In the first scenario, the PC's export supply curve to the HC is determined by the relative prices that the PC exporters receive in its export markets (HC and ROW). Specifically, when the price in the HC's market is less than the price in the ROW's market, the PC will supply all its exports to the ROW and none to the HC. Therefore, the vertical line 0E defines the first segment of the PC's export supply curve to the HC (see figure 3.7). The horizontal line from point E to (say) point Z defines the second segment of the PC's export supply curve to the HC.[19] The segment EZ refers to a situation where there is equality in the price that the PC exporters receive in both export markets. When this equality arises, the PC exporters are indifferent in terms of the price they receive in the two export markets and therefore the volume of exports from the PC to the HC is indeterminate. The third segment of the PC's export supply curve to the HC is determined when the price in the HC's market is greater than the price in the ROW's market. The upward sloping line gives the third segment from (say) point Z to X_B. Therefore, the PC's export supply curve to the HC's market is X_B and not S_B^0.

Assume an initial environment where the HC imposes an MFN tariff on imports. In the MFN tariff environment, the PC exporters receive the world price when they export to the ROW's market. The PC exporters will also receive the world price for their export to the HC as the tariff revenues on all imports entering the HC remain in the HC. Therefore, the PC is indifferent in terms of the price it receives in both export markets. This situation means that in the pre-FTA environment the volume of trade between the HC and the PC is indeterminate and cannot form a basis to assess the welfare effects associated with the formation of an FTA between the HC and the PC.

Next, assume that the HC and the PC form an FTA. As in the standard analysis, the HC imports from the PC increases by $M_1 M_2$ at a price $P_W + T$. Prior to the formation of the FTA, the PC exporters received P_W for its exports to the HC and the ROW markets. However, when the FTA between the HC and the PC is established, the PC exporters can now obtain $P_W + T$ in the HC's market. Thus, the PC exporters will shift all of their exports to the HC's market. In the FTA environment, the PC's export supply curve to the HC will be identical to S_W^0 up to the point where all exports originating from the PC are sold in the HC's market and none in the ROW's market or exports equal to M_4. This point (for example, M_4 or where the PC's export supply curve

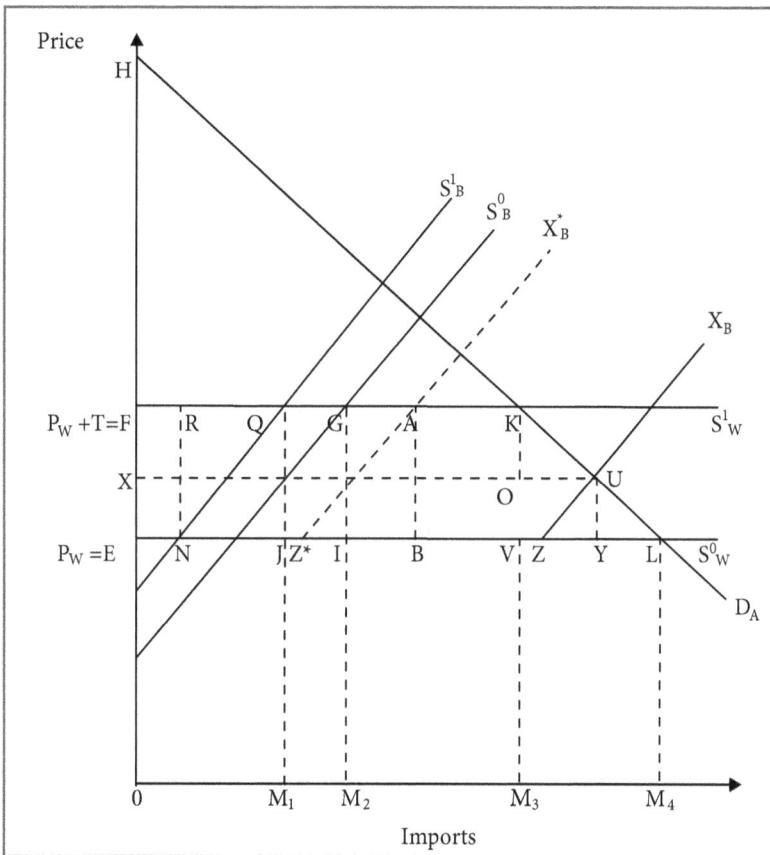

Figure 3.7 Trade complementarity and economic welfare (PC exports to ROW)

begins its upward slope) is important for determining the welfare impact for the HC and the PC in the FTA environment. The possibility that the price in the HC's market will remain at $P_W + T$ or change is determined by the export capacity of the PC to satisfy the HC's import demand in the FTA environment.[20] The change in relative prices in the FTA environment will have an impact on the welfare outcomes for the HC. In this regard, three FTA permutations are possible.

1. The PC's export supply curve intersects the HC's import demand curve at point L or to the right of L.
2. The PC's export supply curve intersects the HC's import demand curve at point U between points K and L.
3. The PC's export supply curve intersects the HC's import demand curve on the horizontal segment FK to the left of point K.

The first FTA permutation is described as the most desirable situation and is analogous to free trade in terms of the welfare gains for the HC. In the first FTA scenario, the PC's export supply curve begins its upward slope at point L and the PC is able to satisfy the HC's import demand at the world price (P_W). Before the FTA is formed, however, the HC imported OM_3 from the PC at the prevailing market equilibrium price of P_{W+T}, that is, where the HC's import demand curve D_A intersects the supply curve of the PC (point K in figure 3.7). Therefore, the HC's pre-FTA welfare would be defined by the area 1+2+3+4+6+7+8, of which area 1 is the consumer surplus and area 2+3+4+6+7+8 is total tariff revenues associated with imports OM_3. The following changes in welfare would occur if the HC and the PC forms an FTA in this first FTA scenario: the HC will initially lose the area 2+3+4+6+7+8 in tariff revenues, but would recoup the same area (2+3+4+6+7+8) due to a resulting lower FTA import price and it would now form part of its consumer surplus (read from figure 3.8). So from a welfare perspective, the area 2+3+4+6+7+8 does not have an impact on welfare for the HC. The HC, however, would now gain the area KLV (5+9+10+11) as part of its new consumer surplus due to an increase in imports (VL) from the resulting lower FTA import price P_W. Thus, the HC's total welfare in this FTA permutation equals its overall consumer surplus HLE. The PC's welfare remains the same, since its exporters continue to reap the same price (P_W) in the FTA environment as they did in the pre-FTA environment.

The second FTA permutation occurs when the PC's export supply curve intersects the HC's import demand curve between K and L (say) at point U (figure 3.7). For the second FTA permutation, the PC is able to satisfy more than the HC's pre-FTA imports demand so that the HC initially loses tariff revenues amounting to 2+3+4+6+7+8. However, the price facing consumers in the HC's market falls from $P_W + T$ to X (figure 3.7). The fall in import prices means that the HC's consumer surplus will increase by 2+3+4+5. Therefore, the impact on the HC's welfare is ambiguous and is determined by the difference between the HC's losses in tariff revenues (2+3+4+6+7+8) and its gains in consumer surplus. According to Schiff (2001), the change in tariff revenues and consumer surplus leads to a net gain and a net loss for the HC.[21] The net gain is given by area 5 and is due to the increase in imports from V to Y because of a lower price X. The net loss is shown by area 6+7+8 and is due to the loss in tariff revenues (2+3+4+6+7+8 of which 2+3+4 is recouped by the HC as consumer surplus) on imports from E to V. In this FTA environment, the PC exporters receive a higher price X when compared to the price (P_W) it received in the pre-FTA environment.

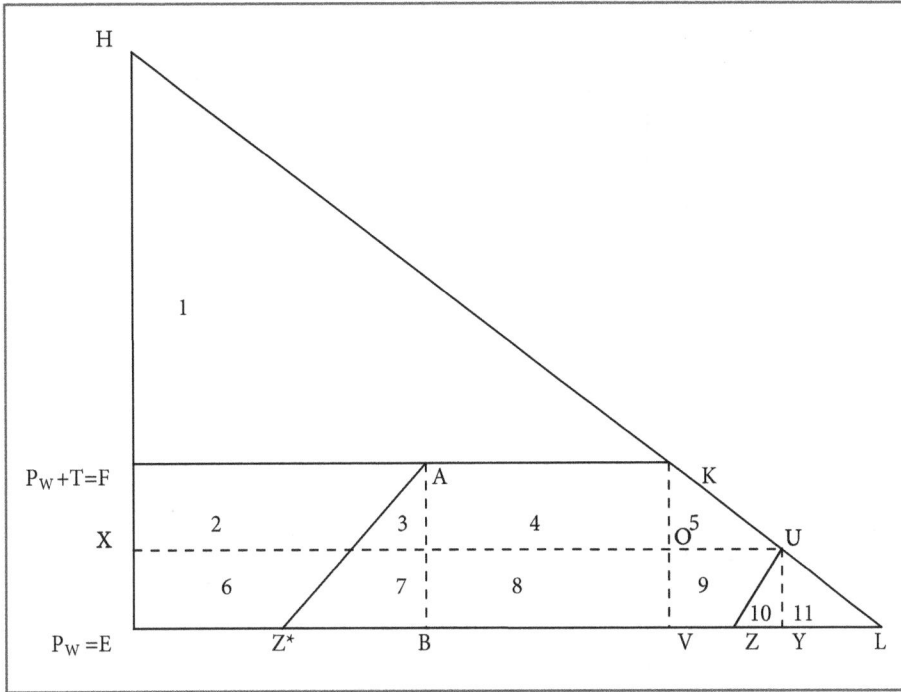

Figure 3.8 Disaggregation of the welfare effects (PC exports to ROW)

Consequently, the PC gains producer surplus amounting to 6+7+8+9 and the FTA as a whole gains 5+9 (read from figure 3.8). The addition to consumer surplus of area 5 occurs as the FTA leads to a fall in the price for HC consumers from P_W+T to X. Area 9 arises from the higher price (X) the producers in the PC receive for its exports to the HC compared to the pre-FTA price (P_W), that is, area 9 represents an increase in producer surplus. Note that area 6+7+8 was part of the FTA welfare as the HC tariff revenues, but was lost due to the FTA; it now forms part of the PC producer surplus in addition to area 9.

The third FTA permutation is the least desirable case and occurs where the PC's export supply curve intersects the horizontal segment of FK to the left of point K (figure 3.7). In this FTA environment, the PC is unable to at least supply the HC's pre-FTA import demand. As such, the price facing the HC consumers will continue to be P_W+T even when the FTA is formed. The FTA effectively removes the tariffs on imports, so theoretically, the HC consumers should pay lower prices (adjusted for the removal of the tariffs). But because the supply capacity of the PC is too small for meet demand in the HC in this scenario, market forces of supply and demand would effectively keep prices at the pre-FTA level although the tariffs have been removed. This means that the HC would not collect tariff revenues which will adversely impact its welfare. The PC would now benefit as a result of the higher prices it receives, that is, the PC received Pw in the pre-FTA but in the FTA it now receives the full P_W+T. To illustrate the welfare effects in this permutation, consider a situation where the PC's export supply curve ($X_B{}^*$) begins its upward slope at Z^* and intersects the horizontal section FK at point A. The HC will lose tariff revenues of the amount (2+3+6+7) on imports EB from the PC. If the HC were to satisfy its pre-FTA import demand ($0M_3$), it will

Table 3.9 Welfare implications of a FTA between the HC and the PC with the PC having export capacity to the ROW

	Pre-FTA (MFN) Environment	Permutation 1	Permutation 2	Permutation 3
Price to the consumer in HC	P_W+T	P_W	X	P_W+T
Price to the consumer in ROW	P_W	P_W	P_W	P_W
Price PC exporters receive from the HC	P_W	P_W	X	P_W+T
Price PC exporters receive from the ROW	P_W	P_W	P_W	P_W
Tariff revenues for the HC	2+3+4+6+7+8	(2+3+4+6+7+8)	(2+3+4+6+7+8)	4+8
Consumer surplus for the HC	1	1+2+3+4+5+6+7+8+9+10+11	1+2+3+4+5	1
Gains to the HC		5+9+10+11	5	
Losses to the HC			2+3+4+6+7+8	2+3+6+7
Gains to the PC			6+7+8+9	2+6
Losses to the PC				
PC exports to HC	Indeterminate	M_4	E to Y	Less than M_3 (B)
Welfare implication		Positive and equal to KLV	Positive but less than Permutation 1	Negative

have to import BV from the ROW and will collect 4+8 in tariff revenues. The producer surplus to the PC will also increase by 2+6 due to the relatively higher price its exporters receive (read from figure 3.8). The net welfare impact of forming the FTA is determined by the changes in welfare for the HC and the PC. So when the FTA is formed in this third scenario, the HC loses 2+3+6+7 in tariff revenues, while the PC gained producer surplus of 2+6 resulting a net loss to the FTA of 3+7. Assuming that the PC's export supply curve in the standard analysis S_B^0 (in figure 3.6) is parallel to the PC's export supply curve in Schiff's analysis (X_B in figure 3.7), then the loss to the FTA as a whole will be equal in both settings, this is given as GIJ (figure 3.6). The welfare implications for the FTA in this scenario will be negative, since the FTA loses from trade diversion. Table 3.9 provides a summary of the analysis.

3.9 Differential Trading Benefits of Small and Large Trade Partners

Many of the ideas and habits that are required for a firm to benefit from multilateral free trade are experimented and learned under a regionalism strategy so that the process of moving onto a multilateral trading agenda is much smoother. In this sense, it is perceived that regionalism may provide the platform from which member states graduate onto multilateralism (Cernat 2003). One would expect that if a globally efficient economy is part of a regionalism thrust, then this will help to narrow the gap between other demonstration effects that are usually associated with regionalism. This includes the fact that government and other officials learn a significant amount of the relevant tricks of the trade which are associated with multilateralism when they participate in regional trading arrangements (RTAs).

In figure 3.9, D^h represents the HC's demand curve for imports and S_{row} is the supply curve of the rest of the world. In the presence of free trade, the HC has a consumer surplus of ACE, which is treated here as W^H. Should the HC implement a most favoured nation tariff then the supply curve of the rest of the world moves to S'_{row} and the supply curve of the partner economy shifts to S'_p. In the context of these types of changes, the HC would consume Q_3 units of which $Q_3 - Q_1$ comes from the rest of the world. In the presence of the MFN tariff, the HC's welfare changes to ABF + BDEF (BDEF is tariff revenues). Let us refer to this new level of welfare as W^{MFN}. So that

$$\Delta W = W^H - W^{MFN} = ACE - [ABF + BDEF] = -BDC$$

If the small HC formed a free trade area with the small partner country then the supply curve of the partner economy will be restored to S_p and the HC will import $0Q_3$, of which $0Q_2$ will originate with the partner economy and the remainder, $Q_3 - Q_2$ will be imported from the rest of the world. In this environment, the welfare level of the HC will be W^P:

$$W^P = ABF + BDIG$$

Because the FTA does not result in a change in the import price level, the consumer surplus does not change from ABF but the HC, however, loses out on the tax revenues that it would have collected from the partner country prior to the formation of FTA. Consequently,

$$W^{MFN} - W^P = EFGI$$

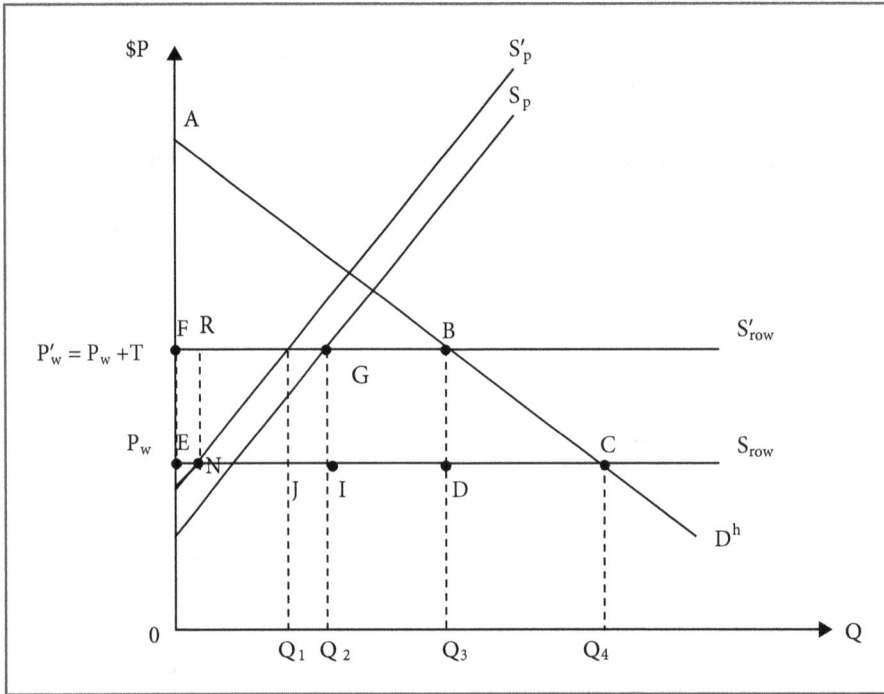

Figure 3.9 FTA between small countries
Source: Schiff (1997)

In the formulation, above EFGI represents the amount of tariff revenues the home country would have collected from the partner economy.

If the HC, however, were to form an FTA with the rest of the world and not with the partner country then the relevant supply curves to the HC becomes S_{row} and S'_p (see figure 3.9). In this scenario, there is an improvement in the welfare of the HC by BCD plus the tariff revenues, FRNE collected from the partner economy. Clearly then, the welfare benefits for the home country from forming an FTA with the ROW are superior to one that involves forming an FTA with the small partner country (Schiff 1997). It should also be noted that the lower the imports from the partner economy and the higher imports from the ROW, the larger the welfare gains for the HC from forming an FTA with the ROW.

The argument being put forward here is that when a small country forms an FTA with a small country it loses, but when it forms an FTA with a large partner economy, it gains. Alternatively said, a small HC is better off when it is a small member of a large trading bloc as compared to a small partner in a small trading bloc or as a large member of a small trading bloc.

This section concludes the first part of this chapter. The main theoretical ideas associated with regional integration theory have been thoroughly discussed. The remainder of this chapter focuses on the application of various aspects of this theory to CARICOM, in particular, a case study of the regional economic partnership agreement signed between the European Union and the CARIFORUM countries.

3.10 The Regional Economic Partnership Agreement: The Cotonou Experience

The Cotonou Agreement,[22] created a new trading regime between the ACP and EU economic blocs, which was designed to be compatible with WTO rules after 2003. Five pillars support the Cotonou Agreement. These are: a wide-ranging political dimension, participatory approaches, an increased focus on poverty reduction, a new framework for economic and trade cooperation as well as a reform of financial cooperation.

The first supporting pillar of the Cotonou Agreement is that there is a wide ranging political dimension. This means that parties of the ACP–EU relationship have agreed to engage in political dialogue to discuss regularly arms trade, excessive military expenditure, drugs and organized crime, and ethnic, religious or racial discrimination. In addition, it assesses the developments concerning the respect for human rights, democratic principles, rule of law and good governance. The aforementioned are expected to govern the behaviour of the European Union and the ACP states both domestically and internationally. Violations of any of these essential elements may ultimately lead to a country facing suspension from the agreement, although full suspension is seen as a measure only of last resort (Holland 2003, 166).

The second pillar is its participatory approaches. The Cotonou Agreement contains provisions to ensure the involvement of the local and regional authorities, civil society and private sector which can benefit directly from grant agreements and funding that has been established. It highlights the significance of non-governmental divisions of society. The design, consultation and implementation of development strategies and programmes are anticipated to include economic and social actors and the civil society. In the stated conclusion of this pillar, the agreement emphasizes the importance of the private sector and the need to define criteria guiding the scope of participation of the different non-state actors (ECLAC 2005).

The third pillar is the increased focus on poverty reduction. This is the main objective of the Cotonou Agreement and in order to achieve this central aim, an integrated approach will be pursued, with strategies emphasizing its three priority areas of economic development, social and human development and integration and regional development cooperation. First, for economic development, the environment for private investment is to be improved through promoting public–private sector relations, developing entrepreneurial skills, technical support, micro-enterprise development and support for financial and non-financial services for enterprises. To achieve macroeconomic growth and stability, the ACP states are to work towards disciplined fiscal and monetary policies and an improvement in the external and fiscal balances, while managing their budgets more transparently and efficiently. The social and human development aspect includes the cooperation in social sector policies in an effort to ensure fair and equitable access to basic social infrastructure and services. It fundamentally addresses education and training, health systems, nutrition, family planning, cultural development, youth issues and children's rights. Furthermore, the Cotonou Agreement strongly supports regional cooperation and integration and thus, focuses on the promotion of the free mobility of persons, goods, services, capital, labour and technology, economic diversification and the promotion of trade.

The fourth supporting pillar is concerned with the establishment of a new framework for trade and economic cooperation. This pillar presents significant alterations in the framework regarding trade relations between the European Union and the ACP states for the purpose of ensuring that the Cotonou Agreement conforms to WTO regulations. This is the reciprocity with regards to trade. In addition, this establishment of a new framework enables the ACP states to fully participate in international trade, the protection of intellectual property rights, trade and standards of work.

Finally, the last pillar of the Cotonou Agreement is the reform for financial cooperation. The allocation of funds is not only based on an assessment of each country's needs but also of its policy performance and it also creates an investment facility to support the development of the private sector.

The Cotonou Agreement was designed with the "objective of reducing and eventually eradicating poverty, consistent with the objectives of sustainable development and the gradual integration of the ACP countries into the world economy" (Cotonou Agreement, "Objectives and Principles", article 1).

The ACP states should be able to achieve these goals through a process of cooperation with the European Union designed to

1. address supply side constraints in the ACP membership,
2. enhance the productive capacities of these economies and
3. attract investment.

The European Union proposes to attain these objectives by the directed use of economic partnership agreements (EPAs). An EPA comprises a reciprocal WTO compatible free trade area between the European Union and the regional groupings of ACP countries.

Before proceeding further, note that the ACP economies can also benefit from the generalized system of preferences (GSP) offered by the European Union. The GSP system was introduced in 1971 by the GATT. The GSP scheme offers up to 178 developing economies duty-free access into the EU market. The GSP preferences are non-reciprocating covering approximately seven thousand products. Just under half of these products are non-sensitive. With the GSP scheme, non-sensitive products are not subject to duty, while sensitive products benefit from a tariff reduction. In 2001, the European Union introduced the Everything But Arms (EBA) initiative. The EBA is lodged in the GSP preference scheme.[23] While the EBA scheme is generally more generous than the Cotonou scheme, in some areas such as cumulation, it is not (Manchin 2006).[24] Because the nature of the GSP is long lasting and the most comprehensive preference scheme, it provides the basis for most other preferential access agreements such as the EBA. One characteristic that all these schemes had was that they applied strict "rules of origin" which required that products be substantially produced within the beneficiary country to qualify (Grimwade 2000, 256). For products that do not fulfil the GSP's "rules of origin" requirements, the normal third country duty rates (MFN duty rates) apply or any preferential duty rate agreed by separate agreement by the country in question and the European Union.

Undoubtedly, the "rules of origin" for the EBA are more restrictive than in the Cotonou Agreement. The difference is that under the Cotonou Agreement, with some exceptions, full cumulation within the ACP countries is granted. Thus, although the original goods may not have originated in the ACP region, if the products undergo further processing in other ACP countries, they are still eligible for duty-free access. However, this is not the case with the EBA agreement – since the EBA is an extension of the GSP, the concept of diagonal cumulation applies, meaning that although products can move within the EBA countries for further processing, sourcing from outside the EBA (including with other ACP countries) is not permitted (Kipe 2003, 5).

3.11 The Structure of Economic Partnership Agreements

The objectives of the EPA extend much beyond expanding ACP–EU trade relations in that a primary objective relates to the expansion of intra-regional trade and increased integration into the global economy. ACP exports fell from 4.4 per cent of total world exports to 1.4 per cent between 1970 and 2012. The share of the ACP exports that go to the EU economies also fell from 48.3 per cent in 1970 to 34.3 per cent in 2012, this in spite of the fact that the European Union has granted preferential market access to the ACP countries throughout the recent history under the various Lomé conventions and now the Cotonou Agreement.

The Cotonou Partnership Agreement (CPA) outlines four principles along which the EPAs are currently being formulated. These are development, reciprocity, regionalism and differentiation. The development aspect of the EPA is that it should lead to the overall development of ACP economies. These EPAs should be development oriented and lead to economic growth and sustainable development, the end product of which should be the elimination of poverty in ACP economies.[25]

The EPA should support the existing integration initiatives in the ACP states. This reinforces regional integration and helps in the consolidating the ACP markets before promoting commercial integration with the European Union. Furthermore, article 2 of the Cotonou Agreement defines regionalization as one of the fundamental principles of ACP–EC cooperation (Cotonou Agreement 2010). The principle of reciprocity is solely to be in compliance with the WTO rules. This means that that the European Union liberates its markets to ACP produced goods and in return, the ACP states would open up themselves to EU exports. The principle of reciprocity itself raises important questions, as the removal of customs duties on imports from Europe could have serious repercussions on the national economies in Africa.

In accordance with article 2 of the Cotonou Agreement, differentiation constitutes one of the fundamental principles of ACP–EC cooperation. The principle of differentiation was understood

Table 3.10 Economic links between the EU and the ACP countries, 1970–2012

	1970	1980	1990	2000	2005	2010	2011	2012
Share of ACP countries in world exports (%)	4.4	3.2	2.1	1.6	1.7	1.2	1.3	1.4
Share of regional ACP groupings exports to the EU(25) in % of groups total	48.3	32.1	36.3	30.7	32.6	25.1	29.4	34.3
CARIFORUM	21.7	19.9	24.6	16.9	20.6	12.5	13.1	12.4
Share of regional ACP groupings imports from the EU in % of total group imports								
ACP countries	50.4	39.2	41.6	32.3	33.3	19.3	19.8	19.1
Caribbean (CARIFORUM)	28.4	15.4	16.8	14.0	17.6	8.8	8.3	8.3

Source: United Nations Commodity Trade Database (UNCOMTRADE) (2014).

Table 3.11 Basic macroeconomic data for CARIFORUM economies, annual averages

Country	GDP Growth			Total Public Debt (% of GDP)			Overall Fiscal Balance (% of GDP)		
	1990–1997	1998–2005	2006–2012	1990–1997	1998–2005	2006–2012	1990–1997	1998–2005	2006–2009
Antigua & Barbuda	3.00	2.50	0.40	102.00	143.00	89.00	–5.00	–9.10	6.10
Bahamas	1.00	3.10	0.02	46.00	49.00	39.00	–2.00	–2.40	–3.40
Barbados	0.10	1.50	–0.30	62.00	87.00	63.00	–3.00	–5.60	–6.40
Belize	6.00	5.20	2.40	41.00	102.00	85.00	–6.00	–11.50	–1.20
Dominica	3.00	–1.10	3.30	61.00	125.00	73.00	–3.00	–8.30	–0.90
Dominican Republic	4.00	4.20	6.30	23.00	63.00	27.00	–3.00	–3.80	2.80
Grenada	3.00	2.20	–0.70	42.00	117.00	98.00	–4.00	–7.40	–4.90
Guyana	6.00	1.40	3.10	211.00	180.00	68.00	–4.00	–6.20	–4.20
Haiti	–0.40	1.20	2.80	NA	47.00	26.00	–4.00	–4.80	–2.20
Jamaica	0.20	1.30	–0.10	103.00	136.00	136.00	0.20	–9.20	–6.30
St Kitts & Nevis	5.00	2.30	1.10	86.00	174.00	138.00	–12.10	–11.00	–2.10
St Lucia	3.00	1.20	2.00	36.00	70.00	62.00	–1.00	–4.10	–4.70
St Vincent & the Grenadines	3.00	2.70	1.10	48.00	77.00	64.00	–1.00	–5.30	–2.30
Suriname	–1.00	2.40	4.20	24.00	47.00	19.00	–4.00	–6.20	–1.20
Trinidad & Tobago	2.00	5.10	2.30	52.00	56.00	31.00	0.20	–3.10	0.70

Source: World Development Indicators (2014).

to imply that reciprocity would not be required from least developed countries (LDCs), participating in an EPA when in reality, the principle of differentiation calls more generally for special treatment for the LDCs and therefore opens the way for negotiations in the EPAs, taking into account the particular constraints and adaptation capacity of the LDC members (Cotonou Agreement 2010).

EPAs should also be socially acceptable and politically sustainable. Table 3.11 provides data that can be used to shed some light on the economic development status of CARIFORUM economies. In particular, the economic growth rate increased either marginally in some CARIFORUM member states or decreased altogether. In the same time interval, the total public debt as a percentage of GDP increased in every CARIFORUM member state except Guyana, where it decreased between the indicated time periods, but still remains worryingly high.

GDP growth and public debt in CARIFORUM countries are generally decreasing. Since 2008, the impact of the global crisis on GDP growth and higher fiscal deficits have resulted in sharply rising debt levels in most Caribbean countries, especially those dependent on tourism (Gendere-Naar 2012). The current account balances worsened during the period 2006–12 with the exception of Belize, Guyana, St Kitts and Nevis, St Lucia, Suriname, and Trinidad and Tobago.

Table 3.12 Selected socio-economic indicators

	Human Development Index Ranking (Out of 175 Countries)	Poverty (% Below the Poverty Line)
	2012	2012 (or most recent year survey)
Antigua & Barbuda	67	12.0
Bahamas	49	NA
Barbados	38	14.0
Belize	96	12.2 (1999)
Dominica	72	33.0
Dominican Republic	96	40.9 (2012)
Grenada	63	32.0
Guyana	118	35.0
Haiti	161	77.0 (2001)
Jamaica	85	17.6 (2010)
St Kitts & Nevis	72	31.0
St Lucia	88	19.0
St Vincent & the Grenadines	83	33.0
Suriname	105	NA
Trinidad & Tobago	68	17.0 (2007)
UK	26	11.4
France	20	14.8

Source: Human Development Indicators (various years), http://hdr.undp.org/en/data.

Using the United Kingdom and France as representative EU economies (these are two of the main former colonial powers in the European Union), the CARIFORUM economies are distinctly behind in terms of their overall HDI ranking and the percentage of their respective populations below the poverty line (see table 3.12).

HDI is a composite statistic of life expectancy, education and income indices. It is observed that the developed countries – United Kingdom and France are ranked in the top thirty in comparison to the developing countries. The small island countries such as those in the OECS (St Vincent and the Grenadines, St Kitts and Nevis, Grenada, and Dominica) have the highest percentage of poverty present in their countries, which contributes to their low rankings in the HDI. Thus, the central objective of the Cotonou Agreement, which was later replaced by the EPA, was to reduce and eventually eradicate poverty and promote sustainable development.

The European Union is pushing for the formation of EPAs with various regional groupings among the ACP membership, on the presumption that regional integration will act as a significant stepping-stone towards the participation of ACP states in more meaningful multilateral liberalization. These EPA negotiations are ongoing between the twenty-five EU economies (hereafter EU-25) and six ACP country groupings. As it stands the combined GDP of the EU-25 is US$16 trillion, while the ACP group includes thirty-nine of the fifty countries categorized as least developed ("MEPs Criticised Delays over ACP Trade Agreement", *Democracy Live,* 11 February 2014, http://www.bbc.co.uk/democracylive/europe-26127606). The extent of this disparity between the European Union and the ACP countries is evidenced in table 3.13.

The European Union is West Africa's main trading partner while the European Union is the Caribbean's second largest trading partner, after the United States. Exports to the European Union from the Pacific region are dominated by palm oil, coffee, coconut, and fish and caviar and imports from the European Union to the Pacific region are dominated by electrical machinery and equipment. Hence, the overall trade between the European Union and the Pacific countries is very small both in absolute and in relative terms. The collection of ACP countries in the EPA comprises 5.77 per cent of the European Union's total GDP as the European Union is the world's largest trading bloc.

Table 3.13 GDP of the EU-25 and various ACP blocs

EPA	GDP (2012) US$ billion	% of EU GDP
EU	16,000	
SADC	63	0.39
ESA	103	0.64
West Africa	395	2.47
Central Africa	224	1.40
Caribbean	130	0.81
Pacific	11	0.07
Total EPA	926	5.79

Source: World Development Indicators (2014).

3.12 Measuring the Welfare Effects of the CARIFORUM Agreement

This section outlines a partial equilibrium model to assess the impact of the CARIFORUM–EU EPA on CARICOM countries. Partial equilibrium models have been widely used in the literature to assess the trade and welfare effects of proposed FTAs (see McKay et al. 2000; Busse et al. 2004; Gasiorek and Winters 2004; Karingi et al. 2005; Greenaway and Milner 2006; Busse and Luehje 2007; Zouhon-Bi and Nielsen 2007; Hosein 2008; Fontagne et al. 2011). The literature identifies two branches of the partial equilibrium model, namely, the perfect substitution model and the imperfect substitution model. The perfect substitution model assumes a homogeneous product is traded. It assumes that markets are perfectly competitive and imported goods are perfect substitutes for domestically produced goods. The perfect substitution model is most applicable in situations, where there are specific markets and where the producers are price takers. On the other hand, the imperfect substitution model is grounded in the Armington (1969) principle of product differentiation.[26] The imperfect substitution variant is more applicable for industrial markets where product differentiation becomes essential to the analysis. One of the distinct advantages of the partial equilibrium model is the facility of being able to discern those aspects of the free trade basket which will be most significantly affected by the formation of an EPA. General equilibrium models, however, can provide insights on foreign exchange and labour markets but require a vast amount of information and assumptions concerning the working of the economy, and failure to include the relevant variables can trigger model misspecification.[27] The first model presented assumes the existence of perfect competition between the outputs of trading partners, while the second model (imperfect substitution) provided thereafter, builds on the work of Greenaway and Milner (2003). A significant assumption associated with both is that tariff cuts are manifested in reduced import prices.

The formation of an RTA affects the export and import performance of member states in the following ways:

1. The HC gets improved access to the partner country's market.
2. The benefits of improved market access are greater, the larger the HC's exports to the partner economy after integration.
3. The benefit is greater for the HC, the larger the tariff reduction of the partner economy.

In this regard, this section emphasizes the impact of the EPA on imports.

3.12.1 Perfect Substitution

Let us subdivide the trading players involved as

HC: home country,
PC: partner country,

and two extra-regional blocs,

EU: European Union,
nEUROW: non-EU Rest of the World.

The perfect substitution case represents the situation in which CARIFORUM producers operate under conditions of increasing costs (CARIFORUM treated as a small economy in relation to the European Union and nEUROW).

In figure 3.10, the production costs of the European Union and nEUROW are assumed to be constant and their supply curves given by S_{EU} and S_{nEUROW}, respectively. $P_{EU} > P_{nEUROW}$ or generically the nEUROW is assumed to be a more efficient producer than the European Union overall.[28] Given that $P_{EU} > P_{nEUROW}$, the imposition of discriminatory trade policy in favour of the European Union will result in both trade diverting and trade creating effects. In the diagram, D_H and S_P represent the demand curve of the HC for imports and S_p the supply curve of the PC. Initial conditions are such that an RTA is formed between the HC and PC and a non-discriminatory tariff (t) is imposed on imports from both the European Union and nEUROW. The tariff-induced price of EU and nEUROW imports becomes P^t_{EU} and P^t_{nEUROW}, respectively. (P^t_{EU} is not shown because it moves above the intersection of S^P and S^H.) With P^t_{nEUROW}, the HC imports $M_1 - M_2$ units of the good from the nEUROW. The PC supplies $0M_1$ units.

In this initial scenario, it is assumed that domestic productive capacity does not exist for the imported good and so welfare can be defined in relation to the level of consumer surplus associated with D_H. In free trade, consumer surplus (W_0) is given by ACP_{nEUROW}. With a non-discriminatory tariff, the welfare level of the HC changes to $W_1 = ABP^t_{nEUROW} + a + b$.

With the formation of an EPA between the RTA (HC and PC) and the European Union, that is, assume that a discriminatory tariff is imposed on the nEUROW. This means that the HC will no longer import from the nEUROW as $P^t_{nEUROW} > P_{EU}$ and so P_{EU} now becomes the substantive

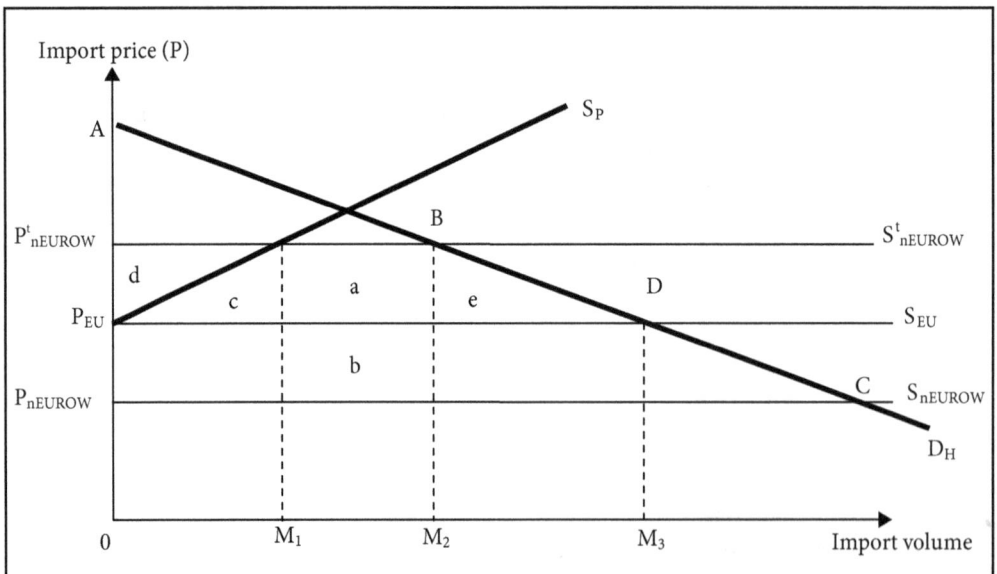

Figure 3.10 Effect of an EU–CARIFORUM EPA with perfect substitution

import price, at which $0M_3$ is imported. The welfare level associated with P_{EU} is ADP_{EU} and all imports now originate from the European Union.

Note that if $P_{EU} < P_{nEUROW}$ then the EPA is equivalent to multilateral free trade, so that there will be no displacement from the nEUROW to the European Union, only trade diversion from intra-CARICOM to the European Union and trade creation with the European Union will result. The trade effects of the formation of an EPA with perfect substitution may be identified as:

1. Consumption effect: imports increase by M_2M_3.
2. Intra-regional to extra-regional trade diversion effect: M_1 is now imported from the European Union rather than PC.[29]
3. Extra-regional to extra-regional trade diversion effect: M_1M_2 which was formerly imported from the nEUROW is now imported from the European Union.

Consumers will gain because of lower import prices, although they are worse off as compared to multilateral free trade, if it is the European Union is less globally efficient than the nEUROW.

3.12.2 The Case of Imperfect Substitution

Greenaway and Milner (2003) are careful to identify that except in the case of highly specific commodities, it will not be practical to presume that all of an economy's imports will come from a single source prior to the EPA or even with the EPA, that all imports will be diverted towards the European Union. These researchers treated goods as being differentiated dependent on their

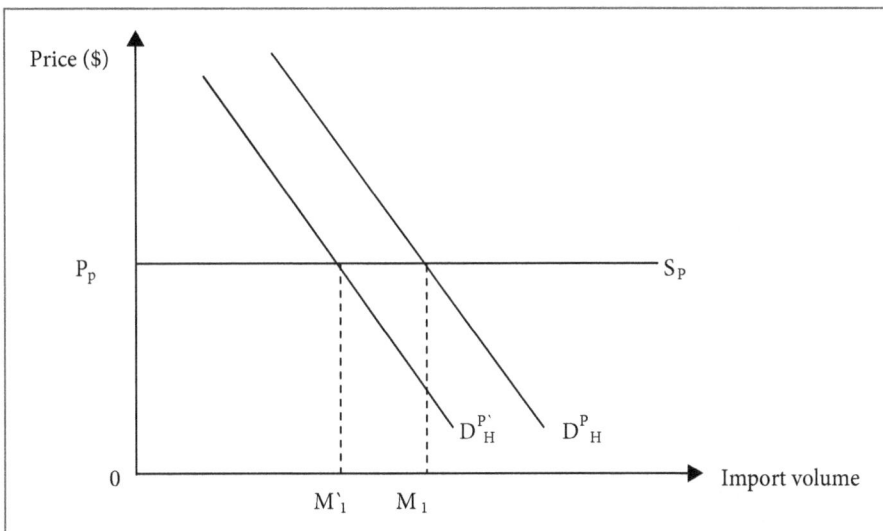

Figure 3.11 Effect of EU–CARIFORUM EPA on Trinidad and Tobago's imports from CARICOM with imperfect substitution

source of origin. In this regard, we can investigate the impact of an EPA as demonstrated in figures 3.11, 3.12 and 3.13.

The fall in the price of EU imports from $P_{EU}(1 + t)$ to P_{EU} implies an increase in the relative price of commodities from other sources. In particular, and as shown in the graph above there is a fall in the demand for intra-regional imports from D^P_H to $D^{P'}_H$ (figure 3.11). For the nEUROW

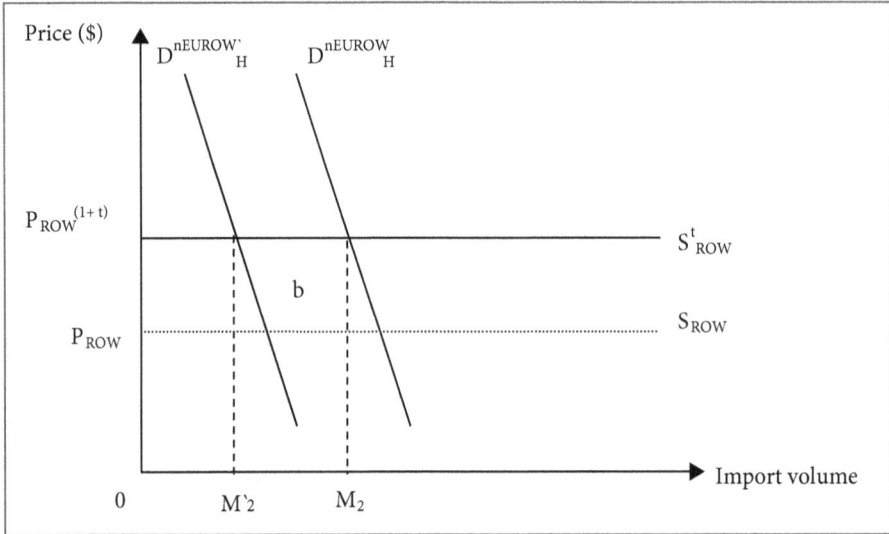

Figure 3.12 Effect of an EU-CARIFORUM EPA on Trinidad and Tobago's imports from nEUROW with imperfect competition

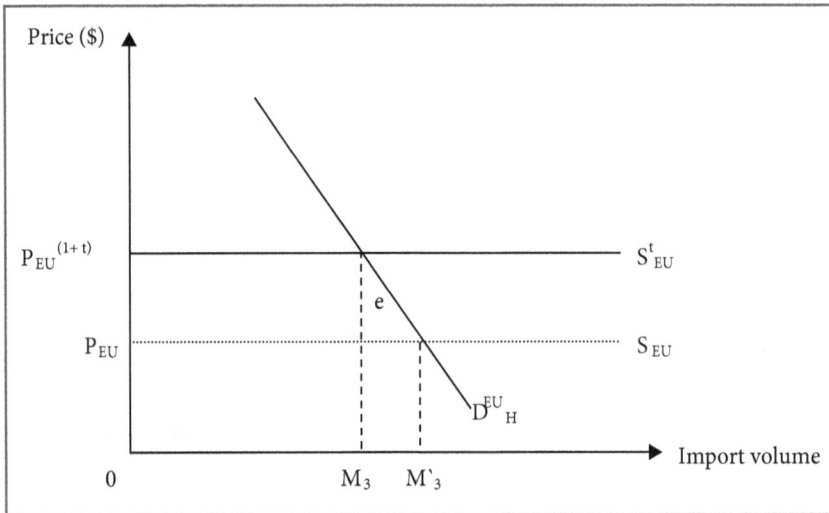

Figure 3.13 Effect of an EU-CARICOM EPA on Trinidad and Tobago's imports from the EU with imperfect competition

a similar element of "trade displacement" occurs, as the demand curve shifts from $D^{nEUROW}{}_H$ to $D^{nEUROW'}{}_H$ so that the volume of imports from the nEUROW falls from M_2 to M'_2 (see figure 3.12).

In the case of imports from the EU market, the direct impact of the fall in the price of EU imports leads to an increase in the volume of goods imported; the area **e** represents the associated increase in consumer welfare (see figure 3.13).

The actual trade-off between trade creation and trade diversion is an empirical matter. The size of these effects will be lower, the lower the HC's imports from the European Union in the list of imports that carry tariffs. As figures 3.11, 3.12 and 3.13 help to illustrate, the extent of net trade creation will depend on

1. the elasticity of demand for EU goods,
2. the initial amount of goods purchased from the European Union,
3. the extent of the fall in the import price from the European Union,
4. the extent of substitution of EU goods for CARIFORUM and nEUROW goods.

3.12.3 Empirical Modelling of the Impact of an EPA

From a modelling perspective,

$$\Delta M_3 = \left(\frac{-t}{1+t}\right) e^d_m M_3$$

where

ΔM_3:	is the change in imports from the European Union,[30]
t:	tariff rate,
e^d_m:	elasticity of demand for imports,
M_3:	the amount of goods imported from the European Union prior to the formation of the EPA.

In the case of trade displacement, there is an induced diversion of exports from intra-regional to extra-regional sources, the extent of which can be measured by

$$\Delta M_i = \left(\frac{-t}{1+t}\right) \sigma_{i3} M_i \, (i = 1,2)$$

σ_{13}:	displacements of imports from region 1 to 3,
σ_{23}:	displacement of imports from region 2 to 3.

In order to ascertain the impact on welfare, Greenaway and Milner (2003) proceeded as follows. In the first instance, it is acknowledged that trade diversion from intra-regional sources to the

European Union does not lead to any loss of customs revenue. At the same time though, any imports that is diverted from the nEUROW towards the European Union will lead to a fall in customs revenue. In this backdrop:

$$\Delta R = t\Delta M_2 - tM_3^0$$

where

$t\Delta M_2$:   is the amount of tariff revenues associated with a change in imports from the nEUROW,

tM_3^0:   is the initial amount of tariff revenues collected from EU imports in the pre-EPA environment.

In this imperfectly competitive world, the change in welfare associated with extra-regional trade creation (e) and trade diversion (b) can be estimated as

$$\Delta W = e + b$$
$$\Delta W = \frac{1}{2}t(\Delta M_3) + \Delta R$$

3.12.4 Trade Effects of the CARIFORUM–EU EPA

This section examines the trade effects associated with an EPA between CARICOM and EU countries.[31] The results indicate that the percentage increase in trade creation ranged from 12.2 per cent for Trinidad and Tobago to 15.8 per cent for Jamaica using 1998 data. The grounding in 1998 is for comparison with a previous study by Greenaway and Milner (2006). When the experiment was performed for 2008, there was a small increase in trade creation (in actual dollars) for ten of the listed countries in table 3.14. This is not a surprising trend as one would expect that over time in a rapidly globalizing world economy, trade source substitution towards the European Union would increase, albeit a small one. Trinidad and Tobago and Jamaica recorded the largest increase in trade creation on EU imports from 1998 to 2008 (see table 3.14). The decline in extra-regional imports ranged from 40.09 per cent for Trinidad and Tobago to 64.89 per cent for St Lucia in 2008.[32] There is a general increase in extra-regional trade diversion (in actual dollars) for all CARICOM countries. Moreover, Trinidad and Tobago recorded the largest increase in trade diversion in actual dollars from the listed CARICOM countries.

3.12.5 Revenue Effects of Full Liberalization of Tariffs on EU

The revenue effects associated with the full liberalization of tariffs on CARICOM countries' imports from the European Union is reported in table 3.15. The results revealed that all CARICOM

Table 3.14 Trade effects associated with the EPA, US$ million, 1998 and 2008

	Trade Creation on Existing EU Imports		Change in CARICOM Imports		Change in Extra-Regional Imports	
	EU (1998)	EU (2008)	EU (1998)	EU (2008)	EU (1998)	EU (2008)
Bahamas	13.62	7.61	−1.49	−8.36	−982.56	−1,500.49
Belize	4.30	5.24	−2.73	−3.38	−121.69	−288.00
Barbados	26.53	32.83	−34.17	−71.81	−311.22	−589.44
Dominica	3.18	3.41	−8.87	−15.72	−41.38	−75.47
Grenada	4.44	5.86	−13.95	−24.59	−62.77	−124.95
Guyana	10.15	14.94	−17.80	−64.81	−171.50	−412.83
Jamaica	44.93	85.32	−89.73	−294.12	−1,310.64	−2,842.30
St Kitts & Nevis	2.57	3.40	−6.55	−12.09	−55.23	−154.85
St Lucia	7.89	9.63	−18.32	−47.30	−112.88	−258.87
Trinidad & Tobago	59.51	150.18	−25.56	−32.47	−969.14	−3,312.19
St Vincent & the Grenadines	6.03	8.77	−12.25	−23.71	−50.26	−119.85

Sources: Own calculations from United Nations Commodity Trade Database (UNCOMTRADE) (2014) and Greenaway and Milner (2006) for 1998 values for EU only.

Table 3.15 Revenue effects associated with the EPA, US$ million, 1998 and 2008

	Change in Revenue	
	EU (1998)	EU (2008)
Bahamas	−133.21	−197.82
Belize	−19.36	−37.58
Barbados	−67.50	−94.85
Dominica	−8.08	−11.82
Grenada	−11.54	−19.98
Guyana	−27.38	−57.72
Jamaica	−234.99	−428.74
St Kitts & Nevis	−9.58	−23.91
St Lucia	−22.35	−41.08
Trinidad & Tobago	−144.33	−461.89
St Vincent & the Grenadines	−10.12	−20.42

Sources: Own calculations from United Nations Commodity Trade Database (UNCOMTRADE) (2014) and Greenaway and Milner (2006) for 1998 values for EU only.

countries are likely to experience a decrease in tariff revenues on account of the EPA. The OECS countries are likely to experience a higher percentage decline on tariff revenues than the larger CARICOM countries. This implies that the loss in tariff revenues would present a greater challenge

Table 3.16 Welfare effects associated with the EPA, US$ million, 1998 and 2008

	Change in Welfare	
	EU (1998)	EU (2008)
Bahamas	−90.64	−146.89
Belize	−16.10	−25.22
Barbados	−48.73	−55.83
Dominica	−5.54	−8.23
Grenada	−8.08	−14.91
Guyana	−18.03	−42.21
Jamaica	−203.61	−313.67
St Kitts & Nevis	−7.54	−18.26
St Lucia	−15.78	−26.10
Trinidad & Tobago	−108.37	−387.55
St Vincent & the Grenadines	−6.05	−14.76

Sources: Own calculations from United Nations Commodity Trade Database (UNCOMTRADE) (2014) and Greenaway and Milner (2006) for 1998 values for EU only.

for the smaller economies since they have a higher dependence on tariff revenues as a source of their total revenues compared to the larger CARICOM countries (see table 3.15).

3.12.6 Welfare Effects of Full Liberalization of Tariffs on EU

The decline in welfare for CARICOM countries on account of the full liberalization of tariffs on EU imports is reported in table 3.16. Trinidad and Tobago, Jamaica and the Bahamas are the three CARICOM countries that are expected to be most affected, while Dominica and St Vincent and the Grenadines reported the least negative effects (in actual dollars) using 2008 data. In comparison to the 1998 experiment, all countries experienced a higher level of welfare decline in 2008.

3.13 Measuring Economic Growth Spillovers from the European Union and the United States in the CARIFORUM Region

This section examines the growth spillovers from the European Union, United States and commodity prices on CARIFORUM countries in the context of the EPA. While a significant body of literature exists on economic growth spillovers from advanced economies to developing countries, there is marginal information on the spillover effects from advanced economies to CARIFORUM countries and specifically from the European Union and the United States on the CARIFORUM region.[33] To assess the impact of growth spillovers from the European Union in the CARIFORUM region, a vector autoregressive (VAR) model is estimated. VARs are generally specified as an *n*-equation and *n* variable system. Each variable in the VAR is regressed on its own lagged values, the lagged values and present values of the remaining $n-1$ variables in the system. The VAR model includes five variables: these are the real GDP growth rates of the European Union, United States, Dominican Republic, CARICOM and real oil prices.[34] The VAR model of order (p) is outlined as follows:

$$V_t = \sum_{i-1}^{m} A_i V_{t-1} + \varepsilon_t$$

where V refers to a vector of endogenous variables that includes the real GDP growth rates of the countries identified above and commodity prices. Before the VAR model is estimated, the stationary properties of each variable in the VAR is examined using the augmented Dickey Fuller (ADF) test (1979), the Phillips-Perron (PP) test (1988) and the Kwiatkowski-Phillips-Schmidt-Shin (KPSS) test (1992). The results of the unit roots are reported in table 3.17 and show that the growth rates of each country is stationary, while the real oil price variable is non-stationary and admits one unit root after first differencing.

The estimated VAR is interpreted using innovation accounting tools such as the impulse response functions and the forecast error variance decomposition. An impulse response function illustrates the response of each variable in the VAR system to a shock in one of the innovations. For example, it measures how a one standard deviation shock in the growth rate of the European Union impact on the real GDP growth rate of CARIFORUM countries. On the other hand, the forecast error variance decomposition shows the contribution of each random shock to variations in an endogenous variable. For example, it measures how much of the change in an endogenous variable is attributed to its own shock and to shocks from other endogenous variables in the system.

In this model, the Cholesky factorization method is used to orthogonalize the residuals in the VAR which may be correlated, since the results of innovation accounting tools are usually sensitive to the ordering of the variables in the VAR model. Specifically, the Cholesky ordering of the

Table 3.17 Results of unit root tests using the ADF, PP and KPSS procedures

Variables	ADF Test Statistic	Level of Integration	PP Test Statistic	Level of Integration	KPSS Test Statistic	Level of Integration
Real oil price	−1.82	I(1)	−1.82	I(1)	0.10	I(0)
Real GDP growth for the Dominican Republic	−6.75	I(0)	−6.75	I(0)	0.11	I(0)
Real GDP growth for the CARICOM	−4.25	I(0)	−4.24	I(0)	0.32	I(0)
Real GDP growth for the EU	−3.61	I(0)	−3.69	I(0)	0.56	I(0)
Real GDP growth for the USA	−5.02	I(0)	−4.89	I(0)	0.39	I(0)

Notes: Critical values for ADF test are −3.6 (1 per cent), −2.9 (5 per cent), −2.6 (10 per cent).Critical values for PP test are −3.6 (1 per cent), −2.9 (5 per cent), −2.6 (10 per cent).Critical values for KPSS test are 0.74 (1 per cent), 0.46 (5 per cent), 0.35 (10 per cent).

Table 3.18 VAR lag order selection criteria

Lag	LogL	LR	FPE	AIC	SC	HQ
0	−570.1105	NA	155,133.7	26.14139	26.34414*	26.21658*
1	−537.1058	57.00823*	108,738.2*	25.77754	26.99403	26.22867
2	−522.8058	21.45002	185,098.2	26.26390	28.49414	27.09098
3	−494.9097	35.50414	182,994.0	26.13226	29.37624	27.33528
4	−471.7354	24.22764	254,638.0	26.21525	30.47297	27.79422
5	−435.3974	29.73110	240,872.4	25.69988*	30.97135	27.65480

Notes: The asterisk "*" indicates Lag order selected by the criterion. LR, sequential modified LR test statistic (each test at 5 per cent level); FPE, final prediction error; AIC, Akaike information criterion; SC, Schwarz information criterion.

Table 3.19 Variance decomposition for CARICOM and the Dominican Republic

Period	United States	European Union	Commodity Price	Dominican Republic	CARICOM
Variance decomposition of Dominican Republic's real GDP growth					
1	5.41	30.65	0.29	63.66	0.00
2	4.58	41.04	0.56	53.82	0.00
3	4.99	39.24	3.23	52.17	0.38
4	5.18	38.76	4.21	51.36	0.52
5	7.89	36.58	5.14	47.45	2.96
6	8.25	35.37	4.88	47.10	4.40
7	7.97	36.12	4.67	46.40	4.84
8	8.05	35.91	4.69	46.21	5.15
9	9.39	35.23	4.66	45.68	5.04
10	9.76	34.95	4.97	45.08	5.24
Variance decomposition of CARICOM's real GDP growth					
1	16.50	17.34	8.06	0.45	57.65
2	24.62	13.83	6.83	0.49	54.23
3	21.71	23.09	7.14	0.41	47.65
4	20.81	22.63	6.83	3.77	45.96
5	19.39	23.29	6.28	9.16	41.87
6	18.37	23.24	7.82	9.91	40.66
7	18.66	22.95	9.28	9.90	39.21
8	17.58	22.29	12.66	9.67	37.77
9	17.28	21.60	12.36	10.48	38.26
10	16.75	20.94	12.63	11.53	38.16

variables is based on the assumption that the higher ordered variables in the VAR have a contemporaneous impact on the variables lower in the ordering of the VAR, but the lower ordered variables do not have a contemporaneous impact on variables higher in the ordering. In this model, the Cholesky factorization is based on the assumption that a large country such as the European Union can have an impact on the growth performance of a small CARIFORUM economy, but a small country is not likely to have to contemporaneous impact on the growth performance of a large economy. The variables are ordered as follows: the real GDP growth rate for the United States, European Union, real oil prices (commodity prices), Dominican Republic and CARICOM real GDP growth rates.

Before estimating the VAR, it is also important to determine the optimal lag length for the variables using the sequential modified likelihood ratio test statistic (LR), the final prediction error (FPE), the Schwarz information criterion (SC), the Hannan-Quinn information criterion (HQ) and the Akaike information criterion (AIC) tests. The results of these tests are provided in table 3.18. Other diagnostic tests on the residuals are also conducted such as tests for normality, serial correlation of the residuals and stability of the VAR. The VAR model to be estimated has satisfied all these tests and is properly specified and stable to estimate the impulse response function and the forecast error variance decomposition.

The results from the forecast error variance decomposition and the impulse response functions are provided in table 3.19 and figure 3.14. The results from the forecast error variance decomposition reveal that the European Union is a larger contributor to GDP growth variations

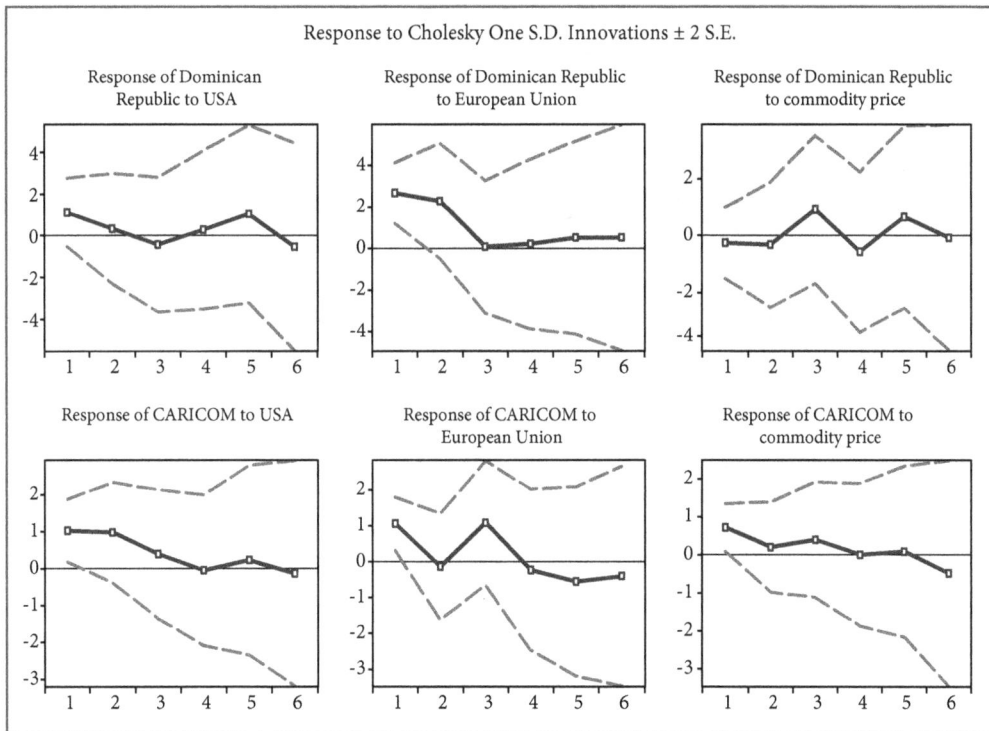

Figure 3.14 Estimated impulse response functions for CARIFORUM countries

in the Dominican Republic compared to the CARICOM region. In fact, over the first ten horizons, the European Union accounted for over 36 per cent of the Dominican Republic's growth variations which increased from about 31 per cent in the first horizon to 41 per cent in the second horizon and gradually declined to approximately 35 per cent in the tenth horizon. On the other hand, on average, only 21 per cent of CARICOM growth variations are attributed to the European Union for the first ten horizons. For the CARICOM region, growth variation from the European Union contributed to 17 per cent in the first horizon which increased to 23.29 in the fifth horizon but marginally declined thereafter to 21 per cent in the tenth horizon. The United States and commodity prices account for a greater share of CARICOM's GDP growth variations compared to the Dominican Republic.

The estimated impulse response functions presented in figure 3.14 indicate that a one standard deviation shock to the EU GDP growth rate has a significant and positive impact on the Dominican Republic and CARICOM GDP growth. For the Dominican Republic, a one standard deviation shock to the EU growth rate leads to an increase in the Dominican Republic's and CARICOM's GDP growth rate by 2.7 and 1.1 per cent, respectively. A one standard deviation shock to the United States only has a significant and positive impact on the GDP growth rate in the CARICOM region by 1.1 per cent, but it is insignificant for the Dominican Republic. For a one standard deviation shock in oil prices, only CARICOM countries revealed a significant and positive response by 0.7 per cent. These results are important in the context of the EPA as it demonstrates that the Dominican Republic is in a better position to benefit from policy changes associated with the EPA compared to the CARICOM region. This may be an indication that the transmission mechanism to facilitate growth spillovers is more effective in the Dominican Republic.

3.14 Conclusion

The eventual negotiating outcome of the EPAs will depend on the level of CARIFORUM's preparedness at the negotiation table. Negotiations should be framed to achieve a win-win outcome as compared to an outcome in which the better negotiating team takes away most of the benefit. The need to help the lesser-developed CARIFORUM economies overcome the transition costs associated with the implementation of the EPA must, however, be acknowledged.

The success of EPAs hinges on the commitment of the CARIFORUM economies to long-term economic sustainability. In particular, these economies would need to develop the relevant institutional, political and economic environment which can facilitate the EPA and the development of these CARIFORUM economies in turn.

One may also argue that the timing, that is, end of December 2007, is a relatively short horizon, and while it may facilitate the completion of the negotiations, it does not have enough width to facilitate the implementation of the negotiated issues.

Even so, an important closing point is that we should not moan and groan about the possibility of an EPA and the various consequences. What we should do is organize and pool our various talents and resources so as to be better prepared to deal with threats and opportunities which the EPA may pose.

<table>
<tr><td>

4

</td><td>

The Rapid Growth of BRICS and Implications for CARICOM

</td></tr>
</table>

4.1 Introduction

The world has witnessed an accelerated growth performance of the BRICS (Brazil, Russia, India, China and South Africa) economies over the past few years. The average growth performance of this group of emerging economies has contributed to a new engine for global economic growth, especially in the presence of a decline in economic activity in advanced economies (UNCTAD 2013). A 2001 Goldman and Sachs report was the first to highlight the potential of the BRICS as an economic superpower using information on GDP predictions and other factors such as macroeconomic stability, institutions, openness and education (Bell 2011). The share of BRICS in global GDP for 2000 was 8 per cent which increased to 20.32 per cent in 2013. South Africa officially became a member of the BRICS in December 2010, changing what was formerly known as BRIC to BRICS. While the BRICS economies share several common features, Almeida (2009) noted that the BRICS differ from each other in terms of natural resources, the level of industrialization and their impact on the global economy. Indeed, of the five members of the BRICS, China has recorded the most success in terms of its share in world output and GDP growth rates. There are a number of similarities between the BRICS economies. The first and most significant characteristic is their large size in terms of land mass and human capital potential. BRICS presently account for approximately 41.5 per cent of the world's population with 19 per cent in China followed by India with 17 per cent, and Brazil and Russia and South Africa with 2.8 per cent, 2.0 per cent and 0.71 per cent, respectively. Da Silva et al. (2011) noted that the reasons for the economic progress of the BRICS are attributed to their generally low labour costs that attract a great share of export oriented foreign direct investment (FDI) into their economies. Furthermore, Cassiolato and Lundvall (2006) have also noted that while China is responsible for decreasing prices in many labour-intensive commodities, India's growth has placed upward pressure on petroleum prices and these occurrences serve to make the growth pattern of BRICS, more interdependent.

In many emerging economies, there is a growing productive skills sector that has tremendous production potential. According to Rao (2008), although China, India and Brazil have records of relatively low literacy and educational attainment rates, but BRICS together have a large and increasing amount of well-educated persons which can strengthen their workforce in the coming years. Rao also highlighted that BRICS, via educational improvements, investments in research and development as well as international collaboration are becoming leaders in technology and innovation. Furthermore, the BRICS represent a main source of outward FDI which can lead to increased economic activity in other developing countries. The expected rise in BRICS middle class represents another opportunity by which tourism inflows and demand for raw materials and consumer goods in developing countries can be increased.

The rise of BRICS has brought about positive changes in the economic landscape within the global economy by creating new economic spaces for developing countries around the world. It has been forecasted that within the next few decades the current G7 may be replaced by the BRICS (Wilson and Purushothaman 2003). Historically, there have not been strong economic relations between the BRICS and the CARICOM bloc. North America and Europe have been CARICOM's main trade and investment partners in the world. These countries, however, are experiencing serious economic and fiscal challenges which are likely to have a ripple effect on CARICOM and other developing countries, where economic growth is driven by external forces. As a result, many developing countries may become more dependent on the growth of BRICS to fuel external demand for trade, as the share of BRICS economies in the global economy continues to rise.

However, over the period 2012–13, there has been a slowing in the growth of emerging economies, but their performance still remains higher than advanced economies. A recent development is the creation of the BRICS Development Bank by the leaders of the BRICS economies in a summit held in Durban, South Africa, on 27 March 2013. The leaders agreed to create a US$100 billion pool of currency reserves to act as a buffer against financial shocks. This bank would also aid in funding infrastructure projects, which would target dilapidated airports, roads and railways and keep their economies on a positive growth trajectory.[35]

It would be prudent on the basis of the discussion above, to include BRICS in the policy sphere for CARICOM and other developing countries. With the onset of globalization and as BRICS gain momentum within the global economy, it is imperative for CARICOM countries to devise strategies that will aid in diversifying their trade markets into emerging economies. In this regard, this chapter provides a deeper understanding and appreciation of the growth and importance of BRICS, possible challenges for CARICOM countries, and determines how the resulting growth of BRICS can feature more in CARICOM's economic development.

4.2 BRICS: A New Engine for Global Growth

This section provides an assessment of the macroeconomic performance of BRICS for the period 1991–2012. All of the countries (see table 4.1) revealed an increase in the GDP (current US$) over the last decade. In particular, the GDP of Brazil, Russia, India, China and South Africa increased

Table 4.1 Macroeconomic overview of BRICS, 1991–2012

Country	1991	2000	2005	2008	2009	2010	2011	2012
				GDP (current US$ billion)				
Brazil	407.34	644.70	882.19	1,653.54	1,620.17	2,143.04	2,476.65	2,252.66
China	379.47	1,198.47	2,256.90	4,521.83	4,991.26	5,930.53	7,321.94	8,227.10
Russian Federation	509.38	259.71	764.00	1,660.85	1,222.65	1,524.92	1,899.09	2,014.77
India	274.84	476.61	834.22	1,224.10	1,365.37	1,710.91	1,872.84	1,841.71
South Africa	120.23	132.88	247.05	273.14	283.99	363.24	401.80	384.31
				GDP per capita (constant 2005 US$)				
Brazil	3,993.06	4,406.71	4,739.31	5,336.08	5,271.14	5,618.32	5,721.29	5,721.23
China	498.83	1,122.29	1,731.13	2,403.31	2,611.40	2,869.09	3,120.93	3,348.01
Russian Federation	5,386.07	3,878.10	5,337.07	6,649.40	6,131.09	6,385.66	6,633.07	6,834.00
India	399.33	578.22	740.11	885.17	947.75	1,034.24	1,085.73	1,106.79
South Africa	4,708.03	4,652.34	5,234.31	5,848.04	5,697.23	5,794.24	5,923.99	6,003.46
				Inflation, consumer prices (annual %)				
Brazil	432.78	7.04	6.87	5.66	4.89	5.04	6.64	5.40
China	3.54	0.26	1.82	5.86	−0.70	3.31	5.41	2.65
Russian Federation		20.78	12.68	14.11	11.65	6.86	8.44	5.07
India	13.87	4.01	4.25	8.35	10.88	11.99	8.86	9.31
South Africa	15.33	5.34	3.40	11.54	7.13	4.26	5.28	5.41
				Unemployment, total (% of total labour force)				
Brazil			9.30	7.10	8.30		6.70	
China	2.30	3.10	4.20					
Russian Federation		10.60	7.10	6.20	8.30	7.30	6.50	5.50
India		4.30	4.40			3.50		3.60
South Africa		26.70	23.80	22.70	23.70	24.70	24.70	25.00

Source: World Development Indicators (2014).

by 249.4 per cent, 675.7 per cent, 268.4 per cent, 586.5 per cent and 189.2 per cent, respectively, from 2000 to 2012. This trend is also observed in the aggregate output of individual members of the BRICS with China being ranked as having the largest GDP (US$8,227.10 billion) in 2012. Furthermore, China's per capita GDP increased almost threefold from US$1,122.29 in 2000 to US$3,348.01 in 2012, accounting for the largest increase in per capita income among the BRICS. Amid these large increases in output, the Chinese economy has managed to maintain a relatively low inflation rate over the last decade compared to Brazil, Russia, India and South Africa. Notably, the inflation rate in India had increased over the last decade from 4.01 per cent in 2001 to 9.31 per cent in 2012. The level of unemployment in the BRICS has generally declined over the period, with the exception of South Africa which continues to post high unemployment rates, above 20 per cent.

The BRICS economies have generally posted higher growth rates compared to the United States, the United Kingdom and Japan over the period 2000–2012 (see table 4.2). The data shows that China and India are among the two fastest emerging economies in the world. It is interesting to note that while three members of the G6 recorded negative and slower growth rates during the post-2008 period, China and India continued to report strong positive growth performance.[36] However, it should be noted that post-2010 the growth performances of emerging economies have slowed (see table 4.2).

Within the last three decades, Brazil, India and China have observed significant progress in poverty reduction via buoyant economic growth and a range of policy reforms. UNIDO (2012) noted that rapid growth and structural change have contributed to the reduction of poverty in all BRICS countries, to varying degrees. The highest decline was experienced by China, where the manufacturing sector absorbed a large number of migrant workers from rural areas.

Table 4.2 Comparison of BRICS growth in GDP (%) with other major economies, 1991–2012

	Brazil	Russia	India	China	South Africa	United States	Japan	United Kingdom
1991	1.51	−5.05	1.06	9.20	−1.02	−0.07	3.32	−1.29
1992	−0.47	−14.53	5.48	14.20	−2.14	3.56	0.82	1.29
1993	4.67	−8.67	4.75	14.00	1.23	2.75	0.17	3.49
1994	5.33	−12.57	6.66	13.10	3.23	4.04	0.86	4.95
1995	4.42	−4.14	7.57	10.90	3.12	2.72	1.94	3.53
1996	2.15	−3.60	7.55	10.00	4.31	3.80	2.61	3.49
1997	3.37	1.40	4.05	9.30	2.65	4.49	1.60	4.35
1998	0.04	−5.30	6.18	7.80	0.52	4.45	−2.00	3.57
1999	0.26	6.40	8.85	7.60	2.36	4.85	−0.20	2.94
2000	4.31	10.00	3.84	8.40	4.15	4.09	2.26	4.36
2001	1.31	5.09	4.82	8.30	2.74	0.95	0.36	2.18
2002	2.66	4.74	3.80	9.10	3.67	1.78	0.29	2.30
2003	1.15	7.30	7.86	10.00	2.95	2.79	1.69	3.95
2004	5.71	7.18	7.92	10.10	4.55	3.80	2.36	3.17
2005	3.16	6.38	9.28	11.30	5.28	3.35	1.30	3.23
2006	3.96	8.15	9.26	12.70	5.60	2.67	1.69	2.76
2007	6.10	8.54	9.80	14.20	5.55	1.79	2.19	3.43
2008	5.17	5.25	3.89	9.60	3.62	−0.29	−1.04	−0.77
2009	−0.33	−7.82	8.48	9.20	−1.53	−2.80	−5.53	−5.17
2010	7.53	4.50	10.55	10.40	3.09	2.51	4.65	1.66
2011	2.73	4.29	6.33	9.30	3.46	1.85	−0.57	1.12
2012	0.87	3.44	3.24	7.80	2.55	2.78	1.94	0.12

Source: World Development Indicators (2014).

The contribution of emerging economies to world output has generally increased over time, especially over the period 2000–2012. BRICS contribution to world GDP averaged about 7 per cent for the period 1961–99, but increased to 20.32 per cent by 2012. This trend is associated with a simultaneous decline in the contribution of the US share in world GDP. In particular, in 1961, the US share in world GDP was 38 per cent, but this declined to 22 per cent by 2012, a similar decline is observed for Japan and the United Kingdom (see figure 4.1).

However, an assessment of the GDP per capita based on purchasing power parity (PPP) (constant 2005 international $) indicated that while the BRICS have made significant improvements in growth and aggregate output, they are still trailing the advanced economies on a per capita basis. Notably, China and India have made significant improvements in comparison to the other members of BRICS. It should be noted that Russia posted the highest GDP per capita PPP in 2012 of US$15,177 among the BRICS, but this was almost three times lower than that of the United States (table 4.3).

The projected growth of BRICS in the coming decades would certainly trigger an expansion in their middle class. At present, only China is recorded in the top seven countries shifting towards middle-income countries but by 2030, all four are projected to be among the top seven middle-income countries in the world (table 4.4). O'Neill et al. (2004) noted that the BRICS middle class is expected to increase fourfold in the next decade, with approximately eight hundred million individuals surpassing the US$3,000 per capita benchmark. Individually, China's middle class is projected to increase tenfold, India's fourteenfold and Brazil and Russia twofold, respectively, in the next decade. This provides a substantial new market of consumers with improved spending power that small developing countries like CARICOM, target for increasing exports (SELA 2013).

Along with the growth experienced by BRICS economies, within the recent past, there have been relative changes in the production structure of these economies. Some of these changes are highlighted in table 4.5. According to the data, there have been continuous contractions in the relative size of the agricultural sector in all of the BRICS economies during the period 1961–2012. In particular, the share of the agricultural sector in GDP for India and China reported the largest decline over the same period. For China, the agriculture sector declined from 35.51 per cent in 1961 to 10.09 per cent in 2012, while that of India declined from 41.77 per cent to 17.39 per cent for the same period. The share of the agriculture sector in GDP for South Africa declined from 11.54 per cent to a paltry 2.57 per cent over the same period.

Brazil, Russia and South Africa experienced considerable decreases in their industrial sector contribution to GDP. More specifically, Brazil's industrial sector contribution to GDP fell from 41.75 per cent to 26.29 per cent, Russia's declined from 48.35 per cent to 36 per cent and South Africa's declined 37.96 per cent to 28.41 per cent over the period 1961–2012. Marginal increases in the industrial sector were observed for China and India over the same period.

In Brazil, the relative size of the manufacturing sector declined from 31.38 per cent in 1961 to 13.25 per cent in 2012. In China, India, Russia and South Africa, a similar trend was observed in the manufacturing sector but in these three countries, the fall was marginal. From the period 1961 to 2012, there was a considerable expansion in the services sector of all five BRICS economies. Specifically, the services sector in the Russian economy witnessed the sharpest increase which was almost twice the amount from 1980 to 2012. Brazil has the largest growing services sector among the BRICS economies followed by Russia, India, China and South Africa (refer to table 4.5).

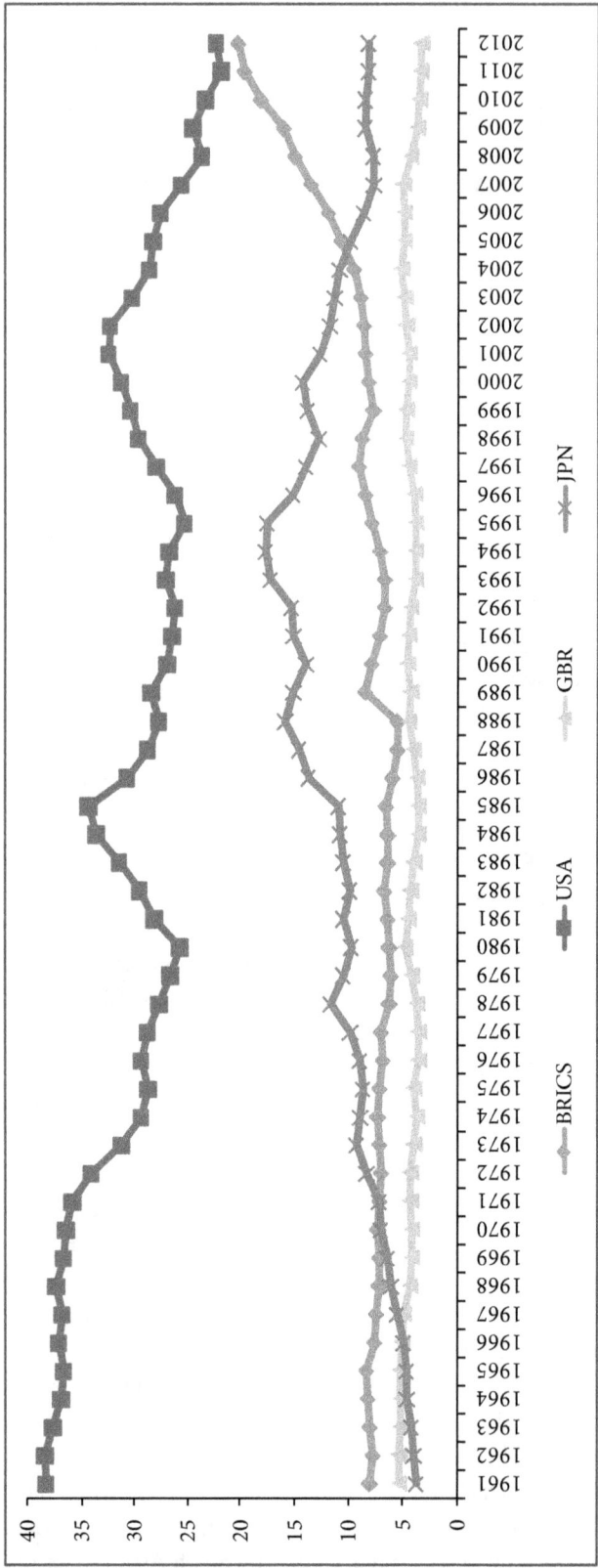

Figure 4.1 BRICS, US, Japanese and UK contribution to World GDP

Table 4.3 GDP per capita PPP (constant 2005 international $), 1991–2012

	Brazil	Russia	India	China	South Africa	United States	Japan	United Kingdom
1991	7,164	11,962	1,205	1,186	7,732	32,504	27,319	22,063
1992	7,017	10,219	1,247	1,338	7,411	33,196	27,475	22,289
1993	7,232	9,344	1,281	1,507	7,346	33,661	27,454	23,011
1994	7,502	8,179	1,342	1,686	7,423	34,592	27,597	24,090
1995	7,714	7,851	1,417	1,849	7,490	35,112	28,026	24,875
1996	7,760	7,589	1,497	2,013	7,641	36,024	28,684	25,678
1997	7,900	7,718	1,530	2,178	7,666	37,190	29,065	26,726
1998	7,784	7,329	1,597	2,325	7,526	38,394	28,411	27,599
1999	7,689	7,829	1,709	2,480	7,520	39,796	28,300	28,315
2000	7,906	8,613	1,745	2,667	7,641	40,965	28,889	29,445
2001	7,898	9,073	1,800	2,868	7,691	40,946	28,928	29,979
2002	7,998	9,546	1,838	3,108	7,864	41,289	28,945	30,554
2003	7,985	10,292	1,952	3,398	7,993	42,078	29,369	31,633
2004	8,338	11,088	2,074	3,719	8,259	43,274	30,053	32,472
2005	8,502	11,853	2,234	4,115	8,597	44,314	30,441	33,324
2006	8,745	12,878	2,406	4,611	8,977	45,059	30,961	34,032
2007	9,187	14,016	2,606	5,239	9,372	45,431	31,636	34,973
2008	9,573	14,767	2,672	5,712	9,605	44,873	31,323	34,474
2009	9,456	13,616	2,861	6,207	9,357	43,234	29,625	32,471
2010	10,079	14,182	3,122	6,819	9,516	43,952	31,030	32,766
2011	10,264	14,731	3,277	7,418	9,730	44,439	30,764	32,878
2012	10,264	15,177	3,341	7,958	9,860	45,336	31,425	32,671

Source: World Development Indicators (2014).

4.3 BRICS and World Trade

Manufactures is the dominant merchandise exports of BRICS, especially for India and China. China's export of manufactured goods as a share in its merchandise exports increased from 75.72 per cent in 1991 to 93.93 per cent in 2012. India's export of manufactured goods accounts for approximately 64.77 per cent of India's merchandise exports in 2012, despite slightly falling over the period. Brazil and South Africa also have a fairly large export of manufactures, relative to their exports from other sectors. Russia, on the other hand, can attribute most of its merchandise exports to fuel. Furthermore, Brazil is the only BRICS member that showed a growing share of food exports while there has been a continuous decrease in food exports by India and China. Russia and South Africa's proportion of food exports stayed fairly low for the last decade (see table 4.6).

All members of BRICS have experienced a significant increase in imports from the world, with regard to total merchandise trade. A large share of BRICS merchandise imports from the

Table 4.4 Top seven: shifting towards middle-income countries

1980	GDP Rank	Income Rank	2030	GDP Rank	Income Rank
United States	1	12	China	1	49
Japan	2	19	United States	2	12
Germany	3	17	India	3	63
France	4	9	Japan	4	29
United Kingdom	5	18	Brazil	5	47
Italy	6	21	Russia	6	35
Canada	7	15	Germany	7	22
2007	**GDP Rank**	**Income Rank**	**2050**	**GDP Rank**	**Income Rank**
United States	1	9	China	1	45
Japan	2	22	United States	2	15
Germany	3	16	India	3	61
China	4	56	Brazil	4	46
United Kingdom	5	10	Russia	5	28
France	6	17	Indonesia	6	60
Italy	7	20	Mexico	7	44

Source: Wilson and Dragusanu (2008).

world during 1990–2012 can be attributed to China and India. In addition, China also has the largest trade surplus among the BRICS economies, while for the period 1990–2012 India and South Africa recorded continuous trade deficits (refer to table 4.7).

According to Markin (2006), China's growing trade surpluses can be attributed to policy initiatives such as China's accession to the World Trade Organization in 2001, tremendous reductions in tariff barriers from over 55 per cent in 1982 to about 9 per cent in 2008, in addition to proper exchange rate controls. According to Hale (2006), China's trade surplus has also grown as a result of FDI from multinationals into export oriented sectors such as the automotive industry.

With regard to India's continuous trade deficit, Palit (2008) posits that this results mainly from industrial imports and rising crude prices. Palit noted, however, that this is not a serious cause for concern for a fast-growing economy like India, and regardless of the increasing crude prices, the Indian economy is in a good position to deal with its current trade deficit. The direction of exports of the BRICS pattern of trade is another interesting phenomenon. There has been a gradual shift of BRICS exports over the last decade from developed economies to emerging markets (figure 4.2).

This point is further illustrated in table 4.8 by an examination of BRICS top five export and import partners for 2012. Notably, in most instances BRICS members are their own top trading partners. Brazil's top export and import market is China. China is also South Africa, Russia and India's top import source and India's third top export market. Although China's major trading partner is not any of the BRICS members, they are from other emerging market economies in Asia, such as South Korea, Japan and Hong Kong.

The ten leading exported goods from BRICS during 2010–12 are shown in table 4.9.[37] The highest share in BRICS merchandise exports from 2010 to 2012 originate from petroleum

Table 4.5 Structure of BRICS economies (% of GDP), 1961–2012

Country	1961	1970	1980	1990	2000	2010	2012
Agriculture, value added (% of GDP)							
Brazil	19.50	12.35	11.01	8.10	5.60	5.30	5.24
Russian Federation	–	–	–	16.61	6.43	4.00	3.87
India	41.77	41.95	35.39	29.02	23.02	17.98	17.39
China	35.51	35.22	30.17	27.12	15.06	10.06	10.09
South Africa	11.54	7.16	6.20	4.63	3.27	2.58	2.57
Industry, value added (% of GDP)							
Brazil	41.75	38.30	43.83	38.69	27.73	28.07	26.29
Russian Federation	–	–	–	48.35	37.95	35.43	36.00
India	19.93	20.48	24.29	26.49	26.00	27.57	25.75
China	32.59	40.49	48.22	41.34	45.92	46.57	45.31
South Africa	37.96	38.18	48.38	40.10	31.78	29.84	28.41
Manufacturing, value added (% of GDP)							
Brazil	31.38	29.32	33.49	–	17.22	16.23	13.25
Russian Federation	–	–	–	–	–	14.99	15.19
India	14.33	13.70	16.18	16.16	15.31	14.87	13.53
China	–	33.75	40.23	32.66	32.12	29.52	–
South Africa	20.65	22.81	21.63	23.64	18.98	14.20	12.38
Services, etc., value added (% of GDP)							
Brazil	38.76	49.35	45.16	53.21	66.67	66.63	68.47
Russian Federation	–	–	–	35.04	55.62	60.57	60.13
India	38.29	37.57	40.32	44.48	50.98	54.45	56.86
China	31.90	24.29	21.60	31.54	39.02	43.37	44.60
South Africa	50.50	54.66	45.43	55.27	64.94	67.58	69.02

Source: World Development Indicators (2014).

products, increasing marginally from 10.37 per cent to 10.92 per cent in 2012. These two sectors can be attributed to the Russian economy. Machinery and other electrical equipment comprise other major export goods from BRICS.

4.4 CARICOM's Trade with BRICS

CARICOM's trade with BRICS can be best described as insignificant on the export side since during the last decade CARICOM's export to BRICS averaged less than 2 per cent. However, BRICS share in CARICOM's exports experienced a slight increase from 1.3 per cent in 2001 to 3.1 per cent in 2012. On average, CARICOM imports more from BRICS as can be observed by the increase in imports from BRICS during the period 2001–12 (table 4.10).

In the last decade, all CARICOM member countries experienced persistent trade deficits with BRICS. The top three countries within the CARICOM region that dominate CARICOM's export

Table 4.6 Exports by broad categories from BRICS (% of merchandise exports), 1991–2012

Country	1991	1995	2000	2005	2010	2012
Agricultural raw materials exports (% of merchandise exports)						
Brazil	3.39	5.23	4.76	3.83	3.94	3.79
Russian Federation	–	–	3.09	2.79	2.07	1.77
India	2.01	1.29	1.26	1.27	2.01	1.95
China	2.82	1.69	1.09	0.52	0.46	0.46
South Africa	–	3.99	3.38	1.98	1.95	1.97
Food exports (% of merchandise exports)						
Brazil	24.93	28.73	23.39	25.77	31.08	32.19
Russian Federation	–	–	1.25	1.60	1.89	3.16
India	16.80	18.68	12.79	8.97	8.26	10.54
China	12.26	8.25	5.44	3.23	2.80	2.75
South Africa	–	7.96	8.47	8.54	8.73	8.47
Fuel exports (% of merchandise exports)						
Brazil	1.37	0.87	1.64	5.98	10.14	11.03
Russian Federation	–	–	50.58	61.77	65.62	70.27
India	2.36	1.66	3.40	10.33	16.95	18.51
China	6.51	3.58	3.14	2.30	1.69	1.50
South Africa	–	8.95	10.04	10.34	9.95	12.50
Manufactures exports (% of merchandise exports)						
Brazil	54.86	53.53	58.43	52.96	37.06	35.04
Russian Federation	–	–	23.59	18.75	14.10	14.20
India	72.04	73.55	77.84	71.07	63.76	64.77
China	75.72	84.13	88.22	91.88	93.55	93.93
South Africa	–	43.51	53.85	56.66	46.55	45.38
Ores and metals exports (% of merchandise exports)						
Brazil	14.35	10.28	9.81	9.61	17.79	15.59
Russian Federation	–	–	9.29	6.66	5.56	3.97
India	5.32	3.29	2.72	7.24	6.99	3.34
China	1.67	2.10	1.90	1.86	1.41	1.28
South Africa	–	8.07	10.75	22.45	32.74	31.52

Source: World Development Indicators (2014).

performance with respect to BRICS are Trinidad and Tobago, Jamaica and Guyana. Furthermore, these three economies are endowed with natural resources such as crude oil, natural gas, asphalt, aluminium and other precious metals necessary for fuelling growth in emerging market economies. There is significant potential for exports in these areas from CARICOM to BRICS in the future, since BRICS demand for natural resources is likely to expand as their economies grow. Trinidad and Tobago, Jamaica, and Guyana also represent a large share of CARICOM's import from BRICS, with Trinidad and Tobago being the top importer in the last decade.

Table 4.7 BRICS merchandise trade with the world, US$ billion, 1990–2012

Country	1990	2000	2005	2006	2007	2008	2009	2010	2011	2012
					Exports US$ billion					
Brazil	31.41	55.12	118.53	137.81	160.65	197.94	152.99	197.36	256.04	242.58
Russia	–	103.09	241.45	301.55	352.27	467.99	301.80	397.07	516.99	524.77
India	17.86	42.36	100.35	121.20	145.90	181.86	176.77	220.41	301.48	289.56
China	–	249.20	761.95	968.94	1,220.06	1,430.69	1,201.65	1,577.76	1,898.39	2,048.78
South Africa	–	26.30	46.99	52.60	64.03	73.97	53.86	71.48	92.98	86.71
					Imports US$ billion					
Brazil	22.46	55.73	73.52	91.26	120.54	172.95	127.44	179.69	225.50	223.15
Russia	–	33.88	98.71	137.81	199.73	267.05	170.83	228.91	306.09	316.19
India	23.80	52.94	140.86	178.21	218.65	315.71	266.40	350.03	462.40	488.98
China	–	217.92	604.79	718.13	870.34	1,040.10	9,19.14	1,289.13	1,620.78	1,675.27
South Africa	–	26.77	55.03	68.08	79.87	87.13	63.77	79.87	99.45	101.61
					Trade Balance					
Brazil	8.95	−0.61	45.01	46.54	40.10	24.99	25.55	17.67	30.54	19.43
Russia	0.00	69.21	142.74	163.74	152.54	200.94	130.97	168.16	210.90	208.57
India	−5.94	−10.58	−40.51	−57.01	−72.75	−133.85	−89.64	−129.62	−160.92	−199.41
China	0.00	31.28	157.16	250.81	349.72	390.59	282.51	288.63	277.61	373.51
South Africa	0.00	−0.47	−8.04	−15.48	−15.85	−13.16	−9.90	−8.39	−6.48	−14.90

Source: World Bank Trade Database, World Integrated Trade Solutions (2014).

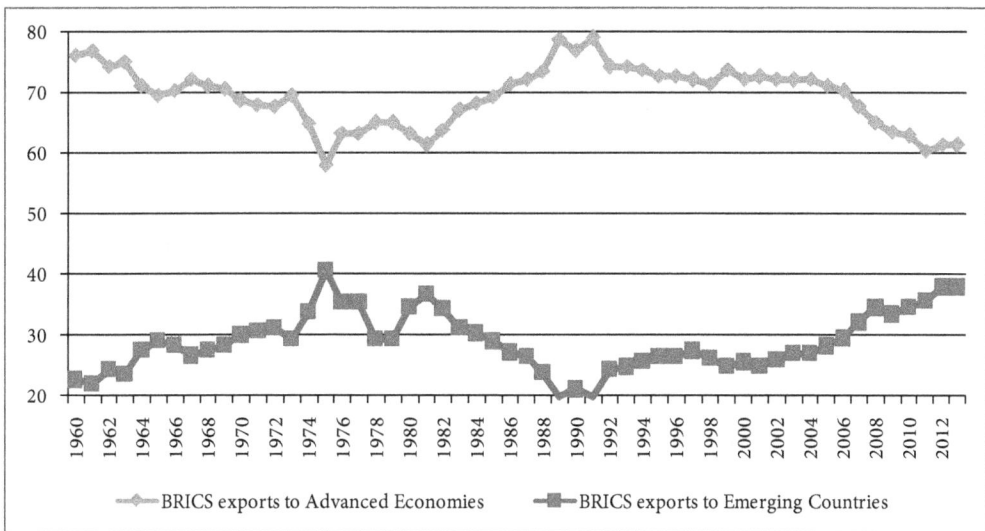

Figure 4.2 Direction of BRICS exports

Table 4.8 BRICS top five trading partners, 2012

Top Export Partners (% of Total Exports)		Top Import Partners (% of Total Imports)	
Brazil			
China	17.00	China	15.30
United States	11.00	United States	14.60
Argentina	7.40	Argentina	7.40
Netherlands	6.20	Germany	6.40
Japan	3.30	Republic of Korea	4.10
Russia			
Netherlands	14.50	China	16.40
Areas, n.e.s.	11.90	Germany	12.10
China	6.80	Ukraine	5.70
Italy	5.30	Japan	5.00
Germany	4.60	United States	4.90
India			
United States	12.80	China	11.10
United Arab Emirates	12.40	United Arab Emirates	7.70
China	5.10	Saudi Arabia	6.70
Singapore	4.70	Switzerland	5.90
China, Hong Kong SAR	4.10	United States	4.90
China			
United States	17.20	Japan	9.80
China, Hong Kong SAR	15.80	Republic of Korea	9.30
Japan	7.40	China Hong Kong SAR	7.90
Republic of Korea	4.30	United States	7.40
Germany	3.40	Other Asia, n.e.s.	7.30
South Africa			
China	11.70	China	14.40
Areas, n.e.s.	10.40	Germany	10.10
United States	8.70	Saudi Arabia	7.80
Japan	6.20	United States	7.40
Germany	4.80	Japan	4.50

Source: United Nations Commodity Trade Database (UNCOMTRADE) (2014).

A look at table 4.11 provides an understanding of the type of export commodities from CARICOM that are able to penetrate the BRICS markets. Some of the top export products include natural gas, ammonia, methanol, aluminium, iron and ores, and lumber and they all come from the top three CARICOM performers: Trinidad and Tobago, Jamaica, and Guyana. More specifically, CARICOM's top exports to BRICS countries represent 3.59 per cent of CARICOM's total exports. Furthermore, CARICOM's top ten export products to BRICS economies represent

Table 4.9 Major exports from BRICS (% in total exports), 2010–2012

HS 6	Description	2010	2011	2012
270900	Petroleum oils	6.32	6.86	6.44
271019	Other petroleum oils and preparations	4.05	4.46	4.48
847130	Portable digital computers	4.15	3.74	3.81
851712	Telephones for cellular networks	2.14	2.35	2.82
851770	Parts of telephone sets, telephones for cellular networks or for other	1.34	1.39	1.35
711319	Articles of jewellery & part thereof /o precious metals w/n platd/ clad w precious metals	0.51	0.81	1.33
901380	Optical devices, appliances and instruments, n.e.s., of this chapter	1.16	1.05	1.22
260111	Iron ores & concentrates, other than roasted iron pyrites, non-agglomerated	1.24	1.41	1.01
847330	Parts & accessories of automatic data processing machines & units thereof	1.35	1.07	1.00
854231	Electronic integrated circuits as processors and controllers	0.67	0.60	0.91
Total		**22.93**	**23.74**	**24.37**

Source: Own calculations from Trade Map (2014).

less than 2 per cent of BRICS total imports. However, interestingly, CARICOM's export of these commodities represents 50.67 per cent of CARICOM's total world exports. This suggests that it is possible to have growth in trade in other product categories from CARICOM countries and that CARICOM would need to recognize and expand possible trade complementarities that may be present between the Caribbean region and BRICS to help expand bilateral trade.

4.5 CARICOM and BRICS Trade in Services

Trade in services accounts for a large portion of CARICOM countries' GDP. During the period 2001–12, trade in services averaged over 35 per cent for nine CARICOM countries and over 60 per cent for two CARICOM countries (table 4.12). During the same period, the share of services trade in GDP for all CARICOM member countries declined with the exception of the Bahamas, Belize, Dominica and Haiti, with some more severely than others. The share in GDP of trade in services for BRICS is considerably less than their CARICOM counterparts in percentage terms.

4.6 BRICS Outbound Tourism and Opportunities for CARICOM

It is anticipated that the middle class of the BRICS economies will experience increase in the coming decades. This should result in a considerable amount of possible tourist outflows particularly from BRICS and other emerging markets, as travel and other leisure activities become more affordable to the consumers in emerging markets. Keohane (2011) suggests that what is more important to note is that the BRICS tourist spends twice the amount as does the non-BRIC

Table 4.10 CARICOM's export & import to BRICS, US$ million, 2001–2012

	2001	2002	2003	2004	2005	2006	2007	2008	2009	2010	2011	2012
						CARICOM's exports to BRICS						
CARICOM	104.70	86.87	187.98	237.16	260.84	461.83	387.86	468.11	262.51	322.52	70.79	114.58
Antigua & Barbuda	0.00	0.00	0.00	0.00	0.00	0.04	0.04	0.00	0.01	0.04	0.00	0.00
Bahamas	0.09	0.01	0.03	0.00	3.11	0.03	10.28	2.91	2.14	0.34	0.70	0.06
Belize	0.11	0.00	0.05	0.02	0.05	0.00	0.00	0.03	0.39	1.17	3.37	3.01
Barbados	0.30	0.42	0.64	0.54	0.88	1.57	4.15	1.60	5.84	3.64	6.37	7.68
Dominica	0.00	0.00	0.00	0.00	0.00	0.00	0.00	0.00	0.00	0.01	0.00	0.02
Guyana	3.56	2.88	3.90	3.49	10.40	22.97	17.34	20.36	15.59	10.75	10.48	23.63
Jamaica	53.13	52.48	115.12	173.41	138.51	325.62	146.42	130.40	23.10	39.88	34.26	80.18
St Kitts & Nevis	0.00	0.00	0.00	0.00	0.00	0.00	0.00	0.00	0.00	0.00	0.00	0.00
Suriname	3.33	6.21	23.96	3.76	28.69	8.93	9.86	18.82	33.58	16.80	15.61	0.00
Trinidad & Tobago	44.19	24.87	44.30	55.93	79.16	102.67	199.77	294.00	181.86	249.85	0.00	0.00
St Vincent	0.00	0.00	0.00	0.00	0.04	0.00	0.01	0.00	0.00	0.02	0.00	0.00
						CARICOM's import from BRICS						
CARICOM	553.60		816.01	1,165.52	1,622.82	1,952.10	2,217.21	3,210.53	2,215.90	2,179.65	1,237.23	1,172.74
Antigua & Barbuda	0.00	0.00	0.00	0.00	9.71	15.88	14.05	0.00	25.20	48.31	19.20	27.08
Bahamas	12.82	5.74	3.60	3.21	15.12	4.32	5.92	2.73	5.27	4.56	10.22	69.17
Belize	9.11	9.38	8.89	10.89	14.62	34.41	50.74	74.71	67.38	75.31	136.57	136.57
Barbados	36.58	46.83	52.85	57.77	86.44	85.65	81.41	92.99	87.77	89.94	103.36	104.70
Dominica	2.17	2.12	2.94	3.99	5.77	8.63	7.78	8.01	11.46	11.61	0.00	7.58
Guyana	23.66	28.74	29.42	43.13	56.31	73.36	117.72	115.42	95.47	129.30	158.28	244.96
Jamaica	143.12	156.40	181.71	285.50	318.83	381.89	563.49	574.07	387.71	474.18	636.15	591.41
St Kitts & Nevis	1.14	1.68	2.02	1.84	3.14	3.99	5.54	5.77	4.92	5.06	8.32	0.00
Suriname	27.31	34.09	45.48	66.52	121.47	83.58	109.44	153.57	145.36	163.66	166.85	0.00
Trinidad & Tobago	294.07	311.47	484.71	684.90	989.06	1,261.55	1,257.96	2,166.33	1,395.66	1,202.48	0.00	0.00
St Vincent	3.62	3.31	4.39	7.77	12.06	14.70	17.21	16.92	14.89	23.56	17.48	18.35

Source: World Integrated Trade Solutions (WITS) (2014).

Table 4.11 CARICOM's top exports to BRICS, US$ million, 2012

HS 6	Description	CARICOM Exports to BRICS	CARICOM Exports to World	CARICOM Exports to BRICS (% of CARICOM Total Exports)	BRICS Imports from World (% of BRICS Total Imports)
271111	Natural gas, liquefied	498	6,540	1.90	0.60
281410	Anhydrous ammonia	231	2,663	0.88	0.05
281820	Aluminium oxide n.e.s.	77	897	0.29	0.14
290511	Methanol (methyl alcohol)	54	1,679	0.21	0.06
440399	Logs, non-coniferous n.e.s.	24	29	0.09	0.13
740400	Waste and scrap, copper or copper alloy	16	32	0.06	0.58
260600	Aluminium ores and concentrates	14	285	0.05	0.07
440349	Logs, tropical hardwoods n.e.s.	11	12	0.04	0.05
721391	Hot rolled bar/rod	11	131	0.04	0.02
720310	Ferrous products	9	1,042	0.03	0.02

Source: Own derivations from Trade Map (2014).

Table 4.12 Trade in services as % GDP, 2001–2012

Country	2001	2005	2008	2009	2010	2011	2012
Brazil	4.80	4.60	4.70	4.60	4.40	4.60	5.40
Russian Federation	10.40	8.30	8.10	8.90	8.20	7.90	8.50
India	7.80	12.00	15.80	12.70	14.10	14.00	–
China	5.50	7.00	7.20	6.10	6.10	5.80	5.70
South Africa	–	9.50	10.90	9.50	8.90	8.60	8.50
Antigua & Barbuda	71.80	67.40	61.70	61.20	61.90	61.50	60.20
Bahamas	49.10	58.30	47.70	45.40	46.60	48.90	52.80
Barbados	58.50	70.20	70.30	61.60	57.70	–	–
Belize	32.90	41.30	40.80	37.50	36.90	35.30	–
Dominica	37.70	37.10	40.40	37.20	43.40	45.40	44.90
Grenada	41.80	30.40	33.90	32.40	32.00	33.20	31.70
Guyana	52.30	42.30	27.90	21.90	26.20	28.40	28.70
Haiti	11.40	16.50	17.00	17.80	22.90	18.90	18.20
Jamaica	37.50	36.30	37.70	37.50	33.80	31.70	31.70
St Lucia	59.20	69.60	49.70	46.50	47.90	48.30	50.30
St Vincent & the Grenadines	44.20	42.90	36.70	34.60	33.70	32.40	32.60
Suriname	30.60	31.00	19.60	14.80	11.50	17.70	16.50
Trinidad & Tobago	10.70	9.00	4.50	6.00	6.10		

Source: World Development Indicators (2014).

tourist. Therefore, it stands to reason that the growth of tourist outflows from BRICS will stimulate further growth in the world tourism industry. Over the past decade, there has been a large increase in the quantity of tourist outflows from BRICS. China's tourist outflows increased from 4.52 million in 1995 to 70.25 million in 2011. This figure is expected to significantly increase with about 25 million first-time travellers annually in the upcoming decade (Min-Hua 2011). India's tourist outflows also increased from about 3.06 million in 1995 to 13.99 million in 2011 and according to the World Tourism Organization, this figure is projected to rise to 50 million by the year 2020. Brazil's tourist outflows reached 6.43 million in 2011, Russia recorded 39.32 million tourist outflows in 2010, while South Africa recorded 5.46 million in 2011 (table 4.13). Tourism Intelligence International (2011) reported that the annual average growth of tourist outflows from both China and India is 13 per cent while according to Kirichenko (2011), Russia is expected to be the third largest outbound market in Europe by the year 2015. Forecasts by Euromonitor International (2011) also suggest that Brazil, Russia, India and China will have outbound travellers that will be more than 6 million, 54 million, 22 million and 62 million, respectively, by the year 2015. According to the Tourism Intelligence International (2011, 3), the new group of outbound tourists from emerging markets are wealthy, young, educated and internet savvy and have significant differences when compared to tourists from traditional markets, so much so that "traditional Western markets have travelled in search of warm weather. They lusted after the sun, sand and sea. Emerging markets have a different take on travel. They are looking for other 'S's. They want shopping, sightseeing and opportunities to gain status/social recognition."

The BRICS tourist is well known for their spending power. According to the World Tourism Organization (UNWTO 2011), China and India are reported to be among the top ten spenders on international travel. In 2011, China was the third largest spender on international travel behind the United States and Germany. Furthermore, China's outbound tourism spending rose from a mere US$3.69 billion in 1995 to an astounding US$72.59 billion in 2011 (table 4.13). This figure is expected to increase as China's economy grows and it is forecasted to reach to US$77 billion by 2015 (Euromonitor International 2011). According to the Kuoni Travel Report India, spending on travel by India is not insignificant either as it experienced increases from US$1 billion in 1995 to US$13.72 billion in 2011. Moreover, Brazil's spending on international travel increased from US$3.39 billion in 1995 to US$21.26 billion in 2011. Therefore, it is important to attract the BRICS tourist as this can certainly help to improve the region's tourism industry. However, currently most of the region's inbound tourism flows originate from North America and Europe.

According to data from the Caribbean Tourism Organization (2012), the United States is a primary source market for many Caribbean countries, representing about 80 per cent of tourist arrivals in the Bahamas, 69 per cent in Haiti, 64 per cent in Jamaica, 60 per cent in Belize, 59 per cent in St Kitts and Nevis, and 54 per cent in Guyana for 2009. Europe is another important source market which represents more than 40 per cent of arrivals in Barbados and Antigua and Barbuda and 31 per cent for Grenada and St Lucia, respectively.

The third largest source market for the CARICOM region is the Caribbean market followed by Canada. It is important to note that the majority of CARICOM's traditional source markets such as Europe are "saturated" and that at best, growth and spending is slow in tourist outflows and tourist spending (Tourism Intelligence International 2011; table 4.13). Because of this, there is a need for policymakers within CARICOM to repackage the Caribbean tourism product to entice

Table 4.13 International tourism, expenditures and departures, 1995–2011

	Brazil	Russia	India	China	South Africa	Germany	Great Britain	United States	Canada
International Tourism, Expenditures for Travel Items (Current US$ Billion)									
1995	3.39	11.60	1.00	3.69	1.85	60.26	24.93	46.26	10.26
2000	3.89	8.85	2.69	13.11	2.09	52.82	38.26	67.04	12.44
2001	3.20	9.29	3.01	13.91	1.88	51.92	37.93	62.82	11.96
2002	2.40	10.92	2.99	15.40	1.81	53.01	41.74	61.74	11.72
2003	2.26	12.88	3.59	15.19	2.89	65.23	47.85	60.94	13.34
2004	2.87	15.29	4.82	19.15	3.16	71.19	56.44	69.63	15.52
2005	4.72	17.31	6.19	21.76	3.37	74.19	59.53	73.32	18.02
2006	5.76	18.11	6.85	24.32	3.38	74.12	63.32	77.53	20.54
2007	8.21	21.22	8.22	29.79	3.93	83.16	71.52	82.12	24.72
2008	10.96	23.78	9.61	36.16	4.40	91.60	69.79	86.08	27.21
2009	10.90	20.77	9.31	43.70	4.15	81.40	50.56	80.10	24.17
2010	16.42	26.52	10.63	54.88	5.60	77.15	48.52	82.05	29.48
2011	21.26	32.47	13.72	72.59	5.28	86.17	51.11	86.18	33.17
% change (2000–2011)	446.50	266.90	410.00	453.70	152.60	63.10	33.60	28.60	166.60
International tourism, number of departures (million)									
1995	2.60	21.33	3.06	4.52	2.52	–	41.35	51.29	18.21
2000	3.23	18.37	4.42	10.47	3.83	74.40	56.84	61.33	19.18
2001	2.67	18.03	4.56	12.13	3.73	76.40	58.28	59.44	18.36
2002	2.34	20.43	4.94	16.60	3.79	73.30	59.38	58.07	17.71
2003	3.23	20.57	5.35	20.22	0	74.60	61.42	56.25	17.74
2004	2.97	24.51	6.21	28.85	0	72.30	64.19	61.81	19.60
2005	3.47	28.42	7.19	31.03	0	77.40	66.49	63.50	21.10
2006	3.93	29.11	8.34	34.52	4.34	71.20	69.54	63.66	22.73
2007	4.68	34.29	9.78	40.95	4.43	70.40	69.45	64.03	25.16
2008	5.18	36.54	10.87	45.84	4.43	73.00	69.01	63.56	27.04
2009	4.95	34.28	11.07	47.66	4.42	72.30	58.61	61.42	26.20
2010	6.43	39.32	12.99	57.39	5.17	0	55.56	60.27	28.68
2011	0	0	13.99	70.25	5.46	0	56.84	58.50	30.15
% change (2000–2011)	99.10	114.00	216.50	571.00	42.60	−2.80	0.00	−4.60	57.20

Source: World Development Indicators (2014) and own derivations.

the large amount of potential tourists from emerging markets. The characteristics of emerging market tourists should be catered for in a CARICOM-BRICS tourism strategy to lure the BRICS tourist and endorse and set the region apart from other tourist destinations. The significance of encouraging the BRICS tourist cannot be ignored. Tourist destinations such as Europe and

Table 4.14 Differences between tourists from emerging markets and traditional markets

Emerging Markets	Traditional Markets
Rapid economic growth	Slow economic growth
Emerging middle class	Wide and even distribution of income
Young and happening	Old and aging
Low and rising income levels	High but slowing income levels
Inexperienced and curious	Experienced and sophisticated
Highly educated with a lust for experiencing new cultures	Highly educated with a lust for the exotic
From shorter to longer trips	From longer to shorter trips
Growing online travel market	Well-established online travel market
Shopping, sightseeing and status-seeking	Sun, sand and sea
Travelling from East to West	Travelling from North to South
To experience a destination	To visit a destination

Source: Tourism Intelligence International (2011).

Australia have understood the significance of this new exploding market and strong competition from various major tourist destinations for the BRICS tourist is imminent.

The Caribbean region has the ability to vie for the BRICS tourist since it is a region of natural aesthetic beauty and can provide rich, vibrant cultural experiences. As a result, the region has much to gain from travellers from emerging markets. According to Bernal (2010), it is not difficult to attract tourists from India and China since there are already about fifty thousand Japanese tourist arrivals to the region yearly.

4.7 BRICS FDI and Development Assistance in CARICOM

According to Rao (2008), FDI is often viewed as an important source of efficient resource allocation and global productivity since transnational firms can get access into factor markets that are relatively efficient. The process of transferring knowledge and technical skills to the host country is aided especially by inward FDI. All BRICS economies have gained significantly from inward FDI, particularly China. In 2011, China's inward FDI peaked at US$124 billion with an increase from 2.8 per cent in 1991 to approximately 8.96 per cent of world inward FDI flows in the year 2012. This increase is not insignificant and other developing countries are threatened by this trend since FDI can be diverted away from their markets. In the last decade, other members of BRICS have increased their share in world inward FDI, but not as much as China. Over the same period, Brazil's share in world inward FDI grew from 0.7 per cent to 4.83 per cent, Russia from 0.6 per cent to 3.81 per cent and India from 0.05 per cent to 1.89 per cent, while South Africa's share has remained below 1 per cent for the same period (table 4.15). According to Duan (2010), the three primary reasons for the growth in inward FDI into BRICS are developed institutions, resources (natural and other) as well as a relatively good business environment.

Moreover, three of the BRICS members are featured among the top fifteen emerging economies on the basis of high FDI outflows. According to Sauvant (2005), Russia occupies fourth

Table 4.15 FDI inflows to and outflows from BRICS, US$ million, 1991–2012

	Brazil	% in World	Russia	% in World	India	% in World	China	% in World	South Africa	% in World
					FDI inflows to BRICS					
1991	1,102	0.72	–	–	75	0.05	4,366	2.84	248	0.16
1995	4,405	1.28	2,066	0.60	2,151	0.63	37,521	10.92	1,241	0.36
2000	32,779	2.32	2,714	0.19	3,588	0.25	40,715	2.88	887	0.06
2005	15,066	1.52	15,508	1.57	7,622	0.77	72,406	7.32	6,647	0.67
2006	18,822	1.27	37,595	2.54	20,328	1.37	72,715	4.91	−527	−0.04
2007	34,585	1.73	56,996	2.85	25,350	1.27	83,521	4.17	5,695	0.28
2008	45,058	2.48	74,783	4.12	47,139	2.60	108,312	5.96	9,006	0.50
2009	25,949	2.13	36,583	3.01	35,657	2.93	95,000	7.81	5,365	0.44
2010	48,506	3.44	43,168	3.06	21,125	1.50	114,734	8.15	1,228	0.09
2011	66,660	4.04	55,084	3.34	36,190	2.19	123,985	7.51	6,004	0.36
2012	65,272	4.83	51,416	3.81	25,543	1.89	121,080	8.96	4,572	0.34
					FDI outflows from BRICS					
1991	1,015	0.51	–	0.00	−11	−0.01	913	0.46	208	0.10
1995	1,096	0.30	606	0.17	119	0.03	2,000	0.55	2,498	0.69
2000	2,282	0.18	3,177	0.26	514	0.04	916	0.07	271	0.02
2005	2,517	0.28	17,880	1.98	2,985	0.33	12,261	1.36	930	0.10
2006	28,202	1.98	29,993	2.10	14,285	1.00	21,160	1.48	6,063	0.42
2007	7,067	0.31	45,879	2.02	17,234	0.76	26,510	1.17	2,966	0.13
2008	20,457	1.02	55,663	2.78	21,147	1.05	55,910	2.79	−3,134	−0.16
2009	−10,084	−0.88	43,281	3.76	16,031	1.39	56,530	4.92	1,151	0.10
2010	11,588	0.77	52,616	3.50	15,933	1.06	68,811	4.57	−76	−0.01
2011	−1,029	−0.06	66,851	3.98	12,456	0.74	74,654	4.45	−257	−0.02
2012	−2,821	−0.20	51,058	3.67	8,583	0.62	84,220	6.05	4,369	0.31

Source: Own calculations from the United Nations Conference on Trade and Development (UNCTAD) (2014).

position, China is ranked right behind at fifth, India is at position thirteen and Brazil is at position 24. FDI outflows from BRICS increased dramatically from US$2.1 billion in 1991 to US$145.4 billion in 2012 (table 4.16).

BRICS total outward stock of FDI has increased over the period 2000–2012 from US$133.9 billion to US$1,355.5 billion, with China accounting for the greatest share followed by Russia in 2012. FDI stock, as a percentage of GDP, for the same period increased for all other BRICS members except Brazil. Russia recorded the greatest increase during the period 2000–2012 from 7.76 per cent to 20.89 per cent, India also showed increases from 0.37 per cent to 6.36 per cent and China experienced increases from 2.33 per cent to 6.29 per cent. However, South Africa's outward FDI stock as a percentage of GDP has declined slightly over the same period.

China and to a lesser extent India are responsible for most of the outward FDI flows from BRICS into the CARICOM region. China's outward FDI to the region has increased from

Table 4.16 Basic indicators for BRICS outward FDI, 2000–2012

	2000	2005	2006	2007	2008	2009	2010	2011	2012
	Outward FDI stock US$ billion								
Brazil	51.95	79.26	113.93	139.89	155.67	164.52	188.64	202.59	232.85
Russian Federation	20.14	146.68	216.47	370.13	205.55	306.54	366.30	362.10	413.16
India	1.73	9.74	27.04	44.08	63.34	80.84	96.90	109.51	118.17
China	27.77	57.21	75.03	117.91	183.97	245.76	317.21	424.78	509.00
South Africa	32.33	37.71	50.83	65.88	49.96	72.58	89.45	78.00	82.37
	Outward FDI stock as a percentage of world outward FDI stock								
Brazil	0.65	0.63	0.72	0.72	0.94	0.84	0.89	0.94	0.99
Russian Federation	0.25	1.17	1.37	1.91	1.24	1.57	1.73	1.69	1.75
India	0.02	0.08	0.17	0.23	0.38	0.41	0.46	0.51	0.50
China	0.35	0.45	0.48	0.61	1.11	1.26	1.50	1.98	2.16
South Africa	0.40	0.30	0.32	0.34	0.30	0.37	0.42	0.36	0.35
	FDI outflows as a percentage of gross fixed capital formation								
Brazil	2.11	1.79	15.76	2.96	6.47	−3.44	2.78	−0.22	–
Russian Federation	7.20	12.97	16.08	16.81	15.04	16.09	16.26	16.90	–
India	0.47	1.13	4.64	4.20	4.86	3.60	2.92	2.03	–
China	0.22	1.35	1.92	1.94	3.03	2.46	2.54	2.24	–
South Africa	1.36	2.24	12.67	5.14	−4.97	1.87	−0.11	−0.33	–
	Outward FDI stock as a percentage of GDP								
Brazil	8.06	8.99	10.46	10.23	9.41	10.15	8.80	8.18	10.33
Russian Federation	7.76	19.20	21.87	28.48	12.38	25.07	24.63	19.49	20.89
India	0.37	1.16	2.85	3.65	4.89	6.06	5.77	5.77	6.36
China	2.33	2.50	2.69	3.37	4.06	4.85	5.33	5.90	6.29
South Africa	24.33	15.26	19.47	23.02	18.24	25.65	24.61	19.11	21.10

Source: United Nations Conference on Trade and Development (UNCTAD) (2014).

US$1.7 billion in 2004 to US$7 billion by 2009, an increase of approximately 300 per cent (Fieser 2011). Bernal (2010) has argued that China's increasing role in the Caribbean is influenced mainly by diplomatic reasons so that the region can continue to support its "One China" policy. In this regard, countries such as Dominica in 2004 and Grenada in 2005 severed long standing diplomatic ties with Taiwan and signed on to the "One China" policy. After this, major investments were made by China in these countries totalling US$100 million and US$55 million in Dominica and Grenada, respectively (table 4.17).

China's interest in the CARICOM sphere is also due to the fact that several CARICOM countries are endowed with raw materials and natural resources. Energy products such as crude oil,

Table 4.17 Snapshot of proposed and/or completed investments and projects from China in CARICOM

Destination	Description	Estimated Value
Dominica	Infrastructural development	US$100 million
Grenada	Cricket stadium	US$55 million
Bahamas	Baha Mar Resort	US$2.4 billion
Suriname	Deep-sea harbour	US$600 million
Dominica	Cash infusion into a stalled beach front resort	US$462 million
Bahamas	Construction and operation of a container port	US$1 billion
Dominica	Cricket stadium	US$17 million
Dominica	Economic assistance	US$122 million
Guyana	Part purchase of Omani Bauxite Mining	US$100 million
Trinidad & Tobago	North Academy of the Performing Arts	TT$480 million
Trinidad & Tobago	Prime minister's residence	TT$243.9 million
Trinidad & Tobago	Brian Lara Stadium	TT$685.1 million
Trinidad & Tobago	South Academy of the Performing Arts	TT$189 million
Jamaica	Infrastructural development	US$500 million

Sources: Sanders (2011) and Fieser (2011).

natural gas, asphalt and other downstream energy products are available in Trinidad and Tobago; Guyana is endowed with minerals, lumber and bauxite and Jamaica also has bauxite. Because of China's growth over the years, its demand for these products has increased and CARICOM is a potential supplier of these resources. Indeed, China has already purchased part of a mining company in Guyana and 10 per cent of the Atlantic Liquefied Natural Gas Company of Trinidad and Tobago, a main producer of liquid natural gas (Watkins 2011). More recently, the president of China visited the CARICOM region in June 2013 and committed over US$3 billion in development assistance to CARICOM countries that have diplomatic relations with China. (Jhinkoo (2013) provides a comprehensive review of CARICOM-China economic and diplomatic relations.) Furthermore, China has approximately US$1.4 trillion in foreign reserves at its disposal and its government offered Chinese based firms more than US$530 million in loans to invest within the Caribbean region, over the period 2007–10 (Sanders 2008).

Though not as extensive as China's investments in CARICOM, India has investments in several areas as well. During 1996–2007, India's total investments in CARICOM (approved by joint ventures and wholly owned subsidiaries) amounted to US$4 million (Fanai et al. 2011). Trinidad and Tobago was the recipient of US$2.7 million or 67.5 per cent of India's outward investment in the CARICOM region. According to Viswanathan (2007), Trinidad and Tobago received the largest share of total Indian investments in Latin America and the Caribbean. Fanai et al. (2011) noted that other countries also gained from India's outward FDI: the Bahamas (US$0.8 million), Belize (US$0.4 million), and St Vincent and the Grenadines (US$0.1 million). India's presence within the region can most clearly be seen in the banking and insurance industries with banks and insurance companies found in the Bahamas, Trinidad and Tobago, and Guyana. India has also made investments in the mining and tourism sectors in the region. According to Horta

(2008), India has significant investments in the steel processing industry in the CARICOM region, for example, Mittal Steel (US$2 billion) and Essar Steel (US$1.2 billion), and owns four hotels in the region.

China and India provide economic assistance to the region in an attempt to gain influence (Montoute 2011). These economic assistance programmes come in the form of soft loans, aid, grants, technical support and lines of credit in strategic areas as well as infrastructural development projects. For instance, India has provided a credit line for Suriname (US$72 million) to carry out development projects and Guyana (US$25.2 million) to modernize its sugar industry. India has also given Suriname financial assistance to develop a cashew-processing plant. Meanwhile, China provided Dominica with economic assistance amounting to US$122 million and carried out infrastructural development projects in Dominica and Jamaica (refer to table 4.17 for a sample of recent projects carried out by China in some CARICOM countries). Brazil's and Russia's outward FDI to the region is not as significant, but they are still essential sources of future investments as they gain influence throughout the developing world. According to Glasgow (2011), Brazil has joined Jamaica and St Kitts and Nevis in the production of ethanol via sugar cane processing and has interest in the energy sector of Trinidad and Tobago. These patterns in FDI outflows from BRICS signify the kind of potential benefits that CARICOM can enjoy. However, it is important to realize that CARICOM's natural resources may become the source of strong competition from BRICS members in the future.

4.8 Challenges Confronting Policymakers in CARICOM as Regards the BRICS

According to the literature, there are two ways by which emerging economies can have an effect on the global economy: these are the complementary effect and the competitive effect. The complementary effect for most CARICOM members is expected to occur via increases in demand for natural resources and other primary products. However, although some CARICOM countries can stand to gain considerably from "commodity booms", they would have to be concerned with the threat of being trapped with a production structure that is strongly inclined towards low value added natural resource–based products. The IMF (2011) stressed the importance of this risk noting that low-income countries (LIC) would have to be concerned about the implications of the traditional Dutch disease, associated with commodity booms particularly from China and India. This was also noted by Jenkins and Peters (2006) and Kaplinsky et al. (2010). Furthermore, Lall and Weiss (2005, 22) noted that the trading patterns between Latin America and China seem to emphasize the "classic . . . colonial trade between developing countries and industrialized regions . . . with the former specializing increasingly in primary and resource based products and the latter in manufactures".

Furthermore, BRICS increasing contribution to world outward FDI can result in complementary growth effects on economies that have little or no capital within the region. The growth likely to be experienced by emerging markets in the upcoming decade would mean an increased demand for energy resources and primary products, which can significantly act as a means to direct their outbound FDI into resource intensive sectors. This pattern is already being noticed in a few CARICOM countries, where there are heavy investments being made by China and India in their energy and resource-based sectors. The concern with this trend, however, is that it is possible that CARICOM countries can be confronted with long term challenges of diversification as BRICS increase their demand and prices for energy and primary products via outward investments and trade.

Traditionally, China and India's outbound investments were largely focused on securing natural resources, but in recent years, according to Mlachila and Takebe (2011), this focus has been redirected to include non-resource intensive sectors. For instance, India's outbound FDI in Africa and Asia are growing in sectors such as manufacturing and services, while Brazil's FDI is focused on energy resources and China is redirecting into sectors such as agriculture, manufacturing and services. In order to encourage investments in these sectors, CARICOM countries would need to cultivate a business friendly environment to entice foreign firms in non-resource intensive sectors to enhance the productive capacity in the region and improve the growth of domestic industries in global supply chains. The tasks for most CARICOM countries is to enhance its export performance to emerging market economies, in areas apart from natural resource-based products, given their forecasted growth potential in the future.

The tourism industry in many Caribbean countries is a major determinant of economic growth and revenue earnings. One of the most significant highlights for CARICOM is BRICS outward tourism flows. In order for the CARICOM region to make the most of outward tourism flows from BRICS, a new CARICOM-BRICS tourism strategy would have to be created to cater to the BRICS tourist, considering that their reason for travelling is different from tourists of traditional market economies. This is particularly important for the resource poor economies in the region.

The competitive effect that emerging markets pose to CARICOM can occur directly or via third markets and can stem from China and India in certain areas in the short to medium term. According to Lall and Weiss (2005), China's competitiveness in labour-intensive technology products depends highly on its low labour cost that encourages export-oriented FDI into technology areas. China embodies a long-term competitive threat to the world's economy, particularly in low-knowledge intensive products like clothing and textile (Welo 2011). Freeman (2008) has argued that the emergence of China and India have had negative effects on labour markets in many developing countries, particularly in low wage sectors. Freeman (2008) also noted that countries such as Peru, El Salvador, Mexico and South Africa have had to deal with difficulties in achieving economic growth through low wage production because of China and India. There is evidence to suggest that approximately 254,000 jobs were lost during 2001 and 2003 in the maquilas of Mexico due to cheap Chinese imports (Lora 2005). Perera (2000) noted that in Sri Lanka, more than 130,000 jobs were lost in its garment industry.

The construction sector in CARICOM is also feeling the effects of cheap Chinese labour. The majority of China's infrastructural projects, investments and economic activities in CARICOM use Chinese raw materials and cheap Chinese labour. This has sparked much concern in the domestic market, particularly in Trinidad and Tobago and Barbados, where domestic workers felt threatened by the influx of Chinese workers, especially in light of high levels of domestic unemployment. Guyana is also facing serious competition from China and India in its clothing and textile industry in both the regional and extra-regional market. These cheaper products can possibly remove CARICOM firms from their usual extra-regional and regional markets. As China and India's competitiveness improves across the production spectrum, these effects will move into other areas and CARICOM firms will have to recognize and act upon these changes.

Although CARICOM countries can benefit in terms of trade and investment opportunities resulting from China's growth, there is a social aspect that can have far-reaching implications for the Caribbean society. This includes issues such as the possible expansion of Chinese criminal networks (Chinese mafia), human trafficking, increased gambling, trafficking of illegal drugs and illicit goods, and money laundering. These are serious matters to take into consideration, bearing in mind the Caribbean's strategic location to North America and Europe.

Evidence infers that the Chinese mafia is in fact carrying out its operations in some Latin American and Caribbean countries with strong links to mainland China. According to El Comercio (2010) and Ellis (2012), some of their operations include extorting protection money from ethnic Chinese businessmen and homicides in countries such as Peru, Argentina, Ecuador, Venezuela and Panama. A report by the *Trinidad Guardian* ("Chinese Triad Expands in T&T", 17 May 2011) noted that regional and national security agencies have been keeping track of the Chinese criminal networks in the region since 2006. Indications of the presence of the Chinese mafia, according to Ellis (2012), can be found in the brutal murder of a fourteen-year-old Chinese boy and the decapitating of a Chinese father and son in Suriname. These incidences can aggravate the already serious crime situation in many Caribbean countries. Furthermore, it can negatively impact tourism and tourist dependent countries in the region and cause other macroeconomic and social problems to arise. Further collaboration between security agencies in the Caribbean and China would have to be developed in an attempt to deal with such a problem.

Another issue with China's growing presence in the region is the problem of human trafficking. Human trafficking of Chinese individuals is an apparently profitable business, where each person can be charged up to US$70,000 to travel from China to the United States (Logan 2009). Logan (2009) also noted that in the year 2008, Chinese criminals were paid approximately US$750 million in trafficking Chinese people to the United States. Although these incidences are more common to Latin and Central America, the Caribbean region may become a target as well. According to Ellis (2012), Trinidad and Tobago's national authorities have warned about the likelihood of human trafficking in light of the increased number of Chinese construction workers brought in to work on development projects. This type of situation increases the probability of human trafficking in the region which may eventually fuel other kinds of criminal activities. For instance, *Kaiteur News* (2012) reported that thirteen undocumented Chinese workers were found working in the gold-mining sector in Guyana.

With investment and financial linkages being developed between CARICOM and China, money laundering activities could become more prominent and easier as criminal organizations may use financial institutions in the region to hide illicitly earned wealth. According to Ellis (2012), the development of Chinese gambling establishments (such as the Baha Mar resort and casino in the Bahamas) may provide opportunities for money laundering to take place and add to the gambling culture in the region. The further development of trading relations between China and the region can lead to possible trade in contraband goods, illegal drugs and ammunition. In Latin America, there is evidence of these incidences. Ellis (2012) noted that illegal ammunition, grenades and other military equipment made in China have been taken from Mexican cartels in some parts of Mexico and the United States. It is suggested that the trade in illicit goods from China to Latin America provides an environment that is conducive to organized crime. In addition, Chan (2003) argued that China is running a race to the bottom, with regards to labour, quality and international standards. The region must be more aware of low priced, substandard products being manufactured in China and coming into the Caribbean and consequently implement stricter trade regulations.

4.9 Conclusion

In this chapter, the rise of the five emerging market economies (BRICS) was examined in order to gain a deeper understanding of their growth dynamics and the probable implications they might have, not only on the world but on the CARICOM region. Of the five BRICS economies, it is anticipated that China and India will dominate in the forthcoming decades. China and India's increasing presence in the region over the last decade can be seen via its natural resource investments, trade, development assistance, services and technical cooperation. This chapter also highlighted some of the main challenges that policymakers may encounter as a result of the increased presence of emerging economies in the CARICOM region.

5 | Intra-industry Trade
Applications to a Small Integration Bloc

5.1 Introduction

Prior to the 1950s, traditional neoclassical trade theory governed the approach taken by researchers in their interpretation of the nature of trade flows among nations. This economic theory, also commonly referred to as the Heckscher-Ohlin theory explains that trade patterns result from differences in factor endowments among trading partners. This implies the exchange of commodities which derive from different industries or the international exchange of unrelated goods. This phenomenon is commonly referred to as inter-industry trade as it reflects "natural comparative advantage". In the early 1960s, an investigation into the economic integration among European nations revealed that trading patterns were inconsistent with the comparative advantage argument. In fact, countries seemed to maintain and expand trade within a given sector, rather than specializing strongly according to comparative advantage. Henceforth, this "empirical anomaly" became widely known as intra-industry trade (IIT) or the international exchange of differentiated products of the same industry or sector. According to Salvatore (1995), "intra-industry trade reflects acquired comparative advantage". IIT can be categorized according to two distinct types: horizontal IIT (HIIT) and vertical IIT (VIIT). While both reveal the same trading pattern, that is the simultaneous exports and imports of goods classified in the same sector, a distinction can be made according to stage of production.

While HIIT is normally defined as the simultaneous exchange of alternative varieties of a particular commodity which differ in their actual or perceived characteristics, for example, ranges of colours or shades of paint, it also reflects the exchange of commodities which belong to the same stage of processing. This is likely based on product differentiation. For example, Finland's simultaneous exchange of mobile phones in final stage of processing. These phones are manufactured using similar technology and perform similar functions, so they can be classified as belonging to the same sector. Nonetheless, the exported Nokia phones differ slightly in physical appearance and product characteristics from the imported Samsung phones (South Korea), catering to the demand and desires of different types of consumers.

Similarly, VIIT is generally defined as the simultaneous exchange of varieties of goods that belong to different levels of quality, for example, the availability of water- and oil-based paints and consumers can be assumed to rank alternatives according to product quality. It also reflects the exchange of commodities which belong to different stages of processing. This is likely based on the fragmentation of the production process into different stages, each performed at different locations by taking advantage of the local conditions. For example, India imports technology-intensive computer components and uses its abundantly available labour force to assemble these components in the labour-intensive final production stage, before the components (as part of a finished computer) are exported again to Europe or the United States.

This chapter undertakes a critical examination of the importance of IIT for CARICOM, by focusing on its many different facets, namely its determinants, main theoretical and methodological frameworks, and empirical applications and also identifies some strategies for boosting IIT within CARICOM.

5.2 Intra-industry Trade: Prospects for CARICOM

The present Caribbean trading environment resonates in large part with its historical background which involved production at the lower end of the value chain or primary production. The pursuit of small scale manufacturing industries in the 1970s failed to generate the required regional support as the survival of many of the region's small islands resided with the primary industry, particularly, agriculture. Thus, dependence on local import regimes and the level of protection afforded domestic production was a priority. Hopes of value-added production fizzled when the region became recipients of preferential treatment (particularly for agricultural commodities) from major extra-regional markets, namely the European Union, and subsequently Canada and the United States, which ultimately exposed the weakness of the industrialization strategy pursued by Caribbean economies. As more efficient global suppliers emerged, trade primarily on the basis of comparative advantage yielded smaller and smaller market shares for the Caribbean region in recent time. The question therefore arises: Can the region develop competitive capabilities to benefit from new forms of specialization? As the natural counterpart of Heckscher-Ohlin trade, IIT represents this new form of specialization, one that is founded on economies of scale, internal efficiency and production along the value chain which encourages deeper regional integration.[38]

Since its establishment in 1973, CARICOM's primary objective of increased economic and functional cooperation underpinned the importance of economic integration by expanding the volume of intra-regional trade flows. However, the degree to which these flows are due to intra-industry trade has been an unexplored subject until now. This chapter focuses on four main CARICOM countries: Barbados, Guyana, Jamaica, and Trinidad and Tobago. These countries engage in some of the highest volume of trade, both imports and exports intra-regionally and among themselves. Table 5.1 shows each country's exports and imports from its respective partner countries as a share of the group's total exports and imports. Panel (a) reveals that for the years 1995, 2005 and 2012, Barbados's exports to Trinidad and Tobago as a share of the group's total exports amounted to 42.5 per cent, 59 per cent and 65.6 per cent, respectively. Trinidad and Tobago's exports to Jamaica also demonstrated high percentages: 55.6 per cent, 51 per cent and 48.3 per cent, respectively. Similarly, Jamaica's exports to Trinidad and Tobago also reflected high percentages with the exception of 2012, which recorded 31.5 per cent. As a share of group imports, Barbados, Guyana and Jamaica all reported percentages above 90 per cent with Trinidad and Tobago for the years 2005 and 2012.

Many regional commentators have voiced concern with the effectiveness of CARICOM in achieving stronger production integration within the region as intra-regional production

Table 5.1 Share of group exports and imports, 1995, 2005 and 2012

	Barbados	Guyana	Jamaica	Trinidad & Tobago
Panel (a): Share of group exports				
Barbados	–	–	30.70	22.80
	–	23.50	33.40	29.50
	–	14.40	50.00	29.20
Guyana	17.20	–	17.10	21.60
	10.30	–	8.20	19.50
	17.10	–	18.50	22.50
Jamaica	40.40	–	–	55.60
	30.70	44.60	–	51.00
	17.40	37.50	–	48.30
Trinidad & Tobago	42.50	–	52.10	–
	59.00	31.90	58.40	–
	65.60	48.10	31.50	–
Panel (b): Share of group imports				
Barbados	–	–	6.80	34.10
	–	2.20	2.30	43.70
	–	5.00	3.40	54.60
Guyana	8.40	–	3.00	21.60
	3.90	–	4.70	33.50
	2.40	–	5.30	35.40
Jamaica	15.30	–	–	44.30
	3.10	1.20	–	22.70
	1.90	5.00	–	10.00
Trinidad & Tobago	76.30	–	90.20	–
	93.00	96.60	93.00	–
	95.60	90.00	91.30	–

Source: Computed from World Integrated Trade Solution (WITS) (2014).

structures diverge and are constituted in the main, by a limited range of indigenous primary commodities. Girvan (2006) remarked that production integration in the Caribbean is best measured by examining inter-industry rather than intra-industry relations. In particular, Girvan (2006, 2) argued that the "extent of production integration in CARICOM is relatively limited, and is growing only in the specific area of supply of energy-based products from Trinidad and Tobago to its CARICOM partners". Balassa (1966) further added that production integration in the region is moving beyond inter-industry relations in productive activities to the movement of factors of production such as finance, entrepreneurship, management and labour for the purposes of engaging in, and organizing production. Balassa (1966, 472), however, argued that "the difficulties of adjustment to freer trade have been generally overestimated because it is apparent that the increased (intra-industry) exchange of consumer goods is compatible with unchanged production in every country". He therefore surmised that these considerations may explain why common market members have not realized the demise of some of their industries. Moreover, trade liberalization between countries with growing IIT levels ought to occur with lower adjustment costs as compared to high inter-industry trade. This became known as the "Smooth Adjustment Hypothesis". Over the next thirty years, both theorists and empiricists have referred to this hypothesis when charting the potential outcomes of integration arrangements. Grant et al. (1993, 32f) in particular expressed that a "purported characteristic of intra-industry trade is its allegedly low adjustment costs in the face of liberalization. It has become the faith that the European Community's early liberalization succeeded because of intra-industry trade."

The importance of this acknowledgement for CARICOM can be significant, as intra-industry factor movements could translate to deeper economies of scale and higher value added market niches. Frankel and Rose (1997), however, refuted this, arguing that the advantages of economies of scale is likely to strengthen inter-industry trade within the region as members lack the size and capacity to transition into other trade patterns. Arguably, the implications elucidated by the CARICOM Single Market and Economy (CSME) since its implementation in 2006 have emerged as a new talking point as increased competition of mobile factors, particularly labour, may be more severe for economies with obsolete production systems, declining growth and limited technical capacity.

The growth experienced by CARICOM economies have been accompanied by changes in their relative production structures. Table 5.2 reports the share of agriculture, hunting, forestry and fishing; mining and quarrying; manufacturing and services in annual GDP for the four countries under consideration. Barbados and Trinidad and Tobago reported a decline in the share of agriculture in GDP while for Jamaica, although there was an improvement between 1994 and 1996, a general downward trend can be observed. Guyana showed growth in this sector between 1990 and 2004 of 9.2 per cent; however, by 2012, the share of this sector had declined to 17.9 per cent from a high of 24.9 per cent in 1999.

Trinidad and Tobago was the only country to report growth in the share of mining and quarrying in GDP of 27.9 per cent between 1990 and 2012, while Guyana and Jamaica reported declines of 32.2 per cent and 41.9 per cent, respectively, for the same period. Trinidad and Tobago reported a marginal increase of 8.3 per cent in its share of manufacturing in annual GDP over the period 1990–2012, while Barbados reported the largest decline of 58.0 per cent. With the exception of Trinidad and Tobago, all countries recorded growth in the share of services. In particular, for Jamaica, a 20.5 per cent growth was observed between 1990 and 2012, while for Barbados and

Table 5.2 Share in annual GDP by activity at current prices, 1990–2012

	Agriculture, Hunting, Forestry and Fishing				Mining and Quarrying				Manufacturing				Services			
	BRB	GUY	JAM	TTO	BRB	GUY	JAM	TTO	BRB	GUY	JAM	TTO	BRB	GUY	JAM	TTO
1990	2.30	16.20	6.60	1.50	0.10	12.10	3.10	36.20	11.20	14.00	11.90	6.00	73.80	53.70	65.60	59.50
1991	2.30	17.10	6.60	1.50	0.10	13.90	3.20	35.50	11.10	14.60	11.00	6.10	74.30	50.60	67.10	60.10
1992	2.20	19.80	7.20	1.50	0.10	11.40	3.10	34.60	11.10	16.20	10.90	6.20	75.10	47.60	69.10	61.00
1993	2.10	19.30	7.80	1.60	0.10	15.70	3.00	32.70	11.10	15.50	10.60	6.10	75.20	45.50	69.20	62.80
1994	2.00	20.20	8.20	1.50	0.10	15.40	3.20	34.40	10.50	15.00	10.50	6.00	75.50	44.80	73.50	62.00
1995	2.00	20.70	8.20	1.50	0.10	13.00	3.00	33.10	10.90	15.70	10.10	6.00	75.30	45.30	74.80	61.10
1996	2.20	20.50	8.60	1.50	0.10	13.90	3.20	33.20	11.10	15.40	9.60	5.80	74.20	44.90	76.00	61.20
1997	2.10	23.50	7.50	1.50	0.20	15.00	3.30	31.10	11.10	8.60	9.40	5.80	74.10	45.00	75.40	63.80
1998	1.80	22.50	7.40	1.30	0.20	15.60	3.40	31.40	8.60	7.80	9.10	6.00	76.30	46.40	75.80	62.70
1999	1.90	24.90	7.50	1.20	0.20	14.00	3.40	35.30	8.20	8.10	8.80	5.20	76.40	44.10	76.30	60.20
2000	2.00	22.50	6.50	1.10	0.20	14.90	3.30	37.10	7.80	7.20	8.80	5.10	76.40	47.40	77.30	59.40
2001	1.80	19.60	6.80	1.20	0.20	15.30	3.40	37.60	7.20	13.30	8.60	5.40	77.30	46.70	77.60	57.40
2002	1.70	24.10	6.30	1.20	0.20	14.10	3.40	39.60	7.20	7.20	8.40	5.20	77.40	46.00	78.60	55.40
2003	1.60	23.80	6.60	0.90	0.20	12.90	3.50	45.40	7.00	7.10	8.10	5.10	77.00	47.20	77.90	51.60
2004	1.50	24.20	5.70	0.50	0.20	11.90	3.50	45.60	7.00	7.00	8.10	5.10	77.80	47.50	78.40	51.70
2005	1.60	21.30	5.20	0.50	0.20	10.00	3.60	45.90	6.90	7.90	7.70	5.50	77.90	52.30	79.30	50.60
2006	1.40	21.60	6.10	0.40	0.20	7.40	3.50	49.80	6.50	7.90	7.40	5.40	78.40	53.80	78.70	47.00
2007	1.40	20.30	5.50	0.40	0.20	8.00	3.40	48.50	6.30	7.60	7.30	5.90	79.00	54.60	79.40	47.90
2008	1.40	19.30	5.20	0.50	0.10	7.80	3.30	46.80	6.10	7.30	7.40	6.00	79.60	56.20	79.60	49.30
2009	1.50	18.90	6.20	0.30	0.10	7.30	1.70	48.00	5.60	7.40	7.30	6.30	81.20	56.90	81.30	48.80
2010	1.40	18.60	6.20	0.60	0.10	6.70	1.60	49.50	5.40	7.10	7.10	6.40	82.10	58.60	80.40	46.60
2011	1.30	18.10	6.80	0.60	0.10	7.50	1.90	48.30	5.00	7.10	7.10	6.40	82.70	58.20	79.20	47.90
2012	1.30	17.90	7.00	0.50	0.10	8.20	1.80	46.30	4.70	7.00	7.10	6.50	83.80	58.00	79.10	48.80

Note: BRB, Barbados; GUY, Guyana; JAM, Jamaica; TTO, Trinidad and Tobago.

Source: United Nations Economic Commission for Latin America and the Caribbean (ECLAC) (2014).

Guyana, growth rates of 13.5 and 8 per cent, respectively were reported. Trinidad and Tobago recorded a contraction in this sector of 17.9 per cent.

5.3 Determinants of Intra-industry Trade: Insights within CARICOM

The most accepted and widely used mode of categorizing the determinants of IIT corresponds to two groups: country-specific determinants and industry-specific determinants (see for example Loertscher and Wolter 1980; Greenaway and Milner 1986; Stone and Lee 1995; Veeramani 2001; Sharma 2004; Byun and Lee 2005; Thorpe and Zhang 2005). This classification has been regarded as the least ambiguous in that the former represents macro determinants while the latter represents micro-determinants.

5.3.1 Country-Specific Determinants of Intra-industry Trade

Per capita income: This is regarded as the most common determinant of IIT. It implies that trading partners with the same/similar income per capita levels will experience an overlap in consumer tastes and demand patterns. The impact of this determinant on the volume and pattern of IIT can be explained from both the supply side and demand side of the economy. In the case of the former, Dixit and Norman (1980), Helpman (1981) and Helpman and Krugman (1985), found a positive relationship between IIT and income per capita. To elaborate, a high income per capita country is assumed to possess factor endowments characterized by a high capital to labour ratio, as this represents the base of its ability to innovate and generate differentiated commodities. It follows that for trading partners with identical factor endowments and equality of income per capita, all trade between this country pair is expected to be IIT.

In terms of the demand side, Linder (1961) asserted that as income increases so too does the demand for variety. This suggests that a high income per capita is positively related to greater differentiated demand patterns, thereby allowing a country to take full advantage of economies of scale in the production of a wide range of individual goods. It therefore implies that greater per capita income levels engender greater IIT, that is, a smaller difference in per capita incomes between two countries implies a greater degree of similarity in their demand structures and a higher potential for IIT between them.

Figure 5.1 illustrates the trends in Trinidad and Tobago's ratio of GDP per capita with that of its regional trading partners. The patterns indicate a large similarity in per capita movements between Trinidad and Tobago and Barbados as demonstrated by a trend line close to unity for the period 1973–2012. Trinidad and Tobago's share of per capita GDP is between 1.4 times and 6.9 times that of Jamaica and between 3.2 times and 11.6 times for Guyana. These trends suggest that IIT may potentially exist between Trinidad and Tobago and Barbados.

Transportation costs and distance: The geographical distance between two trading partners has traditionally been measured by the transportation costs between the two locations. Eichengreen and Irwin (1998) argued that geographic distance is based on the logic of a melting iceberg

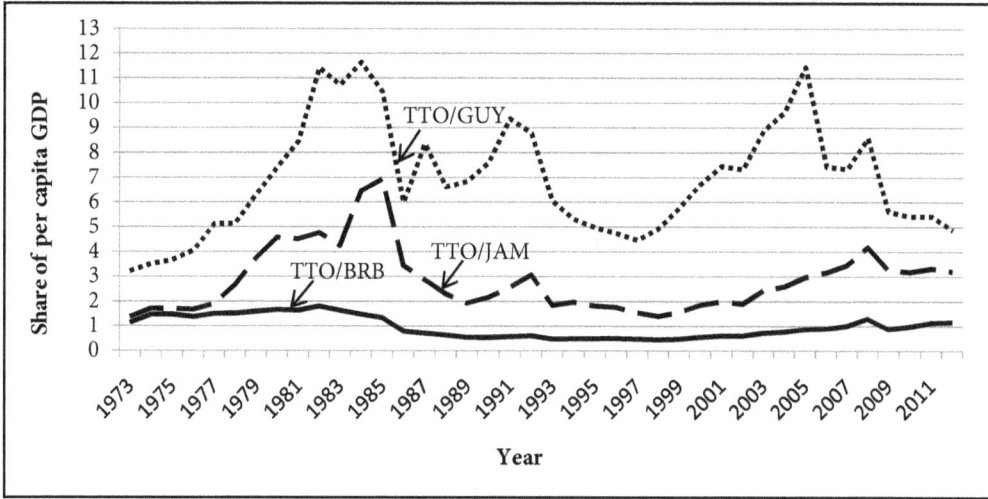

Figure 5.1. Trinidad and Tobago's share of per capita GDP with selected regional partners

where a proportion of the commodity melts away during the transportation between the two countries such that the speed of melting is assumed to be positively related to distance. According to Head (2000), distance can also indicate the time elapsed during shipment. He further argued that for perishable commodities, the probability of remaining intact decreases with a longer transit time. Head also purported that distance is an impediment to communication and therefore gives rise to transaction costs. Krugman (1995, 342) noted that distance "proxies for the possibilities of personal contact between managers, customers, and so on; that much business depends on the ability to exchange more information, of a less formal kind, than can be sent over a wire". Gray and Martin (1980) therefore argued that where demand elasticities for differentiated commodities are high, transport costs is expected to influence IIT in a greater way than inter-industry trade, since more information is required for trading in a differentiated commodity compared to a homogeneous commodity (Balassa and Bauwens 1987).

Trade barriers: Trade barriers including tariff and non-tariff trade barriers have been found to influence IIT flows. Falvey (1981) noted that the amount of IIT between two trading partners is expected to increase as tariff levels decrease. Specifically, import tariffs cause increased demand for domestic varieties of commodities due to the increase in price of foreign varieties of the same commodities. It follows that the intensity of IIT is expected to be smaller the higher the level of trade restriction imposed by one or both of the trading partners.

Economic integration: For countries that enter into economic integration arrangements whether it is a free trade arrangement, a customs union, or a common market, the underlying aim is the promotion of free trade between the members. According to Greenaway and Milner (1986), factors which are correlated to economic integration, namely geographic distance and trade liberalization, are most influential as it pertains to IIT such that it becomes less of the harmonization of policy aspects of integration but rather the increased potential for harnessing economies of scale in enlarged markets that encourages IIT, following economic integration. A positive relationship is usually found between IIT and economic integration.

Other common country-specific determinants include: market size, common border, common language and colonial links, trade imbalance, human capital endowment, technology gap, exchange rate, trade intensity, standard of living as well as monetary agreements and common currency.

5.3.2 Industry-Specific Determinants of Intra-industry Trade

Product differentiation: This variable is often viewed as influencing the demand side of trade but more so for IIT in that differentiated commodities yield satisfaction for the consumers' demand for variety. Several empirical scholars have viewed product differentiation as having a direct effect on IIT specifically; the more differentiated the commodities of an industry, the larger the IIT flows in these commodities (see Krugman 1979, 1980; Lancaster 1980; Helpman 1981). Greenaway and Milner (1986) noted that commodities may be differentiated in three distinct forms: horizontal, vertical and technological differentiation. They argued that all three forms may be simultaneously present in the range of an industry's products and a particular product may be differentiated from other products in the range in more than one fashion. Furthermore, given that products are customarily indivisible into their individual attributes, product differentiation may often appear to be a mixture of the three forms.

Economies of scale: Through economies of scale in production, firms specialize in specific product varieties and to satisfy any demand for other varieties of a given product, the country then imports them thereby constituting an IIT flow. It follows that the larger an industry's economies of scale, the greater the potential for IIT. Caves (1981) and Greenaway and Milner (1984), however, found that these two variables are negatively correlated when an industry's minimum efficient scale of production is small relative to the total market size. This may be due to a large number of firms in the country producing a wide range of differentiated product varieties. The outcome of this is that there would be little or no need for IIT. On the other hand, if the minimum efficient scale were large relative to the size of the market, only a few large dominant firms would coexist in the industry and they would deter the entry of new firms. These firms are likely to produce less differentiated commodities and more standardized commodities, thus impacting IIT negatively. Helpman and Krugman (1985) argued that "scale economies is an essential condition for the existence of IIT" while others argue that "some degree of scale economies may be needed to enhance IIT" (Somma 1994; Davis 1995; Bernhofen 2002); however, high levels of economies of scale may inhibit IIT if they lead to the standardization of commodities.

Foreign direct investment: This determinant is recognized as possessing a dual relationship with IIT. Greenaway and Milner (1986) argued that if there is demand for different varieties of the same product and the production of these goods are subject to economies of scale there may be the tendency for a greater amount of FDI to be associated with a greater amount of IIT. At the same time, if the purpose of FDI flows are to fragment the production process into geographic blocs according to different stages of the commodity (VIIT), then the tendency will be for FDI to promote a greater amount of inter-industry trade as compared to IIT (Markusen 1995; Fukao et al. 2003).

Another common industry-specific determinant of IIT is market structure. All these determinants are grounded in theoretical models that emerged over time to explain the existence and volume of IIT between country pairs. The next section provides a brief review of the main theories of IIT.

5.4 Theoretical Models of Intra-industry Trade

The theory of IIT spans from perfectly competitive models to models of multiple products and multiple firms. While each model is distinct in its own right, all possess features that enable comparison with each other. Figure 5.2 provides an illustration of these features according to various criteria. Level one distinguishes according to the differentiation of products, level two market structure and level three the determinants of trade. Level four depicts the main contributors to each framework.

The single obvious assumption of the classical theories of international trade resides with structural differences between countries, more so their natural pattern of comparative advantage as the basis of trade. Theories explaining IIT largely emerged as a consequence of Adam Smith's theory of absolute advantage, David Ricardo's theory of comparative advantage and the Heckscher-Ohlin factor endowment model[39] and in more formal terms, depicted an expansion of these highly proclaimed works of study.

While David Ricardo was credited with providing the first theoretical exposition of mutually beneficial trade, it is the Heckscher-Ohlin-Samuelson (H-O-S)[40] model that is regarded as the most famous model of international trade (Gomes 2003). The H-O-S model is premised on the notion that a country's trade is determined by its relative factor endowments, namely, capital and labour, and specific assumptions act to isolate the idea that all trade is driven by factor endowment differences.

The inability of the H-O-S theorem to explain exchanges of an intra-industry nature has provided the stimulus for a search for new trade theories, particularly those which lay emphasis on the role of decreasing costs and product differentiation. In developing alternate approaches, some models have retained the notion that factor endowment differentials may have a deterministic role to play in non-autarkic trading practices and can therefore be reasonably described as neo-H-O-S models. These models investigate the role of product differentiation, particularly, vertical differentiation yet still factoring in the key assumptions of the H-O-S theorem. The crucial distinction between these two groups of models is that of factor mobility and sector specific factors.

Falvey (1981) explained that a theoretical model could be unearthed if one factors into the analysis each industry producing differentiated commodities, with IIT occurring when a country imports some commodities and export others, within a given industry. He went on to develop such a model, one that it is based on a two-country, two-factor framework where endowments of capital and labour differ in each country at the initial stage. Like the traditional theory, factor endowment differentials effect different factor prices in the two countries which are reflective of a relatively low domestic price of capital and a relatively low foreign price of labour. Falvey, however, argued that this approach presents a modification to the traditional H-O-S framework

Total trade

Inter-industry trade

Intra-industry trade

Homogenous products

Vertical differentiation

Horizontal differentiation

Homogenous products

Multi-product/plant

Perfect competition

Perfect competition   Oligopoly

Monopolistic competition   Oligopoly

Oligopoly   Multi-product   Multi-plant

Comparative advantage   External economies of scale

Comparative advantage   Fixed costs in R&D

Demand for variety   Diversity of tastes   Demand for unique variety   Reciprocal dumping   Demand for new product varieties   OLI paradigm

Heckscher Ohlin   Helpman Krugman

Falvey Kierzkowski   Gabszewicz Shaked Sutton Thisse

Dixit Stiglitz Krugman   Lancaster   Eaton Kierzkowski   Brander Krugman   Spence Scherer   Norman Dunning

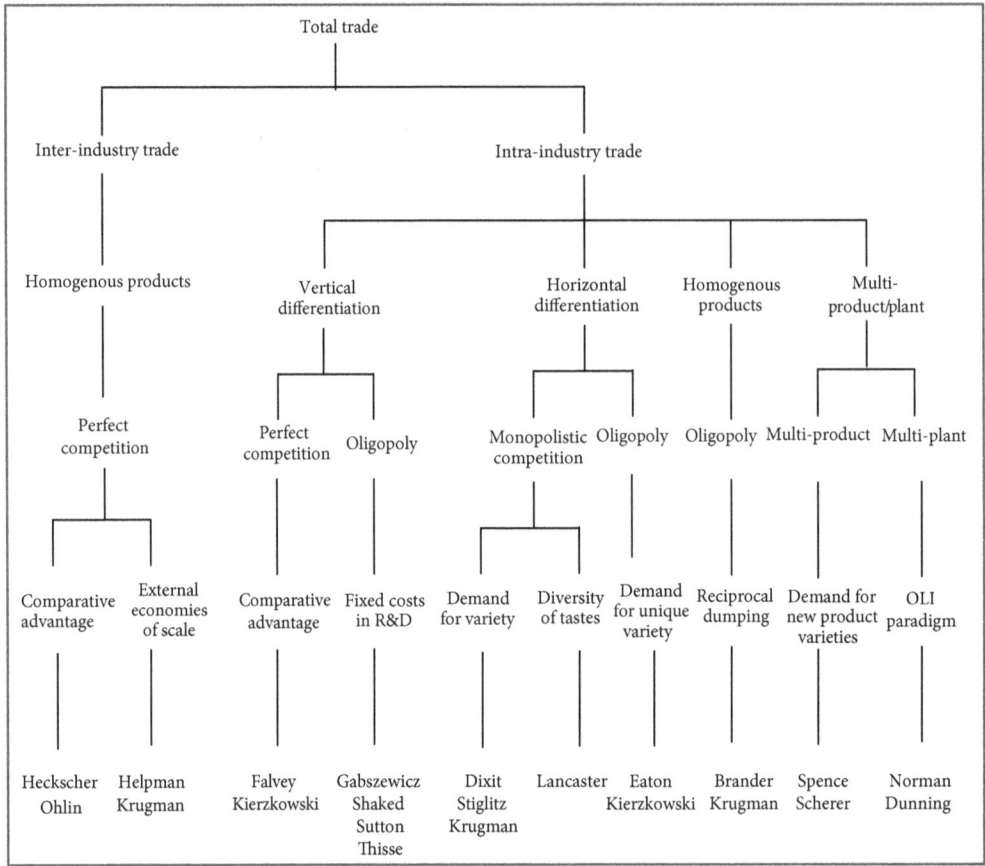

Figure 5.2 Intra-industry trade theoretical frameworks

in two unique aspects. In the first instance, of the two factors, capital is regarded as industry specific;[41] mobile within a given industry/sector but immobile among industries/sectors. Second, each industry can produce a range of products, differentiated vertically using as inputs, labour and its own industry-specific capital, and where "verticalness" or quality is determined by the size of the capital to labour ratio used in producing the commodity. IIT then occurs if countries specialize in production within this range of vertically differentiated products.

Following Falvey (1981), Falvey and Kierzkowski (1987) extended this model retaining the full cadre of assumptions applied in the earlier model with the fundamental assumption of vertical product differentiation also driving demand. The source of distinction between the two models resides with consumer preferences and their income levels. Falvey and Kierzkowski (1987) paid greater attention to the demand side of the system, and took the position that the consumer's choice of quality is income constrained and that some consumers may be initially confined to a low quality variety and as income increases, they switch to a higher quality.

Alternative theories of IIT were developed by researchers who looked beyond perfect competition for the explanation of consumer choices given differentiated commodities. Such studies led to an examination of the merits of applying the concept of production differentiation in an imperfectly competitive framework and more so, to monopolistic competition. This genre comprises two distinct models, neo-Chamberlinian and neo-Hotelling, and are collectively classified as "large number" models. Each of these models is grounded in certain properties which broadly consist of independence from relative factor endowment arguments and absence of barriers to trade and relies on decreasing costs in production, locational theory and horizontal product differentiation.

The neo-Chamberlinian model was derived from Spence (1976) and Dixit-Stiglitz (1977) analyses of monopolistic competition. However, the features of the neo-Chamberlinian model can be illustrated by reference to Krugman (1979).[42] While the model is underpinned by several key assumptions, the defining assumption is that all consumers have identical utility functions, and all varieties enter the utility function symmetrically. This means that there is an equal increase in utility from the consumption of one unit of any variety and total utility increases as more varieties are consumed. Comparative advantage does not exist within this framework such that the gains from trade will be measurable mainly on the basis of consumer surplus due to the increases in variety choices. Free trade creates one large market space so that if two countries already produce vastly different varieties, then IIT is likely to dominate between this country pair and like countries within this market. On the other hand, if a country produces a good that is identical to another country then it is assumed that one of these countries will alter the characteristics of its good, thus creating a different variety of the same good. This therefore also generates IIT.

The neo-Hotelling model differs from the neo-Chamberlinian model in one crucial aspect, that being the modelling of the utility function. Unlike the neo-Chamberlinian approach, the neo-Hotelling model assumes an asymmetric utility function for all horizontally differentiated varieties of a commodity. Originally articulated by Lancaster (1966), this approach is deemed to be an extension of Lancaster consumer behaviour model reformulated for the IIT case. The crux of the Lancaster (1979) model lies with the deviation of goods as the object of utility but rather as combinations of characteristics or attributes. The broad propositions by Lancaster (1966) that first, goods are comprised of combinations of characteristics or attributes; second, when faced with diverse preferences, each consumer will express different preferences for alternative varieties of a given commodity; third, consumers will demand more of their most preferred or ideal variety rather than some of all varieties; and fourth, the non-combinability[43] of different varieties were applied in an IIT setting.

The rest of this section considers oligopolistically competitive behaviour in an open economy setting, or "small number" models. While there is no single general oligopolistic model, alternate assumptions regarding conjectural variation,[44] entry conditions and product specifications result in different patterns and directions of trade flows.

Regarded as the first real attempt to formally model oligopolistic behaviour, Cournot (1838) postulated that in a two-firm setting, speculative behaviour on the part of each firm to the other's productive output will not exist, thus, effectively reducing the model to a two firm perfectly competitive market. Although being chastised for its inability to explain real world adjustment processes, the Cournot method holds relevance in an IIT setting specifically owing to its ability to produce stable and determinate outcomes for a market structure for which there exists no general model (see Brander 1981; Brander and Krugman 1983; Krugman 1984; Neven and Phlips 1985). Using this framework, Brander and Krugman (1983) based their model on several fundamental assumptions: there are two identical countries with each country having one firm producing a single homogeneous commodity, the countries are identical in every respect, that is, demand and costs are identical and consumers have identical demand functions, state legislation or natural barriers impede trade, and there is a constant return to scale.

The fundamental premise of this model is that each firm regards each country as a separate market, thereby choosing the profit maximizing quantity for each country separately. Quantity is therefore viewed as the "strategy variable" from a Cournot perspective; that is, each firm assumes that the other firm will keep their output fixed in each country. By introducing transportation costs, Brander (1981) and Brander and Krugman (1983) subsequently found that a proportion of exports is absorbed by freight charges and the IIT that ensues is described as "reciprocal dumping", since firms charge lower effective prices in export markets than in the home market.

An alternative mode of analysis to the Cournot approach was developed by Gabszewicz, Shaked, Sutton and Thisse (GSST) in 1981 and by Shaked and Sutton (1982, 1983, 1984). They assumed pricing behaviour (that is, the strategic variable is price rather than quantity)[45] where commodities are differentiated by quality and where sunk costs and entry considerations are essential. Differences in product quality characterize vertical differentiation in this model such that if consumers are offered all products at the same price, they would be assumed to rank products according to quality with the eventual choice of the highest quality product. Furthermore, quality is a function of research and development expenditure, that is, the greater the amount spent on research and development the better the perceived quality. Consumer behaviour is defined by income levels with higher income earning consumers willing to expend more for a higher quality product. It follows then that in a closed economy scenario with a product defined by two different qualities, the market can be segmented into two consumer groups: those willing to purchase the higher quality product and those willing to purchase the lower quality product, with the marginal consumer indifferent between the two. In autarky, each market is comprised of two firms; however, with free trade, one firm from each economy will depart leaving the remaining two firms to engage in vertically differentiated IIT.

Eaton and Kierzkowski (1984) examined product differentiation within an industrial structure similar to that articulated above. The key assumption of this model is entry, and pricing decisions are typically taken sequentially rather than simultaneously, that is, before entering the market the firm must decide on the variety of good it will produce, following which output and pricing decisions will be made. This implies that by choosing the variety first, the firm protects the position of its product variety in the market as well as its associated profits. Subsequent potential entrants take this variety as given, then decide whether or not to enter. Additionally, products are horizontally differentiated and utilize semi-reactive Bertrand pricing to model conjectural variation.[46]

The models discussed thus far have considered production by single product firms whose production facilities are located in one country. Empirical evidence has suggested that in markets where IIT is substantial, firms engage in the production of more than one variety or quality of a given product and in some cases possess production and/or distribution facilities in more than one country. Firms can therefore be classified as multi-product and/or multinational. A multi-product firm refers to a firm that produces more than one variety or quality of a particular commodity. While horizontally differentiated commodities are more predominantly produced from multi-product firm activity, it is not uncommon for vertically differentiated commodities to be produced in this environment as well. Spence (1976) and Scherer (1979) commenced the debate on multi-product firms from an industrial organization perspective following which Greenaway

(1982) extended the analysis in an open economy framework. A multinational firm is defined as a single owner of two or more production facilities set up in a foreign territory. Hymer (1976) and Hirsch (1976) have been credited as having produced pioneering work in this genre. Thereafter, Dunning (1981) proposed the "Ownership, Location and Internalization (OLI) paradigm." This approach requires that three conditions must be fulfilled in order for not only FDI to occur but also for foreign production to be rendered more profitable than trade. These are Ownership, Location and Internalization.[47]

While the OLI generally explains inter-industry trade, it can also be applied to IIT interpretations. Cited heavily in the literature, is Norman and Dunning (1984), who discussed the relationship of IIT in goods to one-way and two-way FDI (intra-industry FDI). The precise nature of these relationships is dependent on whether goods are close substitutes in production, consumption or both. However, the parallel theme of each case is that of the OLI paradigm where ownership may take the form of brand image, locational advantages may follow from factor price differences across countries as well as the response rate to taste changes through its geographical presence in the foreign market, while internalization may enable the exploitation of vertical scale economies (Greenaway and Milner 1986). These researchers added that IIT and FDI tend to complement each other in the context that significant scale economies can be reaped from the production of specific product variants, although the possibility exists for all varieties to be sold in all markets.

5.5 Measuring Intra-industry Trade

For several decades, scholars have been creating empirical measures of IIT. Balassa (1966) produced the first empirical evidence that addressed the relationship between the relative magnitudes of export and import balances of individual countries. Thereafter, Grubel and Lloyd (1975) developed an index, which is perhaps still the most prominent "static" measure of IIT. The search for a "dynamic" index was started by Hamilton and Kniest (1991). Measures of IIT have since been accepted as indispensable tools by policymakers in the developed world and although its importance has grown over time, there is a lack of urgency in the use of these measures within the Caribbean region. This section outlines some of the main measures of "static" and "dynamic" IIT. Moreover, a detailed assessment of IIT for selected Caribbean countries is undertaken using these measures.

5.5.1 Static Intra-industry Trade

Static indicators of IIT broadly measure the simultaneous exchange of commodities within a particular industry for single-time periods only, usually annually, such that they lack flexibility and comparability when applied to several time periods. Nonetheless, this branch of the literature has been widely regarded as an empirical breakthrough that motivated numerous structural modifications culminating in the creation of the dynamic school of indicators. The contribution by Grubel and Lloyd (1975) in this genre remains the most popular even today. The GL index (B_j index) measures the degree to which exports (X) match imports (M) in absolute terms and expresses this trade overlap as a proportion of total trade in the same commodity grouping (j).

$B_j = 0$ (perfect inter-industry trade) when $X_j = 0$ or $M_j = 0$ and there is no trade overlap in industry (j). On the other hand, $B_j = 1$ (perfect IIT) when X_j and M_j match perfectly ($X_j = M_j$).

5.5.2 Marginal Intra-industry Trade

Marginal intra-industry trade (MIIT) was first introduced in the early 1990s when scholars found the GL index unsuitable for measuring changes in adjustment costs. MIIT or dynamic IIT as it is sometimes referred to, analyses trade patterns in terms of the structure of the change in trade flows from period to period, by focusing on the importance of changes in "new trade" rather than that of Heckscher-Ohlin trade. Among the most notable contributors to the MIIT literature are Brulhart (1994), Menon and Dixon (1997) and Azhar and Elliott (2003).

Brulhart (1994) proposed three alternative measures of MIIT dubbed the "A", "B" and "C" indices. The "A" index and GL index share similar statistical characteristics, that is, the same theoretical range and interpretation of range. According to Brulhart and Elliot (1998), the "A" index is a "transposition" of the GL index of first differences. Furthermore, given that the index is dynamic by construct, it makes the link between adjustment costs and changes in trade patterns.

Brulhart's "B" and "C" indices represent subsets of his "A" index. The "B" index corrects for A's shortcoming and is most useful for investigating sectoral trade patterns (Brulhart and Hine 1999). The B index in particular measures the asymmetry between the growth of net exports and imports of a specific industry. The index ranges between −1 and 1 where a value closer to zero indicates higher MIIT and values tending to −1 or 1 denote greater marginal inter-industry trade. According to Azhar and Elliott (2003), these positive and negative outcomes of the B index are reflective of expansionary and contractionary adjustment pressures that occur within sectors. The B index provides an indication of the sectors a country "specialized into" and sectors "specialized out of", as well as those sectors with trade flows that do not affect international adjustment patterns and inter-industry specialization.

The C index produces an absolute value of MIIT relating to matched trade changes and can take only positive values (in absolute terms). Menon and Dixon (1997) explained that Brulhart's approach for the C index was premised on the idea that if an increase in exports is matched by an increase in imports of a similar magnitude, then adjustment costs would be low as factor movements remain relatively unchanged in the domestic industry. From table 5.3 case 1, C = 2 meaning that an increase of one unit of exports is matched by a one unit increase of imports. It implies that for a change in total trade $\Delta TT = 3$, two units require no inter-industry factor movements. The same logic applies for C = 4 such that a contraction of two units of exports is matched by a similar contraction of two units of imports. Therefore, given that $\Delta TT = -5$ then four of these five

Table 5.3 Comparisons of measures of matched and unmatched changes in trade: hypothetical data

Case	ΔX	ΔM	ΔTT	A	B	C	UMCIT
1	1.0	2.0	3	0.67	−0.34	2	1
2	−3.0	−2.0	−5	0.80	−0.20	4	1
3	−0.5	0.5	0	0.00	−1.00	0	1

Source: Menon and Dixon (1997).

Table 5.4 Static and dynamic measures of IIT

Author	Index	Strengths	Weaknesses
Grubel and Lloyd (1975)	$B_j = 1 - \dfrac{\left\| X_j - M_j \right\|}{\left(X_j + M_j \right)}$	First accepted measure of IIT. Remains the most popular indicator of IIT today.	Categorical aggregation – this is associated with the inappropriate classification or aggregation of commodities from the same industry such that products that possess different factor ratios are produced in the same industry resulting in an overvaluation of the index. Trade imbalance – the specific weighting effect within industries is contingent on the consistency of the signs of trade imbalances ($X_{ij} - M_{ij}$) of each sub group i within industry j.
Brulhart (1994)	A index $A = 1 - \dfrac{\left\| \Delta X - \Delta M \right\|}{\left\| \Delta X \right\| + \left\| \Delta M \right\|}$	The A index is a "transposition" of the GL index of first differences. Furthermore, given that the index is dynamic by construct, it makes the link between adjustment costs and changes in trade patterns.	The A index though useful for multilateral studies lacks relevance for single country studies as it does not incorporate information on the dispersal of sectoral or country specific trade-induced gains. It also does not capture the change in trade associated with adjustment costs i.e. marginal inter-industry trade.
	B index $B = \dfrac{\Delta X - \Delta M}{\left\| \Delta X \right\| + \left\| \Delta M \right\|}$	The B index is most useful for investigating sectoral trade patterns. The B index provides an indication of the sectors a country "specialized into" and sectors "specialized out of" as well as those sectors with trade flows that do not affect international adjustment patterns and inter-industry specialization.	Contingent upon varying signs of all industries, the B index cannot be aggregated across industries since the outcome of such a task would produce a value closer to 0 (high MIIT). In addition, when ΔX and ΔM take on opposite signs, the B index is non-responsive to variations in ΔX and ΔM. When compared to the S index, the latter is superior since it can distinguish between the relative sizes of diverging changes in net trade.
	C index $C = \left(\left\| \Delta X \right\| + \left\| \Delta M \right\| \right) - \left\| \Delta X - \Delta M \right\|$	C produces an absolute value of MIIT relating to matched trade changes and can take only positive values. C can also be scaled at the disaggregated level by using scaling factors.	The C index computes only balanced trade changes without providing any meaningful insights into the nature of unmatched trade changes.
Menon and Dixon (1997)	$UMCIT = \left\| \Delta X - \Delta M \right\|$	This measure assumes only positive values and can be scaled and aggregated.	The UMCIT index together with the Brulhart A and B indices are criticized for their delay in responding to variations in adjustment changes especially when opposite signs are apparent. Further, when there is an equal change in exports and import $UMCIT = \left\| \Delta X - \Delta M \right\| = \left\| \Delta M - \Delta X \right\|$ such that it is impossible to determine whether adjustment pressures are due to expansionary or contractionary effects.
Azhar and Elliott (2003)	$S_t = \dfrac{(\Delta X - \Delta M)}{2 \left(\max \left\{ \left\| \Delta X \right\|_t , \left\| \Delta M \right\|_t \right\} \right)}$	The S index allows for scaling by the largest value for a particular time scale (months, years, decades) thus enabling policy makers to track the progression of adjustment pressures over the time period considered.	Although the S index can differentiate between the "relative sizes of opposing net trade changes" in contrast to the Brulhart B index, under certain ranges, a clear interpretation of its value is difficult.

Source: Author's compilation.

units require intra-industry factor adjustment while only one unit require inter-industry factor movements. Lastly, for case 3 where C = 0, the changes in imports and exports are in opposite directions implying that all of this change in trade is unmatched. On this basis, Menon and Dixon (1997), criticized the C index since it computes only balanced trade changes without providing any meaningful insights into the nature of unmatched trade changes.

According to Menon and Dixon (1997), existing measures of IIT are only appropriate when the focus is on trade theory literature. When, however, adjustment costs are considered then the focus should be on unmatched trade or marginal inter-industry trade. They therefore provided an alternative measure for Brulhart's C index, one that investigated the degree of marginal inter-industry trade in absolute terms and its associated factor movements. The index provides an indicator of the positive and negative trade changes requiring factor movements between rather than within industries. Referred to as the unmatched changes in trade (UMCIT) index, this measure assumes only positive values and can be scaled and aggregated. This index adopts the latter part of the Brulhart C index.

Menon and Dixon (1997) maintained that for all the cases identified in table 5.3, UMCIT = 1 because for the production of one unit of output, its associated factors must move out of the industry to make way for a surplus of import expansion over export expansion. Menon and Dixon maintained that the UMCIT measure is also superior to the Brulhart B index, in the sense that case (3) as defined in table 5.3, requires greater inter-industry factor movements than case (2) and case (2) requires greater inter-industry factor movements than case (1).

Azhar and Elliott (2003) devised an index that measures expansion induced adjustment or contractionary adjustment pressure. The index ranges from −1 to 1. The index is positive (negative), if sectoral trade balance is improved (deteriorated).

Table 5.4 provides a summary of these measures and also outlines some of the main strengths and weaknesses of each measure.

5.6 CARICOM's Intra-industry Trade: Merchandise Trade and Services

In this section, IIT trends for both merchandise trade and services were assessed by employing the GL index. A detailed analysis of MIIT for the selected countries was undertaken using the methodology outlined above. All indices were calculated at the three-digit aggregation level using data extracted from the United Nations commodity trade (UN Comtrade) database for the period 1973–2012. Calculations are conducted for the entire data period as well as for selected sub periods.

A general inspection of the data in table 5.5 suggests that merchandise trade is more inter-industry than intra-industry in nature. Many researchers have employed a 0.5 threshold value of the GL index to discern inter-industry trade from IIT where scores equal to and above 0.5 suggest increasing IIT (see Faustino and Silva 2002; Crespo and Fontoura 2004; Mamoon et al. 2011). IIT (0.52) was observed in 1977 between Trinidad and Tobago and Barbados; however, by 1978 scores had declined to 0.47. Only in 1991 did these countries again report IIT with a score of 0.51. In subsequent years, the GL index declined continuously settling at 0.16 by 2012. For all of the countries analysed, a tendency towards IIT was apparent in the earlier years of trade liberalization.

An analysis of IIT in services reveals a much different picture particularly for Guyana and Trinidad and Tobago.[48] Specifically, trade in services for Guyana with the rest of the world (ROW)

Table 5.5 IIT in goods between selected CARICOM countries, 1973–2012

	Barbados			Guyana			Jamaica			Trinidad & Tobago		
	GUY	JAM	TTO	BRB	JAM	TTO	BRB	GUY	TTO	BRB	GUY	JAM
1973	0.196	0.238	0.269	0.189	0.056	0.169	0.296	0.060	0.421	0.288	0.201	0.424
1974	0.180	0.209	0.339	0.148	0.059	0.159	0.277	0.055	0.415	0.370	0.160	0.379
1975	0.170	0.224	0.398	0.141	0.089	0.147	0.237	0.063	0.356	0.452	0.125	0.381
1976	0.210	0.240	0.442	0.194	0.089	0.154	0.220	0.094	0.352	0.470	0.148	0.390
1977	0.223	0.230	0.484	0.183	0.073	0.152	0.148	0.073	0.215	0.518	0.121	0.238
1978	0.175	0.218	0.413	0.076	0.029	0.075	0.208	0.032	0.207	0.471	0.093	0.212
1979	0.199	0.288	0.372	0.076	0.035	0.127	0.226	0.064	0.284	0.396	0.139	0.281
1980	0.175	0.290	0.386	0.000	0.000	0.000	0.332	0.014	0.264	0.371	0.095	0.255
1981	0.230	0.342	0.328	0.000	0.000	0.000	0.379	0.015	0.282	0.321	0.062	0.290
1982	0.166	0.301	0.255	0.000	0.000	0.000	0.365	0.075	0.202	0.241	0.020	0.193
1983	0.247	0.307	0.271	0.000	0.000	0.000	0.347	0.215	0.178	0.248	0.024	0.184
1984	0.099	0.213	0.292	0.000	0.000	0.000	0.270	0.246	0.070	0.265	0.068	0.096
1985	0.096	0.100	0.182	0.000	0.000	0.000	0.152	0.088	0.096	0.352	0.049	0.086
1986	0.174	0.162	0.396	0.000	0.000	0.000	0.163	0.011	0.158	0.419	0.162	0.130
1987	0.185	0.188	0.303	0.000	0.000	0.000	0.150	0.002	0.231	0.334	0.241	0.225
1988	0.314	0.219	0.404	0.000	0.000	0.000	0.205	0.021	0.300	0.415	0.175	0.312
1989	0.308	0.417	0.412	0.000	0.000	0.000	0.326	0.162	0.276	0.402	0.143	0.296
1990	0.272	0.376	0.418	0.000	0.000	0.000	0.295	0.027	0.315	0.417	0.071	0.306
1991	0.246	0.320	0.414	0.000	0.000	0.000	0.258	0.028	0.294	0.511	0.079	0.290
1992	0.234	0.298	0.417	0.000	0.000	0.000	0.254	0.015	0.273	0.410	0.132	0.279
1993	0.113	0.241	0.363	0.000	0.000	0.000	0.199	0.023	0.272	0.346	0.150	0.302
1994	0.197	0.275	0.326	0.000	0.000	0.000	0.219	0.022	0.229	0.331	0.170	0.244
1995	0.222	0.205	0.314	0.000	0.000	0.000	0.237	0.160	0.233	0.262	0.171	0.229
1996	0.220	0.166	0.336	0.000	0.000	0.000	0.222	0.053	0.195	0.354	0.121	0.244
1997	0.230	0.191	0.291	0.000	0.050	0.123	0.214	0.032	0.163	0.278	0.109	0.199
1998	0.158	0.208	0.301	0.000	0.021	0.076	0.235	0.026	0.143	0.299	0.078	0.148
1999	0.176	0.197	0.250	0.087	0.033	0.076	0.270	0.043	0.138	0.239	0.092	0.162
2000	0.145	0.179	0.193	0.261	0.030	0.087	0.263	0.018	0.166	0.154	0.086	0.202
2001	0.143	0.137	0.198	0.114	0.016	0.093	0.215	0.019	0.138	0.168	0.077	0.146
2002	0.154	0.178	0.165	0.081	0.010	0.083	0.389	0.024	0.141	0.125	0.070	0.130
2003	0.190	0.157	0.156	0.099	0.006	0.087	0.240	0.011	0.139	0.163	0.065	0.155
2004	0.203	0.143	0.123	0.066	0.007	0.059	0.405	0.004	0.124	0.120	0.056	0.134
2005	0.179	0.110	0.116	0.230	0.005	0.093	0.209	0.003	0.098	0.096	0.061	0.112
2006	0.135	0.162	0.120	0.059	0.039	0.068	0.213	0.018	0.112	0.115	0.049	0.115
2007	0.100	0.194	0.144	0.054	0.014	0.130	0.353	0.013	0.108	0.092	0.048	0.109
2008	0.118	0.209	0.129	0.063	0.020	0.081	0.306	0.062	0.093	0.100	0.066	0.104
2009	0.088	0.233	0.147	0.055	0.049	0.073	0.271	0.041	0.108	0.147	0.055	0.104
2010	0.099	0.205	0.174	0.044	0.042	0.067	0.315	0.064	0.090	0.179	0.058	0.095
2011	0.120	0.242	0.158	0.074	0.011	0.046	0.283	0.054	0.100	0.037	0.022	0.022
2012	0.121	0.267	0.165	0.076	0.019	0.055	0.309	0.115	0.125	0.167	0.048	0.028

Source: Computed.

Table 5.6 IIT in services for selected CARICOM countries with the ROW, 2000–2010

	Barbados	Guyana	Jamaica	Trinidad & Tobago
2000	0.39	0.83	0.39	0.79
2001	0.41	0.80	0.42	0.72
2002	0.41	0.72	0.46	0.72
2003	0.39	0.68	0.47	0.59
2004	0.38	0.74	0.48	0.52
2005	0.38	0.67	0.42	0.66
2006	0.34	0.58	0.39	0.55
2007	0.35	0.62	0.37	0.5
2008	0.34	0.63	0.36	0.45
2009	0.37	0.56	0.34	0.55
2010	0.39	0.65	0.32	0.49

Source: Trade Map (2014) and own calculations.

reflects entirely IIT, with the highest score reported in 2000. Similarly, Trinidad and Tobago posted scores that for the most part are indicative of IIT, though falling below the 0.5 threshold at times (table 5.6).

At a more disaggregated level, of the six services sectors, IIT is concentrated in communications, insurance and government services for Barbados. For Guyana, travel reported the largest IIT score, followed by communications and other business services. Jamaica demonstrated IIT in three areas, government services, transportation and communications services. Trinidad and Tobago displayed three sectors that were intra-industry in nature: other business services, transportation and travel in that order (table 5.7).

5.6.1 The Structure of Matched Trade Changes: MIIT

The extent to which trade patterns correspond to marginal inter-industry trade or marginal IIT can be articulated by employing the Brulhart A index. Based on our analysis thus far inter-industry

Table 5.7 IIT for selected CARICOM countries with the ROW disaggregated by services sector, annual average 2000–2010

	Transportation	Travel	Communications Services	Insurance Services	Other Business Services[a]	Government Services, n.i.e.
Barbados	0.30	0.27	0.51	0.72	0.45	0.83
Guyana	0.23	0.92	0.81	0.57	0.79	–
Jamaica	0.71	0.27	0.53	0.16	0.13	0.81
Trinidad & Tobago	0.80	0.54	0.31	0.16	0.87	0.48

[a]Merchanting and other trade-related services, operational leasing (rental), miscellaneous business, professional and technical services, and other services.

Source: Trade Map (2014) and own calculations.

trade appears most prevalent among all the countries investigated. For all of the bilateral relationships examined, in the MIIT case, the aggregate A index assumed low values. The A index scores for Barbados's bilateral trade with Guyana, Jamaica, and Trinidad and Tobago for the period 1974–2012 were recorded as 0.074, 0.089 and 0.120, respectively. A similar observation was made for Guyana's trade with Barbados (0.063), Jamaica (0.075), and Trinidad and Tobago (0.131). Jamaica and Trinidad and Tobago reported lower scores for all two way cases for the same time period.[49] The most promising of the outcomes was observed for Barbados's MIIT with Trinidad and Tobago. The data reveals that about 12 per cent of total trade was intra-industry in nature (see table 5.8). Furthermore, MIIT as documented for the manufacturing sector surpassed that of the primary sector, with the former constituting 13 per cent of MIIT between 1974 and 2012. For the eight sub-periods considered, MIIT ranged between 10.8 per cent and 16.9 per cent, with scores for the primary sector residing within a 6.5 per cent and 11.9 per cent interval, inclusively. However, for consecutive sub-periods, MIIT scores for both the primary and manufacturing sectors fluctuated though largely demonstrating a declining trend. The highest reported score was 27 per cent for SITC sector 5 (chemicals) during the 1976–80 subperiod. These findings demonstrate

Table 5.8 Barbados's MIIT (A index) with Trinidad and Tobago by SITC section, 1974–2012

Sub-Period	74–75	76–80	81–85	86–90	91–95	96–00	01–05	06–12	74–12
SITC Section									
0. Food and live animals	0.1098	0.1448	0.0869	0.0562	0.1321	0.1469	0.0691	0.1113	0.1031
1. Beverages and tobacco	0.1129	0.1205	0.2803	0.2186	0.1849	0.0804	0.1654	0.1901	0.1613
2. Crude materials, inedible, except fuels	0.0385	0.0767	0.0169	0.0348	0.1002	0.1994	0.0897	0.1161	0.0877
3. Mineral fuels, lubricants and related materials	0.0000	0.0000	0.0000	0.0000	0.0000	0.0000	0.0000	0.0000	0.0000
4. Animals and vegetable oils and fats	0.0000	0.0157	0.0915	0.0000	0.0000	0.0491	0.0552	0.0128	0.0313
5. Chemicals	0.2088	0.2691	0.2634	0.1222	0.1479	0.1198	0.0682	0.1277	0.1627
6. Manufactured goods classified chiefly by material	0.1144	0.1232	0.0929	0.0907	0.0826	0.1269	0.1195	0.1782	0.1431
7. Machinery and transport equipment	0.0559	0.1099	0.0876	0.0781	0.0903	0.1966	0.2418	0.1537	0.1376
8. Miscellaneous manufactured articles	0.1655	0.1747	0.1313	0.1373	0.2010	0.2197	0.1492	0.2160	0.1698
0–8. All sectors	0.1007	0.1293	0.1313	0.0981	0.1096	0.1423	0.1143	0.1229	0.1159
0–4. Primary sectors	0.0653	0.0894	0.1172	0.0867	0.0916	0.1189	0.0877	0.0861	0.0851
5–8. Manufacturing sectors	0.1362	0.1692	0.1438	0.1071	0.1304	0.1657	0.1447	0.1689	0.1345

Source: Own calculations from the World Integrated Trade Solution (WITS) (2014).

Table 5.9 Trends in the share of Trinidad and Tobago's GDP per capita and MIIT (A index) with regional partners, 1994–2012

	Trinidad & Tobago/Barbados	MIIT	Trinidad & tobago/Guyaa	MIIT	Trinidad & Tobago/Jamaica	MIIT
1994	0.48	0.12	5.31	0.07	1.97	0.11
1996	0.50	0.21	4.74	0.06	1.76	0.10
1998	0.44	0.17	4.92	0.04	1.40	0.10
2000	0.55	0.12	6.72	0.05	1.85	0.13
2002	0.60	0.06	7.33	0.06	1.90	0.13
2004	0.77	0.13	9.62	0.04	2.59	0.07
2006	0.90	0.04	7.43	0.03	3.17	0.06
2008	1.30	0.05	8.59	0.05	4.18	0.06
2010	0.98	0.06	5.41	0.04	3.18	0.09
2011	1.14	0.02	5.43	0.01	3.32	0.02
2012	1.17	0.04	4.87	0.03	3.20	0.02

Source: Own calculations from the World Integrated Trade Solution (WITS) (2014).

convincingly that marginal inter-industry trade comprise a larger share of intra-regional trade for the entire data period as well as for all sub-periods examined.

A rudimentary assessment of the likely pattern of IIT when the ratio of per capita GDP varies in size was undertaken in section 5.3.1. The focus is now on applying the data to explicitly investigate this relationship for the marginal case in an attempt to gauge whether or not the underlying theories hold for the selected CARICOM cases and identify reasons for the outcomes observed. Table 5.9 depicts trends in Trinidad and Tobago's ratio of income per capita and MIIT with Barbados, Guyana and Jamaica. The most marked relationship is that of Trinidad and Tobago and Barbados which reveals that for the period 1994–98 a positive relationship for the most part exists between the two variables. Thereafter, an inverse relationship can be observed where, as per capita GDP increases, MIIT deteriorates. Arguably, the potency of these trends has been influenced by Trinidad and Tobago's oil wealth, which would have masked the rate of per capita income convergence and at the same time fostered a migration to different commodities thereby making MIIT less feasible. However, the results of table 5.9 suggest that the possibility exists for Trinidad and Tobago and Barbados to intensify matched trade between them particularly in the manufacturing sector. A closer look at the disaggregated results for manufacturing MIIT between the two trade partners reveals that there may be scope for greater MIIT in light manufactured commodities such as nitrogen-function compounds (514), organic chemicals, n.e.s. (516), medicinal and pharmaceutical products, other than medicaments (541), medicaments (including veterinary medicaments) (542), soap, cleansing and polishing preparations (554), fertilizers (562), textile yarn (651), pottery (666), paper mill and pulp mill machinery, paper cutting machines and machinery for the manufacture of paper articles, parts thereof (725), articles, not elsewhere specified, of plastics (893) among others.

Table 5.10 Decomposing the B index

Category	Range	MIIT	Specialization
I	B < −0.5	Low	} Specializing out
II	−0.5 ≤ B < 0	High	
III	0 ≤ B ≤ 0.5	High	} Specializing in
IV	B > 0.5	Low	

Table 5.11 Trinidad and Tobago's sectoral performance and specialization pattern with Jamaica (B index), 1974–2012

	Number of Industries								
Category	74–75	76–80	81–85	86–90	91–95	96–00	01–05	06–12	74–12
I	27	24	6	3	9	7	8	11	0
II	11	36	38	27	22	27	41	35	40
III	14	23	27	37	38	44	39	37	53
IV	33	10	8	17	12	12	8	7	1
Total	85	93	79	84	81	90	96	90	94
Specializing out (y)	38	60	44	30	31	34	49	46	40
Specializing in (x)	47	33	35	54	50	56	47	44	54
"High" MIIT	25	59	65	64	60	71	80	72	93

Source: Own calculations.

5.6.2 MIIT and CARICOM's Sectoral Trade Performance

Brulhart and Hine (1999) proposed that the B index can be further evaluated by categorizing its values according to different ranges such that specific sectors or commodities can be identified as having been specialized "into" or specialized "out of". Table 5.10 classifies these ranges.

Table 5.11 illustrates that for the aggregate period 1974–2012, Trinidad and Tobago specialized into ($\Delta X > \Delta M$), an estimated fifty-four of the ninety-four commodities, that is, 57 per cent with Jamaica. For the periods 1974–75, 1986–90, 1991–95 and 1996–2000, a higher proportion of commodities were specialized into. For all the sub-periods high MIIT scoring commodities were reported. In particular, approximately 16–70 per cent of total commodities reported high MIIT.

5.6.3 Evaluating Matched and Unmatched Trade Changes

The last two measures, the C index and the UMCIT index are instrumental in evaluating inter-industry versus IIT and comparisons of adjustment costs post trade liberalization. A possible limitation in the assessment of these indices is that they assume only "non-negative values" and do not occur within a fixed range (Brulhart 2002). Table 5.12 documents the results of the C and UMCIT calculations for the period 1974–2012. Lewis (2008) found that the sum of the UMCIT

Table 5.12 Jamaican sectors with "HIGH MIIT" during trade with Barbados and Trinidad and Tobago, 1974–2012

	Barbados				Trinidad & Tobago		
	C index	UMCIT index	Cat.		C index	UMCIT index	Cat.
513	284.86	21,803.65	II	511	2,059.84	80,511.24	III
514	356.54	72,005.92	III	513	8,846.65	382,983.97	III
515	272.70	27,658.24	III	514	44,598.27	333,226.65	III
516	333.14	6,617.68	III	515	3,974.16	361,105.78	II
541	68,668.54	181,721.46	II	532	502.05	6,983.35	III
542	41,162.54	247,508.08	II	541	54,830.32	360,711.97	II
554	22,585.73	104,791.32	III	542	95,611.35	296,793.38	II
562	101,656.49	390,175.89	II	553	2,205.57	143,746.24	III
582	15,637.14	54,777.62	II	554	165,449.78	534,476.97	III
625	58.86	1,126.68	II	562	174,951.95	871,717.43	II
633	2,981.41	133,688.03	III	582	79,904.81	262,565.19	II
642	1,778.27	46,837.78	III	625	160.65	19,038.51	II
651	84,510.59	428,421.54	III	633	60,971.78	391,817.95	III
653	96.00	2,222.19	III	642	37,957.73	159,775.16	II
654	144.16	7,527.00	III	651	148,299.62	983,428.89	II
656	342.32	1,544.73	II	652	1,045.78	23,999.68	II
657	3,317.08	31,302.89	III	653	48,886.86	144,522.22	III
662	4,081.89	335,404.95	II	654	12,628.43	153,380.92	II
663	60.32	7,161.95	II	655	207.35	7,718.11	III
664	523.89	7,298.24	II	656	11,488.00	85,665.08	II
665	372.27	37,000.86	III	657	8,598.38	58,204.76	III
666	2,091.78	72,250.05	II	658	75.24	19,894.73	II
667	723.57	13,370.51	II	662	829.84	252,788.89	II
683	447.41	7,018.70	II	663	1,568.65	38,099.46	II
685	243.68	25,004.38	III	664	577.84	16,735.11	II
689	755.08	36,576.22	III	665	2,361.14	80,514.24	III
692	8,643.14	83,635.73	III	666	143,569.78	790,207.46	III
693	11,953.03	431,261.30	II	667	30.54	3,446.95	III
695	330.70	35,621.24	II	673	15,240.43	565,709.38	II
696	129.14	3,818.59	II	674	6,377.89	921,331.41	III
697	0.43	15,640.32	III	675	21,356.00	582,694.97	III
699	4,992.81	52,975.73	II	678	330.81	435,192.65	II
712	8.27	569.43	III	679	6,405.03	103,036.38	III
716	3,738.59	15,300.81	III	681	237.30	18,029.08	III
721	5,796.86	75,981.19	II	683	1,130.70	19,752.68	II
724	3,250.70	95,646.95	II	685	50,611.68	245,495.03	II

Table 5.12 Jamaican Sectors with "HIGH MIIT", 1974–2012 (*continued*)

	Barbados				Trinidad & Tobago		
	C index	UMCIT index	Cat.		C index	UMCIT index	Cat.
725	109,595.78	218,208.08	II	689	4,608.70	211,153.38	II
726	350.00	18,475.05	III	692	27,133.46	330,588.51	III
813	5,522.86	22,815.81	III	693	36,977.14	204,258.95	II
831	29,949.73	155,523.70	III	694	4,494.86	96,419.49	II
841	7,206.97	33,364.84	II	695	23,504.65	178,779.49	II
842	61,385.30	252,887.00	III	696	8,739.03	28,370.08	III
871	252.16	56,647.81	III	697	81.68	64,634.62	II
892	4,600.32	16,155.81	II	699	38,026.05	130,097.19	II
893	22,856.54	266,534.05	II	712	321.46	15,356.03	III
894	39,019.35	158,351.19	III	716	11,476.86	47,885.38	II
895	201.89	14,303.68	III	721	17,909.30	67,836.84	III
896	779.35	5,601.16	III	723	60,404.76	167,543.43	III
897	54.05	1,828.86	II	724	91,998.59	622,673.70	II
898	720.32	14,793.49	II	725	10,263.14	149,775.65	II
				726	74,760.11	460,240.95	III
				735	712.65	14,244.73	II
				737	35.14	14,704.05	II
				813	17,606.00	66,800.54	II
				831	36,335.68	562,486.62	II
				841	4,079.73	25,119.76	III
				842	130,727.30	519,945.32	III
				871	42,604.16	263,647.03	III
				892	4,590.38	80,569.00	II
				893	64,045.62	341,627.68	II
				894	102,056.22	369,898.30	II
				895	1,803.30	43,181.30	II
				896	7,182.00	48,180.57	II
				897	68.70	2,447.65	II
				898	824.16	14,077.16	III

Source: Own calculations.

values outperformed that of the C index in the time period investigated. He further commented that these findings imply that the adjustment costs due to IIT were less than that from inter-industry trade. The findings below concur with these results. In particular, for trade between Jamaica and Barbados, the UMCIT index reported US$4,346,758.38 while the C index posted US$674,824.55. For Jamaica's trade with Trinidad and Tobago, the UMCIT outweighed the C index by US$3,671,933.83.

5.7 Boosting Intra-industry Trade in CARICOM

From the analysis above, IIT in merchandise trade and more so in services are evident among the countries considered. The data revealed that Trinidad and Tobago and Barbados have the largest scope to strengthen and increase MIIT between themselves. Notwithstanding this finding, efforts must be intensified to address the low volume of IIT between these two countries as well as the weak performances of the other CARICOM countries in the IIT sphere. Some proposed strategies in this regard can comprise, establishing suitable transportation networks, an industrial cluster initiative based on an agro-tourism cluster, the development of special economic zones (SEZs), public private partnership initiatives, aid for trade and the expansion of IIT in a multi-product and multinational firm setting.

According to Kendall (2008a), "of critical importance is the development of efficient air and sea transport. After years of struggle, the Caribbean is yet to develop an efficient means of transportation among the island states. Yet without this, the level of market integration possible, especially in the case of the goods market, will continue to be limited". It follows that one way of boosting matched trade is through maritime and air transportation networks between islands (and this is elaborated in detail in chapter 8). Geographic distance has traditionally been a determinant of IIT where lower transportation costs between economies of proximity should engender increased trade intensity and stimulate IIT as per unit cost falls. Caribbean nations have long been contending with geographic dispersion, namely, the consequent challenge of building inter-island ties and the development of regional distribution and transportation systems. It is important that the region agree on ways to establish suitable transportation systems especially for small and medium sized enterprises (SMEs) that are also agents conducting the trade which are the most adversely affected by costs and wait time.

Presently, containers need to be filled before they can be shipped. This time lag is a disincentive for regional trade especially if commodities have short shelf lives. Furthermore, the costs associated with lengthy transportation processes ultimately limit IIT in the region. It is therefore necessary for horizontal expansion of shipping policy to allow for economically small lots to be shipped in a timely manner. Perhaps the implementation of a regional shipping policy in this regard can be aligned with and incorporated within the CSME framework, thereby facilitating ease of movement of goods from the upper islands. Certainly, through the Caribbean's many existing and emerging trading agreements, this policy can be applied and extended for the extra-regional market. In particular, parts I and II of the 2008 CARIFORUM–EU EPA (namely, trade partnership for development, and trade in goods, investment, trade in services and e-commerce, current payments and capital movements and trade-related issues, respectively) take on an important role here as the EU commitment to assist in developing the physical and technological infrastructure in the region provides a tremendous opportunity for CARIFORUM countries. This may also aid in CARIFORUM economies streamlining trade logistics and communication with trading partners intra-regionally and extra-regionally.

Second, an industrial cluster initiative can be established whereby industries engaging in the production and trade of similar commodities form its membership. Phase II (2009–15) in the implementation of the CSME speaks to the "implementation of common policies in Energy-related industries, Agriculture, Sustainable tourism and agro-tourism, Transport, and Small and medium enterprises", inter alia. An easily adaptable and implementable strategy for the Caribbean is an agro-tourism cluster where IIT is promoted by agents from the tourism sector embracing the supply industries located within the agriculture sector. This can occur in two ways: first, firms with similar product ranges in the agriculture sector, for example, vegetables, ground provisions, dairy and the like form linkages and trade among themselves thereby ensuring that each firm procures a greater variety of commodities demanded by its targeted tourism product; second, the promotion of IIT in services, particularly marketing and communication services where agents within the tourism sector of each island engage in the promotion of the output of their respective country's agriculture sector in accordance with a standardized procedure such that both the domestic and tourist markets are informed of the product ranges available to them regardless of the Caribbean island travelled.

In 2006, the Organization of American States (OAS) and the Inter-American Institute for Cooperation on Agriculture (IICA) organized a project entitled "Strengthening of the Tourism Sector through Development of Linkages with the Agricultural Sector in the Caribbean". By 2009, fourteen projects were undertaken in seven Caribbean countries (two in each country), namely Barbados, Dominica, Guyana, Jamaica, St Kitts and Nevis, Suriname, and Trinidad and Tobago. These programmes promoted backward and forward linkages between agriculture and tourism by engaging and strengthening inter-relationships between producers and hotels. In late 2010, a new agro-tourism initiative was launched in Trinidad and Tobago based on cocoa and coffee. Cocoa and coffee have in the past been mainstream cash crops for Trinidad and Tobago, but production has declined dramatically over the last two decades. Accordingly, the IICA has great interest in this project as it links agriculture and tourism through marketing, trade in products, and the development and use of farms and other places for unique visitor experiences. Partnerships have since been established between Trinidad and Tobago and the Belmont Estate in Grenada for assistance in the preparation of labels for the cocoa and coffee products. Four specific examples of agribusiness ventures have been identified in the literature, which has the potential to significantly boost agri-tourism linkages and IIT within the region. These include: Goodfellows Farms (Bahamas), the Sandals Model for Farmer/Hotel Partnerships (Jamaica), the Nevis Model for Farmer/Hotel Partnerships (St Kitts and Nevis) and the Oxfam Market Access Initiative (St Lucia).

According to the theory of fragmentation, countries attempting to attract fragmented production blocks can do so by improving the advantages of their location. For instance, the development of special economic zones (SEZs) which essentially are geographic areas that offer special economic policies and more flexible government measures, that is, free market oriented. SEZs are usually established to attract foreign direct investment flows from international enterprises and multinational corporations. Thus, the host economy in addition to building a vibrant local investment climate, offers tax incentives, the opportunity for payment of lower tariffs and improvements in trade and transport facilitation. As it applies to CARICOM, SEZs can assist in deepening bilateral relations through infrastructure investment, manufacturing, trading and service activities and if implemented throughout the region, it can strengthen and diversify intra-regional trade as foreign funds, expertise and technology kick-start production processes. Certainly with the incentives offered through SEZs, significant research and development can occur which can ultimately result in the development of many new closely differentiated product lines with the added benefit of a domestic and regional test market especially if like SEZs are established in bilateral regional trading markets.

In addition, the SEZs can better pursue a more efficient and coordinated exploitation of natural resource based comparative advantages and may be able to prioritize efforts to promote industrial development by improving the corresponding regional and international competitiveness of manufacturing sectors. Certainly, emphasis can be placed on export diversification through business initiatives that draw on the competitive advantage of each country. In so doing, targeted investment flows centred on value chains involving regional firms can be explored.

One of the newest branches of IIT is that of multiproduct firms and multinational firms. Multiproduct firms in this context refer to firms producing several varieties or several qualities of a particular commodity. The literature informs us that economies of scope may be a stimulant to IIT for single product firms that lengthen production runs by reducing unit costs and prices and in so doing, provide an incentive for firms in different countries to specialize in different varieties. Although economies of scope can prove to be a deterrent for domestic producers, they may be less important for potential foreign entrants. As long as there exists taste overlap between the two countries and their varieties are differentiated, then each has an incentive to enter each other's market and stimulate IIT. This can be achieved from the construction of a complex network of vertical supply chains between domestic firms and multinational corporations which ultimately benefit the region by way of a larger volume of trade and a wider variety of trade.

CARICOM can embark on more public-private partnership initiatives such that greater entrepreneurial talent can be nurtured perhaps via incentivized training programmes. In this way, innovation can be fostered thereby promoting and strengthen the prospects for vertical IIT within the region. Existing training programmes within the individual economies though facilitation of new trade in some regards, require a more targeted approach if an initiative of increased IIT is to be pursued. An alternative approach could be to integrate these objectives in the curriculum of institutions (vocational, technical and otherwise) that specialize in manufacturing activities such as at the University of Trinidad and Tobago. Certainly, individuals who are equipped with the relevant industry competencies are better positioned for smoother transitions into industries that require adept technical skills to produce commodities with subtle differences. Furthermore, both the public and private sectors must be prepared to allow their companies to build ties with successful regional firms by forming part of their supply chains.

5.8 Conclusion

This chapter investigated the importance of IIT in merchandise trade and services trade for four CARICOM economies: Barbados, Guyana, Jamaica, and Trinidad and Tobago. Subsequently, a detailed assessment of the extent of MIIT in commodity trade was investigated among these countries by employing five established indices for the period 1973–2012. Each of these measures was explored rigorously both at the aggregate and commodity levels.

The results have confirmed unequivocally that for the CARICOM countries examined, inter-industry trade predominates in merchandise trade for the most part, but trade in services appear to have some promise in the IIT sphere. An analysis of per capita shares and IIT between Trinidad and Tobago and Barbados revealed that as income per capita converged or approached unity, MIIT tended upwards only marginally as Trinidad and Tobago's oil wealth may have masked its true per capita shares. Moreover, an investigation of the A index showed more pronounced MIIT patterns for the manufacturing sector between Barbados and Trinidad and Tobago, suggesting that there may be scope for greater IIT in light manufactured commodities between the two economies. An assessment of the B index at the commodity level showed that for all the selected countries, the majority of commodities were specialized into. With regards to the C and UMCIT trends, the data revealed that the adjustment costs due to IIT were less than that from inter-industry trade.

Based on these findings, policy suggestions were proposed to boost IIT levels for the CARICOM region. These included: establishing suitable and efficient networks for air and maritime transportation, an industrial cluster initiative based on agro-tourism, the development of special economic zones (SEZs), the expansion of IIT in a multiproduct and multinational firm setting and public-private partnership initiatives. A further suggestion can be the investigation of the extent of IIT in services trade for the region on a bilateral level. This area appears to have considerable breath in the IIT sphere; however, data deficiencies prevent assessment at this time.

6

Market Access

Trade Facilitation and Aid for
Trade Integration in CARICOM

6.1 Introduction

With the GATT developing countries did not need to sign on to new disciplines nor were they required to participate fully in reciprocity in concessions. Under the GATT, developing economies benefited from MFN and national treatment. However, with the creation of the WTO in 1995, developing countries became subject to a large number of obligations. The new set of rules associated with the emergence of the WTO was broad and ultimately impacted on the number of policy interventions that the governments of the developing world could deploy. The implementation of these new rules also carried high costs for decision makers in several of these economies; many ascertained that it compromised their development. Increasingly, developing economies raised their development concerns and this motivated the decision by the WTO to label its first round, the Doha Development Agenda – a central facet of which was addressing the various developmental concerns raised by developing economies.

One of these concerns was market access. The developing economies argued that benefits from participating in the multilateral trading framework, presumes the existence of a certain level of infrastructural and institutional capacity. However, many developing countries, including small vulnerable economies, may not be able to exploit some of the opportunities that may be available through market access opportunities because of their high operating costs and weak levels of infrastructure. Even though the Doha Development Round has not made significant progress, a number of new initiatives have been introduced that have the potential to make a difference, one such is the multilateral Aid for Trade (AfT) initiative which was launched in 2005. This chapter investigates the AfT initiative in the context of the small and vulnerable CARICOM economies as an effective avenue to bolster their productive capacity and to help enhance their market access and to greater utilize foreign markets.

There is a wide ranging consensus among economists that the benefits from trade liberalization can be substantial. Simply argued, the improvement in the allocation of scarce factors of production can enhance output performance. Trade liberalization also has the attribute that it can help to improve the degree of competition on the domestic market and in so doing reduce wastage. Also via a process of sharper competition, free trade encourages domestic firms to improve on the quality of their products. By reducing import costs, an economy may gain easier access and lower cost access to relevant factors of production and this in turn could help to expand their capabilities.

The Organisation for Economic Co-operation and Development (OECD 2007) has identified five avenues through which trade impacts innovation within an economy. These are: increased competition, enhanced technology transfer, greater economies of scale, the globalization of value chains and the use of intellectual property rights. Each of these points is briefly discussed below.

Free trade exposes firms to a greater degree of competition which affects the amount of economic rents that the firm earns as well as enhances how the domestic firm behaves in that it provides greater incentives for the firm to innovate so as to preserve its market share from the roving foreign firm. Trade helps to facilitate technology transfer when a nation buys capital goods and benefits from the technology embedded within it. Free trade also helps to facilitate the transfer of technology and increases the number of techniques available to developing and developed economies. Smith (1776) also noted that trade leads to specialization and allows firms to benefit from economies of scale. Specifically, free trade leads to an expansion in the market size served by an economy. By expanding the market base, free trade offers a firm a greater incentive to innovate as the market to which it can sell the innovated products will be much larger. This raises the potential that there is a much greater scope for expanded profits.

In some regards, freer trade has helped to promote the harmonization of technical standards used by firms participating in a fragmented value chain. Additionally, Park and Lippoldt (2007) in a recent study illustrated that there is a strong positive correlation between patent protection levels in developing economies and innovation. Increasing the output of an economy has two fundamental aspects: either increase the deployment of factors of production for the productive process or innovate and find ways to cull from the same number of units of factor inputs, a greater element of commodity output. Many economies have subscribed to the perspective that more liberal trade is indeed beneficial.

6.2 Market Access: Free Trade Necessary but Not Sufficient for Growth

It has become accepted in most quarters that free trade is not a magic wand.[50] While it has been established that trade is necessary for enhancing economic growth, this section suggests that it is not sufficient. Simply put, while trade may help an economy benefit from economic growth, other factors help trade to be meaningful. Furthermore, while trade would generate benefits, these benefits have to be taken against the backdrop that trade also generate costs, which arise when resources are moved around from one segment of an economy to another. Even more, while the adjustment costs are immediate, the benefits from free trade takes a long time to accrue.

When countries get improved market access opportunities, say via a newly negotiated free trade arrangement, they would need to undertake the relevant adjustment costs in order to benefit from the improved market opportunities. Consequently, they may need to find resources to spend on the relevant trade facilitating infrastructure: including ports, roads, electricity and water supply. To illustrate, in the 1960s Trinidad and Tobago was in the midst of its energy boom and so it became necessary to construct adequate facilities to support increases in its trading activities. In this regard, the Point Lisas Industrial Port was built as it was believed that the absence of a deep-water harbor in the south of the island would hinder the development of new export oriented manufacturing industries and contribute to problems for importers accessing their goods in different parts of the economy (Driver 2008).

On the other hand, a member state within an FTA may not have the technical and requisite knowledge to meet the type of product standards as may exist in the partner economy. In order to benefit from liberalization on the whole therefore, developing economies would need to build up the relevant stock of public investments, both in physical infrastructure and in productive capacity.

Improving market access for its participating countries has long been one of the priorities of the WTO. Through the WTO secretariat and in particular, its market access division, all relevant bodies, namely the Council for Trade in Goods, the Committee on Market Access, the Committee on Customs Valuation, the Committee on Rules of Origin, the Committee on Import Licensing and the Committee of Participants on the Expansion of Trade in Information Technology Products (ITA), oversee all procedures related to global market access and the issues raised by member countries in this regard (WTO Secretariat 2011).

The WTO has defined the market access for goods as the conditions, tariffs and non-tariff measures, agreed by members for the entry of specific goods into their markets (WTO 2011). Furthermore, the commitments made by each member country including specific tariff concessions in the context of international trade negotiations are noted in the "Schedules of Concessions". This document enlists the maximum tariff levels also referred to as "bound tariffs" or "bindings" according to GATT article II for the trade in goods. The rate charged by developed country states is usually the binding rate; however, developing member states charge a higher rate than what is actually charged, so the binding rate acts as a ceiling.

In simple terms, individual participating governments that enter into a commitment binds itself from intervening in the market to prevent entry or the operation of a service. Thus, foreign member countries are assured that entry conditions and market operations in the "committed" country will not change to its disadvantage. Modifications or the withdrawal of such a commitment can only be undertaken if an agreement of compensatory adjustments is achieved and no further changes be made until three years have passed since entry into the new agreement (Hoda 2002).

Market access in the context of non-tariff measures are distinguished under the following subjects: agriculture, anti-dumping, balance of payments, customs valuation, import licensing, information technology agreement, rules of origin, safeguards, sanitary and phyto-sanitary measures, state trading enterprises, subsidies and countervailing measures, technical barriers to trade, textiles and trade facilitation.[51]

The AfT agenda reflects the realization that, for developing countries, the necessary investments are particularly large and the capacity of developing economies to meet them is particularly, small. There is the growing consensus that the current WTO Doha Round will require adequate trade-related assistance to mitigate the adverse effects of trade reforms, and to enhance the trading capacity of developing countries.

6.3 The Role of Aid

Aid represents a voluntary transfer of resources from one economy to another and the general intention of aid is to benefit the receiving economy. Many times aid comes attached with conditionalities, and when it does, it tends to stifle the use and developmental outcomes it can facilitate. With aid there is an erosion of accountability; this means that when a government receives aid, its accountability becomes partly compromised as the recipient economy tends to favour satisfying the donor economy as compared to its own citizens. Even more aid can promote a dependency mentality (Svensson 2003).

When poor economies are dependent on the hand out of donors they may not always take the appropriate block of proactive steps to generate resources for themselves. In this regard, aid helps to create a chronic syndrome of dependency with all types of attendant consequences. Some of the governments receiving aid may engage in corrupt practices. Aid can also help to perpetuate authoritarian regimes where the political dysfunctionality that characterizes the system can reduce the level and extent of transparency and accountability so that the extent of corruption in the economy increases. However, aid can also be wasted by the recipient economy, in glorifying the aid where the aid granting organization can be given too much leverage in the decision making process of the home country. As noted by Okaru-Bisant (2009) in many instances, donor organizations leverage control in selecting, designing and implementing the economic development initiative that is being financed. Another issue with aid is that it can hinder the emergence of an entrepreneurial class. According to Majewski (1987), for third world countries, aid has the tendency to increase the role of government and bureaucracy while minimizing the role of markets and private entrepreneurship.

Another form of aid is preferential trade agreements which until recent developments, many Caribbean islands benefited from, particularly in the trade of bananas.[52] According to Stoeckel and Borrell (2001), trade preferences can be an inefficient method of giving assistance to countries in need. This is because these arrangements actually divert attention and resources away from addressing structural shortcomings. These shortcomings explain why the countries are experiencing poor economic performances; however, they are masked by the preferential trade agreements.

With time, it was recognized by many donors that aid as a developmental tool was not working and what was needed was trade, not aid. The petition for Trade Not Aid[53] was first made at the UNCTAD's conference in Geneva in 1964, and again some four years later in 1968 in New Delhi. AfT was not part of the WTO Doha Multilateral Declaration in 2001 that marked the start of the Doha Development Round.[54] However, as the negotiations progressed, it became clear that developing economies would require assistance to help build up their trade capacity and to take advantage of improved market access in the developed world.

6.4 Why Aid for Trade Matters

An important basis on which the AfT initiative was launched was that while market opportunities were being made available to developing economies in a number of developed economies, they were simply unable to capitalize on these improved market access opportunities. One of the principal reasons was that developing economies did not have the requisite level or quality of infrastructure to take advantage of the various market access opportunities they were being offered in the developed world. This introduces one of the most important and identifying traits of AfT, which is that it is targeted at attempting to lower the cost of production and enhancing the level of productivity in benefiting economies. The presumption is that by focusing on improving public investment and the plethora of complementary factors which goes along with it, AfT can help receiving economies benefit from improved market access opportunities in the developed world.

AfT can also help poor economies recover from negative shocks. The OECD and WTO noted that the developing economies in the context of the slowdown of global economic growth are not likely to be in a position to adequately respond to the global economic crisis (OECD/WTO 2009). In this setting, donor support in the form of AfT may be required to help pull these developing economies out of their crisis. AfT can also be used to help expand and improve on trade-related infrastructure and help to reduce institutional inefficiency, both of which are critical for enhancing the environment where export diversification thrives. Because export diversification tends to be associated with a lower degree of export volatility, it is usually a favoured strategy for AfT.

6.5 Aid for Trade and Productivity in Low-Income Countries

Many developing countries also have tremendous problems implementing agreed parts of the WTO trade liberalization agenda. Some of these WTO agreements are not only technically complex, but also costly to implement, which promoted arguments for the need of AfT in helping to reform developing economies. It was in this type of setting that the AfT initiative gained importance. With the establishment of the WTO, trade-related technical assistance (TRTA) has continued to rise.

The focus on TRTA for the LDCs was strengthened when the Integrated Framework for Trade-Related Technical Assistance to Least Developed Countries was established at the first ministerial conference in Singapore in 1996.[55] In many regards, the Integrated Framework provided the basis for the formation of an AfT agenda. Indeed, the Doha Declaration has noted that international trade can make a significant contribution to economic development and poverty reduction. As overseas development assistance (ODA) began to falter, AfT emerged as a politically rational option.

At this point, it was realized that some form of North–South gestures was required to help extend the benefits of trade to all. Indeed, it is correct to say that the Doha Round of trade negotiations has shifted away from a narrow focus on trade liberalization to the much more important recognition, that many economies would need a range of complementary reforms in order for them to benefit from opportunities with global trade. In Hong Kong at the sixth WTO ministerial conference it was emphasized that "AfT should aim to help developing countries, particularly

LDCs to build the supply side capacity and trade-related infrastructure that they need to assist them to implement and benefit from WTO agreements and more broadly to expand their trade" (WTO 2001, para 57).

Most commentators would readily agree that AfT is not a new phenomenon, as Caribbean economies have received assistance to help develop their trade regimes and infrastructure from international and multilateral donors for many years. The difference between what occurred in the past and the current configuration is the explicit coverage of AfT in the Doha Development Round and the coordination of the aid that countries receive for trade from the various donors. A taskforce appointed by the Hong Kong ministerial declaration to operationalize AfT reported on 27 July 2006 that "the scope of the Aid for Trade should be defined in a way that is both broad enough to reflect the diverse needs identified by countries, and clear enough to establish a border between Aid for Trade and other development assistance of which it is a part" (WTO 2006, 2). The taskforce identified that AFT could be used for:

1. trade policy and regulation
2. trade development, including infrastructure
3. building productive capacity
4. trade-related infrastructure
5. trade-related adjustments
6. other needs

All the factors listed above, are areas of concern in the Caribbean, which are impeding the islands from improving their export and growth performance (Tsikata et al. 2009). This is not unique to the Caribbean, but rather is applicable to all low-income countries.

6.6 Trade Competitiveness and Trade Facilitation

At the fourth WTO ministerial conference in November 2001, in Doha, Qatar, trade ministers from member countries agreed to undertake a new round of multilateral trade negotiations with respect to agriculture and services. These negotiations were already under discussion before the Doha conference and were even required under the last round of multilateral trade negotiations (Uruguay Round 1986–94). The United States, in particular, was of the view that having a new round of multilateral trade negotiations would help the global economy, which was weakened by recession and uncertainty because of the terrorist attack. As the WTO noted, the year 2001 showed the lowest growth in world output compared to the previous two decades and world trade also contracted for that year. With respect to trade facilitation, the Doha negotiations focused national policy attention on trade costs.

Trade facilitation subsumes regular simplifications of the various procedures and documents that are utilized in international trade. There are both broad and narrow interpretations of trade facilitation. According to the United Nations (2006, 7), the broad definition of trade facilitation focuses on improving the commercial and policy environment associated with international trade transactions but not limited to "narrow" trade facilitation. The narrow definition of trade facilitation refers to the reduction of transaction costs on the border, which essentially involves the

Table 6.1 Various definitions of the term "trade facilitation"

Authorities	Definition
UNCTAD (2001)	"simplification and harmonization of international trade procedures, including activities, practices and formalities involved in collecting, presenting, communicating, and processing data required for the movement of goods in international trade".
OECD (2001)	"simplification and standardization of procedures and associated information flows required to move goods internationally from seller to buyer and to pass payments in the other direction".
UN/ECE (2002)	"comprehensive and integrated approach to reducing the complexity and cost of the trade transactions process, and ensuring that all these activities can take place in an efficient, transparent and predictable manner, based on internationally accepted norms, standards, and best practices".
APEC (2001)	"trade facilitation generally refers to the simplification, harmonization, use of new technologies and other measures to address procedural and administrative impediments to trade".
APEC (1999)	"the use of technologies and techniques which will help members to build up expertise, reduce costs and lead to better movement of goods and services".

Source: Wilson et al. (2003, 23).

standardization of documentary and administrative formalities as it relates to the requirements of international trade.

Table 6.1 provides brief and simple definitions of trade facilitation, by various international authorities.

Collectively, trade facilitation measures include policies to lower the port handling aspects of trade and those to ease compliance with the relevant set of rules and associated documentation needed at the border.[56] Whether trade reforms help to improve trade outcomes or not, hinges on their effects on both rent creating and cost evaluating activities. The importance of trade facilitation is that it simplifies the process by which goods move in a trade liberalized environment.[57] Border issues are critical for the development of an economy's long run export competitiveness. This involves the exporting economy being able to produce goods and services up to international standards and the management of the export process. Some of the most critical border issues are bottlenecks in the trade-related infrastructure, ranging from transportation of cargo to the actual port-based handling of cargo.

Wilson et al. (2002), Alaba (2006), Zaki (2010) and others have argued that improving trade facilitation can offer more gains than further multilateral trade liberalization. In most countries, the main border agency is the customs.[58] ECLAC has referred to these types of regulatory barriers as non-tariff barriers (NTBs). As NTBs decline, businesses are becoming more aware of the cost of these NTBs. With the passing of time and the persistent reduction in tariff levels, trade transaction costs in many economies have become higher than the actual average tariff level in these economies.[59]

Table 6.2 lists annual data for two proxies for trade transaction costs in CARICOM, namely the costs to export and import, respectively. The trends in this dataset indicate that for most of the listed countries there has been a steady increase in both aforementioned indicators.

Table 6.2 Trade transaction costs in selected CARICOM economies, 2006–2013

	Cost to Export (US$ per Container)								Cost to Import (US$ per Container)							
	2006	2007	2008	2009	2010	2011	2012	2013	2006	2007	2008	2009	2010	2011	2012	2013
Trinidad & Tobago	693	693	693	866	866	808	843	843	1,100	1,100	1,100	1,100	1,100	1,250	1,260	1,260
Antigua & Barbuda	1,057	1,057	1,107	1,133	1,133	1,133	1,202	1,440	1,967	1,967	1,674	1,633	1,633	1,633	1,633	1,870
Belize	1,700	1,700	1,700	1,710	1,710	1,710	1,505	1,355	1,855	1,855	1,855	1,870	1,870	1,870	1,650	1,600
Guyana	530	530	530	730	730	730	730	730	530	530	530	730	730	745	745	745
Jamaica	1,750	1,750	1,750	1,750	1,750	1,750	1,410	1,500	1,350	1,350	1,350	1,420	1,420	1,420	1,420	1,560

Source: World Bank (various years), Doing Business reports (http://www.doingbusiness.org/reports/global-reports/doing-business-2015).

Table 6.3 Trends in average MFN applied tariff rates in selected CARICOM countries (weighted in %), 1986–2008

Country	1986	1996	2006	2007	2008
Trinidad & Tobago	17.10	11.30	9.40	8.20	8.20
Antigua & Barbuda	12.00	22.80	11.60	11.60	11.60
Belize	17.30	20.70	11.80	11.60	11.60
Guyana	17.40	21.10	11.40	11.10	10.80
Jamaica	17.30	21.10	9.10	7.30	–

Source: World Development Indicators (2014).

Table 6.3 shows the trends in average applied tariff rates for the countries listed in table 6.2. It is clear that over the time period 1986–2008, there has been a significant decline in tariff rates for all countries listed. As such, the proportional burden of trade transaction costs has to be addressed. Figure 6.1 highlights the positive impact that trade facilitation can have not only on trade competitiveness, but also on overall economic growth. Given that trade transaction costs are the sum of tariff and trade facilitation costs, then at a point in time with the continuous reduction of tariffs, trade facilitation costs can eventually outweigh tariff costs.

Some studies such as the OECD (2003, 6) have shown that trade transaction costs account for as much as 2 per cent to 15 per cent of the value of goods and services that are traded in developed countries.[60] Table 6.4 provides some empirical references from the literature which reflect on how trade facilitation impact on trade flows.

When an economy is characterized by tedious and cumbersome procedures regarding the trade facilitation process they are at a relative disadvantage to economies which perform better in those areas when international trade expands (Francois and Manchin 2007).

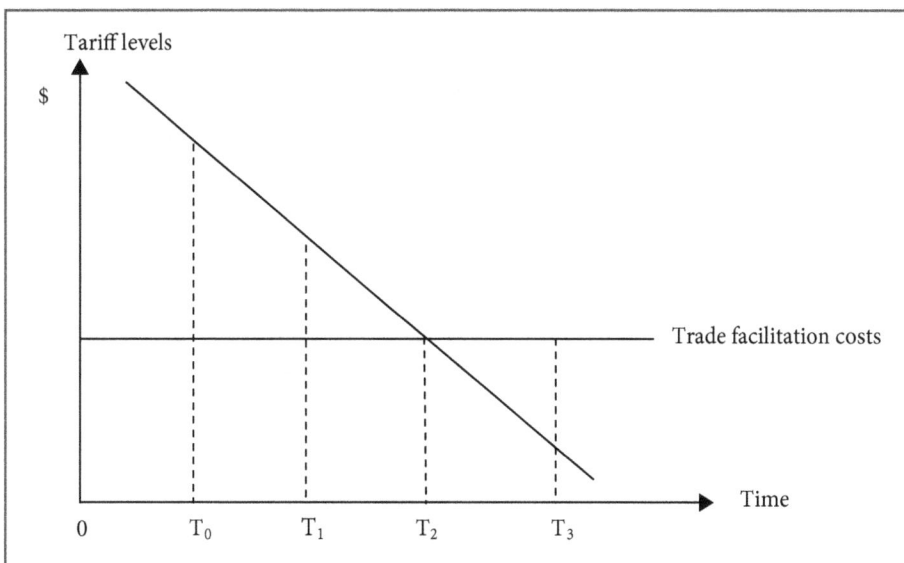

Figure 6.1 The positive impact of trade facilitation

Table 6.4 The impact of trade facilitation on trade flow

Study	Key Findings
Viet (2015)	This study examined the impact of trade facilitation as measured by the number of documents and days required to facilitate exports and imports on poverty and inequality in low- and middle-income countries. This study found that trade facilitation helps to reduce poverty and inequality in low- and middle-income countries and also increases per capita GDP.
Portugal-Perez and Wilson (2010)	Based on building four new indicators (physical infrastructure, information and communications technology, border and transport efficiency, business and regulatory environment) for 101 countries over a period of 2004–2007 estimating the impact of soft and hard infrastructure on the export of developing countries the authors concluded that trade facilitation reforms do improve the export performance of developing countries.
Njinkeu, Wilson and Powo Fosso (2008)	Using trade data from 2003 to 2004, they found that improvement in ports and services infrastructure promise relatively more expansion in intra-African trade than other measures.
Wilson and Otsuki (2007)	Based on the data of trade performance for the past two decades on South Asia and comparing East Asia, the authors came to the conclusion that South Asia expansion of trade will be more significant if they implement concrete programmes to address barriers to trade facilitation.
Martinez-Zarzosa and Marquez-Ramos (2007)	Overall, the results indicated that multilateral initiatives, as that in the WTO, are potentially beneficial in terms of increasing trade. Trade facilitation efforts are supposed to have positive effects on not only the country that improves trade facilitation, but also on its trading partners.
Dollar et al. (2004)	Based on survey results from 7,302 companies in eight developing economies (including Brazil, China, India), the authors find that "customs clearance times . . . are key determinants of . . . export status". Maximum likelihood estimates show that customs clearance times for both imports and exports have a significant negative effect on exportation.
Kim et al. (2004)	Based on a gravity model exercise for APEC economies, the authors conclude that an improvement in customs procedures performance by 50 per cent would increase imports by 1.7–3.4 per cent in industrialized APEC economies, 2.0–4.5 per cent in newly industrialized APEC economies, and 7.7–13.5 per cent in industrializing APEC economies, respectively.
Wilson et al. (2004)	Based on a gravity model exercise for seventy five countries, the authors find that improvements in port efficiency and customs administration for below-average efficient countries half-way up to the global average would increase trade flows by US$107 billion and US$33 billion respectively. Improvements in customs administration would benefit all regions but in particular developing countries importers. Port efficiency improvements would also greatly benefit developing countries.

Batra et al. (2003)	Based on survey results from 8,560 companies in some eighty countries, "customs/foreign trade regulations" were identified as the second most serious "tax and regulatory constraint" on operations and business growth/trade in Latin America, Africa, Developing East Asia and the Middle East. In 44 per cent of non-OECD countries, half or more of the companies reported that "customs/foreign trade regulations; were moderate or major obstacles to operations and business growth/trade. SMEs were particularly affected".
Fox et al. (2003)	Based on General Trade Analysis Project (GTAP) model estimates, the authors concluded that a removal of the frictions in border crossings (delays) between Mexico and the United States would lead to US$7 billion rise in trade, with southbound trade estimated to increase by US$6 billion and northbound trade by US$1.4 billion in Mexico and by US$1.4 billion in the United States.
Wilson et al. (2004)	Based on a gravity model exercise for APEC economies, the authors found that enhanced port efficiency has a large and positive effect on trade. Improvements in customs significantly expands trade but to a lesser degree than the effects of ports improvements. If port efficiency and customs environment in below-APEC-average members were brought halfway to the initial APEC-average, intra-APEC trade is estimated to increase by 11.5 per cent. A 9.7 per cent gain (US$117 billion) is expected from increased port efficiency and 1.8 per cent (US$22 billion) from an improved customs environment.
Hummels (2001)	The author estimates that each additional day spent in transport reduces the probability that the United States will source from the country by 1–1.5 per cent for manufactured goods while no effect is found for commodities. Each day saved in shipping time is worth 0.8 per cent ad valorem for manufactured goods.
APEC (1999)	Based on CGE analysis, the authors find that a 1 per cent reduction in import prices (from reduced TTCs) for the industrial and newly industrializing countries of Korea, Chinese Taipei and Singapore, and a 2 per cent reduction for the other developing countries yields an increase in APEC merchandise trade of 3.3 per cent.
Moïsé, Sorescu, Hummels and Minor (2013)	Based on the findings of the OECD, it was found that the policy areas that had the most significant effect on trade volume and trade costs include: the availability of trade related information, simplification and harmonization of documents, streamlining of proce- dures as well as the use of automated procedures. Combined, the impact of improvements in these areas was close to a 14.5 per cent decrease in total trade costs for low-income countries, 15.5 per cent for the lower-middle-income countries and 13.2 per cent for those upper-middle-income countries.

Source: Author's compilation.

6.7 Arguments for a Greater Flow of AfT Programmes for Trade Facilitation in the Caribbean

Arguments supporting a greater degree of AfT support are centred on the following five (5) areas: (1) assistance to offset adjustment costs, (2) technical assistance, (3) capacity building including support for trade facilitation, (4) institutional reform and (5) investments in trade-related infrastructure. This chapter singles out one of these five areas: assistance to offset adjustment costs.

6.7.1 Assistance to Offset Adjustment Costs

The adjustment costs associated with trade liberalization are not trivial and include the following:

1. **Costs of preference erosion**: The erosion of preferences often involves a large-scale loss of income to the private sector in an economy and to the balance of payments, as public administrations are often required by external donors to undertake the management of a major expansion of external assistance programmes, which can overwhelm local administrative capacities. For small countries, these losses can be quite significant (Goodison 2007, 20).

   Using banana as an example, the erosion of preferences on bananas entering the European Union from the various CARICOM economies would no doubt adversely affect their economies. Table 6.5 shows the extent of the implicit assistance lost by these economies on account of the decline in preferences. These are large margins of decline in the level of implicit assistance received by these economies and this no doubt would compromise their ability to make adjustments (Mlachila et al. 2010). Indeed for Dominica and St Lucia, the correlation between the implicit subsidy received by both countries and their per capita GDP growth rates was positive, providing indicative evidence that a decline in the value of the implicit subsidy would likely be associated with a decline in the growth rate of these economies. For these small Caribbean banana-exporting economies, the incomes and employment of the banana farmers and their economic inter-linkages would have been adversely affected (Mlachila et al. 2010). In this context, these economies would need AfT assistance to help strengthen their non-banana export base.

2. **Costs of compliance with product standard requirement**: For the various extra-regional markets targeted by CARICOM economies, sanitary and phyto-sanitary assurances are required especially with regards to food products. When CARICOM food producers have to meet these standards, it imposes a further adjustment cost burden on their respective economies. These burdens may take the form of a further thinning of the economies' existing resource base in terms of land, human capital and financial constraints (FAO/WHO 2002). To meet these new standards in general, AfT would be definitely helpful.

3. **Costs of implementing WTO agreements**: The implementation of these trade agreements in these small economies to meet WTO compatibility usually involves a significant change in policy and legislation. Countries are still struggling to implement agreements concluded in the Uruguay Round; for example, those dealing with trade-related

Table 6.5 Subsidy and GDP comparisons in Dominica and St Lucia, 1995–2008

	Implicit Subsidy in Dominica (% of GDP)	GDP Growth in Dominica	Implicit Subsidy in St Lucia (% of GDP)	GDP Growth in St Lucia
1995	6.20	2.01	7.90	4.67
1996	6.40	2.64	7.00	5.42
1997	6.40	1.49	5.50	0.40
1998	5.60	4.98	5.70	6.35
1999	4.90	0.68	4.50	2.36
2000	2.90	0.68	2.90	0.00
2001	1.30	–3.75	1.00	–5.12
2002	1.50	–4.01	1.60	3.11
2003	1.60	2.18	1.90	4.31
2004	1.60	6.28	1.90	5.18
2005	2.10	3.37	2.00	5.80
2006	0.80	5.15	0.80	4.03
2007	0.70	3.43	1.10	0.84
2008	0.80	4.31	1.40	0.51
Correlation	0.055		0.87	

Source: World Development Indicators (2014) and own derivations.

investment measures (TRIMS), trade-related intellectual property rights (TRIPS) and the general agreement on trade in services (GATS) (Parsan 2006). Implementation of trade agreements usually involves costly changes in policies and legislation. These implementation costs have a public aspect which arises from the process of harmonizing the participating economy's policy instruments with the type of policy instruments required by the WTO. The process of becoming WTO compliant is not simply one of adopting new laws and regulations but also include the establishment of new administrative capacity, sometimes adopting newer and different types of technology and sometimes even new investments. One source notes that using the agreement on sanitary and phyto-sanitary measures and on technical barriers to trade as referenced examples would require the establishment and development of administrative capacity, educating customs officers, accumulating knowledge of business practices, and establishing systems to address issues relating to risk analysis and auditing (Drabek and Bachetta 2004, 1110).

4. **Costs of tariff revenue losses as a result of tariff reductions**: Using a partial equilibrium model founded on the Armington (1969) principle, Greenaway and Milner (2003) estimated the welfare impact of the economic partnership agreement (EPA) between the European Union and the CARIFORUM economies. These researchers estimated the losses (shown in table 6.6) in customs revenues for the named CARICOM economies. These are not trivial losses. AfT can help CARICOM economies deal with these adjustment losses (this was elaborated in chapter 3).

5. **Costs related to factors of production**: With trade liberalization, some workers are factored out of the market and these workers would take time to learn the new relevant

Table 6.6 Changes in customs revenue by country

	EC$ million
Barbados	182.40
Belize	52.80
Dominica	21.80
Grenada	31.20
Jamaica	635.10
St Kitts	25.90
St Lucia	60.40
St Vincent	27.30
Trinidad	390.10

Source: Greenaway and Milner (2003).

skills that may be necessary to re-enter a different segment of the market. The South Centre (2006) in "Elements for the Architecture of Aid for Trade" notes that this situation could be costly to both the individual and the society as a whole.

6.8 The Experience of AfT in the Caribbean

There are two main sources of AfT funds in CARICOM, these are the AfT provided by the Caribbean Aid for Trade and Regional Integration Trust Fund (CARTfund) and the AfT provided by major donor countries.[61]

6.8.1 CARTfund

The CARTFund was established at the Caribbean Development Bank (CDB) in March 2009 with the initial funding from the UK Department for International Development (DFID) to support Caribbean implementation of the EPA programme and the deepening of the Caribbean Single Market and Economy (CSME). The fund was motivated by the commitment of the United Kingdom to provide a greater flow of development funds for the Caribbean. The CDB manages the fund from the stage of application to the completion of the project. The fund has so far dispensed US$6.06 million. Table 6.7 provides some relevant details regarding the distributed funds.

6.9 AfT and Regional Integration

In December 2008, the WTO and OECD circulated self-assessment, revised and more user-friendly questionnaires to donors and partner countries regarding AfT. These questionnaires were used by donor economies to help them identify from partner countries, priority areas that would help them better integrate and participate in the developing world. The WTO–OECD partner country questionnaire was completed by fourteen Caribbean economies. Table 6.8 drawn from

Table 6.7 CARTFund approved projects

No.	Approval Date	Country	Grant Recipient	Project Title	CARTFund Resources Approved US$
1	4 September 2009	Regional	CARICOM Secretariat	Support for the Establishment of a Unit to Facilitate Implementation of the CARIFORUM EC Economic Partnership Agreement (EPA) in the Caribbean Community (CARICOM) Secretariat	1,647,265
2	4 September 2009	Guyana	Government of Guyana	Single Window Automated Processing Systems (SWAPS) for Trade Transactions in Guyana	874,500
3	4 September 2009	Guyana	Government of Guyana	Establishment of the Competition and Consumer Protection Commission of Guyana	746,225
4	18 December 2010	Regional	Caribbean Export Development Agency	Processed Food Sector Development: The Specialty Food Industry of the CARIFORUM Member States	1,094,082
5	18 December 2010	Regional	Caribbean Export Development Agency	Development and Promotion of the Caribbean Health and Wellness Tourism Sector	659,887
6	18 December 2010	Regional	Caribbean Hotel and Tourism Association	EPA Manual and Awareness Building Programme for the Caribbean Tourism Sector	108,879
7	18 December 2010	Barbados	Barbados Private Sector Association	Barbados Private Sector Project Proposal Hub	190,655
8	18 December 2010	Barbados	Barbados Private Sector Association	Barbados Private Sector Communication Enhancement Project	170,725
9	18 December 2010	Antigua & Barbuda	Government of Antigua & Barbuda	Support for the Establishment of a Unit to Facilitate Implementation of the CARIFORUM–EC Economic Partnership Agreement, Antigua & Barbuda	363,361
10	18 December 2010	Grenada	Grenada Hotel and Tourism Association	CARIBCERT – Grenada	288,115
11	10 May 2010	Dominica	Government of Dominica	Implementation of the Dominica National Export Strategy	561,780
12	10 May 2010	Dominica	Government of Dominica	Dominica Coalition of Service Industries	347,667
13	10 May 2010	Regional	CARICOM Development Fund	CARICOM Development Fund Capacity Development Project	500,000
14	10 May 2010	Jamaica	The Private Sector Organization of Jamaica	Improving CARICOM Market Access for Jamaican Goods and Services	217,389
Total					7,770,530

Source: CARICOM Secretariat (www.CARICOM.org).

Table 6.8 AfT flows in Latin America and the Caribbean by sub-region

	Commitments US$ Millions		Disbursements US$ Millions	AFT as % of Total Sector Allocable
	2002–2005	2007	2007	2007
Antigua & Barbuda	2.10	0.20	0.20	15.40
Bahamas	0.00	0.00	0.00	0.00
Barbados	0.40	15.20	0.00	77.30
Belize	9.40	3.10	4.50	16.20
Dominica	12.30	6.30	10.30	42.60
Grenada	6.40	0.20	0.60	7.40
Guyana	40.70	94.80	9.80	38.60
Haiti	81.60	54.50	48.50	12.20
Jamaica	33.80	50.80	40.50	50.70
St Kitts & Nevis	1.40	0.00	0.60	0.00
St Lucia	7.50	8.90	5.80	45.40
St Vincent & the Grenadines	4.40	7.80	9.10	26.50
Suriname	23.00	21.80	26.70	46.60
Trinidad & Tobago	15.40	11.50	3.60	71.40

Source: OECD/WTO (2009).

OECD/WTO (2009) shows the AfT flows to the Caribbean region. In 2007, this amounted to US$160.2 million. There is a wide degree of variation in the AfT received by these various states, thus Haiti, Jamaica and Suriname received US$48.5 million, US$40.5 million and US$26.7 million in disbursements, respectively, in AfT in 2007.

In accordance with the classifications of the responses in the WTO–OECD partner country questionnaire, table 6.9 illustrates the national development plans of CARICOM economies. CARICOM member states such as Dominica, St Kitts and Nevis, St Lucia, St Vincent and the Grenadines, Suriname, and Trinidad and Tobago received in excess of 80 per cent of their AfT in productive capacity. Haiti, Jamaica and Dominica received more aid towards economic infrastructure as opposed to productive capacity in 2007.

According to table 6.10, the main AfT priority area is competitiveness followed export diversification and trade facilitation. These priority areas were determined by the responses of the islands to the AfT questionnaire sent out by the World Trade Organization. This is followed by trade policy analysis, export diversification, and regional integration (AfT in Latin America and the Caribbean).

Within CARICOM, the National Export Strategy in Grenada was singled out as an AfT process that provided good results. This is an inter-sectoral and inter-ministerial strategy to promote Grenadian exports.[62] In St Kitts and Nevis, the Trade Facilitation and Capacity Building Project was cited by OECD/WTO (2009) as a good project that helped to remove bottlenecks and impediments in the supply chain of St Kitts and Nevis. For St Lucia, it was noted that their Bureau of Standards established via an AfT grant, was critical in helping agroprocessors and other companies in meeting international standards. In Guyana, the establishment of the Guyana Revenue

Table 6.9 AfT by category to Caribbean countries' commitments, US$ million, constant 2007 prices

	Trade Policy and Regulations		Economic Infrastructure		Building Productive Capacity		Trade Related Adjustment	Total	
	2002–2005	2007	2002–2005	2007	2002–2005	2007		2002–2005	2007
Antigua & Barbuda	0.00	0.00	0.00	0.00	2.10	0.20	0.00	2.10	0.20
Bahamas	0.00	0.00	0.00	0.00	0.00	0.00	0.00	0.00	0.00
Barbados	0.00	0.00	0.00	0.00	0.40	15.20	0.00	0.40	15.20
Belize	0.00	0.00	0.10	0.00	9.20	3.10	0.00	9.40	3.10
Cuba	0.10	0.00	1.40	0.70	7.40	7.60	0.00	8.80	8.30
Dominica	0.00	0.00	6.20	6.00	6.10	0.20	0.00	12.30	6.30
Grenada	0.00	0.00	1.90	0.10	4.50	0.10	0.00	6.40	0.20
Guyana	0.40	0.80	31.80	24.30	8.40	69.60	0.00	40.70	94.80
Haiti	0.00	1.40	32.80	36.60	48.70	23.70	0.00	81.60	54.50
Jamaica	1.50	0.40	9.30	28.70	23.00	21.60	0.00	33.80	50.80
St Kitts & Nevis	0.00	0.00	0.00	0.00	1.40	0.00	0.00	1.40	0.00
St Lucia	0.00	0.80	3.80	0.30	3.60	7.10	0.80	7.50	8.90
St Vincent & the Grenadines	0.00	0.20	0.00	0.00	4.40	7.50	0.20	4.40	7.80
Suriname	0.00	0.00	11.30	7.40	11.70	14.40	0.00	23.00	21.80
Trinidad & Tobago	0.30	0.00	0.70	0.00	14.30	11.50	0.00	15.40	11.50

Source: OECD/WTO (2009).

Authority and the National Procurement and Trader Administration Board has helped to promote trade, and established through AfT assistance. When asked to identify areas in which the effectiveness and implementation of AfT could be improved the areas identified in the table 6.11 were listed as priority areas.

6.10 The Way Forward: Getting More Out of AfT in CARICOM

CARICOM ministers at the seventh WTO ministerial conference (2009) argued that the fast tracking of AfT programmes was of particular significance to CARICOM economies in light of the erosion of long standing preferential agreements. Ministers expressed the opinion that CARICOM countries are not receiving a fair proportion of AfT, as they are not perceived as being poor economies. This chapter recommends the following:

1. CARICOM economies when requesting AfT should look for programmes which address their trading capacity. Specifically, this would include focusing on avenues to improve

Table 6.10: AfT priority areas for Caribbean countries

	Priority 1	Priority 2	Priority 3
Antigua & Barbuda	Trade policy analysis	Competitiveness	Network infrastructure
Bahamas	Trade policy analysis	Value chains	Export diversification
Barbados	Competitiveness	Trade policy analysis	Regional integration
Belize	Trade facilitation	Export diversification	Regional integration
Dominica	Competitiveness	Regional integration	Trade policy analysis
Grenada	Export diversification	Trade policy analysis	Competitiveness
Guyana	Network infrastructure	Competitiveness	Export diversification
Jamaica	Network infrastructure	Competitiveness	Export diversification
St Kitts & Nevis	Competitiveness		
St Lucia	Adjustment costs	Other transport	Competitiveness and export diversification
St Vincent & the Grenadines	Competitiveness	Network infrastructure	Regional integration
Suriname	Trade policy analysis	Regional integration	Network infrastructure
Trinidad & Tobago	Export diversification	Competitiveness	Regional integration

Source: OECD/WTO (2009).

their trade-related infrastructure and their trade infrastructure such as roads, ports, bridges and so on.

2. CARICOM economies should lobby aid donors and negotiate at relevant new avenues such as the pending CARICOM-Canada free trade agreement for improved disbursement conditions of AfT flows. The OECD and WTO (2009, 54) noted that disbursements generally lag behind in commitments since the latter are multi-year in nature. In particular, investment projects have the longest implementation time frame, usually lasting five to six years. There are several reasons why some commitments do not translate into disbursements:

> For instance, a change of government in a partner country often leads to a change in priorities. Reassigning existing commitments to newly established priorities takes time to negotiate with donors, and will very likely extend disbursement schedules. Furthermore, the requirements for the release of some donor funds have proven to be burdensome, resulting in very low disbursement rates for these programmes. Finally, numerous delays in disbursements are related to the low absorption capacity of partner countries OECD and WTO. (WTO 2009, 54)

While this may be true, slow disbursements can undervalue the adjustment process in developing economies including those that are small and vulnerable.

3. Cali and te Velde (2009) have also argued it would be desirable that donors organize their trade-related initiatives to cater for a longer time frame and encourage a greater level of involvement from the recipient countries and stakeholders. This approach would result in a greater level of ownership of AfT resources and increased predictability.

Table 6.11 Priority areas for effective aid for trade investments

	Antigua & Barbuda	Bahamas	Barbados	Belize	Dominica	Dominican Republic	Grenada	Guyana	Jamaica	St Kitts & Nevis	St Lucia	St Vincent & the Grenadines	Suriname	Trinidad & Tobago
Greater say in design of AFT		x	x	x	x	x	x				x			
Stronger donor focus on local capacity development	x		x			x	x	x	x	x		x	x	
Better predictability of AFT funding		x	x	x	x	x	x	x	x		x			x
More extensive use of budget support	x							x	x		x	x		
More regular joint-donor implementation actions			x											
More harmonized reporting requirements		x								x				x
More frequent joint donor implementation efforts	x				x									
More systematic use of joint donor-partner monitoring/evaluation												x		
Other priorities			x											

Source: OECD/WTO (2009).

4. CARICOM economies should lobby for a greater amount of AfT for trade facilitation as trade facilitation has real benefits for reducing the cost of trade.
5. AfT helps to improve economic infrastructure; one of the most direct effects of engaging in international trade is the reduction in production costs, which leads to improved infrastructure. Improving infrastructure by reducing water shortages, electricity outages and bad roads can result in a shift from private resources to more productive sectors, thus shifting from non-tradables to tradables or from agriculture to manufacturing and services. Another advantage of improved infrastructure is that it facilitates the movement of people and goods which can result in higher investments in the rural sectors and greater diversification of the agricultural sector in the medium term.

Many studies, particularly in Africa, have been done showing the importance of good infrastructure on trade and export performance (Iwanow and Kirkpatrick 2008; Freund and Rocha 2010; Rippel 2011; Portugal-Perez and Wilson 2012). The African Development Bank in the late 1990s found that freight charges on exports as a percentage of cost, insurance and freight (CIF) value for countries of the region to the United States were around 20 per cent higher than similar products in other low-income countries. Another study by Yoshino (2008) found that poor quality public infrastructure, in terms of the average number of days per year for which firms experience disruptions in electricity, had an adverse effect on exports in sub-Saharan Africa. Yoshino noted that Rwanda farmers only received 20 per cent of the price of their coffee and the other 80 per cent disappeared into the cost of poor roads and red tape between Rwanda and Kenya (Naudé and Matthee 2007). The WTO (2001, para 57) notes that "Aid for Trade should aim to help developing countries, particularly LDCs, to build the supply-side capacity and trade-related infrastructure that they need to assist them to implement and benefit from WTO agreements and more broadly to expand their trade".

The international donors, both at the multilateral and country level, could collaborate more with CARICOM economies to identify the relevant areas in which AfT would be most useful. As Cali and te Velde (2009, 9) noted "aid seems to work better in certain sectors in SVEs, such as tourism and minerals". Many Caribbean islands such as Trinidad and Tobago, Saint Lucia, Jamaica, Belize and Grenada have already completed or are in the process of completing national export strategies using the template provided by the International Trade Centre. The use of these strategies will allow for a more targeted approach to AfT and facilitate the monitoring and measurement of the impact of the aid on trade.

Enhanced AfT initiatives for the purpose of furthering market access opportunities for CARICOM is a policy option which can serve to strengthen the economic relations between CARICOM and its major extra-regional trading partners. This option was mainly derived from facts such as the United States (30.43 per cent) and the European Communities (38.22 per cent) are the largest contributors to AfT funds globally. Therefore, it is essential that AfT be well targeted in an attempt to assist the region to overcome its underdeveloped trade-related infrastructure. The need for AfT funds are thus critical given that Caribbean economies are fragile with production structures that are highly vulnerable and largely characterized by a polarization in its range of export items (Lord 2011).

Jamaica's export sector has long been recognized as having significant earning potential; however, openness and market access alone were not sufficient factors for expanding trade. Where there has been greater market access, this economy has been faced with a limited capacity to produce for trade. Therefore, Jamaica has sought AfT funding from the Inter-American Development Bank in an attempt to sustainably develop its existing inadequate infrastructure, its weak facilitating framework and non-modernized sanitary and phyto-sanitary regime. According to Baugh (2011, 3):

> For Jamaica, Aid for Trade is an essential element that can strengthen our ability to adjust to changes in the trading environment, build productive capacity and enhance our competitiveness in the production of goods and services, with a resultant increase in exports [however] Aid for Trade is predicated on the understanding that improved market access opportunities do not automatically translate into increased investment, production and exporters penetrating global markets.

In this regard, three pillars have been identified as AfT targeted areas that can potentially spur some substantial market access opportunities in the medium to longer term. These areas included network infrastructure, competitiveness, export diversification, and trade development should be aggressively pursued and promoted by CARICOM member states.

6.11 Conclusion

Many economists agree that there are many advantages of trade liberalization; most notably, it can help to efficiently allocate scarce factors of production and increase output levels. There are five main ways in which trade impacts on innovation within an economy: these include increased competition, enhanced technological transfer, greater economies of scale, globalization of value chains and the use of intellectual property rights. However, while trade liberalization offers many significant opportunities for countries, it does not come without associated costs. Free trade alone is not sufficient to enhance economic growth levels and the benefits can take a long time to be realized.

In order to reform the world trading system, the Uruguay Round of Multilateral Trade Negotiations was initiated in 1986. This served to bring about substantial progress in market access by developed as well as developing countries. The Doha Development Round was also initiated to deal with the issues of preferential treatment and reciprocity. These preferences would be gradually removed as free trade becomes the focus. This will affect CARCIOM countries directly as the region's exports are generally uncompetitive and dependent on preferential agreements.

With the realization that developing countries cannot adequately deal with the effects of the Doha discussions and would require assistance to dampen the effects and enhance their trading capacity, the AfT initiative was launched. The AfT initiative aims to lower the cost of production and enhance productivity in low-income countries.

Within the Caribbean region, there are a number of factors which hinder the islands from improving their growth and export performance. Among these are (1) trade policy and regulation, (2) trade development, (3) building productivity capacity and (4) trade-related infrastructure and adjustment, among others. By improving trade facilitation, as discussed in the Doha negotiations, there will be a smoother and easier movement of goods within a liberalized environment.

There is a need for a greater flow of AfT programmes for trade facilitation in the Caribbean. However, CARICOM countries do not have the adequate and necessary conditions to meet the various adjustment costs accompanying trade liberalization, by themselves. Slow and low growth rates, high and rising public sector debt as well as fiscal imbalances are some of the challenges faced by these economies.

The CARTFund was initiated to help Caribbean economies deepen the integration movement via CSME in the region, as well as support the implementation of the EPA in the region. The inherent characteristics of CARICOM economies, as small island developing states, combine to result in the cost of business being higher than elsewhere. Therefore, the importance and necessity for a greater amount AfT facilitation cannot be underscored.

7 | Strengthening CARICOM Regional Integration in the Twenty-First Century
Key Studies and Their Recommendations

7.1 Introduction

Recognizing the deteriorating economic performance of CARICOM member states, several important studies identifying the urgency for a change in policy action among CARICOM member states over time have been undertaken.

This chapter provides a synthesis of six reports, namely the Compton Bourne report, the OECS Development Strategy report, the Bonnick report, the Caribbean Trade and Adjustment Group (CTAG) report, the World Bank report and the Regional Transformation Task Force (RTTF) report. Some of these reports were written more than ten years ago and so where possible the data sets relevant to the arguments made in these policy reports are updated.

7.2 Bourne Report (1988)

The Caribbean Community Secretariat together with the Commonwealth Secretariat, commissioned in November 1986, a study on the medium to long-term prospects of the Caribbean economy. The mandate required that a general study be conducted on the development prospects of CARICOM within the context of the structural changes taking place in the global environment. This study was led by Compton Bourne from the University of the West Indies. In addition, several unnamed short-term consultants were credited with inputs on various aspects of this exercise. The document, as designed, was targeted at professional economists and policy advisors. The idea being that this target audience would facilitate a filtering down of the information to policymakers in particular. For the rest of this section, the study is referred to as the Bourne report.

The Bourne report provides some foundational information for the development of the CARICOM economy by the year 2015. Bourne undertook an extensive discussion of the various prospects and problems facing the Caribbean and summarized his policy prescriptions under a number of subheadings, including the following:

1. Growth opportunities
2. Employment
3. Finance
4. Foreign trade
5. Production

Growth opportunities: The Bourne report suggested that CARICOM economies needed to align themselves with the production of commodities in greater demand by the global community. In order to penetrate export markets for these new commodities, CARICOM economies needed to improve their external competitiveness and through a deliberate process of intervention, seek new export items on the upswing of the international product cycle. In this regard, table 7.1 shows the top ten exports of goods and services from the CARICOM region. Notably, the data shows that the top merchandise exports from the CARICOM region is made up of minerals and other primary products while transportation, travel and communication comprise the main service exports.

At the same time, he argued that CARICOM economies will need to improve on their export marketing thrust and the various processes involved in financing new exports. Bourne noted that international demand for services demonstrates an upward trend and emphasized that some growth opportunities existed in tourism as well as in a few other services. He added that tourism services have emerged as having "demonstrable comparative advantage" in many Caribbean countries. Knowledge-intensive services demonstrating this feature for the region included law,

Table 7.1 CARICOM's top ten exports (merchandise goods and services), 2011

Merchandise Goods	Value US$	Services	Value US$
Mineral fuels, oils, distillation products, etc.	12,373,134	Transportation	7,226,258
Inorganic chemicals, precious metal compound, isotopes	3,206,456	Travel	5,392,593
Commodities not elsewhere specified	2,114,919	Communication	908,545
Organic chemicals	1,968,659	Construction	243,795
Iron and steel	1,588,806	Insurance	217,546
Fertilizers	758,936	Financial	166,032
Articles of apparel, accessories, knit or crochet	621,386	Computer and info services	47,712
Beverages, spirits and vinegar	611,973	Royalties and licence fees	39,351
Pearls, precious stones, metals, coins, etc.	394,329	Other business services	37,304
Ores, slag and ash	328,479	Personal, recreational and cultural services	14,830

Source: Trade Map (2014).

medicine, higher education and engineering design and construction. Bourne argued that for these four services, competitive advantage existed or can be readily developed through the promotion of private initiatives, dispensing of incentives and the support of institutional facilities.

Bourne advanced that CARICOM should also seek out markets and new trading opportunities in the Pacific Rim, given its emergence as a new international growth centre. He added that Latin American countries had also displayed longer-term growth prospects. These two trends presented scope for the Caribbean region to widen and deepen links with these blocs of economies. This report then argued that CARICOM member states should engage in some degree of technological leap as "new and improved technologies and their increasing accessibility make it possible for the Commonwealth Caribbean to significantly upgrade its own production technology" (p. xxxix). At the same time though, this report noted that attention should not altogether be diverted away from the need to promote local technological capabilities. Specifically, the report suggested that "even where such 'leapfrogging' is possible, concerted efforts need to be made to promote the sustained development and enhancement of local technological capabilities" (p. xxxix). Bourne proposed that incentives be offered to enterprises for research and technology, and innovation and adaptation. He also referred to models of technology used in Western Europe, which facilitate regional cooperation.

Employment: This report recognizes the need to increase the supply of jobs in the region given the expected growth of the population over the medium term period. Table 7.2 shows the collective population of CARICOM's member states. It can be observed that CARICOM's population has grown more than twofold over the last five decades (obviously this is also in part due to the addition of new members as the integration arrangement widened).

Emigration has a significant influence on the labour markets within CARICOM. This report argued that opportunities formerly available through emigration will decrease, as developed economies preserve their own domestic labour markets. Table 7.3 illustrates the number of educated people who have migrated from the English-speaking Caribbean between 1990 and 2000. From this table, it is evident that a significant proportion of migrants have tertiary-level education, confirming that the Caribbean diaspora is made up of highly skilled and educated people.

Bourne argued that as the more advanced economies mature, the size of their service sectors will expand and so the type of emigration opportunities that may be available to CARICOM

Table 7.2 CARICOM population, 1960–2012

Year	Total
1960	8,056,261
1970	9,621,784
1980	11,152,700
1990	13,072,695
2000	15,009,614
2010	16,778,036
2012	17,138,233

Source: World Development Indicators (2014).

Table 7.3 Migration from the Caribbean by education level, 1990 and 2000

	Primary		Secondary		Tertiary		Overall	
	1990	2000	1990	2000	1990	2000	1990	2000
Antigua & Barbuda	7.00	6.00	31.70	35.90	65.30	70.90	27.60	36.70
Bahamas	3.70	1.50	11.70	12.10	38.30	36.40	11.00	12.10
Barbados	14.10	9.90	24.80	24.30	63.50	61.40	26.40	27.80
Belize	5.00	3.60	48.60	49.20	62.60	51.00	22.80	18.40
Dominica	16.60	8.00	62.10	60.60	58.90	58.90	32.00	32.10
Grenada	7.50	9.90	61.10	69.50	68.80	66.70	30.50	40.10
Guyana	10.90	13.70	30.60	34.10	89.20	85.90	28.00	34.50
Jamaica	11.00	8.30	28.90	30.00	84.10	82.50	25.60	29.00
St Kitts & Nevis	10.80	10.30	21.40	37.10	89.90	71.80	28.90	38.50
St Lucia	1.90	2.60	46.80	32.10	80.40	36.00	11.60	14.00
St Vincent & the Grenadines	5.90	6.30	56.70	53.40	89.80	56.80	22.40	28.00
Suriname	15.70	17.50	54.00	43.90	92.00	89.90	42.10	43.30
Trinidad & Tobago	5.70	6.10	19.30	20.60	77.20	78.40	18.90	23.70

Note: By country of birth, figures represent percentages.

Source: International Monetary Fund (IMF) (2014).

workers may become progressively more knowledge intensive. This idea is partly illustrated in table 7.4 which shows that the services sector's contribution to GDP (where the knowledge sector activities arise) has increased for Canada, United States and the United Kingdom over the period 1970–2012, and these are the economies where CARICOM nationals migrate to most frequently.

Table 7.4 Services, value added (% of GDP), 1970–2012

	Canada	United Kingdom	United States
1970	60.20	55.04	61.22
1975	59.09	58.33	62.69
1980	58.80	57.17	63.57
1985	61.43	60.00	66.70
1990	65.83	64.38	70.05
1995	66.37	67.59	72.08
2000	64.52	71.67	75.37
2005	65.80	76.04	76.60
2010	66.46	77.66	79.02
2011	67.32	78.38	78.60
2012	68.16	78.83	79.21

Source: World Bank Development Indicators (2014).

In this type of macroeconomic environment, Bourne noted that it is necessary for CARICOM economies to strive hard to improve their export revenues faster than their import demand so as to preserve and even improve on the inflow of pertinent capital goods.

Bourne also argued that CARICOM economies should undertake longer term strategic planning, which caters for a greater degree of local content usage in the production process. To facilitate this thrust, the Bourne report noted that local and regional R&D efforts would have to widen. As it stands, the R&D effort in the region is at best rudimentary and fragmented. Comparing Trinidad and Tobago with Singapore, table 7.5 shows that R&D expenditure as a percentage of GDP for Trinidad and Tobago is far below that of Singapore and in fact, for Trinidad and Tobago, this trend has been declining while for Singapore, R&D expenditure as a percentage of GDP has almost doubled from 1996 to 2012.

Bourne recognized that these small highly open developing economies imported a considerable amount of goods and services, and thus recommended that when the price of imported goods increased, all attempts should be made to control the growth of domestic factor prices, to preserve the general level of price competitiveness of domestic output. An improvement in domestic competitiveness in turn can lead to an improvement in employment conditions in the CARICOM region.

Recognizing the role of technological competitiveness, the Bourne report argued that CARICOM economies needed to facilitate an improvement in the technological capabilities of the region by providing fiscal and other types of financial assistance to encourage domestic firms to improve on their degree of technological deployment.

Table 7.5 Research and development expenditure (% of GDP), 1996–2012

	Trinidad & Tobago	Singapore
1996	0.10	1.34
1997	0.12	1.43
1998	0.13	1.75
1999	0.12	1.85
2000	0.13	1.85
2001	0.12	2.06
2002	0.13	2.10
2003	0.11	2.05
2004	0.11	2.13
2005	0.09	2.19
2006	0.06	2.16
2007	0.05	2.36
2008	0.03	2.64
2009	0.06	2.20
2010	0.05	2.05
2011	0.04	2.23
2012	–	2.10

Source: World Development Indicators (2014).

The report also emphasized that an important part of the way forward involved the development of the human capital fabric of the region. Human capital, the report noted, is not only necessary for the absorption of technology but also for its adaptation. In this regard, table 7.6 shows the Caribbean Examination Council (CXC) pass rates in mathematics and English language by Caribbean country for the period 1995–2013. CXC does not have a pass/fail system but refer to acceptable grades which are usually grades 1–3. To calculate the pass rates, the number of candidates attaining grades 1 through 3 is summed and a percentage taken using the total number of registered candidates that wrote the exam, in each case. The data reveals that subsequent to 1996, several countries recorded significant declines in the pass rate for mathematics. In particular, Grenada recorded a 37.6 per cent contraction in 1997 relative to its 1996 rate. Significant declines between 1996 and 1997 were reported by Guyana (20.4 per cent) and St Lucia (15.4 per cent). By 2013, the trends were even worst, as all countries experienced tremendous declines from their 1995 pass rates.

Pass rates for English language were observably high for all countries between 1995 and 1996. Contractions were recorded for the majority of countries thereafter; however, by 2001, a reversion occurred with pass rates steadily climbing. For the full data period, Guyana was the only country to report an increase in the pass rate by 24.6 per cent. Montserrat, St Kitts and Nevis, St Vincent and the Grenadines, Grenada, and St Lucia recorded the largest declines in pass rates for English by 53.2 per cent, 28.2 per cent, 27.7 per cent, 24.8 per cent and 24.2 per cent, respectively.

Finance: Table 7.7 shows the gross national savings as a per cent of GDP in CARICOM economies for selected years. Economies such as Dominica and Grenada reported negative levels of gross national savings for a number of consecutive years.[63] The data also shows that the highest gross national savings level as a per cent of GDP among CARICOM economies for these years occurred in Trinidad and Tobago in 2006, while Grenada realized the lowest amount in 2012.

The Bourne report infers that in order to improve the growth performance of the CARICOM economies, it is necessary to increase the extent of capital deployed and also to increase the domestic savings rate in CARICOM. The report noted that an important part of the developmental process requires the availability of finance on which firms can draw upon for investment purposes. It identified the following broad set of policy measures to assist in the expansion of the amount of financial flows:

1. striking the right balance between profits and labour incomes as corporate savings rates are generally in excess of personal savings rates;
2. designing a system of tax subsidies to transfer incomes towards enterprises away from individuals.

The report acknowledges that any attempt to improve the financial transformation coefficient region must include financial instrument innovation. This is necessary to

1. increase the amount of risk bearing in the financial sector;
2. increase the overall liquidity of financial assets;
3. improve the overall efficiency of financial institutions.

Table 7.6 CXC pass rates in mathematics and English language by country (%), 1995–2013

	TTO	BRB	GUY	JAM	ATG	BLZ	DOM	GRD	MONT	LCA	KNA	VCT	SUR
	English A pass rates												
1995	65.40	78.00	36.10	60.10	85.00	76.50	73.90	71.50	97.60	77.10	84.50	70.30	–
1996	72.30	81.40	55.20	71.70	86.40	82.60	80.20	80.00	91.90	87.20	83.50	82.60	–
2000	44.90	50.90	23.40	40.60	56.90	54.60	62.70	38.20	77.10	52.70	53.20	57.20	35.70
2005	54.00	63.10	56.10	50.70	69.20	63.80	68.00	50.50	78.40	59.20	62.30	59.10	42.90
2010	55.50	69.20	57.80	61.80	73.60	81.10	73.70	59.00	74.10	66.90	70.70	66.30	40.90
2011	57.80	75.50	59.60	61.00	77.30	81.30	75.00	62.80	85.40	67.10	73.30	63.40	61.10
2012	42.00	56.10	36.10	44.30	56.40	60.50	54.80	40.20	50.70	49.60	47.40	43.00	18.20
2013	52.50	65.60	45.00	54.50	67.10	71.50	67.80	53.70	45.60	58.40	60.60	50.80	53.30
	Mathematics pass rates												
1995	36.70	55.10	28.50	43.20	55.70	62.30	51.50	53.70	60.20	52.80	50.10	54.90	–
1996	38.60	55.80	31.40	39.90	41.40	58.30	49.30	60.60	56.50	47.60	42.50	50.80	–
2000	31.10	38.20	23.00	30.10	31.70	49.10	42.10	23.60	38.90	36.50	27.10	31.50	–
2005	38.00	41.90	30.10	31.80	38.90	49.40	37.80	29.50	50.00	37.10	41.10	32.40	16.70
2010	34.30	42.50	33.40	36.30	33.90	56.00	36.10	34.80	41.30	38.30	40.10	30.60	11.10
2011	30.90	37.80	29.40	30.70	26.80	50.20	32.50	27.80	31.00	27.00	35.80	24.30	5.30
2012	31.40	37.30	28.70	29.50	25.40	43.50	25.50	26.10	37.00	27.70	37.20	24.20	35.70
2013	33.60	39.20	28.30	31.90	25.70	41.10	31.00	31.90	33.80	29.00	37.60	23.90	45.50

Note: TTO, Trinidad and Tobago; BRB, Barbados; GUY, Guyana; JAM, Jamaica; ATG, Antigua and Barbuda; BLZ, Belize; DOM, Dominica; GRD, Grenada; MONT, Montserrat; LCA, St Lucia; KNA, St Kitts and Nevis; VCT, St Vincent and the Grenadines; SUR, Suriname.

Source: CXC Headquarters (2013).

Table 7.7 Gross national savings (% of GDP), 1990–2012

Country	1990	1995	2000	2005	2006	2007	2008	2009	2010	2011	2012
Antigua & Barbuda	25.30	31.15	24.03	12.17	15.38	9.21	13.18	25.84	21.52	20.47	24.91
Bahamas	39.73	36.03	10.19	21.87	18.62	19.81	18.81	15.99	13.97	11.95	8.41
Belize	33.28	22.46	22.94	26.57	13.47	13.60	12.61	14.04	15.77	15.77	–
Barbados	13.39	9.91	12.34	7.29	9.26	11.76	6.78	8.29	8.39	–	–
Dominica	15.36	15.31	2.09	−0.80	6.54	−1.20	−5.98	−1.63	4.24	4.27	10.79
Grenada	17.37	22.95	20.84	18.36	3.15	0.58	−2.45	−0.52	−7.03	−6.00	−10.15
Guyana	NA	23.56	8.45	8.00	15.42	10.87	7.54	15.46	14.51	9.54	11.09
Jamaica	18.94	24.71	16.77	15.18	17.48	15.53	6.26	13.04	13.43	8.44	8.28
St Kitts & Nevis	25.74	26.46	26.74	32.39	31.10	30.51	18.58	18.75	18.06	21.83	18.35
St Lucia	9.05	13.25	14.87	15.44	7.72	−2.29	2.09	16.42	17.44	13.75	12.96
Suriname	19.81	12.01	−1.51	9.10	–	–	–	–	–	–	–
Trinidad & Tobago	21.46	26.51	26.64	52.57	55.03	36.71	42.62	–	–	–	–

Source: World Development Indicators (2014).

The Bourne report also noted that if the capital markets of member states are both nationalized and regionalized within the context of an appropriate set of support policies, then this should facilitate an improvement in international and regional funds to finance domestic investment.

This continues with the suggestion that there is need to consider the relationship between the private and public sector, as concerns the provisioning of some services. This is necessary so as to help improve deteriorating fiscal conditions. In this same vein of reasoning Bourne noted that there is need to redesign the tax structure and the way taxes are administered within the region in order to improve the extent of tax compliance and overall fiscal buoyancy.

To provide proper management of international transactions, Bourne cited that it is necessary to improve the capability of the region to assess foreign and financial market transactions. Caribbean economies, the report argues, should try to turn more to rigorous and sound macroeconomic policies, a subset of which may be exchange rate policies as a basis to attract FDI.

Foreign Trade: The Caribbean trading environment is characterized by a high degree of export revenue volatility. Noting this, the report identified the necessity for

1. a greater degree of stability in the foreign exchange earnings process;
2. using a currency basket approach to maintain exchange rate stability;
3. a switch away from a narrow dependence on a few geographically concentrated markets (see table 7.8).

Table 7.9 provides evidence of the relative costs of labour in Barbados, Guyana, Jamaica and Mauritius for the year 2012. It shows that the hourly rate in Barbados is US$3.13 which is much higher than the other economies, while Mauritius experiences the lowest hourly rate (US$) of the

Table 7.8 Exports of goods and services (% of GDP): export market dependence, 1990–2011

Country	1990	1995	2000	2005	2010	2011
Antigua & Barbuda	88.95	85.30	62.90	54.42	46.13	47.74
Bahamas	54.16	49.55	44.36	45.19	40.86	43.59
Barbados	49.10	61.97	50.47	59.38	47.34	–
Belize	62.22	47.97	52.99	54.63	58.37	65.57
Dominica	54.54	49.81	44.54	35.77	35.75	34.92
Grenada	42.43	44.81	45.05	21.25	21.84	23.60
Guyana	62.71	101.21	96.08	84.62	–	–
Jamaica	48.06	50.52	–	35.29	31.31	30.91
St Kitts & Nevis	51.75	51.15	36.04	42.25	27.86	30.48
St Lucia	72.56	67.55	49.30	57.77	52.43	46.20
St Vincent & the Grenadines	65.82	51.15	45.14	36.37	26.96	26.95
Suriname	42.05	22.85	19.73	30.42	–	–
Trinidad & Tobago	45.36	53.77	59.22	65.82	58.57	–

Source: World Development Indicators (2014).

listed economies. The Bourne report identifies that part of the reason for the high costs of production, stems from inefficiencies in the scale of the plants deployed by most firms. Often times, the report noted, multiple suboptimally sized plants exist in the same industry. Significantly, the report recognized that while exchange rate policy may play a role in improving the export performance of member states, the significant reliance should be on appropriate changes in domestic factor markets and commodity markets. Part of the reason for the poor performance of the export sector is because of excessive protection and so the report argued in favour of a greater degree of trade liberalization.

Table 7.10 illustrates the level of merchandise trade as a percentage of GDP in the various CARICOM economies over a thirty-three-year period. The data suggests that from 1980 to 2012, trade as a percentage of GDP have substantially declined in most member states. Over the first decade, 1980–90, these CARICOM economies, with the exception of Antigua and Barbuda and Dominica, experienced a decline in the amount of national trade. By 2012, all economies continued to show lower levels of trade as a percentage of GDP, except Trinidad and Tobago. Over

Table 7.9 Relative costs of labour

Country	Annual (US$)	Annual PPP (Int$)	Standard Work week (hours)	Hourly (US$)	Hourly (Int$)	Per Cent of GDP per capita	Effective Time
Barbados	6500	7065	40	3.13	3.40	0.28	2012
Guyana	2056	3214	44	0.99	1.55	0.95	2013
Jamaica	3281	3844	40	1.58	1.85	0.42	2014
Mauritius	1050	1379	45	0.45	0.59	0.09	2012

Source: http://en.wikipedia.org/wiki/List_of_minimum_wages_by_country#cite_note-2.

Table 7.10 Merchandise trade (% of GDP), 1980–2012

Country	1980	1990	2000	2010	2011	2012
Antigua & Barbuda	107.21	70.49	58.27	47.09	48.16	51.58
Bahamas	636.71	88.06	41.88	41.75	48.25	54.61
Barbados	87.16	45.47	45.78	45.07	52.19	55.39
Dominica	98.14	104.01	61.95	53.99	50.92	48.99
Grenada	80.13	59.71	54.85	43.61	43.92	48.27
Guyana	126.16	143.22	150.28	100.78	112.05	112.26
Haiti	–	–	36.95	56.15	51.54	46.15
Jamaica	76.81	67.20	51.40	49.63	57.21	56.25
St Kitts & Nevis	143.75	86.68	54.97	44.68	41.70	35.85
St Lucia	136.42	100.20	52.06	72.55	68.40	71.85
St Vincent & the Grenadines	119.39	110.49	52.84	56.24	53.80	55.29
Suriname	128.07	243.11	103.68	78.37	94.07	83.80
Trinidad & Tobago	116.34	60.56	92.98	84.49	95.71	96.48

Source: World Development Indicators (2014).

the next year, trade as a percentage of GDP for Antigua and Barbuda, Dominica, St Kitts and Nevis, and St Lucia further declined, while the remaining economies showed signs of growth. This report also emphasized the significance of targeting other economies in the Western Hemisphere, with rapid economic progress. However, the report is also careful to observe that the growth of South-South trade will require a considerable amount of innovative skills, and CARICOM economies will need to improve on the relevant endowment of these skills in order to make these types of trading adjustments meaningful. Bourne argued in the report that "trade growth can be actively pursued by targeting the markets of other least developed economies, especially fast growing economies, within the Western Hemisphere. Growth of South-South trade requires careful market identification, and the exercise of innovative market skills, not yet displayed among CARICOM countries. This too is an area of critical human resource deficiency, to which urgent attention should be given" (p. 122).

Production: To increase overall output levels with regards to agriculture in the region, this report suggests that

1. Land distribution has to be effected to provide farm plots of the appropriate size, and so on, so that economic returns from farm based activity, rivals non-farm activity;
2. Establishing commodity price levels can help to influence farm incomes directly. Similar effects can be obtained by stimulating farm outputs;
3. It was also imperative to provide technical assistance and marketing assistance for the agricultural sector;
4. There was also the need for the rationalization of existing production on a region wide basis and further for a greater degree of regional training, research and development.

As concerns tourism, the Bourne report identified the need to

1. Incorporate a greater quantum of local content in preparing consumption goods for the tourism sector. One success story in this regard is Walkerswood Caribbean Foods Limited, which is a Jamaican company registered in 1978. This company aided by the Jamaica Industrial Development Corporation (JIDC) employed two persons at the time it started to sell jerk-seasoned pork locally. Since then, it has broadened its product lines to fourteen, ranging from seasoning, sauces, spices and other food products. Of its sales, approximately 80 per cent (US$4 million) is exported. Raw materials such as thyme, scallion and peppers are purchased fresh from farmers. Further, the company has established a farming and restaurant division and created in 2005 the "Walkerswood Jerk Country Tour : A Jamaican Epicurean Experience". Walkerswood employs a full-time staff of over hundred people of which fourteen local persons are employed as guides. Even further, since 2006, an estimated hundred local farmers had a guaranteed market for all their produce (CTO 2007).
2. Improve on the amount of culture specific goods provided for the tourist market, for example, cultural souvenirs, cultural clothing, and aggressively identifying and determining the size of the diaspora (table 7.11).
3. Organize and orchestrate an improved tourism marketing strategy which is cognizant of changing types of tourists. Indeed, the presence of both the US twin deficits and the

Table 7.11 The Caribbean diaspora by country of residence, 1996

Country of Residence	Countries of Emigration & Diasporic Affiliation[a]	Estimates of Population (Million)
United States	Cuban born and Cuban Americans	1.90
	Puerto Rico born and born in continental USA	2.85
	Dominican born and born in the USA	1.52
	Haitian born and born in the USA	1.52
	West Indian[b] born and born in the USA	1.14
	Sub-total	8.93
Canada	Haitian-born and born in Canada	0.18
	West Indian born and born in Canada	0.27
France	French Antillean born and born in France	0.29
Netherlands	Netherlands Antilles born and born in Netherlands	0.07
	Surinamese born and born in Netherlands	0.29
	Sub-total	0.36
United Kingdom	West Indian born and born in the UK	0.93
	Total	**9.30**

[a] Caribbean diaspora includes foreign-born and persons with one or both parents of Caribbean origin.
[b] West Indies includes Barbados, Guyana, Jamaica, Belize, Trinidad and Tobago, the Bahamas, and the Eastern Caribbean islands.

Source: Segal (1996).

Table 7.12 Tourism expenditures (BRICS), US$ billion, 2000–2012

	2000	2005	2009	2010	2012
China	13.10	21.80	43.70	54.90	102.00
Russia	8.80	17.30	20.90	26.60	42.80
Brazil	3.90	4.70	10.90	16.40	21.30[a]
India	2.70	6.20	9.30	10.60	13.70[a]

[a] It represents 2011 data.

Source: UNWTO (2013).

European Crisis in 2012 was still not enough to prevent international tourist arrivals from exceeding the billion figure marker for the first time. More specifically, there were 1.035 billion tourist arrivals, which amounted to an increase of 39 million or 4 per cent more than that of the previous year, 2011. Advanced and emerging economies accounted for 550 million and 485 million of the 1.035 billion tourist arrivals in 2012, respectively. It is expected that such growth will continue in 2013, but on a slightly slower rate between 3 per cent and 4 per cent per year to 2020 (UNWTO 2013). It was also reported that there was a strong positive correlation between tourist arrivals and receipts (UNWTO 2013).

On the expenditure side, there was also impressive growth, with the emerging markets leading the way (see table 7.12). In particular, China was first overall, with its tourists spending US$102 billion, a 37 per cent increase from 2011, thus overtaking the perennial leaders Germany (US$83.8 billion) and the United States (US$83.5 billion). Rounding out the top ten spenders were: United Kingdom, Russian Federation, France, Canada, Japan, Australia and Italy, respectively.

International tourist arrivals to the Caribbean grew by over 83 per cent from 1990 to 2012 (table 7.13), with arrivals to Trinidad and Tobago increasing twofold by 2010. Moreover, tourist expenditure in Trinidad and Tobago amounted to an estimated US$449 million in 2010, an increase of 22.6 per cent from the previous year (see table 7.14).

4. Bourne also suggests an integrated multi-product strategy for some of the services required by the local tourist industry.

7.3 OECS Report (2000)

The OECS report commenced by noting that the OECS bloc of countries is at a crossroads because of the changes in the international community. Recognizing this, the OECS Secretariat and Eastern Caribbean Central Bank were mandated by the OECS Authority at its thirty-first meeting to

Table 7.13 International tourist arrivals to the Caribbean, million, 1990–2012

	1990	1995	2000	2005	2010	2011	2012
International tourist arrivals	11.40	14.00	17.10	18.80	19.50	20.10	20.90

Source: Caribbean Tourism Organization (2014).

Table 7.14 International tourist arrivals and expenditures to Trinidad and Tobago, 1990–2010

	1990	**1995**	**2000**	**2005**	**2008**	**2009**	**2010**
International tourist arrivals	194,021	250,784	398,550	463,190	437,452	418,864	388,300
Expenditure (US$ million)	–	–	–	453.00	396.90	366.60	449.50

Source: Central Statistical Office of Trinidad and Tobago and Caribbean Tourism Organization (2014).

organize a number of consultations in the OECS member states so that civil society and other social partners could participate in the design of an OECS development strategy (hereafter ODS). In planning the ODS, inputs were drawn from a broad range of planning instruments at the official, national and regional levels. The report identifies that the OECS subset of economies have prospered despite the high number of external circumstances which make these economies vulnerable (see chapter 2: tables 2.1–2.4 for the GDP performance of OECS countries). According to Kaly and Pratt (2000) Grenada, St Kitts and Nevis, and St Vincent and the Grenadines are classed as highly vulnerable[64] while St Lucia is categorized as extremely vulnerable (see tables 7.15 and 7.16).

This prosperity was partly on account of the coincidence of a number of favourable circumstances, including the following:

1. An increase in agricultural output, because of preferential trade markets in North America and Europe. This is partly reflected in the improvement of export revenues for two main agricultural commodities (nutmeg and banana) illustrated in table 7.17. The exports of nutmegs and bananas from the OECS to the United States and Canada increased by 200 per cent and 670 per cent, respectively over the period 1991–2008.

Table 7.15 Classification of environmental vulnerability index

Extremely vulnerable	365+
Highly vulnerable	315+
Vulnerable	265+
At risk	215+
Resilient	<215

Source: Kaly and Pratt (2000).

Table 7.16 Environmental vulnerability index for selected CARICOM countries

Country	**EVI**	**Classification**
Antigua & Barbuda	307	Vulnerable
Dominica	–	–
Grenada	316	Highly vulnerable
St Kitts & Nevis	359	Highly vulnerable
St Lucia	393	Extremely vulnerable
St Vincent & the Grenadines	337	Highly vulnerable

Table 7.17 OECS nutmeg and banana exports to Canada and the United States, US$ 000s, 1995–2012

	Nutmeg[a] Exports from OECS		Banana Exports from OECS	
	Canada	**USA**	**Canada**	**USA**
1995	247.93	310.33	8.81	42.88
2000	825.65	2626.54	9.06	22.72
2005	696.35	1292.33	3.00	5.23
2010	3.27	–	0.04	9.64
2011	5.78	–	0.02	2.11
2012	3.45	0.04	–	2.62

[a]Nutmeg represented by SITC 07524, Banana represented by SITC 0513.

Source: World Integrated Trade Solution (WITS) (2014).

However, in the post 2008 period there was a sharp decline in the exports of these two commodities from the OECS which were caused by several factors, such as the end of preferences in the EU market and greater price competition from other countries. In addition, nutmeg, banana and cocoa plantations in Grenada were destroyed by Hurricane Ivan in 2004. In 2005, Hurricane Emily hampered efforts to rebuild the industry. Further, in 2007, Hurricane Dean obliterated 80 per cent to 100 per cent of the banana crop in St Lucia, Martinique, Dominica and Guadeloupe (Mohan and Strobl 2012).

2. The OECS countries have had stable nominal exchange rates as illustrated in the table 7.18. This stable exchange rate system reduces risks associated with international trade (transactions), reduces inflationary pressures and encouraged foreign investments.

3. Favourable tourism arrival traffic in part has also helped to ramp up increases in growth within this small regional bloc. Table 7.19 shows that the number of international tourist arrivals has increased for all of the listed OECS economies over the period 1995–2012. St Lucia experienced the largest increase in international tourist arrivals from 231,000 in 1995 to 307,000 in 2012, an increase of 33 per cent.

4. Greater economic integration among OECS membership and also a stronger degree of integration of the OECS subset of economies within CARICOM.

5. Improved fiscal conditions in most of these states founded on strong macroeconomic policies.

6. A large amount of concessionary financing assistance.

Table 7.18 Official exchange rate (LCU per US$, period average), 1980–2012

	1980	**1990**	**2000**	**2010**	**2011**	**2012**
Antigua & Barbuda	2.70	2.70	2.70	2.70	2.70	2.70
Dominica	2.70	2.70	2.70	2.70	2.70	2.70
Grenada	2.70	2.70	2.70	2.70	2.70	2.70
St Kitts & Nevis	2.70	2.70	2.70	2.70	2.70	2.70
St Lucia	2.70	2.70	2.70	2.70	2.70	2.70

Source: World Development Indicators (2014).

Table 7.19 International tourist arrivals, 000s, 1995–2012

	Antigua & Barbuda	Dominica	Grenada	St Kitts & Nevis	St Lucia	St Vincent & the Grenadines
1995	220	60	108	79	231	60
2000	207	70	129	73	270	73
2005	245	79	99	141	318	96
2010	230	77	110	92	306	72
2011	241	76	118	–	312	74
2012	247	79	116	104	307	74
% change 1995–2012	12	32	7	32	33	23

Source: World Development Indicators (2014).

Even so, the report noted that the OECS economies contracted during the 1990s, principally because of a number of structural flaws, which included the following:

1. These economies lacked resilience. They did not have the ability to regain economic momentum after a downturn in the economy.
2. The report highlighted the lack of diversification in these economies. Indeed, the data in table 7.20 shows that the top ten exports from the OECS countries accounted for more than 75 per cent of the group's total exports over the period 1981–2012.
3. The report emphasized that these economies were not internationally competitive.
4. A significant amount of the growth in these economies is founded on public sector expenditures. Government expenditure makes up more than 10 per cent of GDP in each economy for any given year. The OECS countries (with the exception of St Kitts and Nevis) generally have a greater share of government expenditure in GDP among the listed countries in table 7.21. Note though there is some indication that the share of government expenditure in GDP has declined over the period 1980–2011.
5. The ODS report emphasized that the external sector's viability was conditioned by a variety of trading preferences.
6. These countries exported to a fix bloc of economies.
7. The current account balances of these economies deteriorated as their import demand increased alongside waning export performance (see chapter 2: table 2.7).
8. The private sector within these economies did not display a significant amount of efficiency and dynamism.

The vision of the ODS (formed via a series of public consultations) includes:

1. The attainment of sustainable human development based on the widest degree of participation by the people using their own resources - this is summarized in the report as market driven sustainable development;

Table 7.20 OECS top twenty-five exports, US$ million, 1981–2012

1981	US$ million	%	2000	US$ million	%	2012	US$ million	%
Fruit, fresh and nuts excl. oil	24.80	28.40	Fruit, fresh, and nuts excl. oil	58.40	24.70	Soaps, cleansing and polishing	16.40	23.00
Sugar and honey	15.00	17.20	Electric power machinery	33.90	14.30	Meal and flour of wheat	11.60	16.20
Clothing except fur clothing	9.60	11.00	Soaps, cleansing and polishing	15.70	6.60	Vegetables, roots and tubers, fresh	6.20	8.70
Soaps, cleansing and polishing	7.80	8.90	Spices	14.30	6.00	Rice	4.30	6.10
Articles of paper, pulp, paperboard	5.60	6.40	Office machines	14.00	5.90	Fruit, fresh, and nuts excl. oil	3.70	5.30
Alcoholic beverages	3.00	3.40	Equipment for distributing electric	13.70	5.80	Feed. Stuff for animals excl. unmil	3.70	5.20
Other fixed vegetable oils	2.90	3.30	Meal and flour of wheat	10.00	4.20	Alcoholic beverages	3.60	5.10
Footwear	2.30	2.70	Alcoholic beverages	8.20	3.40	Stone, sand and gravel	3.60	5.00
Margarine and shortening	1.60	1.80	Perfumery, cosmetics, dentifrices	7.20	3.00	Non-alcoholic beverages, n.e.s.	2.30	3.20
Household equipment of base metals	1.50	1.70	Sugar and honey	5.80	2.40	Universals, plates and sheets of iron	1.90	2.70
Non-alcoholic beverages, n.e.s.	1.50	1.70	Vegetables, roots and tubers, fresh	5.50	2.30	Pigments, paints, varnishes	1.70	2.40
Other electrical machinery	1.10	1.30	Fish, fresh and simply preserved	4.70	2.00	Articles of paper, pulp, paperboard	1.70	2.40
Furniture	1.10	1.30	Clothing except fur clothing	4.70	2.00	Fish, fresh & simply preserved	1.20	1.70
Electric power machinery	1.10	1.20	Rice	4.50	1.90	Musical instruments, sound recorder	1.10	1.50
Domestic electrical equipment	0.80	0.90	Articles of paper, pulp, paperboard	4.30	1.80	Manufactures of metal, n.e.s.	0.90	1.30
Telecommunications apparatus	0.60	0.70	Non-alcoholic beverages, n.e.s.	4.10	1.70	Iron and steel scrap	0.80	1.20
Food preparations, n.e.s.	0.50	0.60	Pigments, paints, varnishes	3.10	1.30	Spices	0.80	1.10
Pigments, paints, varnishes	0.50	0.60	Chemical materials and products	2.90	1.20	Telecommunications apparatus	0.70	1.10
Manuf. of leather or of artif.	0.50	0.50	Universals, plates and sheets	2.60	1.10	Finished structural parts	0.70	1.00
Vegetables, roots and tubers, fresh	0.40	0.50	Feed. Stuff for animals	2.60	1.10	Articles of artificial plastic mate	0.60	0.90
Essential oils, perfume and flavour	0.40	0.40	Stone, sand and gravel	2.30	1.00	Other electrical machinery	0.40	0.50
Fish, fresh and simply preserved	0.30	0.30	Other electrical machinery	1.90	0.80	Essential oils, perfume and flavour	0.30	0.50
Plastic materials, regenerd.	0.30	0.30	Food preparations, n.e.s.	1.60	0.70	Nails, screws, nuts, bolts, rivets	0.20	0.30
Printed matter	0.20	0.30	Ships and boats	1.60	0.60	Food preparations, n.e.s.	0.10	0.20
Cereal preps and preps of flour	0.20	0.30	Cocoa	1.60	0.60	Fruit, preserved	0.10	0.20

Source: World Integrated Trade Solution (WITS) (2014).

Table 7.21 General government final consumption expenditure (% of GDP), 1980–2011

	1980	1990	2000	2010	2011
Antigua & Barbuda	19.30	17.95	19.37	–	–
Bahamas	12.51	12.86	10.75	14.58	14.84
Barbados	14.92	20.16	21.19	20.31	–
Belize	17.15	12.93	12.91	–	–
Dominica	27.29	20.46	18.76	16.89	17.62
Grenada	20.40	21.58	11.65	16.70	17.08
Guyana	24.20	13.62	24.67	15.11	15.45
Jamaica	20.24	13.04	14.29	16.09	15.98
St Kitts & Nevis	20.90	18.05	11.07	10.72	10.44
St Lucia	17.54	14.72	17.14	16.92	16.56
Suriname	21.32	30.01	37.49	–	–
Trinidad & Tobago	12.06	11.94	11.95	–	–

Source: World Development Indicators (2014).

2. The attainment of an economy in which there is an abundance of work opportunities provided by the free market and the state;
3. Economic agents can operate in an environment in which they can utilize the fruits of their labour;
4. The education stock of this region must be enhanced by making higher education available to all persons, irrespective of social standing;
5. The interaction of people, in the various facets of their life without social disruption;
6. An improved governance system with respect for democracy and law. At the same time, the ODS report acknowledges that the law of the land must be fair and just;
7. Human capital preservation takes on an important role and high quality, affordable health care is easily accessible to all;
8. A sense of unity with all social partners working together to attend to any emerging development problem.

7.3.1 Objectives of the Development Strategy for the OECS

This study included the following objectives:

1. To guide the developmental planning in the OECS membership;
2. To set a framework for the attainment of particular human development levels;
3. To establish guidelines for the improvement of the level of international competitiveness of the OECS bloc of economies;
4. To cater for a wider degree of social participation in the developmental thrust of the OECS;

5. To ensure more substantial use of scarce resources, wherever they may be located; and
6. To define various means through which the capabilities of the peoples of the OECS could sustain their livelihoods.

This report recognized that in this type of environment the OECS bloc of countries will need to

1. Accelerate transition away from protection for main export items to one founded in a greater degree of competition;
2. Decrease dependence on concessionary aid flows;
3. Be guided by the realities of globalization in their adoption of growth strategies; and
4. Involve a process of capacity building in all areas to improve the likelihood of selecting the best subset of policy choices.

This report consisted of ten programme areas, with each area carrying a programme goal basis for action. The stated programme areas are the following:

1. Managing the external environment
2. Sustainable economic development
3. Integrated production and marketing
4. Education and training
5. Poverty eradication
6. Job creation
7. Access to quality health services
8. Sustaining the stock of natural capital
9. Empowering disadvantaged groups
10. Implementing the strategy

As concerns the attainment of sustainable economic development, the ODS uses the following measuring rods:

1. A minimum central government savings of 2.5 per cent
2. A minimum public sector savings rate of 7 per cent of GDP
3. The attainment of an 85 per cent level of liquidity within the banking system
4. Realizing moderate economic growth of not lower than 7 per cent
5. A current revenue to GDP ratio of 29 per cent
6. A current expenditure to GDP ratio of 25 per cent
7. A capital investment to government expenditure of at least 30 per cent

7.3.2 Economic Sectors

Reflecting on the ten programmes for sustainable human development, the services sector was identified as a high-priority economic sector.

Services: The report noted that the development benefits include sustainable employment opportunities for a wide range of skills, a reduction in vulnerability to external shocks by fostering a greater degree of diversification and the attainment of a greater degree of foreign exchange earnings alongside the benefit of attaining a higher level of economic growth. The study identifies that the development of the services sector requires improvements:

1. Transportation, telecommunications, intellectual property rights and computerization. An improvement in air transportation is also very important in order to improve the attractiveness of the OECS bloc of economies for investment. The study also identifies financial services as a potential growth pole. The report notes that the offshore financial services sector can help to earn foreign exchange for CARICOM economies and can also help improve fiscal revenue intakes, overall employment levels, as well as help improve the technological base. In a 2010 press release, the prime minister of Antigua and Barbuda, Baldwin Spencer, indicated the importance of the financial services sector, an area in which Antigua and Barbuda has demonstrated competitive advantage. He also stated that the offshore financial sector was crucial to the provision of employment, not only for Antiguans, but also for nationals of the OECS. He boasted that the offshore financial sector had a "significant multiplier effect on our economy" (speaking at the opening ceremony of Conference of Financial Services of the CARIFORUM of ACP states and the European Union). The study also suggested that the information services sector is an important area for intervention which can help to improve the competitiveness of the OECS set of economies.

2. In targeting the attainment of sustainable income, this report noted that the output of the agricultural sector (especially bananas and sugar) should be improved. The report also cited that domestic agriculture should be promoted in the OECS bloc, so as to reduce current account pressures.

3. The fisheries sector was also listed in the ODS as another area which should be improved. The objective here was to improve the fisheries sector so as to stabilize fishermen's income.

On the whole, this report is proposed to assist civil society and other social partners to "build and sustain the requisite capacity to manage the transition to international competitiveness and to develop systems of governance that will support the attainment of the Vision".

7.4 Bonnick Report (2000)

The Bonnick report was prepared at the request of the steering committee of the Caribbean Group for Cooperation in Economic Development (CGCED). The intent was to provide a framework to guide policy actions and efforts towards the continued economic, social and political development of the Caribbean region. The main author of this report was Gladstone Bonnick (2000, vii). This Caribbean Vision 2020 (hereafter CV 2020) report outlined "an emerging consensus regarding the principal challenges and opportunities facing the region and the main components of a strategy to create a region of participatory democracies, cohesive societies with reduced poverty, and dynamic economies generating employment for a growing population".

The CV 2020 was founded on a projection of the labour force in the region considering the growth of population and the various participation rates in member states.[65] The report at that time identified a number of favourable factors contributing to the possibility that the CARICOM economy will move into the twenty-first century as a viable, economically strong and politically secure economy:

1. The political environment remains stable (this is illustrated by the democracy index in table 7.22). Specifically, all of the listed CARICOM economies had generally free and experienced fair elections in the given years. Although the figures have fluctuated over the six-year period, each economy managed to maintain the same level of democracy ranking in both 2006 and 2012.
2. Social decay based on ethnic, religious, economic or other bases are not prevalent in the region.
3. Economic growth of the quantity and quality necessary to stimulate employment and reduce poverty has occurred in these economies in the past.
4. Strong traditional linkages between CARICOM and developed economies in North America and Europe persist, and these will continue to embrace the development plans of the CARICOM sphere.

In the pursuit of this vision, a number of risks exists which could erode the attainment of the Vision 2020 thrust. These risks are:

1. Governments may change and so the political will and political directive may change. Indeed, table 7.23 provides some basic data of changes in the political regimes in the listed member states. In Trinidad and Tobago and Jamaica in particular, there have been fluctuations in political regimes.

Table 7.22 Democracy index of selected CARICOM countries, 2006–2012

Country	2006	2008	2010	2012
Trinidad & Tobago	7.18	7.21	7.16	7.18
Suriname	6.52	6.58	6.65	6.52
Guyana	6.15	6.12	6.05	6.15
Jamaica	7.34	7.21	7.21	7.34

Key:

$8 \leq DI \leq 10$ (Full Democracy – free and fair elections)

$6 \leq DI \leq 7.9$ (Flawed Democracy – generally free and fair elections)

$4 \leq DI \leq 5.9$ (Hybrid Regime – highly unreliable parliamentary elections)

$0 \leq DI \leq 3.9$ (Authoritarian Regime – complete concentration of power to one leader)

Source: Economist Intelligence Unit (2013).

Table 7.23 Changes in political parties, 1980–2013

Barbados		Guyana		Jamaica		Trinidad & Tobago	
1981	Barbados Labour Party (BLP)	1980	People's National Congress (PNC)	1980	Jamaica Labour Party (JLP)	1981	People's National Movement (PNM)
1986	Democratic Labour Party (DLP)	1985	People's National Congress (PNC)	1983	Jamaica Labour Party (JLP)	1986	National Alliance for Reconstruction (NAR)
1991	Democratic Labour Party (DLP)	1992	People's Progressive Party (PPP)	1989	People's National Party (PNP)	1991	People's National Movement (PNM)
1994	Barbados Labour Party (BLP)	1997	People's Progressive Party/Civic (PPP/C)	1993	People's National Party (PNP)	1995	United National Congress (UNC)
1999	Barbados Labour Party (BLP)	2001	People's Progressive Party/Civic (PPP/C)	1997	People's National Party (PNP)	2000	United National Congress (UNC)
2003	Barbados Labour Party (BLP)	2006	People's Progressive Party/Civic (PPP/C)	2002	People's National Party (PNP)	2001	People's National Movement (PNM)
2008	Democratic Labour Party (DLP)	2011	People's Progressive Party/Civic (PPP/C)	2007	Jamaica Labour Party (JLP)	2002	People's National Movement (PNM)
2011	Democratic Labour Party (DLP)			2011	People's National Party (PNP)	2007	People's National Movement (PNM)
2013	Democratic Labour Party (DLP)					2010	People's Partnership (PP)

Sources:

Barbados: http://www.caribbeanelections.com/elections/bb_elections.asp;

Guyana: http://www.caribbeanelections.com/gy/elections/default.asp;

Jamaica: http://uca.edu/politicalscience/dadm-project/western-hemisphere-region/jamaica-1962-present/; http://www.eoj.com.jm/content-183-179.htm;

Trinidad and Tobago: http://www.ebctt.com/reports_in_pdf.php; http://en.wikipedia.org/wiki/History_of_Trinidad_and_Tobago.

2. Some economies, for example, Haiti are at risk of political unrest. According to the Haiti Crime and Safety Report (2012 and 2013), frequent protests are held in Port-au-Prince for reasons due to dissatisfaction in infrastructure and utilities as well as disapproval of Haitian government entities or UN presence. These protests have been known to turn violent, averaging multiple incidents in weeks since 2009 and totalling 360 in 2011. In November 2010, a few Cholera-related protests were held in Cap Haitian, Haiti's second largest city, which prevented operations in the city for days. Early December riots concerning presidential elections led to the shutdown of Port-au-Prince and Les Cayes (Haiti's third largest city) for three days. In December 2012, the "quality of life protestors" together with students held demonstrations in Cap Haitian.

   Social upheavals are not new to the country. In fact, since the 1900s demonstrations were being made by different segments of the population in reaction to events that appeared to disadvantage the people. In particular, between 1807 and 1820 civil war broke out in the country, in 1957 a military controlled elections resulted in tens of thousands killed or exiled, in 1976 there were widespread protests against repression of the country's press, in 1980 hundreds of human rights workers, journalists and lawyers were arrested and exiled from Haiti, in 1984 more than two hundred peasants were massacred after demonstrating for access to land, and 1985–86 saw widespread anti-government demonstrations. In 1987 dozens of people were shot and killed by soldiers after the approval of a new constitution, in 1989 massive repression against political parties, unions, students, and democratic organizations were ordered by the then president, in 1990 a state of siege was declared by the president, in 1991 a military led coup resulted in thousand people killed in the first days of the coup, in 1994 violence continued as human rights violations persisted and in 1994 a rebel group successfully initiated an uprising and seized control of several towns, the result of which led to the resignation of President Aristide on 29 February 2004.[66] In November 2013, political demonstrations were held in Port-au-Prince and in late January 2014, protests concerning quality of life occurred in north eastern Haiti.

3. In some member states crime and violence continue to create social challenges that impact on the development efforts. In a 2010 study by the UNDP, an average of 16.7 per cent of Caribbean people reported being the victim of at least one crime, table 7.24.

4. There has been in some cases a legacy of lethargic responses to serious issues and problems such as slow rates of economic growth, high levels of unemployment and high levels of poverty.

5. Educational reform has progressed at a slow pace.

6. Land use has been irrational and poorly managed in some economies.

7. The quality of the environment has deteriorated in some Caribbean economies. A key indicator of environmental erosion in the Caribbean is beach erosion associated with rising sea levels. In a UNDP report prepared by Simpson et al. (2010) the impact of beach erosion on the highly vulnerable tourism resorts and sea turtle nesting beaches were investigated. Tourism resort infrastructure is often highly vulnerable to beach erosion. For example, 693 tourism resorts were sampled of which 307 were found to be vulnerable to a 50-metre erosion scenario associated with 1-metre sea level rise (SLR), table 7.25. Comparatively, a 100-metre erosion associated with a 2-metre SLR was found

Table 7.24 Self-reported criminal victimization, Caribbean 7 and by country (%)

Number of Crimes Interviewee was Victim of	Caribbean 7	Antigua & Barbuda	Barbados	Guyana	Jamaica	St Lucia	Suriname	Trinidad & Tobago
No crime	77.9	77.6	73.4	79.9	82.6	77.0	76.0	77.4
1 crime	16.7	14.7	20.2	17.9	14.2	15.8	14.8	19.9
2 crime	3.2	4.4	4.4	1.5	2.0	4.2	5.0	1.4
3 crimes or more	2.2	3.3	2.0	0.7	1.2	3.0	4.2	1.3

Source: UNDP Citizen Security Survey (2010).

to place an additional 79 resorts at risk. The countries which demonstrate the most vulnerability as relating to tourism infrastructure under the 50-metre erosion scenario are Belize, St Kitts and Nevis, and St Vincent and the Grenadines while the countries with the largest number of tourism resorts likely to be damaged by SLR-induced erosion are the Bahamas, Belize and Barbados (77, 42 and 42 resorts, respectively, at 1-metre SLR and 93, 44 and 50 resorts, respectively, at the 2-metre SLR).

Beach nesting sites for sea turtles are also at great risk to beach erosion associated with SLR. In particular, 331 sea turtle nesting beaches were examined, of which 146 were

Table 7.25 Impact of beach erosion associated with 1-metre or 2-metre sea level rise (SLR) in CARICOM nations

	Tourism Resorts (n = 673)		Sea Turtle Nesting Beaches (n = 331)	
	50 metres	100 metres	50 metres	100 metres
	(1m SLR)	(2m SLR)	(1m SLR)	(2m SLR)
Antigua & Barbuda	34	44	24	31
Bahamas	77	93	4	4
Belize	42	44	7	7
Dominica	5	6	6	7
Grenada	14	19	7	7
Guyana	0	0	0	–
Haiti	14	17	6	8
Jamaica	34	52	18	24
Montserrat	0	0	0	2
St Kitts & Nevis	15	18	15	15
St Lucia	5	9	9	16
St Vincent & the Grenadines	8	16	16	22
Suriname	2	2	0	–
Trinidad & Tobago	15	16	29	34

Source: Simpson et al. (2010).

found to be at risk with a 50-metre erosion scenario and 185 at risk with a 100-metre erosion scenario. Further, if 50 metres were to erode, 100 per cent of the turtle nesting sites in Belize would be at risk, followed by 80 per cent in the Bahamas and 79 per cent in St Kitts and Nevis.

The Bonnick report noted that the achievement of these CV 2020 goals would be conditioned by a number of challenges, including:

1. The creation of the relevant type of political environment;
2. The creation of the relevant type of social fabric;
3. An economic growth rate which can swamp the projected growth of the population in the region;
4. Coping with a changing international environment in which margins of preference are earmarked to be further dismantled as globalization proceeds;
5. Coping with the rapid progression of technology in virtually all areas of productive activity;
6. Managing the increasing pressure of expanding economic activity and population mass on the fragile physical environment;
7. Coping with a cycle of natural disasters, including hurricanes which affect the region more frequently. The Caribbean region has always been susceptible to natural disasters, mainly affected by hurricanes, earthquakes and volcanic eruptions. The Caribbean region has seen this as an additional challenge to their economic and sustainable development. Recalling events such as hurricanes in Barbados (1955), Cuba, Trinidad and Tobago, Jamaica and Haiti (1964), Dominica and the Dominican Republic (1979), St Lucia, Haiti and Jamaica (1980), and Antigua and Barbuda, St Kitts and Nevis, and Montserrat (1989) show successive impacts on the Caribbean economies due to natural disasters.

    Furthermore, volcanic eruptions were extensive in Guadeloupe (1976), St Vincent and the Grenadines (1979) as well as earthquakes in the Dominican Republic (1946) and Antigua and Barbuda (1974). The devastating 7.3 magnitude earthquake in Haiti in 2010 also shed light on the region's helplessness and unpreparedness toward the occurrence of a massive natural disaster;
8. Coping with the general disadvantages that small size poses for development and planning;
9. Coping with a strained and underdeveloped physical infrastructure;
10. Coping with a strained and underdeveloped institutional infrastructure.

In the context of these strengths, risks and challenges, the CV 2020 in summarizing the response of a variety of experts suggested a holistic approach for the attainment of CV 2020. This approach must recognize that the way forward:

1. Must understand the synergistic relations among politics, economics and the social fabric of the region;
2. Must emphasize as its dominant goals the growth, equity and wellbeing and participation of all the people in their development;

3. Would need to recognize the tremendous contribution human development efforts can foster; and must not ignore the knowledge that improving human development will require the production of psychological goods as part of the output basket.[67]

In the attainment of the CV 2020 objective, the experts interviewed raised a number of concerns including:

1. Adapting and adjusting to the changing international environment in which margins of preference are being increasingly eroded;
2. Adapting and adjusting to the economic conditions within individual states;
3. The need to implement second generation reforms. Second generation reforms play a critical part in strengthening the democratic process and contributes significantly to improving transparency and accountability in the practices of the state;
4. The need to address poverty in a more head on manner;
5. A more sustained effort will have to be made to improve the international competitiveness of member states improves;
6. The private sector will have to be unbridled even further and encouraged to play a greater role in carving the economic growth dynamic of member states;
7. Growth inhibiting factors which limit the ability of economies to initiate meaningful changes will have to be aggressively resolved;
8. It will be necessary to improve on the physical and social capital in each of the member states of the OECS bloc. If these stocks that are diminished, then this will affect the sustainability of the growth process in these economies.

In a reassessment of the CV 2020 policy guidelines, Bonnick (2000) notes that

1. Between 2000 and 2005 the international environment had shown distinct signs of change, with the direction of change providing a greater degree of challenge for Caribbean economies. Economic growth in the world economy appears to have peaked in 2000 and growth into the medium term is projected to weaken principally because of slower growth in investment in Europe and Japan.
2. There have been significant changes in the period since 2000, in terms of the share of world production accounted for by some countries and their influence on world economic affairs. China's ascendance on the ladder of economic output has continued. Significantly, China can produce most non-traditional goods cheaper than Caribbean economies. China's increasing output level has no doubt been partly responsible for the improvement in global oil prices. Caribbean economies should try to capture niche markets in China, India and the general Asian bloc.
3. Many developed economies which posted positive net saving flows in the past, continue to realize decreases in their net savings pool. China, however, continues to accumulate substantive increases in savings. This infers in part, that the Caribbean may need to turn more attention to the Asian bloc for securing FDI for the medium and longer term periods.
4. If other net suppliers of savings in Asia do not continue to lend prolifically to countries like the United States, the cost of borrowing on the international market will increase.

This infers that over the longer term period, Caribbean countries will need to improve their net savings, which can be facilitated by: greater budgetary prudence and higher private savings.

In the context of the changing global environment, Bonnick (2000) identifies that

1. Caribbean economies will need to place a greater amount of attention on increasing net national saving flows in the region;
2. Weak, stagnant or recessive growth in the region seems to be linked to a variety of factors including natural disasters, crime and socio political instability, and all attempts should be made to reduce the magnitude of impact from these disruptions; and
3. Investment in human capital is absolutely critical for the development of efficiency and competitiveness in the region.

7.4.1 Economic Sectors Identified by Bonnick Report

The Bonnick report identified a holistic development plan. Significantly, the report singled out the vast possibilities offered by service exports. The report emphasized that the specific export of services based on technological advances in computer technology, information transfer and bio-medical research represented distinct niche opportunities. Successes by the Bahamas, Barbados, the Cayman Islands, St Vincent and the British Virgin Islands have lent themselves to replication by other Caribbean countries. Furthermore, the report cited that subsequent to the 1996 Caribbean Group for Cooperation in Economic Development (CGCED), substantial developments in communication technology and information management may have influenced the location and impact of such services. Moreover, the report made mention of some factors that constrain service exports and private sector development. These comprised the ineffectiveness of education reform, work permit requirements, obsolete telecommunications legislation and regulatory capacity. The Bonnick report added that while policy discussion of means to develop service exports tend to be constantly focused on incentives, these incentives are insufficient, as they will not make up for fundamental challenges to establish and operate a competitive service export enterprise.

The report also acknowledged the need to continue to improve on the tourism product. The report was clear that in order for tourism to be regarded as one of the Caribbean's leading sectors by 2020, an assessment must be conducted on the basis of whether an approach can be devised to properly manage the implications of the growth targets for the sector. The report indicated that it expected future tourism activity in the Caribbean to be characterized by the following traits:

1. Private investors will drive development in the sector;
2. The tourism product will be mainly recreational;
3. Diversification of the tourism product into areas such as health and retirement with a flexible cost structure;
4. A greater domestic ownership of the tourism sector;
5. An expansion of capacity in complementary sectors such as domestic transportation, utilities and other services;

6. Greater predictability and stability in transportation-related matters such as airfare, seating accommodation and flight scheduling;

7. Greater focus on environmental issues.

In addition to those highlighted above, some indicative target for tourism growth would be required in formulating a strategy for tourism development in the region. The report identified the usefulness of past and expected stopover visitors. The report noted that if tourism is to be a leading sector, then its growth should be greater than the required minimum GDP growth.

7.5 Caribbean Trade and Adjustment Group Report (2001)

The Caribbean Regional Negotiating Machinery and the CARICOM Secretariat, in a joint meeting in October 2000, teamed up to evaluate the development in the key negotiating areas in which CARICOM economies were involved. Out of this exercise, it was determined that a Caribbean trade and adjustment group be formed to examine the main trade and adjustment issues emerging because of these negotiations.

The CTAG report (2001) started by acknowledging that CARICOM, while vying for "most over-researched" community in the world, seems to be characterized more by talk than action.[68] The CTAG report very early, noted that many of the reports and reviews undertaken in the past, lacked a sense of craftsmanship and explicitly states, "they were too vague, shapeless and timeless to be a useful guide to action: devoid of appreciation of how to move from one step to the next; maps without contours" (CTAG 2001, x).

The CTAG's immediate mandate therefore, was to detail both the ongoing and forthcoming set of trade negotiations in which CARICOM economies are involved. The group started with the observation that as it stands the Caribbean sphere hosted nothing like a regional development strategy (RDS). The consequence of this is a general inability to forge an international trade policy position, which in turn, potentially inhibits the rational allocation of scarce resources within the region. In the absence of a RDS, there is no clear cut directive regarding how to distribute the net gains from a market driven regional trading arrangement among member states.[69] The CTAG focused on supply side changes which will redound to the benefit of CARICOM people, including creating employment for them and reducing the incidence of poverty. This report focused on identifying the main challenges and opportunities which the region faced in the context of its various multilateral negotiations and outlined a variety of adjustment policies that catered to the circumstances.

A substantive suggestion proposed by the CTAG was that there was a greater need for improving the competitiveness of the region. This study recognized that the competitiveness of the firm was dependent on the relationship between the cost of production and the rate of output, which in turn depended on

1. exchange rate stability;
2. the efficiency of the tax system;
3. the effectiveness of the public system;
4. the quality of the public infrastructure;

5. the orientation of trade unions and the structure of labour policy;
6. the quality and quantity of physical infrastructure;
7. the availability and quality of R&D facilities;
8. the governance structure; and
9. the general participation of the wider society.

7.5.1 The Way Forward

With a process of adjustment, this study recognized that the major traditional sectors such as: export agriculture, import substituting manufacturing, retailing, customs revenues, commodity type tourism and offshore financing will lose out. Apart from improving the extent of international competitiveness and grabbing any opportunities new markets may offer, CARICOM economies will have to take advantage of services to help improve developmental options for the region. The CTAG identified seven priority areas for heads of governments:

1. On international trade policy, the community should define an international position and should build institutional capacity to support its trade policy stance. The CTAG suggested that competitiveness can be cultivated by a Competitiveness programme in business schools and a human resource retention programme.
2. The Caribbean Development Bank (CDB) should become the main financier of the development process in the region.
3. An overall plan for the revival of the traditional agricultural sector in the region is urgently required. The report specifically emphasized the need for common policies for sugar and rice. The level of international competitiveness of the banana sector should also be improved within the relevant perimeters of the Cotonou Agreement.
4. A Caribbean tourism development strategy should be established and operationalized. This strategy will need to cover
   a. the marketing of the Caribbean brand of the tourism product;
   b. expanding tourist inflows;
   c. the financing of a human development programme for the tourism sector;
   d. minimum standards for the tourism product in the CARICOM sphere;
   e. practising sustainable tourism so that host communities do not experience deterioration of the very environments which encouraged tourism in the first place;
   f. promoting tourism research.
5. Recommendation that a competitive strategy should be established with collaborative support from the business schools linked to the universities and with support from multilateral institutions particularly, the Inter-American Development Bank, the World Bank and the European Investment Bank.
6. Formulation of a Caribbean economic forum (CEF). This CEF should be coordinated by a regional private sector entity and should be patterned after the World Economic Forum. The objective of the CEF, the CTAG noted, was to eventually take over from the CGCED with initial support originating with the World Bank.

7. The need to develop a strategy to retain scarce human capital resources. This strategy should include the assistance of key international organizations and bilateral partners to help coordinate the process.

The CTAG report went on to detail some of the principal challenges that the agriculture, manu-facturing, mining and services sectors are presented with in the context of globalization.

Agriculture:

1. The CTAG recognized that external demand for key traditional export crops such as sugar, bananas and rice had waned in the past and growth in demand was insignificant. Although these sectors benefited from a considerable amount of margins of preference, they have not prospered, and are likely to fall behind in the face of free and fair competition.
2. Because of the heterogeneity of CARICOM member states, there is some basis for Heckscher-Ohlin type trade within the region, with member states such as Jamaica, Guyana and Belize carrying comparative advantage in the production of agricultural goods. The CTAG noted that this can be facilitated by further lowering the intra-regional trade barriers and an improvement in intra-regional maritime services. It is also depend-ent on the stance the region takes in the extra-regional community.

Sugar: As concerns sugar, the CTAG noted that there are four policy options confronting CARICOM economies:

1. A gradual downsizing of sugar production in Barbados, Jamaica and Trinidad and Tobago as sugar production in these economies were not cost effectively produced. The report identified that this type of change would require financial assistance for those economies which have to reduce their output levels.
2. Allowing the market to determine which of the Caribbean sugar producers remained viable. This would lead to the elimination of higher cost producers. Indeed, for over three decades, Trinidad and Tobago has benefited from preferential access to the European market for the export of its sugar cane. Through the "Sugar Protocol", Trinidad and Tobago fetched a considerably higher price for sugar sold to Europe, when compared to the world market price. By 2003, Trinidad and Tobago's cost of production for sugar was among the highest in the Caribbean (table 7.26).

   This led to the restructuring of the sector by the government of Trinidad and Tobago. However, by mid-2008, the state responded to the European Union's decision to cut European subsidy by closing down the Trinidad government-owned sugar company Caroni (1975) Limited.[70] Previously, the sugar industry in St Kitts was closed in 2005 and on this, the then minister of housing, agriculture, fisheries and consumer affairs, stated that "we have done all that we can to save the sugar industry, but because of the high cost of production in relation to monies received, and the pending 39 per cent reduction for sugar bought from the ACP countries including St Kitts and Nevis, we had to take that decision".[71]

Table 7.26 Comparative cost of sugar production, US cents per pound, 2003

Country	Cost of Production
Belize	15.63
Guyana	20.37
Barbados	38.30
Jamaica	39.67
St Kitts	41.98
Trinidad & Tobago	56.40

Source: Cardno Agrisystems Limited Report (2007).

3. Because of the social benefits (for example, employment) the sugar sector offers in various CARICOM economies, the CTAG proposes that there may be adequate basis for the government of relevant member states to provide some amount of subsidies for the sector.
4. Injecting capital into the industry to facilitate the production of more downstream products like specialty sugars, branded rums, and so on.
5. The report recommended the formation of a regional task force to design a CARICOM Common Sugar Policy which would extend the work on the sugar market done for the intra-regional sphere, to longer term planning for the extra-regional market.

Rum: To cope with the pressures of freer trade, the CTAG report specified that Caribbean distilleries will need to

1. Upgrade existing equipment;
2. Seek technical assistance and access to resources to renovate and upgrade plants;
3. Enter an aggressive marketing thrust to not only retain, but also expand on existing markets;
4. Prepare and submit to the appropriate EU authorities, development proposals for the rum sector;
5. Rather than export bulk rum, Caribbean producers should now try to target export markets with branded rum products. The "brand or value addition approach" would result in more benefits for Caribbean countries as it would require the use of domestic marketing managers to assist with branding initiatives in target markets (Braun-Munzinger and Goodison 2010). Moreover, the brand approach would enable Caribbean rum producers to differentiate their rum products in the rum market which can also effectively improve the recognition of Caribbean rum products by consumers. Table 7.27 illustrates some recent revenues from rum exports.

Banana: The report noted that apart from Belize, the banana producing economies of the Caribbean are not cost competitive and their prospects for survival after 2006 are dismal. The CTAG report highlighted that because the banana industry was a large employer, there was a need for a gradual downsizing. If CARICOM economies do not make accelerated adjustment, then the

Table 7.27 CARICOM exports of alcoholic beverages, US$, various years

Antigua & Barbuda	2000	505,420
	2012	1,210,248
Bahamas	2000	30,972,417
	2011	913,755
Belize	2000	1,004
	2012	153,011
Barbados	2000	12,526,758
	2012	44,964,340
Dominica	2000	21,573
	2012	103,093
Grenada	2000	79,931
	2008	216,504
Guyana	2000	3,592,033
	2012	42,464,502
Jamaica	2000	43,857,098
	2012	94,081,092
St Kitts & Nevis	2000	17,299
	2011	1,775,194
St Lucia	2000	6,720,702
	2008	14,326,420
Montserrat	2000	110
	2008	387
Suriname	2000	252,406
	2011	584,424
Trinidad & Tobago	2000	33,656,388
	2010	30,319,052
St Vincent & the Grenadines	2000	241,929
	2012	2,358,770

Source: World Integrated Trade Solution (WITS) (2014).

industry is likely to collapse, with the implementation of a tariff only system in 2006. Certainly, as the export volumes of banana in the table 7.28 illustrates, the industry has already started to collapse.

Rice: Rice is produced for export by two CARICOM economies, Guyana and Suriname. The formation of the EBA Agreement between the European Union and the forty-nine Least Developed Economies of the World represents a real threat to the market prospects for Guyana and Suriname. In this regard, the CTAG proposed that these two particular CARICOM economies vigorously pursue alternative geographical markets in the Caribbean and Central and South America, particularly Brazil. Certainly, from the data in the table 7.29, Guyana and Suriname have over

Table 7.28 Banana export quantity, tonnes, 1965–2011

	Dominica	Grenada	St Lucia	St Vincent & the Grenadines	OECS Total	Jamaica
1965	49220	20997	81451	28846	180514	182900
1970	36240	19131	37439	30489	123299	136410
1975	27550	13129	30695	13586	84960	68099
1980	8222	12459	33496	19773	73950	33124
1985	33866	8137	73962	40570	156535	12490
1990	58603	8398	135166	79010	281177	61073
1995	33071	4098	112834	54788	204791	82753
2000	30611	705	50072	43400	124788	40900
2005	12732	0	30630	27470	70832	11713
2010	4652	59	26234	12103	43048	1
2011	4554	59	8101	12200	24914	1

Source: Food and Agriculture Organization of the United Nations Database (FAO) (2014).

time, sent much more of their rice to the intra-regional market. Guyana has sent a pronounced amount, extra-regionally.

The CTAG report also suggested that CARICOM should pursue the formation of an intra-CARICOM common rice policy so that the CARICOM market, which procures a significant

Table 7.29 Rice exports, US$ million, 1997–2012

	Guyana				Suriname	
	Intra-Regional	Extra-Regional			Intra-Regional	Extra-Regional
1997	33.37	46.10	1996		0.37	33.40
1998	24.55	44.22	1997		1.41	25.56
1999	24.83	32.89	1998		1.27	16.90
2000	18.89	21.97	1999		1.82	11.39
2001	21.49	22.02	2000		1.33	9.82
2002	15.68	25.59	2001		1.59	9.39
2003	12.57	23.20	2002		2.89	13.21
2004	24.12	24.87	2003		3.92	7.66
2005	23.21	22.77	2004		5.16	7.02
2006	27.26	22.79	2005		1.84	7.01
2007	37.33	38.12	2006		8.09	3.34
2008	58.23	55.49	2007		8.77	6.58
2009	59.97	53.38	2008		12.43	19.89
2010	48.48	103.69	2009		12.53	8.67
2011	43.00	105.11	2010		19.77	18.08
2012	43.95	152.09	2011		26.45	4.43

Source: World Integrated Trade Solution (WITS) (2014).

amount of its rice requirements from extra-regional sources, would now be serviced mainly by intra-regional producers.

Manufacturing: In the CARICOM sphere, manufacturing is mainly a non-tradable sector. The two notable exceptions are; Trinidad and Tobago and Jamaica. It is projected that as the Common External Tariff (CET) is dismantled, alongside other globalization changes, such as the proposed Free Trade Area of the Americas, the share of manufacturing sector in GDP and exports will continue to decline. The CTAG further emphasized that the manufacturing sector of CARICOM economies can be improved through the following policy interventions:

1. an industrial training programme;
2. a retooling programme; and
3. increased levels of research and development (R&D) within the region.

Textile/Apparel Industry: This report noted that for the apparel industry of the CARICOM sphere to survive it must implement a structural adjustment programme (SAP). This SAP will need to

1. consolidate and rationalize the sector so that it can benefit from economies of scale;
2. implement backward integration consistent with the output requirements of the apparel industry;
3. upgrade the technological requirements of this sector;
4. expand the marketing thrust of the sector; and
5. improve the amount of credit available to the sector to facilitate the expansion of e-commerce, capital financing and crime prevention.

Mining: The main mining economies of the CARICOM region are Jamaica, Suriname, and Trinidad and Tobago. The CTAG report made a number of policy suggestions for the mining sector including the following:

1. The need to define policies and regulations for the mining industry. Particularly, the report argued that there is the need for a clear and effective legal framework, which will outline in detail the perimeters involved in such important areas as
   a. security of tenure;
   b. tax codes; and
   c. access to mineral resources.
2. The report also emphasized the need to promote small-scale domestic mining companies, of the type which can specifically focus on the extraction of complex ore bodies. The CTAG suggests that this may be facilitated by highlighting the prospects and opportunities in this field of economic activity to local banks. This would also require investments in the relevant human capital base to provide a ready workforce for these types of small mining companies. Additionally, the report noted that policymakers should consider offering more training options in educational institutions revolving around mining, and encouraging a greater degree of entrepreneurial effort targeted at the mining sector.

The study is careful to point out that these interventions should not occur at the expense of the environment.

Services: The CTAG report also emphasizes the need to initiate changes in the services sector, especially within the following:

1. tourism services;
2. financial services;
3. telecommunications services;
4. information services;
5. entertainment services;
6. health and education export services.

As concerns tourism in particular, the CTAG report noted that what is required is an effective marketing strategy between the public and private sectors.

Fiscal Reform: The CTAG recognized that the Caribbean is in dire need of fiscal reform given the widening gap between fiscal revenues and expenditures. The data in table 7.30 provides some guideline information along these lines.

The report provided a list of reform options that can help alleviate fiscal deficits among CARICOM economies in the medium and long term into the future including:

1. Governments should try to use increased government savings to finance key projects rather than relying on "the availability of foreign grants".
2. Because trade liberalization will lead to a loss of tariff revenues, there is the need to find compensating sources of revenues, especially in the OECS bloc such as VAT or general consumption taxes.

Table 7.30 Fiscal revenue and fiscal expenditure (% of GDP), 1980–2012

	Fiscal Revenue (% GDP)			Fiscal Expenditure (% GDP)		
	St Kitts & Nevis	St Vincent & the Grenadines	Jamaica	St Kitts & Nevis	St Vincent & the Grenadines	Jamaica
1980	40.92	22.14	18.49	47.38	26.78	24.73
1985	19.77	28.25	19.20	28.18	24.25	24.32
1990	20.10	27.71	25.52	19.47	26.55	23.25
1995	24.80	22.98	21.83	23.89	22.41	19.48
2000	23.42	24.81	23.49	35.09	26.41	26.79
2005	32.22	23.59	24.51	35.53	28.04	28.50
2010	31.04	27.42	26.02	38.85	32.85	36.53
2011	37.10	26.73	25.33	35.29	30.35	31.31
2012	35.93	25.62	24.42	30.74	28.34	30.53

Sources: International Monetary Fund (2013) and World Development Indicators (2014).

3. The harmonization of indirect taxes in the context of regional integration efforts would reduce the administrative burdens of affecting these tax regimes and will also improve the efficiency of regional indirect tax systems.

4. There is a need to simplify the tariff system, transport valuation and to hasten the implementation of machinery to conduct its transactions via a computerized process. This can have two benefits: it can widen the degree of trade and it can also reduce tax evasion. The CTAG report also adds that "reform in the customs area should in fact, be one aspect of the overall simplification and streamlining of the tax regimes in order to reduce discretion and rent seeking" (p. 27).

5. The governments of the region should try to extend their formal taxation regimes to cover the self-employed and those in the underground economy.

6. In some member states, the report proposed that a reduction in the level of direct taxation can stimulate private sector savings.

7. The report argued that the region wields too many tax incentives that are overly generous to attract investments. In this regard, there is the need to remove ineffective taxes as they weaken the amount of tax revenues collected by the governments of the region.

8. CARICOM governments will have to consider, at some point, implementing user fees so as to recover some of its financial outlays on public investment. Governments in the region will also need to list its support for any state owned entities in a transparent manner and will also need to monitor the debt of these institutions.

9. Governments in the region should establish special funds into which they siphon any windfall gains so as to smoothen revenue flows.

10. Governments in the region will also need to downsize their public sectors. Even more they will need to control the growth of public sector wages as these have a demonstration effect on private sector wages, and in so doing influence the overall competitiveness of the economy.

11. Where possible, regional governments should privatize state owned entities in an effort to improve more efficient and competitive levels of output.

12. There should be a prioritization of government spending on public sector programmes.

The CTAG report acknowledged that some of these policy recommendations are being practised in individual states. However, what is required is that multilateral assistance should be engaged to coordinate "A Plan for Caribbean Fiscal Reform".

Exchange Rate Management and Regional Monetary System: The CTAG report noted that in the Caribbean sphere, there did not appear to be any real political support for a monetary union. In this regard, the report purported that any inclination towards monetary union in the region must be looked upon as a long-term strategy. The group recommended that as things stood, the CARICOM region should persist in aiming for a greater degree of convergence among its membership. Beyond this, the study notes that a significant underlying reason for the formation of a single economic market within the region should be the need for a single market for investment intra-regionally.

Capital Markets: In order for CARICOM economies to benefit from a greater block of international capital flows, they will have to address a number of structural and other obstacles which exist in their respective domestic economies. The CTAG report proposed the formation of a regional action plan for the liberalization and development of CARICOM capital markets. The study argued that this plan would attend to both the national requirements of individual member states, and also set out proposals for the development of the regional capital market.

Competitiveness, Public and Private Sector Developments: The CTAG report noted that the public sector had a crucial and very significant role to play in the enhancement of the competitiveness of the firms in the CARICOM sphere. Specifically, the report outlined that

1. Negotiating strategies must reflect the dynamic capabilities of regional firms and the pace at which they can adapt to globalization;
2. The governments of the region need to strive hard at achieving macroeconomic stability;
3. Government's investment in improving the national scientific standard can also assist with improving the competitiveness of domestic firms;
4. Policies that help to improve workplace flexibility also help to improve the competitiveness of firms; and
5. The government can also provide an environment in which workers can be easily upgraded and can help in the training and upgrading of skills.

The CTAG emphasizes the acute importance of human resource development if CARICOM firms are to become more competitive. Even more so, the group noted that without a tremendous improvement in human resource development, the CARICOM sphere is unlikely to be able to position itself to take advantage of changes in the global economy. In this regard, the CTAG argues in favour of a comprehensive regional programme for human resource development. The report urged that the IDB or another major organization take the lead and help to make such a program a reality.

Labour: The CTAG report recognizes the need for labour market reform in the region and argued that

1. Existing labour market policies have to be reviewed;
2. Reforms which increase the extent of labour market flexibility (for example, unemployment relief and retraining programmes) have to be implemented;
3. An effective system of tripartite consultations, covering labour, management and the government, has to organize various programmes including
    a. national skills development
    b. business development
    c. institutional development and strengthening
    d. dispute resolution

Public Sector Modernization. In the CARICOM sphere, the public sector has become increasingly modernized through the influence of an expanding middle class and increasing and persistent pressure from non-governmental organizations. This report argued for greater transparency

in government decision making and transparent legislation on financial and personnel procedures. There is the need to devise clear accountability criteria for evaluating public sector officials. There is also the need to strengthen the region's parliaments. The report recommended the
formation of a comprehensive regional public sector modernization plan which "would include
for each country and also at the regional level a detailed reform agenda and timetable, and commitment to the resources needed, mainly financing, training and technical assistance" (p. 38).

Private Sector Development: The private sector has a key role to play in the development of the
region. To facilitate private sector growth, the CTAG report recommended the formation of a
formal mechanism for cooperation between the government and the private sector.

The Informal and Small Business Sector: In order to improve on the income and productivity
of the people working in the informal and small business segment of the economy, the government will have to take more direct measures to improve on the productivity of employees in this
sector and improve the business opportunities for this category of employees.

This report cited that an alternative policy option that revolves around pumping more
resources into the informal sector with the explicit intention of bringing the informal sector into
the mainstream part of the economy. A significant part of this whole process involves widening
the access of the informal sector to ready markets.

The report made the critical point that there is a dearth of informal sector economy information. To improve policymaking decisions for this sector the CTAG argued, it is necessary to
have a comprehensive region-wide programme of data collection and analysis of the informal
sector.

The Caribbean Diaspora: This report recognized the tremendous potential that the CARICOM
diaspora represents to the region, but acknowledged that it is a principally underutilized
resource. The report argued that the consular services of Caribbean economies in the big cities
of New York, Miami and the like should pool resources to maximize the region's capacity to tap
into the diaspora. Significantly, the report is careful to note that the relationship between CAR-
ICOM economies and the diaspora should be reciprocal.

Indeed, it is well known that there exists a large amount of untapped potential in the diaspora
with regards to economic development. The diaspora has the potential to contribute to the wellbeing of the Caribbean region via investments in human capital; financial investments, which
include economic remittances, diaspora bonds/stocks, insurance and savings; also real sector
investments in the form of foreign direct investment which can take the form of trade in nostalgic
goods and entrepreneurial investments. The diaspora contributes to foreign direct investments
in the home country, which enables the development of various sectors and overall stimulates
economic growth. The diaspora via hometown associations and other voluntary groups helps to
develop communities as well as help to reduce the level of poverty in various countries (Hosein
et al. 2010).

Recently, the World Bank conducted a survey engaging over 850 members of the Caribbean diaspora from over thirty-one countries, including, London, New York/New Jersey, Miami
and Toronto. The results revealed that approximately 80 per cent of the diaspora group had
higher education degrees and 95 per cent of the respondents indicated that they earn at least

US$100,000–US$200,000, annually. Moreover, 84 per cent of the diaspora respondents are engaged with CARICOM, of which 48 per cent send money back home to family and friends, 32 per cent donate money to charities, 22 per cent, 13 per cent and 8 per cent invest in property, companies and the stock market, respectively. Additionally, 14 per cent indicated that they work for a Caribbean entity. Furthermore, social instability (crime) and weak legal frameworks have been found to be the largest barrier to increased engagement of the diaspora in the Caribbean. In terms of investments, 40 per cent indicated that they have already invested in a business venture that is any company in its early stages. Of these investments, 57 per cent were based in the Caribbean. With regards to accredited investors, 26 per cent have made investments of US$100,000 or more in new business ventures, and 40 per cent of accredited investors have indicated their willingness to invest over US$100,000 each year for a five-year period in start-ups, and specifically, high-potential growth-oriented start-ups in the Caribbean (World Bank 2013).

Infrastructure: The CTAG report argued that there is a greater need for the participation of the private sector in the development of the region's infrastructure and emphasizes the need for a regional infrastructure advisory agency. This agency, the report cited, should only act in an advisorial capacity, independent of government influence.

The group specifically requests the formation of a Caribbean infrastructure and training facility with collaborative support from the University of the West Indies. The main purpose of this facility would be to pool information and to assist with appropriate research and analysis.

Governance and Institutions: This report identified that a policy intervention which can improve on the governance of the region is education. Education can help identify best policies and practices to follow, can help CARICOM governments to assess technical and financial resources, and also assist with setting appropriate targets.

The CTAG report also identified trade policy as another significant area of policy intervention. Increasing the degree of openness of their respective economies has already been posted as a key target for CARICOM economies to reach single market and economy status.

Civil Society: The civil society movement in CARICOM economies is underfunded and depends almost singularly on funding from foreign non-governmental organizations. This potentially exposes regional non-governmental organizations to a compromise of their independence. Lamentably, the report notes that the non-governmental organization community in CARICOM is not striving. Specifically:

> CARICOM Governments provide little or no funding to support and strengthen their national and regional NGOs. At the same time, near total dependence on dwindling external funding – itself provided by NGOs in developed countries that are themselves funded by their own governments…CARICOM governments have also done little or nothing to assist in creating a more structured approach incorporating the beneficiaries and their organizations, as well as branches of decentralized ministries and local government. The NGO community therefore, despite high appreciation of its useful role, does not seem to be thriving. (CTAG 2001, 68)

This report argued that to develop the non-governmental organization community there is the urgent need for a joint conference of ministers of local government and community development.

7.6 World Bank Report (2005)

This report commenced by acknowledging that "the Caribbean[72] is at a development crossroads. Decades of reliance on traditional markets and on trade preferences, have given way to a new reality, where traditional agriculture plays a much smaller role in most economies, and where a much harsher and more competitive international wind blows. In such an environment business as usual will no longer suffice" (p. xi).

In this environment, the World Bank (2005) noted, there was the need to germinate a debate among key stakeholders, concerning the provision of proper directions for a development strategy to embrace both the national and regional levels and to take CARICOM economies forward into the twenty-first century.

This report acknowledged that CARICOM economies, like all small economies, are characterized by a variety of problems that make them particularly vulnerable. Even so, the report acknowledged that some of these Caribbean economies have gone on to attain middle-income developing country status. The report cited the following block of factors which have contributed to the favourable growth of CARICOM economies:

1. The Caribbean economies are located close to the North American market;
2. The climatic and environmental conditions in most CARICOM economies are excellent and form a significant basis for attracting large inflows of tourists;
3. Most of the economies of the Caribbean use English language as their first language;
4. These economies have attained generally high levels of primary school enrolment and also high rates of secondary school enrolment;
5. The political fabric and democratic structure of most Caribbean economies remains stable, and so decision-making and longer term planning have not been significantly disrupted;
6. Integration has progressed in the region with CARICOM progressing onto the doorstep of a common market, this notwithstanding the gaps in income and other social and economic attributes of Caribbean economies.

The World Bank report identified that there is the perception that the Caribbean sphere will find it increasingly difficult to replicate its past accomplishments. The report also added that the CARICOM economies are partially underachievers, as even their past accomplishments were below what these economies should have attained. Into the twenty-first century, the World Bank has identified a number of challenges which can adversely affect CARICOM economies from replicating their past growth performances:

1. Poverty remains high in some Caribbean economies.
2. Unemployment rates in most Caribbean economies remain in double digit terms. This remains a formidable challenge, and if not addressed urgently, will continue to pose as an obstacle for the management of poverty levels and the pattern of income distribution. This report also links unemployment in the region to an increased degree of drug addiction.

3. Many of the region's best and brightest brains continue to leave the Caribbean perimeters. While remittances may prove partially counterbalancing, it indicated a lack of access to suitable employment opportunities. Mishra (2006) indicated that the Caribbean region receives the most remittances in the world as a per cent of GDP. In 2002, approximately 13 per cent of the region's GDP are made up of remittances. Evidence for brain drain from the Caribbean can be seen in the losses due to high-skill migration outweighing the official remittances to the Caribbean.

4. Natural disasters seem to be occurring with increased frequency in the region.

5. The crime situation in many Caribbean economies has persistently deteriorated during the last few years. Significantly, survey work identified crime as an important factor influencing investment decisions in the Caribbean.

6. Maintaining growth has also been compounded by the magnitude of the public debt carried by economies from the region. Caribbean economies have the ill fate of ranking among the most indebted economies in the world. The high debt levels of some CARICOM member states places a strain on these economies to appropriate the fullest use of their human potential, and compromises the economic growth process by stifling the volume of resources available for productive deployment.

The World Bank report emphasized that the development challenges enveloping the region can be overcome with a sustained improvement in the degree of international competitiveness of each CARICOM economy and an overall improvement in its economic growth performance.

In terms of the ways forward, the World Bank report pointed to the following:

1. A greater degree of integration will help to improve the competitiveness of Caribbean economies. Greater integration for example, will ease unemployment problems in various parts of the region and would help to promote
   a. an improvement in wage rates;
   b. the extent of skill arbitrage;
   c. if investment is promoted at the regional rather than national level, the region as a whole would become much more attractive for investments;
   d. a greater degree of integration manifested in a harmonization of tax rates can reduce tax competition in the region; and
   e. a greater degree of intra-regional integration in the provision of some services can result in a fall in the cost of government in the region.

2. Tariffs throughout the region should be further dismantled. The global economy is becoming increasingly liberalized and CARICOM economies should join this bandwagon because of the gains on offer. Ideally, the CARICOM economies should negotiate greater technical support and financial assistance in return for the lowering of their tariffs.

3. There is the need to improve the economic climate in the region to foster a greater degree of private sector investments. This World Bank report identified that an important part of the investment climate required an improvement of the custom procedures, a reduction of high corporate taxes and a switch away from subsidies as a basis for attracting investment. An important part of this whole process would also require

an improvement in physical and institutional infrastructure. It acknowledged that an important aspect of private investment should remain FDI and so greater efforts should be made to woo FDI.

4. The public sector has to become more cost effective and make a stronger thrust at delivering public sector services more efficiently. Where possible and feasible, some public goods should be delivered by the private sector. Attempts should be made to attain cost efficiencies in the production and delivery of some public services by forging regional alliances. The basic argument behind the World Bank's reasoning is to reduce the extent of the crowding out of private sector investment by public sector investment.

5. There is the need to improve the human capital fabric of the region. This can help to widen the comparative advantage base of the region and may facilitate the production and export of some knowledge intensive service sector goods.[73]

6. In the post-independence era, CARICOM governments took the lead role to initiate change and so considerably expanded its participation in the economy. In the aftermath of the debt crisis of the 1980s, however, some of the region's governments made a switch towards a minimalist state. The way forward required a greater degree of cost efficiencies in government expenditure. Overall, the aim is that the private sector plays a greater role in providing important services, including those in the health and education sectors.

7. CARICOM economies would need to take advantage of emerging opportunities, especially in services. The World Bank report cites Ireland and Singapore as two exemplar economies from which the services sector has played a key catalytic role in propelling economic growth. In the report, an illustration on a variety of influences of ICT on products and services including, higher end tourism, offshore education and health services is provided. The report acknowledged that the traditional sun, sea and sand product that the region has produced in the past has now matured and that the region should capitalize on growing demand for cultural and adventure tourism. To be successful in these areas, the report recognized that regional governments will need to

    a. improve investment conditions in the tourism sector. This could be attained through improved management and marketing of the region;

    b. improve the quality of the tourism product on offer;

    c. target a wider range of "source" economies, including India and China;

    d. address any areas of skill deficiencies which inhibit the sector's growth.

This report also points out that offshore education, especially in health services represent a new dynamic area of demand for services by the developed world. It is noted that given existing demographic patterns in the United States, there will continue to be a great demand for physicians and the region should tap into producing these "services", while they are on the upswing of the international product cycle. To initiate this type of change,

    a. The region should try to improve on its investment climate by refining and improving its accreditation stature and also provide support for these regional accreditation centres and

    b. Create a harmonized and transparent investment regime to help promote FDI targeted at the tertiary level education sector.

The report also recognized the potential offered by cross border provision of health services. To improve the amount of opportunities in this area, the governments of the region would need to encourage growth in providing health care services and seek to close gaps in terms of the variations in the quality of health care services in the region. The report also suggested that economies of scale may be obtained if some of the offshore medical university facilities are utilized for the purpose of providing medical services for citizens of the host economy.

8. This study also identified a number of weaknesses in the labour markets of the region, and noted that addressing these various weaknesses in these labour markets are critical for improving the welfare of economic agents and reducing poverty rates in CARICOM. In particular, this study prescribed the following:

   a. There is a need to restructure the compensation paid to the public sector so that work remuneration will be founded on merit and productivity. This will have the effect of reducing the size of the public sector wage premium and will also help to minimize the overall amount of distortions in the labour market;

   b. Increasing employment in the public sector crowds out skilled employees for the private sector, so that a downsizing of the public sector will create a greater pool of skilled workers for the private sector;

   c. The labour market of Caribbean economies has a number of rigidities. However, these rigidities can be reduced if more modern labour market regulations which increase the employer's flexibility can help increase employment in the formal sector over time;

   d. As concerns migration, this report suggested that because of the tremendous benefits that the developed economies garner from migration, it is in the interest of CARICOM economies to try to engage some kind of cost sharing arrangement for educational training. CARICOM economies should also lobby for better terms for temporary migrant workers from its perimeters, as this type of policy action in the developed world can help to reduce the extent of permanent skills depleted from CARICOM economies.

9. This World Bank report expressed that CARICOM firms would need to try and target higher value added niche areas of production to facilitate their economic viability. In order to sustainably penetrate these niche markets, CARICOM economies would find it increasingly necessary to employ a greater amount of skilled labour. In this regard, the World Bank report noted:

   a. There is a need to improve the quantity of skills and the quality of skills produced in the region;

   b. That all children are equipped with a basic degree of education;

   c. The need to reduce the level of real starting salaries in the primary school system so as to make available more resources for teaching equipment, etc. In those CARICOM economies where it is necessary, the government should make greater use of the private sector;

   d. Greater attention should be paid to aligning private and public sector teaching with private sector needs;

    e. Investing in new products necessitates closer ties between research institutions and firms. There is also need to provide an FDI enabling environment.

10. Recognizing the importance of infrastructure for the development of the Caribbean sphere. This World Bank report noted that to bring the quality and quantity of infrastructure up to the required standards which facilitates the growth needs of the region, it would require substantial investment in infrastructure. The study noted that air services stood out as one definite area where the private sector can play a greater role. It is the recommendation of this study, that the government can offer contracts for air services rather than provide subsidies to domestic and regional carriers. The report also cited electricity as another area in which the private sector or an independent regulator can play a greater role.

11. Improving macro stability in the CARICOM sphere will require CARICOM economies to improve on their fiscal balances by reducing their expenditures, reducing the share of the public debt in total GDP, increasing taxes on the informal sector and reducing tax incentives. Other policy interventions can include more emphasis on privatization and a prioritization of public sector expenditures.

The World Bank report closed by emphasizing that because of the challenges facing CARICOM economies, action and not talk is required.

7.7 Regional Economic Transformation Task Force

The Regional Transformation Task Force (RTTF) was confirmed at the Fifteenth Meeting of the Bureau of the Conference of Heads of Government. The RTTF addressed the following purposes/objectives:

1. To determine the changes the private sector in the region has to make in order to prepare for the CSME;
2. To identify the constraints which prevented the private sector from being more meaningfully involved in productive activity;
3. To provide a greater utilization of non-debt financing instruments;
4. To provide recommendations to address points (1) to (3) above;
5. To outline the investment requirements of the CSME.

The arrangement was that the RTTF would be convened by the Caribbean Association of Industry and Commerce (CAIC). Four working groups were formed with the following portfolios:

1. Working Group 1: Upgrading industry competitiveness (responsibility carried by CAIC and the Caribbean Tourism Organization);
2. Working Group 2: Improving the Caribbean business environment (CARICOM Secretariat);
3. Working Group 3: Financial mobilization of infrastructure development (Caribbean Development Bank);

4. Working Group 4: Strategic planning (including fiscal and financial reform) for sustainable economic growth (Caribbean Centre for Monetary Studies).

Working Group 1: Upgrading Industry Competitiveness

1. The following sectors were identified as key areas for development emphasis:
   a. agriculture;
   b. manufacturing;
   c. textile and apparel;
   d. mining other than petroleum;
   e. oil and gas;
   f. tourism;
   g. services: financial, telecommunications, information services, entertainment services and health export services.
2. For these sectors it was agreed that there is the need to
   a. investigate the competitiveness of each sector;
   b. review their cost structures and product qualities so that areas of uncompetitiveness can be identified;
   c. identify best practices in these sectors.
3. For these sectors, Working Group 1 recognized the need to
   a. examine intersectoral and cross cutting linkages;
   b. identify synergies and policy issues which help to contribute to the efficiency of production;
   c. the intersectoral linkages should consider backward and forward linkages, and also physical infrastructure and research;
   d. the Working Group also carried the responsibility for designing a Caribbean business transformation plan.

Working Group 2: Improving the Caribbean Business Environment
This working group, which operated under the chairmanship of the CARICOM Secretariat, recommended the following programme of work:

1. ameliorating the investment environment in the region;
2. restructuring the sectoral investment framework;
3. reforming important economic policies.

Working Group 3: Financial Mobilization of Infrastructure Development
This working group focused on those areas where financial mobilization for infrastructural development was necessary and identified the following main areas:

1. Physical infrastructure:
   a. communications;
   b. transportation;
   c. roads;

    d. airport and seaport;

    e. water supply;

    f. waste management and disposal;

    g. environment;

    h. disaster preparedness and management.

2. Social infrastructure:

    a. health;

    b. education and training;

    c. housing;

    d. recreation;

    e. security.

3. Institutional infrastructure:

    a. public administration capacity;

    b. laws, regulations, rules, procedures and policies.

This working group recognized that in mobilizing finance needed to help develop the infrastructure base of the region, a number of issues should be kept in mind, namely:

1. Identifying areas of investment;
2. Determining investment volumes;
3. Identifying constraints;
4. Investment productivity;
5. Maintaining productive capacity;
6. Maintaining focus on the overall environment (Working Groups 3, 4).

Working Group 4: Strategic Planning (including Fiscal and Financial Reform) for Sustainable Economic Growth

This working group focused on the formulation of strategic planning for sustainable economic development. This group identifies the following five programme areas which could help reform the Caribbean region:

1. entrepreneurial development;
2. cultural activities;
3. intellectual property development;
4. joint venture activities and strategic alliances;
5. self-help improvement projects.

7.8 Summarizing the Gaps

Table 7.31 provides a summary of some of the key policy suggestions to address gaps in the economic development process within the CARICOM sphere, as indicated by the various policy documents.

This section closes by identifying the common areas identified by all the studies reviewed.

Table 7.31 Summary of major findings from the various reports

Bourne Report (1988)		
	1.	CARICOM economies need to align themselves with the production of commodities in greater demand by the global community. In order to penetrate export markets for these new commodities, CARICOM economies will need to improve their external competitiveness and through a deliberate process of intervention seek out new export items on the upswing of the international product cycle.
	2.	CARICOM economies will need to improve on their export marketing thrust and the process involved in financing new exports.
	3.	Growth opportunities exist in tourism. Other services which are currently experiencing a rapid upward increase in demand are: law, medicine, higher education, engineering and construction
	4.	CARICOM should also seek out growth opportunities connected to strongly growing economies in the Western Hemisphere. These newer markets with growing demand can provide new opportunities in trade, etc.
	5.	These economies will need to engage in some degree of technological leapfrogging. Technological improvement is critical to improve productive competitiveness CARICOM.
	6.	There is also the need to develop regional level technological capability.
	7.	Because of the expected demographic progress of the region there is the need to increase the amount of employment opportunities available to its people.
	8.	The region will need to ensure that its export revenues expand in real terms so as to maintain a stable and even improving inflow of capital goods as necessary for development.
	9.	There is the need for a greater degree of local content usage in the production process. This in turn will require strategic longer term planning on the behalf of regional governments.
	10.	The way forward significantly requires a greater degree of linkages between local factors and productive activity.
	11.	There is a need for the governments of the region to provide assistance by way of fiscal and other type of financial assistance to encourage domestic firms to improve on their technological deployment.
	12.	An improvement of the human capital fabric of the region is critical for the enhancement of the developmental prospects for the region. Economic growth into the future will also require a greater degree of capital deployment which can be facilitates by an increase in domestic savings rates.
	13.	A critical part of the developmental process requires the availability of finance for productive enterprises to call upon to make investment.
	14.	To increase the amount of financial inflows to the region:
		a. Striking the right balanced between profits and labour incomes as corporate savings rates and in excess of personal savings rates.
		b. Designing a system of tax subsidies to transfer incomes towards enterprises away from individuals.

Bourne Report (1988)	15.	To improve the cost competitiveness of the region, there is need to change both unit factor costs and also the extent of technological deployment. In this regard, wage policy in member states play a significant role as does the extent of research and development undertaken.
	16.	Whilst exchange rate policy may play a role in improving the export performance of member states, the significant reliance should be on appropriate changes in domestic factor markets and commodity markets.
	17.	Greater tariff liberalization in the region can help to reduce some of the inefficiencies caused by excessive protection.
	18.	The report acknowledges the significance of targeting other economies in the western hemisphere with rapid economic progress.
	19.	The report identifies that because the growth of export revenues is not pronounced every, attempt should be made to restrict import expenditures so as not to widen current account imbalances.
	20.	The report identifies that in the agricultural sector,
		a. Land distribution has to be effected to provide farm plots of the appropriate size, etc., so that economic returns from farm based activity, rivals non-farm activity.
		b. Establishing commodity price levels can help to influence farm incomes directly. Similar effects can be obtained by stimulating farm outputs.
		c. It is also imperative to provide technical assistance and marketing assistance for the agricultural sector.
OECS Report (2000)	1.	Accelerate transition away from protection for main export items to one founded on more competition
	2.	Decrease dependence on concessionary aid flows
	3.	Growth strategies in the region must be guided by the realities of globalization
	4.	Must involve a process of capacity building in all areas to improve the likeliness of selecting the best subset of policy choices
	5.	Managing the external environment
	6.	Sustainable economic development
	7.	Integrated production and marketing
	8.	Education and training
	9.	Poverty eradication
	10.	Job creation
	11.	Access to quality health services
	12.	Sustaining the stock of natural capital

(Table 7.31 continues)

Table 7.31 Summary of major findings from the various reports (*continued*)

Bonnick Report (2000)	1.	Adapting and adjusting to the changing international environment in which margins of preference are increasingly being eroded
	2.	Adapting and adjusting to the economic conditions within individual states
	3.	The need to implement second-generation reforms. Second-generation reforms are a fundamental part of the target the strengthening the democratic process and improve transparency and accountability in the practices of the state
	4.	There is the need to address poverty in a more front on manner
	5.	A great effort will have to be made to improve on the international competitiveness of member states
	6.	The private sector will have to be unbridled and will need to take a greater role in carving the economic growth dynamic of member states
	7.	Growth inhibiting factors which limit the ability of economies to initiate meaningful changes will have to aggressively resolved
CTAG Report (2001)	1.	CARICOM should define an international position and should build institutional capacity to support its trade policy stance.
	2.	The CDB should become the main financier of the development process in the region.
	3.	There is the need for the revival of traditional agricultural sector. The report specifically emphasized a common policy for sugar and rice. The level of international competitiveness of the banana sector should be improved within the relevant perimeters of the Cotonou Agreement.
	4.	A Caribbean tourism development strategy should be established and operationalized. This strategy will need to cover:
		a. The marketing of the Caribbean brand of the tourism product
		b. The facilitation of tourism traffic
		c. The financing of a human development programme for the tourism sector
		d. Minimum standards for the tourism product in the CARICOM sphere
		e. Practicing sustainable tourism so that the host communities do not experience deterioration of the environment encouraging tourism
		f. Promoting tourism research
	5.	A programme of competitiveness should be established, using the business schools of the universities as the institutional base. This programme would initially concentrate on enterprise case studies, particularly of successful businesses and move to organizing self-financing advisory services for improving competitiveness.
	6.	A Caribbean economic forum should be organized by an appropriate regional private sector body with the aim of bringing together Caribbean and multinational corporations, the public sector and multilateral financial institutions. The intention is that CEF would be patterned after the Davos (World Economic) Forum, would be initially supported by the World Bank as a successor to the CGCED, and would become a self-supporting institution.
	7.	A human resource retention and development programme should be prepared in a region wide sector comprehensive basis, and selected international organizations and bilateral partners invited to participate on a long term coordinated basis.

World Bank Report (2005)	1. A greater degree of integration will help to improve the competitiveness of Caribbean economies. Greater integration for example, will ease unemployment problems in various parts of the region and would help to promote:
	
	    a. an improvement in wage rates
	
	    b. the extent of skill arbitrage
	
	    c. if investment is promoted at the regional rather than national level, the region as a whole would become much more attractive for investments
	
	    d. a greater degree of integration manifested in a harmonization of tax rates can reduce tax competition in the region
	
	    e. a greater degree of intra-regional integration in the provision of some services can result in a fall in the cost of government in the region
	
	2. Tariffs in the region need to be further dismantled. For lowering tariffs, the region should negotiate greater technical and financial assistance.
	
	3. There is the need to improve on the investment climate in the region so that private investment can strive. An important part of the investment climate requires an improvement of the custom procedures, a reduction of high corporate taxes and a switch away from subsidies as a basis for attracting investment. Physical and institutional infrastructure also has to be improved. An important aspect of private investment should remain FDI and so greater efforts should be made to woo FDI.
	
	4. Where possible and feasible, some public goods should be delivered by the private sector. Attempts should be made to attain cost efficiencies in the production and delivery of some public services by forging regional alliances. The perspective here is to reduce the extent of the crowding out of private sector investment by public sector investment.
	
	5. Improving government finances and the role of government.
	
	6. Improving the investment climate so as to encourage more efficient private sector growth.
	
	7. Changes in the international environment.
	
	8. Emerging opportunities, especially in services.
	
	9. CARICOM firms will need to try and target higher value added niche areas of production to facilitate their economic viability.
	
	10. Renewed focus needed on education and skill development.
	
	11. Recognizing the importance of infrastructure for the development of the Caribbean sphere this report notes that to bring the quality and quantity of infrastructure up to the required standards which facilitates the growth needs of the region; it will require substantial investment in infrastructure.
	
	12. Improving macro stability in the CARICOM sphere will require CARICOM economies to improve on their fiscal balances by reducing their expenditures, reducing the share of the public debt in total GDP, increasing taxes on the informal sector and reducing tax incentives.

(Table 7.31 continues)

Table 7.31 Summary of major findings from the various reports (*continued*)

World Bank Report (2005)	**Regional transformation task force**
	a. Diversify the economies. Shift economic dependence to a wider export basket.
	b. Expand the existing capacities of the traditional sectors; manufacturing, agriculture, textile and apparel, mining, petroleum and oil and gas, and tourism.
	c. Tap into the existing niche markets of the financial services sector, the emerging informatics sector, entertainment services, health and education services, and telecommunications.
	d. Industry-level planning premised on modern planning methodologies, e.g., foresighting and backcasting.
	e. Planning should be participative, i.e., it should be a process which includes all stakeholder issues.
	f. Improve access to development funding for entrepreneurs.
	g. Increase the incentives for investment, e.g., with regards to taxation regimes.
	h. Improve the mechanisms for attracting FDI.
	i. Improve the quantity and quality of the human capital base of the region, through education and health care services.
	j. Increase the amount of backward and forward linkages between and among regional and domestic firms and institutions.
	k. Improve the physical, social, institutional and technological environment.

Source: Compiled from the various reports reviewed in the text of this chapter.

1. Identifying an international trade policy stance and effecting institutional capacity to support this stance.
2. The CDB should become the main financier of the development process in the region.
3. Revival of the traditional agricultural sector with special emphasis on common policies for rice and sugar. The banana sector should seek to make adjustments within the perimeters of the Cotonou Agreement.
4. There is need to improve on the tourism product. The sun, sand and sea image has matured and culture, adventure and other higher end tourism products is now in greater demand.
5. Human capital on every front has to be improved. Greater use has to be made of the University of the West Indies and the business schools in the region to help provide the appropriate type of entrepreneurial skills required by the region. Support for this can be sourced from the multilateral lending agencies such as the IDB.
6. The development effort of the region should be sustainable and people-centred.
7. There is the need to create jobs which are driven by the free market. The state should play an increasingly smaller role.
8. There is a need to address the crime situation in the region so that economic agents can benefit from the fruits of their labour.
9. The governance system of the region has to be improved.
10. There is a greater role for civil society and the need for a sense of unity with all social partners working together to attend to development challenges.
11. There is need to hasten the integration process as this will improve on the competitiveness of the region and even more, can help to ease unemployment problems in various parts of the region by an improvement in wage rates, increasing the degree skill arbitrage and helping to increase the attractiveness of the region as a basis for the attraction of investments, and so on.
12. CARICOM economies need to become even further liberalized so that they can reap more of the gains on offer from trade liberalization. In return for greater market access and reciprocity, the CARICOM economies should lobby for greater technical support and financial assistance.
13. There is the need to improve on the infrastructure of the region.
14. Greater efforts should be made to woo FDI into the region. The attraction of foreign investment should be done along alternative routes such as improving on customs procedures and reducing corporate taxes rather than through excessive subsidies.
15. Significant growth opportunities for the region exist in the services sector including offshore education and health services. To promote the growth of these "new" service sectors will require building the capital stock in these sectors, improving on the quality of the product on offer, improving on the stock of relevant human capital and targeting new and emerging significant markets such as India and China.
16. These studies also collectively looked at the labour markets of the regions and emphasized the need to improve on the economic welfare of the region and to reduce the rate of poverty in the society. The various reports recognized that in the public sector there was the need to premise the growth of wages on merit and productivity. It was also noted that by decreasing the size of the public sector there is the creation of a

greater pool of resources for the private sector to utilize. To overcome labour market rigidities it was recommended that more modern day labour negotiations needed to be deployed.

17. Concerning migration it was noted that the CARICOM sphere should try to negotiate some type of cost sharing arrangement with the developed world, while at the same time CARICOM should negotiate better terms for temporary migrant workers from the region in order to try and reduce the amount of permanent skills, lost from the CARICOM sphere.

18. These reports recognized the infrastructural deficiencies of the region for the development of the CARICOM sphere and recommended the privatization of air services and electricity.

19. All of these reports emphasized the importance of improving macroeconomic activity. Although their positions had some degree of variations their general consensus was that CARICOM member states needed to improve their fiscal balance, reduce the size of their public debt relative to the overall level of economic activity, privatize selected industries and improve the efficiency of public sector investments.

20. There is urgent need to improve the competitiveness of the region.

7.9 Conclusion

One of the main issues highlighted by all of the reports was the need for the region to improve its macroeconomic conditions. Subsequent to the publication of the latest summarized report (World Bank 2005), regional macroeconomic conditions have experienced improvements in some aspects and worsened in others. For instance, real GDP growth rates for most of the islands were less in 2012 as compared to 2005 with the exception of Guyana. This decline can be attributed to the region experiencing the residual effects of the global recession that occurred in the wake if the US financial crisis in 2008. Implications can be observed more pointedly for heavily tourism dependant islands and in debt stricken islands. These notwithstanding, there has been a slight increase in the size of the services sector for most of the islands which has led to a general increase in commercial service exports. There was also an improvement in the current account balance as a percentage of GDP for the majority of countries in the region when compared to 2005. For most of the countries there was some improvement in external competitiveness as well as net barter terms of trade.

In 2013, the regional aid for trade strategy was developed to show donors, investors and regional development partners that the region was taking a more organized approach to resource utilization and diversification of regional economies. This strategy was drafted taking into account all the different factors and vulnerabilities of the region in an effort to ensure maximum effectiveness.

8 | Unpausing the CARICOM Single Market and Economy

8.1 Introduction

This book covered a wide range of theoretical and practical issues associated with regional integration. However, it is clear that CARICOM is not doing well as a regional economic arrangement. Recall that CARICOM itself has four pillars, with the other three being foreign policy coordination, functional cooperation and security.

Foreign policy: The intention of the CSME is to have a common trade agreement among members on matters linked to internal and international trade and a coordinated external trade policy that is mutually negotiated. A major feature of the CSME's foreign policy is its common external tariff. This tariff implements a uniform tax on the imports of goods from non-member states into the single market.

Functional cooperation: The existence of the CSME depends on functional cooperation. This entails the synchronizing of policies and regulations on companies and intellectual property rights to ensure the smooth and effective management of the CSME. Moreover, this addresses the issues of economic, monetary and fiscal policy harmonization, to coordinate and promote the convergence of macro-economic policies and performance, coordinate exchange rate, interest rate, indirect taxes, commercial banks and national budget deficit policies.

Security: Security is of critical importance to the region. Certainly, policymakers are charged with the task of espousing regulations that will address domestic and maritime affairs of the CSME. On 3–5 July 2005, the community agreed to establish a management structure for its Crime and Security agenda. CARICOM is convinced that a cooperative approach is a very effective way to confront and address crime and security issues. The management structure of CARICOM security is comprised of the commissioners of police, chief of immigration, chiefs of the military, comptroller of customs and heads of intelligence and financial intelligence units. These heads collectively manage the region's security and advise political heads. Additionally, the CSME's security aspirations include food and nutrition safety. A recent study revealed that member countries suffer from a lack of access to nutritious, healthy food and not an inadequacy of food. In particular, the overview of vulnerability and food and nutrition security in the Caribbean (CFNI 2007) noted that food and nutritional issues can be addressed through several measures, including countries establishing national food and nutritional goals, the expansion and targeting of programmes that provide micronutrient supplementation, policy planning and coordination, strengthen food security, social policy as well as natural resource and environmental sustainability.

8.2 Regional Dissatisfaction with CARICOM

According to Stoneman et al. (2012), CARICOM is in crisis.[74] This is for three reasons: long-standing problems of slow progress have continued to escalate; a progressive weakening in its structure and operation; and continuing economic cutbacks since the 2008 financial crisis. The CARICOM crisis is a result of the indebtedness of many of its member countries, which means that further global economic downturns will compromise their ability to fund CARICOM. The secretariat and CARICOM institutions are not stable enough to address any large cutbacks in funding. In spite of this, evidence indicates that CARICOM would collapse if fundamental changes are not made. "Fundamental changes in the Secretariat's structure, operation and staffing need to be introduced gradually over a period of about 3 years" (Stoneman et al. 2012). Stoneman et al. highlighted five main recommendations that may generate this change. In particular, Stoneman et al. noted that, first, CARICOM and its secretariat require refocusing and restructuring and proposed that this be facilitated through a "transitional Change Office working directly with the Secretary General". Second, the secretariat requires refocusing in order to formulate strategic regional policies that have the potential to benefit member states beyond that which they can achieve individually. Third, the secretary general's role should be redefined as an executive rather than representational one. Fourth, emphasis should be placed on implementation, and this should be placed under the purview of the deputy secretary. Fifth, the appointment of a new chief operating officer with the responsibilities of maintaining efficiency in support functions (Stoneman et al. 2012).

8.3 Status of CSME Twenty-Five Years after Its Launch

After twenty-five years of its launch the CSME is nowhere near to completion (see chapter 1, table 1.5). Even more troubling is that "we do not know when it will be completed. Progress has slowed to a virtual standstill; the momentum has been lost; interest has waned. It is not yet officially dead; but it certainly appears to be comatose" (Girvan 2013a, 7).

In 2011, the CSME was put on pause. According to Girvan (2013b), in 2006, an "indicative target" was agreed to by the then twelve participating CSME countries for the establishment of a "single economy" by 2008. By 2007, these members agreed to the phased implementation of the single economy by 2015. Thereafter, information on CSME implementation was not forthcoming resulting in the single economy being placed on pause in 2011. In July 2012, a new schedule of implementation was reported agreed to by the members but by July 2014 no mention has been made to this effect.

According to Ralph Gonsalves, prime minister of St Vincent and the Grenadines:

> CARICOM's current mode of marking time, at an historical moment of overwhelmingly awesome challenges for our region which compellingly demands a more profound integration, is mistaken . . . "pausing" is but a euphemism for standing still, which in a dynamic world is sliding backwards. That, to me, is the evidence before us in CARICOM since its leaders, including me, decided at a special conclave in Guyana about a year ago to put the "single economy" process "on pause". (Letter to the secretary general of CARICOM, 29 February 2012, cited in Girvan 2013b, 4)

Jamaica has been calling for a suspension of its obligation in CARICOM. The *Trinidad Guardian* (9 October 2013) reported that in an address at the forty-fifth annual awards banquet of the Jamaican Manufacturers' Association, former minister Claude Clarke declared that Jamaica had losses of US$15 billion in revenues from subsidizing imports from the region. Indeed, table 8.1 shows that Jamaica's imports from the CARICOM region has increased by more than 2,500 per cent during the period 1972–2012. Jamaica's top import partners are the United States, Venezuela, and Trinidad and Tobago, respectively. Clarke urged that Jamaica should suspend the common external tariff on CARICOM imports for the duration of the payback period of Jamaica's IMF loan.[75] "It is time for the Jamaican Government to assert its sovereign authority and suspend the Common External Tariff of CARICOM, at least for the duration of the IMF programme," he said.

The free movement of CARICOM nationals has not been occurring as regional policy-makers may have hoped. Under article 45 of the Revised Treaty of Chaguaramas (RTC), member states committed themselves to the goal of free movement of its nationals within CARICOM. In a 2012 study conducted by CARICOM, findings reveal that the CSME is operating at an estimated 64 per cent level of compliance (CARICOM Secretariat 2012). A closer look at the CSME's five regimes reveals that while functional, they lack the required level of effectiveness. In particular, the freedom of movement of skills recorded a 66 per cent level of compliance, the free movement of goods recorded an 80 per cent level of compliance, the free movement of services reported a compliance level of 37 per cent, the free movement of capital reported a compliance level of 72 per cent, while the right of establishment reported a 64 per cent level of compliance. Perhaps the most ground-breaking development by CARICOM standards on the issue of free movement within CARICOM was the ruling of the Caribbean Court of Justice (CCJ) against the Government of Barbados, for breach of the aforementioned article of the RTC in 2013. On 14 March 2011, a Jamaican woman was denied entry into Barbados. The lawsuit filed against the Barbadian government for this action claimed that the Jamaican national was denied entry into Barbados on the basis of nationality and was subjected to inhumane treatment by immigration officials in Barbados. The CCJ ruled in favour of the Jamaican national (awarding damages which amounted to BD$77,240) citing the right to freedom of movement within CARICOM as outlined in article 45 of the RTC. A second related incident occurred in November 2013 when thirteen Jamaican nationals were refused entry into Trinidad and Tobago despite the fact that these individual are owners of CARICOM passports. The incident was purportedly motivated by the murder of a Trinidadian national in Jamaica a few days prior. However, many commentators claimed that these actions were a breach of the RTC and CCJ laws (Boodram 2013).

Table 8.1 Jamaica's import and export from/to CARICOM, US$ million, 1972–2012

	Export to CARICOM	Import from CARICOM	Trade Balance
1972	26.86	33.66	−6.80
1973	28.04	35.57	−7.53
1974	33.38	72.31	−38.92
1975	35.50	97.52	−62.02
1976	44.48	64.34	−19.86
1977	51.44	42.40	9.03
1978	49.66	50.26	−0.60
1979	72.69	57.30	15.39
1980	59.75	85.38	−25.63
1981	70.91	113.36	−42.45
1982	80.88	80.00	0.87
1983	102.60	70.88	31.72
1984	56.88	36.65	20.23
1985	50.63	43.11	7.52
1986	45.95	36.27	9.67
1987	50.24	59.26	−9.02
1988	61.52	58.40	3.13
1989	68.62	95.99	−27.36
1990	73.70	88.54	−14.84
1991	65.59	67.77	−2.18
1992	61.57	67.43	−5.86
1993	60.20	115.81	−55.61
1994	59.57	152.99	−93.42
1995	59.00	239.85	−180.85
1996	53.55	288.54	−234.99
1997	46.54	318.08	−271.53
1998	44.10	311.13	−267.04
1999	41.73	368.18	−326.45
2000	43.41	401.35	−357.93
2001	48.41	433.88	−385.47
2002	45.41	366.35	−320.93
2003	47.20	475.81	−428.61
2004	45.28	563.40	−518.13
2005	41.78	827.56	−785.78
2006	48.53	672.77	−624.24
2007	49.06	1,192.43	−1,143.38
2008	60.76	1,636.53	−1,575.77
2009	64.93	660.77	−595.84
2010	62.07	833.51	−771.44
2011	62.11	1,032.29	−970.18
2012	94.59	904.23	−809.64

Source: World Integrated Trade Solution (WITS) (2014).

On the basis of the deportation of Jamaican nationals from Trinidad and Tobago, several calls within Jamaica were made to boycott the imports of Trinidadian goods. However, Sanders (2013) noted that "an organised boycott of Trinidad and Tobago products that is currently being proposed in Jamaica is not the answer". The minister of foreign affairs for Trinidad and Tobago, Winston Dookeran, also noted that a "trade war" will lead to adverse outcomes for both countries. In an attempt curb this action, a meeting between the foreign ministers of the two islands led to an agreement to cooperate in an effort to preserve the integrity of CARICOM. Additionally, they have agreed to the recognition of skills certificates and the adoption of relevant legislation to allow for the hassle-free travel of all ten categories of skilled nationals.[76] Indeed different member states seem to have different immigration and tourism regulations for entry. Movement of labour in the region is still an issue to be addressed.

Leeward Islands Air Transport (LIAT) has issues with Caribbean Airlines (CAL) especially as regards fuel subsidy. On 4 May 2013, LIAT accused CAL of being in breach of the RTC that governs the regional integration movement. Chairman of LIAT's stakeholder governments, Prime Minister Ralph Gonsalves noted that due to Trinidad and Tobago's fuel subsidies, CAL is in violation of the common air service agreement among CARICOM member states, which has caused magnanimous losses for LIAT. Indeed, data over the five-year period 2008–12 reveal that LIAT spent US$106.1 million on jet fuel, but CAL spent only US$43.64 million which suggests that LIAT paid US$62.4 million more on fuel than it would have paid if it enjoyed the same subsidy as CAL ("CARICOM Heads Vex over CAL", *Trinidad Guardian*, 13 May 2013). CAL enjoyed a low average fuel price of US$53 per barrel of jet fuel over the five-year period while LIAT paid US$127 on average per barrel of jet fuel. Gonsalves estimated that the subsidy led to the loss of seventy-eight thousand passengers for LIAT to CAL as a result of the unfair competition. Gonsalves noted that the facts and laws regarding this matter are clear, so a sensible resolution must be forthcoming, particularly on the part of the Trinidad and Tobago government (ibid.).

The OECS is advancing at a pace beyond CARICOM. Girvan (2013b), in particular, noted that the OECS bloc has already commenced with the establishment of their own economic union, having signed the Revised Treaty of Basseterre in 2010. This treaty

> establishes the OECS economic union, making possible the creation of a single financial and economic space within which goods, people and capital move freely, monetary and fiscal policies are harmonized and countries continue to adopt a common approach to trade, health, education and environment, as well as to the development of such critical sectors as agriculture, tourism and energy . . . the Treaty paves the way for the introduction of legislative competence at the regional level, so that Member States of the Organisation act in concert to develop and enact legislation in certain areas specified in the Treaty.[77]

The strengthening of the relationship between some CARICOM member countries and the Venezuelan Bolivarian Alliance for the Peoples of Our America (ALBA) – Peoples' Trade Treaty initiative as well as the Petrocaribe initiative is one of the most notable occurrences in modern regional matters. Petrocaribe is a partnership between some Caribbean states and Venezuela to purchase oil at a preferential rate.[78] It began on 29 June 2005, in Venezuela by Hugo Chavez.

One of the major consequences of Petrocaribe for CARICOM is its emergence as the largest source of concessional financing for the CARICOM bloc in comparison to US foreign assistance and financing from the Inter-American Development Bank. Box 8.1 highlights the added benefits that ALBA member countries accrue from Petrocaribe.

Box 8.1 Petrocaribe projects

Jamaica – Supply of 23,500 b/d. Agreements signed in education, science, technology, medicine, and tourism. Agreement to upgrade the Petrojam refinery.

Grenada – Agreements to supply 340,000 barrels per year of products; 55,000 gasoil, 85,000 thousand gasoline and 200,000 fuel oil.

Cuba – Inauguration of the Cienfuegos Refinery in Cuba with a capacity of 70,000 b/d.

Belize – Mixed enterprise between Petróleos de Venezuela, S.A. (PDV) and Belize Petroleum.

Nicaragua – 80,000 gallons of Venezuelan diesel per day.

Dominica – 1,200 barrels of asphalt. Warehouse 1,000 b/d hydrocarbons.

Antigua & Barbuda – This is a strategic place for warehouse and distribution of fuel to the Eastern Caribbean.

New projects:

Expansion of the Kingston refinery, Jamaica;

Building of the refinery in Leon, Nicaragua;

Construction of the refinery in Dominica;

Construction of the refinery in Belize;

Conclude the construction of the PLG (liquefied petroleum gas) in St Vincent & the Grenadines;

Construction of fuel distribution plants in Dominica, St Kitts & Nevis, St Vincent & the Grenadines, Grenada and El Salvador;

Electricity generation plants in Nicaragua, Haiti, St Kitts & Nevis, and Antigua & Barbuda.

Source: Girvan (2009).

The rise in world oil price post 2008 has strengthened the strategic role of the Petrocaribe for CARICOM. Girvan (2009) noted that if the current importation rate stands at 72 million barrels/year), for every dollar increase in the oil price, $72 million/year is added to the oil bill of importing countries. Assuming a base price of $30/barrel and the world market price of $135/barrel, this signifies an addition amounting to $7.6 billion/year to the oil bill of the sixteen importing countries. It follows that between 25 per cent and 50 per cent could be financed by Petrocaribe credits, which for the smaller member countries provides a level of energy security.

It is also clear that the enthusiasm of Owen Arthur, P.J. Patterson, Michael Manley and Eric Williams has not been replicated by their successors. The painstaking slow pace of CARICOM is a testament to the loss in enthusiasm in the Caribbean's present leaders in the drive towards regional integration. The absence of will to implement policies and missed deadlines would convince the masses that Caribbean leaders are not as passionate as they once were about the issue of regional integration. The 2005 deadline of free movement of labour has not been met; the CARICOM passport has only been issued by Suriname; and there are other signs that indicate a loss of passion and enthusiasm to make the CSME a reality.

Trinidad and Tobago appears more interested in the extra-regional markets, notwithstanding its position as a major player within CARICOM (see chapter 4 for details on CARICOM-BRICS relations). By 2012, Trinidad and Tobago accounted from approximately 37 per cent of regional GDP, 67 per cent of regional exports but only around 33 per cent of regional imports (see chapter 2, table 2.24).

Jamaica has been overburdened by its debt position. The Jamaican economy has long been plagued by a cycle of low growth and high debt. In particular, over the past two decades, average GDP per capita growth has reported a negative value of 0.1 per cent, the lowest percentage reported for the Caribbean region, with the exception of Haiti. Furthermore, as a consequence of the global financial crisis, Jamaica's growth performance has weakened in the last four years. Moreover, the unemployment and poverty rate have been on the rise, such that the gap between the rich and the poor has expanded substantially and the poverty rate has almost doubled. During this time, multilateral agencies such as the IMF, World Bank and the Inter-American Development Bank have all extended support to the island's developmental goals. Specifically, in 2010, the IMF loaned Jamaica US$1.27 billion. Additional funding was sourced from the World Bank and the Inter-American Development Bank, which together with the IMF's loan amounted to over US$2 billion. In an effort to address its unsustainable debt situation and as a pre-condition for this loan, the country engaged in a debt exchange. Implications to this loan agreement included severe austerity measures, freezing of wages and cutting of spending. According to Johnston (2013), subsequent to the debt exchange, interest payments on the loan climbed to 11 per cent of GDP representing the world's highest debt interest burden. Following Jamaican court rulings that departed from the ideals of the IMF, the agreement collapsed, however, to a large extent, Jamaica has maintained the austerity measures from the IMF agreement. Slow growth was recorded in 2011–12; however, a year later Jamaica had again slipped back into a recession due to its government's move to cut non-interest expenditure by over 2 per cent of GDP. In 2013, Jamaica again entered into an agreement with the IMF, the result of which affected domestically held debt while the principal remained fixed. The IMF now required Jamaica to:

> run primary surpluses (revenue minus expenditure, excluding interest costs) of 7.5 per cent of GDP, which . . . would mean Jamaica would have the highest primary surplus in the world outside of oil exporting countries in 2013 [Oil-exporting countries that run large primary budget surpluses are doing so because of excess oil revenues, not budget tightening as in the case of Jamaica]. And even after the second debt exchange in three years, Jamaica is projected to have the highest average interest burden in the world over the next six years. (Johnston 2013, 1–2)[79]

This second IMF agreement coupled with funding from the World Bank and the Inter-American Development Bank make approximately US$2 billion dollars of loans available to Jamaica over the next four years.

Change of political regimes has perhaps prompted a lowered political will (see chapter 7, table 7.23). The region has also been hammered by the 2008 financial crisis. According to Downes (2009), the main effects of the global economic crisis on Caribbean economies can be seen in a decline in export demand for both goods and services, in particular, bauxite, tourism and offshore finance, a fall in remittance flows, reduction in FDI capital inflows, changes in credit ratings the consequence of which is a reduction in access to financial credit, exchange rate depreciations, an increase in unemployment levels as well as some deterioration of fiscal balances and balance of payments. In addition, the region has experienced a variety of natural disasters in the last fifteen years. Table 8.3 lists the frequency of the Caribbean's most prevalent natural disaster, hurricanes.

Table 8.2 Jamaica's growth and debt overview, 1970–2012

	GDP (Constant LCU$ Million)	Current Account Balance (US$ Billion)	Total Net External Debt (US$ Million)	Net Internal Debt (US$ Million)
1970	539,214.20	–	–	–
1975	588,624.90	–	–	–
1980	498,771.70	−0.11	–	–
1985	508,858.90	−0.25	–	–
1990	649,234.40	−0.33	33,068.80	1,140.44
1995	787,901.20	−0.08	33,361.70	16,362.98
2000	774,573.90	−0.35	34,465.50	47,914.91
2005	0.00	−1.07	54,511.00	86,715.50
2006	873,129.20	−1.20	58,287.40	94,784.46
2007	885,353.00	−1.97	61,512.60	92,031.10
2008	879,031.00	−2.43	63,895.40	85,767.12
2009	840,255.00	−1.33	65,007.30	92,524.30
2010	827,819.00	−1.15	71,126.30	109,283.30
2011	841,918.00	−1.93	70,694.20	116,986.20
2012	838,116.00	−1.92	73,896.60	122,348.40

Source: World Development Indicators (2014).

According to ECLAC (2010), for the period 1990–2008, the Caribbean region experienced losses (loss of crop harvests or industrial production) and damages (immovable assets and stock) from natural disasters amounting to an estimated US$136 billion (see table 8.4).

The economic impact was most severe in productive sectors including agriculture, tourism and manufacturing. In terms of agriculture, countries such as St Lucia and Dominica experienced damages to their respective banana crop and subsistence agriculture, Guyana in its sugar and rice industries and Belize in its sugar, banana, citrus and papaya crops. With regards to tourism, countries such as Anguilla, the Bahamas, Cayman Islands and Grenada experienced infrastructural damage along the coastlines. Housing and human settlements constituted the main social impact with damages ranging between 35 per cent and 99 per cent of total national damage costs for most of the affected islands. In terms of the environmental impact, an estimated US$3.5 billion was incurred by the region between 1990 and 2008. Countries experienced differential impacts depending on their level of resilience. Haiti experienced the largest damage which amounted to approximately US$53 billion. Suriname followed with an estimated US$51 billion in total damage costs. Cumulatively, the total subregional rehabilitation costs from natural disasters were estimated at US$1.3 trillion of which Haiti alone accounted for 99 per cent of this sum (ECLAC 2010).

Some argue that the secretariat is under resourced and therefore has little financial effectiveness. CARICOM itself has no executive authority. At the inter-sessional summit in St Vincent in March 2014, the head of CARICOM, Prime Minister Gonsalves, made it clear that CARICOM was not designed as a central government for a "bundle of disparate territories", neither was it a unitary state of federation or confederation. Gonsalves faulted the RTC by saying that it "conceives CARICOM as a community of sovereign states. Its centre has been deliberately designed as

Table 8.3 List of hurricanes in the Caribbean within the last fifteen years

Date	Wind Speed and Hurricane Category	Hurricane Name
22 August 2000	81 mph Category 1	Debby
01 October 2000	40 mph thunderstorm	Joyce
17 August 2001	40 mph thunderstorm	Chantal
22 August 2001	58 mph thunderstorm	Dean
06 October 2001	58 mph thunderstorm	Iris
08 October 2001	52mph thunderstorm	Jerry
24 September 2002	69 mph thunderstorm	Lili
08 July 2003	46 mph thunderstorm	Claudette
10 August 2004	46 mph thunderstorm	Charley
15 August 2004	52 mph thunderstorm	Earl
31 August 2004	127 mph Category 3	Frances
08 September 2004	138 mph Category 4	Ivan
15 September 2004	69 mph thunderstorm	Jeanne
05 July 2005	46 mph thunderstorm	Dennis
15 July 2005	127 mph Category 3	Emily
15 November 2005	40 mph thunderstorm	Gamma
02 August 2006	63 mph thunderstorm	Chris
25 August 2006	40 mph thunderstorm	Ernesto
18 August 2007	167 mph Category 5	Dean
02 September 2007	98 mph Category 2	Felly
11 December 07	52 mph thunderstorm	Olga
16 October 08	132 mph Category 4	Omar
03 September 2009	46 mph thunderstorm	Erika
04 August 2010	46 mph thunderstorm	Colin
30 August 2010	132 mph Category 4	Earl
01 September 2010	63 mph thunderstorm	Fiona
31 October 2010	98 mph Category 2	Tomas
02 August 2011	40 kt tropical storm	Emily
22 August 2011	65 kt Category 1	Irene
10 September 2011	45 kt tropical storm	Maria
28 September 2011	40 kt tropical storm	Ophelia
03 August 2012	40 kt tropical storm	Ernesto
22 August 2012	40 kt tropical storm	Issac
14 October 2012	45 kt tropical storm	Rafael
24 October 2012	75 kt Category 1	Sandy
09 July 2013	55 kt tropical storm	Chantal
04 August 2014	70 kt Category 1	Bertha

Sources: Caribbean Hurricane Network (2011) and National Oceanic and Atmospheric Administration (2014).

Table 8.4 Impact of natural disasters in the Caribbean, 1990–2008

Impact	Amount (US$ Billion)	% of Total Impact
Economic	63.00	46
Social	57.00	42
Infrastructural	12.00	9
Environmental	3.50	3
Total	135.50	100

Source: United Nations Economic Commission for Latin America and the Caribbean (ECLAC) (2014).

a weak superstructure which constantly gropes consensus." CARICOM was deliberately designed to be weak at the executive level. This is further substantiated by the fact that CARICOM has no executive authority, which accommodates the lack of political will to implement CARICOM policies. Gonsalves made this clear when he said that, "invariably, the CARICOM Secretariat is excoriated for this implementation deficit. However, the Secretariat is not CARICOM, it is the central administrative instrument of CARICOM but it possesses no authority to compel enforcement of decisions of the various Councils of Ministers and the Heads of State and Government conference."

Overall and following Girvan (2013b), CARICOM economies may not be able to see the economic benefits of the CSME because of the cost of implementation in the context of their current economic realities and the realities of benefits from extra-regional entities and because implementation may be beyond their capacity. In many regards, the acid test of the CSME is what changes has it brought as regards to improving the economic outcomes in CARICOM. The new secretary general of the secretariat has outlined that in his perspective, the time has arrived for us to, "recalibrate and focus more on the productive sector and making our economies more competitive. I am of the view that we do. We probably have adopted a too theoretical model of economic integration" (LaRocque 2013, 6).

8.4 The Way Forward

The CSME must be more proactive. It should seek to address the economic realities of the region and in so doing enhance its economic welfare. In closing this chapter, three areas are suggested here: maritime transport, food security and regional energy cooperation.

8.4.1 Maritime Transport

One of the main challenges that firms in the developing world encounter in moving up the value chain of production is the unpredictability of the international supply chain. With the global production chain, the problem is compounded as not just exports enter into the equation but also imports. From this perspective, improving the quality of the supply chain is critical for economies trying to improve their trade competitiveness. Arvis et al. (2008) have demonstrated that the competitiveness position of economies at lower levels of economic development is eroded by high logistics cost. Arvis et al. (2008) have argued that for lesser developed economies it is more expensive to move goods to their destination. Lowe (2002) describes logistics as the total concept of planning and organizing the supply and circulation of materials and supplies from the original source through the stages of production, assembly, packaging, storage, handling and distribution to the final consumer. Hausman et al. (2013) noted that countries are dependent on trade to increase sales of domestic products in world markets. However, in emerging economies, trade is regarded as a tool for economic development. Yildiz (2014, 63–64) argued that the "high costs (to trade) are driven by the unreliability of logistics suppliers and low predictability, which result primarily from rent-seeking and governance issues". Moreover, it is this underlying unreliability of supplies that reduces the competitiveness of lesser developed countries (see chapter 6, table 6.2, which provides an indication of various indicators of ease of trading in various economies and comparative rankings for listed Caribbean economies). This data reflects that in the Caribbean trading is relatively difficult.

Indeed, no less a person than the prime minister of Grenada, Tillman Thomas, at a retreat of CARICOM Heads of Government in Grenada on 3 April 2011, argued on the urgency and significance with which CARICOM should treat with the issue of maritime transport. Specifically, Prime Minister Tillman noted

> Caribbean regional maritime transport service is both inadequate and very expensive compared with other parts of the world. Yet substantial opportunities are available for intra-regional cargo and passenger shipments, trans-shipment services, cross roads, port and shipping services and containerization. Substantial investments are required and need to be organized around a holistic approach to expanding and modernizing maritime assets, creating larger scale, specialized vessels and upgrading seaports, and that at the same time would be facilitated by a regionally harmonized, regulatory, legal and policy framework. (p. 4)[80]

The CARICOM Secretariat (2013) noted that the majority of Caribbean islands are characterized as being small and fragmented, with only Guyana and Suriname sharing a border. This underscores the importance of maritime transport as a crucial factor in strengthening the region's competitiveness. In particular, McLean added that approximately 90 per cent of the world's merchandise trade takes place via containers and overall containerized shipping costs in the Caribbean are approximately 30 per cent above the global average. Moreover, CARICOM countries are price takers and are less vocal on decisions of intra-regional and international shipping frequency. It follows that CARICOM views an efficient regional maritime transport system as prerequisite for boosting regional production, strengthening and transforming intra-regional trade and accelerating the region's integration into hemispheric and global supply chains. This can be achieved through regional cooperation in maritime infrastructure development, specifically, that of port facilities and shipping technology.[81]

There are several interventions which have been recognized by regional policymakers and international development partners as having the greatest potential for improving the efficiency and reducing the cost of regional maritime transport. These, according to McLean (2014, 17) include

    1. Establishment of a pan-Caribbean maritime corridor:
        a. Upgrading Caribbean port infrastructure and services, as well as freight logistics; and
        b. Establishing an intra-CARICOM fast-ferry service.

2. Development of a common shipping policy for the small vessel fleet in the Eastern Caribbean (OECS countries);
3. Formulation of a cohesive regional maritime safety and security strategy for small vessels that operate among CARICOM member states; and
4. Establishment of innovative regional transport networks.

The possibility for an inter-island fast ferry service has been recognized as a facility for increasing the efficiency of the CSME and intra-regional commerce; however, no solid initiative has taken fruition. In 2001, a feasibility study for the establishment of a fast ferry service in the southern Caribbean was conducted, with countries such as Barbados, Grenada, St Vincent and the Grenadines, St Lucia, and Trinidad and Tobago targeted as the main beneficiaries in the first instance. Accordingly, private-public partnership was envisioned as the mode through which this initiative would become operational, with Port of Spain the proposed base. Moreover, the establishment of an inter-island fast-ferry has been highlighted as a major AfT project and therefore crucial for strengthening regional integration under the CSME framework (McLean 2014).

It is also important to note that Guyana and Suriname are also members of the Union of South American Nations (UNASUR). The UNASUR was established in 2008 and facilitates regional integration projects through its common initiatives fund. Under the Initiative for the Integration of Regional Infrastructure of South America (IIRSA), Guyana and Suriname form a vital part of three agenda of priority integration projects, which include: the Boa Vista–Georgetown roadway between Brazil and Guyana; the Ciudad Guyana–Georgetown roadway between Venezuela and Guyana; and the South Drain–Apura–Zanderu–Moengo–Albina linkage, which includes a bridge over the Corentyne River (McLean 2014).

Tables 8.5–8.7 reveal that Jamaica and the Bahamas are regional leaders in liner shipping connectivity. Jamaica boasts an average quality of port index of 5.21 over the six-year period. Indeed, evidence suggests that as Jamaican port infrastructure improved, so did its trading activity and liner connection. However, the Barbadian infrastructure was 5.53 over the same period as Barbadian liner connectivity worsened. In spite of this, trade activity grew sporadically in Barbados. With a port infrastructure index of 1.85, Haiti has the worst port equipment in the region, but surprisingly Haiti is not the worst destination for liner connectivity. Trinidad and Tobago has an average infrastructure index of 3.76 but has one of the most active ports in the region. Countries like Trinidad and Tobago and Haiti can improve trading activity by improving port infrastructure and this in turn will strengthen trading opportunities within CARICOM.

The attendant benefits that strengthening regional maritime shipping will have for regional economic integration are broadly threefold. Perhaps the most profound benefit for the region will be the harmonization of national shipping policies. CARICOM's Protocol IV addresses transport policy, specifically, the need for individual countries to formulate specific maritime and port policies which in their fundamentals allow for transport policy issues to be surmised within a general framework (Sánchez et al. 2009). This becomes particularly important in the context of the expansion of the Panama Canal. Rodrigue and Notteboom (2011) noted that the expansion of the Panama Canal is opening a new phase for transhipment in the Caribbean in what has been dubbed the "transhipment triangle". The authors added that the growth in Caribbean transhipment activities is linked to the growth in Latin America and to this end the need for shippers to reconcile within their national and regional shipping networks the large volume of north–south trade flows.

Table 8.5 Maritime profiles of selected Caribbean economies port moves, national total (TEU), 2000–2012

	Antigua & Barbuda	Bahamas	Barbados	Belize	Dominica	Guyana	Jamaica	Dominican Republic	St Vincent & the Grenadines	St Lucia	Trinidad & Tobago
2000	–	572,224.0	68,600.0	25,537.0	–	–	894,779.0	561,266.0	–	41,037.0	347,934.0
2001	–	570,000.0	67,203.0	27,074.0	7,726.0	39,894.0	983,400.0	583,390.0	–	22,836.0	352,758.0
2002	–	860,000.0	68,260.0	30,312.0	7,201.0	38,994.0	1,065,000.0	541,932.0	–	23,067.0	385,233.0
2003	–	1,057,879.0	70,146.0	33,789.0	–	–	1,137,798.0	480,650.0	–	25,000.0	396,368.0
2004	–	1,059,581.0	82,028.0	35,565.0	–	–	1,356,034.0	537,316.0	–	24,965.0	449,468.0
2005	–	1,121,285.0	88,758.0	35,891.0	–	–	1,670,800.0	355,404.0	–	60,747.0	322,466.0
2006	–	1,390,000.0	98,511.0	38,005.0	–	–	2,150,408.0	366,255.0	–	30,656.0	632,266.0
2007	–	1,636,000.0	99,623.0	39,191.0	–	–	2,016,792.0	309,344.0	–	32,339.0	357,486.0
2008	32,562.0	1,702,000.0	87,255.0	38,211.0	–	–	1,830,000.0	1,129,680.0	–	70,201.0	560,000.0
2009	31,332.0	1,323,000.0	82,832.0	31,344.0	–	52,000.0	1,728,042.0	1,262,943.0	14,704.0	51,942.0	565,389.0
2010	26,366.0	1,125,000.0	80,430.0	31,917.0	–	59,850.0	1,891,770.0	1,382,045.0	15,569.0	52,497.0	573,217.0
2011	21,824.0	1,116,000.0	77,053.0	34,200.0	–	–	1,756,832.0	1,479,455.0	16,419.0	60,342.0	550,418.0
2012	24,449.0	1,202,000.0	72,163.0	36,651.0	–	–	1,139,418.0	1,751,758.0	16,826.0	89,080.0	–

Source: United Nations Economic Commission for Latin America and the Caribbean (ECLAC) (2014).

Table 8.6 Quality of port infrastructure, WEF, 2007–2012

	2007	2008	2009	2010	2011	2012
Antigua & Barbuda	–	–	–	–	–	–
Bahamas	–	–	–	–	–	–
Barbados	5.42	5.51	5.49	5.55	5.60	5.60
Belize	–	–	–	–	3.30	–
Dominica	–	–	–	–	–	–
Grenada	–	–	–	–	–	–
Guyana	2.70	3.02	3.21	3.50	3.70	3.30
Haiti	–	–	–	–	1.80	1.90
Jamaica	5.21	5.05	5.27	5.34	5.30	5.10
St Kitts & Nevis	–	–	–	–	–	–
St Lucia	–	–	–	–	–	–
St Vincent & the Grenadines	–	–	–	–	–	–
Suriname	2.69	2.94	3.32		4.50	5.00
Trinidad & Tobago	3.21	3.38	3.98	4.33	3.90	3.80

Note: 1 = extremely underdeveloped to 7 = well developed and efficient by international standards.

Source: World Bank Development Indicators (2014).

Table 8.7 Liner shipping connectivity index (maximum value in 2004 = 100), 2004–2012

	2004	2005	2006	2007	2008	2009	2010	2011	2012
Antigua & Barbuda	2.33	2.56	2.43	3.76	3.82	2.66	2.40	2.40	2.41
Bahamas	17.49	15.70	16.19	16.45	16.35	19.26	25.71	25.18	27.06
Barbados	5.47	5.77	5.34	5.79	5.36	4.75	4.20	5.85	4.82
Belize	2.19	2.59	2.62	2.61	2.32	2.30	3.95	3.85	9.99
Dominica	2.33	2.51	2.33	2.40	2.31	2.73	1.88	2.08	2.08
Grenada	2.30	2.52	3.37	4.09	4.20	4.13	3.71	3.93	4.04
Guyana	4.54	4.37	4.60	4.51	4.36	4.34	3.95	3.96	4.06
Haiti	4.91	3.43	2.91	2.87	3.44	4.40	7.58	4.75	5.08
Jamaica	21.32	21.99	23.02	25.50	18.23	19.56	33.09	28.16	21.57
St Kitts & Nevis	5.49	5.32	5.59	6.16	6.19	3.08	2.84	2.66	2.67
St Lucia	3.70	3.72	3.43	4.21	4.25	4.25	3.77	4.08	4.55
St Vincent & the Grenadines	3.56	3.58	3.40	4.34	4.52	4.13	3.72	3.95	4.02
Suriname	4.77	4.16	3.90	4.29	4.26	4.16	4.12	4.16	4.48
Trinidad & Tobago	13.18	10.61	11.18	13.72	12.88	15.88	15.76	17.89	18.90

Source: World Bank Development Indicators (2014).

One of the most popular arrangements occurring within the maritime sector in the region is that of private-public partnerships (PPPs). Through PPPs the design, financing and execution of maritime infrastructure projects by the private sector has been found to be one of the mechanisms that can be used to reduce the large gap between infrastructure needs and the limited investment resources that government have at their disposal to meet them (Aggarwal 2009). Rodrigue and Notteboom (2011) argued that the standards of infrastructure in some Caribbean countries can be considered acceptable; however, the biggest problem has been its maintenance. UNECE (2008) outlined the three phases of a PPP lifecycle model. The last phase: the concession phase constitutes the PPPs role of design and construction, facility operation and maintenance and asset hand back. The logic follows that by maintaining port facilities, PPPs effect stronger maritime shipping in the region. Moreover, port activities are conducted with greater efficiency, greater adherence to compliance standards and collectively a reduction of bottlenecks.

The strengthening of regional maritime shipping engenders enhanced regional competitiveness as commodity and container trade are boosted. There would be shorter lead and wait times and reduced transaction costs. The benefit in the longer term would be a streamlining of activities along the regional production line and the supply chain. This should encourage greater productivity and improved quality along all levels of the value chain. Within the CSME framework, the end result could be the attraction and greater movement of labour, capital (investments) and the stimulation of new business activities.

8.4.2 Food Security

The FAO (2003) noted that "food security is traditionally discussed in terms of either food self-sufficiency or food self-reliance". The former refers to a low degree of reliance on imports for food supply and the latter has to do with the availability of food based on the amount of resources in an economy and the extent of comparative advantage. During the period 1998–2005, the prices of some commodities escalated, especially that of maize, rice and wheat, which form an important part of the diet of developing economies. A variety of factors motivated this including fluctuations in the demand and supply of these food commodities (De Schutter 2010).

Table 8.8 Average annual prices of maize, rice and wheat, dollars per tonne, 1998–2005

Year	Maize	Rice	Wheat	Year	Maize	Rice	Wheat
1998	102.20	215.16	128.53	2006	121.07	216.65	199.65
1999	91.76	191.46	114.41	2007	162.65	272.98	263.80
2000	88.22	142.96	118.63	2008	223.13	507.65	344.58
2001	89.61	135.38	129.65	2009	165.64	328.10	235.69
2002	99.25	151.15	150.83	2010	184.56	388.44	240.81
2003	105.07	151.33	149.64	2011	292.33	466.12	330.08
2004	111.94	207.27	161.31	2012	298.32	540.69	327.15
2005	98.39	218.52	157.81	2013	280.76	510.65	324.07

Source: Food Security Portal (2013).

8.4.2.1 Food Export and Import Patterns of CARICOM Countries

This rapid increase in food prices have adversely affected CARICOM economies as they are net food importers and over time this trend has become a bit more pronounced. Implications of the sharp increase in the FAO's global food price index between 2008 and 2010 laid the context in which the CARICOM Regional Food and Nutrition Security Policy (RFNSP) was developed.

In October 2010, at the special meeting of the CARICOM Council on Trade and Economic Development (COTED) in Grenada, the RFNSP was validated and endorsed. Its formulation was a collaborative effort on the part of CARICOM member states, regional technical institutions, the CARICOM Secretariat and the FAO, in a technical working group which comprised Antigua, Belize, Dominica, Jamaica, Grenada, Guyana, OECS, Caribbean Food and Nutrition Institute (CFNI), Caribbean Farmers Network (CaFAN), the University of the West Indies, and IICA (Garcia and Smart 2011).

This initiative demonstrates member states' reaffirmation of their commitment to the Liliendaal Declaration on Agriculture and Food Security (July 2009). Accordingly, the RFNSP is consistent with national food security policies and complements the goal of the common agricultural policy from the RTC as well as the Jagdeo initiative. Moreover, it demonstrates the region's adherence to the 2009 World Food Summit declaration and the 2025 Caribbean initiative for a hunger free Latin America. Even further, this policy is in concert with the Millennium Development Goals, which focus on hunger eradication and poverty, environmental sustainability and the fostering global partnerships for development (Flores 2013).[82]

The RFNSP established four goals:

1. Food availability – Promote the sustainable production,[83] processing, preparation, commercialization and consumption of safe, affordable, nutritious, high quality Caribbean food commodities/products. This concerns food, agricultural, rural, infrastructural development, land use and trade issues;
2. Food access – Ensure regular access of Caribbean households, especially the poor and vulnerable, to sufficient quantities of safe, affordable, quality food at all times, particularly in response to diverse socioeconomic and natural shocks. Prices, incomes, agricultural public health, food safety and social development issues;
3. Food utilization/nutritional adequacy – Improve the nutritional status of the Caribbean population, particularly with respect to non-communicable diseases (NCDs) including diabetes, hypertension, overweight and obesity. Healthy lifestyle choices from early childhood-education, health, nutrition and social welfare issues; and
4. Stability of food supply – Improve the resilience of the region's national communities and households to natural and socio-economic crises Information and early warning systems, disaster preparedness and management, and adaptation to climate change issues (see Garcia and Smart 2011, 8).

At the 2011 COTED meeting in Dominica, a 2012–26 action plan[84] was endorsed which set priorities to implement several of the goals of the RFNSP. These include

1. the promotion of a greater availability of regionally produced nutritious and quality food;

2. identification and mapping of vulnerable food insecure groups coupled with the establishment of national and regional databases documenting the same;

3. the removal of non-commercial barriers to trade and the formulation of strategies to improve regional transport;

4. the promotion of healthy Caribbean diets, especially in the education system;

5. reduction of NCDs, obesity and malnutrition;

6. the building of resilience to recurrent threats to food security such as natural disasters through the establishment of information and early warning systems for food and nutrition security and the building of risk profiles for the major crops in support of risk management, emergency preparedness and crop insurance. (Flores 2013)

Seven steps have been recommended for immediate action for the implementation of the food and nutrition security action plan in member states:

Step 1: Establish or strengthen a multi-sector government institution dealing with food and nutrition policy;

Step 2: Revise current food and nutrition security action plans and sector policies;

Step 3: Prioritize the implementation of specific actions;

Step 4: Operationalize the action plan through a combination of macro-economic policies, regulatory frameworks (legislation, regulations, etc.) and fiscal and other measures;

Step 5: Establish dialogue and partnerships with all stakeholders;

Step 6: Allocate resources;

Step 7: Monitor implementation and accountability.

Subsequent to the agreement of the RFNSP, COTED emphasized the need for both the RFNSP and the Regional Food and Nutrition Security Action Plan (RFNSAP) to be reinforced by national food and nutrition security (FNS) policies and programmes in each CARICOM member state, thereby ensuring that there is consistency and harmonization among national and regional policies and the RFNSP. It is within this context that in 2012, Antigua and Barbuda initiated the preparation of a national food and nutrition security policy (Government of Antigua and Barbuda 2012).[85]

Caribbean countries cannot produce wheat because of weather conditions but they can produce rice and maize. Table 8.10 shows that for Barbados, maize production fell drastically while for Guyana, maize and rice production both increased. Indeed, some tropical produce such as cassava, yam and sweet potatoes are excellent sources of carbohydrates and some Caribbean countries with large land masses such as Guyana, Suriname, Belize and Jamaica can be encouraged to produce more of these commodities (table 8.11).

For a variety of reasons, food security in the region has proven to be a challenge. Mathews (2010, 5) states that advocates of food self-sufficiency, "warn of the dangers of relying on international markets for food supplies and advocate policies to ensure that a high proportion of food supplies are sourced domestically". Regional food integration can have several benefits for CARICOM regional economic integration. First, there will be reduced food instability and regional food independence. This implies a reduction in the region's food import bill, which requires investment in harnessing

Table 8.9 Food imports and exports of selected CARICOM countries, US$ million, 1997–2012

	Food Imports				Food Exports			
Year	Barbados	St Kitts & Nevis	St Lucia	Guyana	Barbados	St Kitts & Nevis	St Lucia	Guyana
1997	115.69	20.46	58.57	57.25	47.99	0.99	40.30	25.79
1998	111.31	0.00	60.50	63.06	37.14	0.00	38.56	33.25
1999	116.80	20.62	58.80	58.10	34.96	0.94	42.01	31.34
2000	123.65	26.70	59.41	55.55	36.05	1.53	31.37	57.81
2001	121.71	23.79	52.14	62.42	43.78	0.78	31.47	74.60
2002	122.80	23.19	53.98	60.43	42.82	0.67	32.16	74.66
2003	136.93	25.06	68.05	58.03	34.04	0.94	28.48	72.62
2004	143.83	26.55	74.56	61.40	36.21	1.21	33.08	84.44
2005	170.34	28.98	77.68	79.94	46.52	1.37	28.93	82.15
2006	166.83	34.30	84.02	76.27	40.16	3.09	34.26	93.95
2007	168.60	37.57	90.31	89.96	50.13	3.34	34.07	100.22
2008	203.22	42.88	99.67	120.25	58.43	4.61	46.25	102.26
2009	172.19	46.33	0.00	107.12	52.83	3.44	0.00	88.92
2010	193.01	38.88	0.00	128.57	58.83	3.31	0.00	82.89
2011	206.23	42.41	0.00	146.88	54.26	4.55	0.00	101.05
2012	211.26	0.00	0.00	168.41	80.43	0.00	0.00	128.94

Source: United Nations Commodity Trade Database (UNCOMTRADE) (2014)

the large productive capacity of Guyana and perhaps, Belize, and also providing a regional export market for the Eastern Caribbean islands which have seen their historical agricultural export markets decline (Bishop et al. 2011).

Food integration also implies the adherence to common sanitary and phyto-sanitary standards (SPS) controls and a harmonization of food safeguard mechanisms. These measures set the standard for food, in terms of safety and health standards. This technical barrier can indirectly improve the quality of food produced in the CARICOM economies hence making if safer for consumption. Within an integration framework, a greater level of information on these issues can be disseminated and more laboratory facilities could be established, which can in some way assist exporters to overcome these challenges. To this end, the region can move up the value chain into the production and export of more high value added, innovation-intensive food products.

Food integration, particularly, for the Caribbean region coexists within an environment of climate change and the potential for climatic food security risks. Perhaps one of the greatest benefits of food integration on regional economic integration within a context of climate change, is the ease at which a comprehensive study on local and regional food security vulnerability to climate change can be designed and executed. Mathews (2003) noted that this information could be incorporated in the development of information systems that also focus on changes in agricultural production in the presence of climate variability; available technologies for mitigating these impacts; assessments of each island's food supply needs; and raising awareness of various stakeholders, including policymakers about food security risks. Further, these information systems

Table 8.10 CARICOM countries' production of rice and maize, tonnes, 1992–2012

	Barbados	Guyana		Suriname		Belize		Jamaica		Trinidad	
Year	Maize	Maize	Rice	Maize	Rice	Maize	Rice	Maize	Rice	Maize	Rice
1992	1,800	3,200	28,4962	159	261,080	26,462	6,644	3,828	506	3,500	–
1993	1,600	3,500	345,637	260	216,890	27,188	9,745	3,295	269	5,000	–
1994	1,300	3,300	391,251	349	218,000	23,263	6,490	3,828	253	5,404	–
1995	1,100	3,800	527,977	336	242,000	28,204	9,628	3,741	158	6,188	–
1996	800	3,100	543,500	167	228,650	36,877	12,756	4,037	30	7,892	–
1997	650	7,900	568,188	137	213,050	37,358	16,726	3,121	29	9,905	–
1998	520	3,100	522,907	110	188,410	37,606	9,452	2,198	30	8,811	–
1999	390	3,200	562,260	33	180,296	40,639	12,619	2,133	31	1,000	–
2000	300	3,829	449,181	40	163,655	31,722	9,868	1,769	12	975	–
2001	250	2,023	495,862	70	191,370	36,736	12,121	2,083	33	1,811	–
2002	218	2,000	444,290	61	157,105	33,459	12,500	1,755	10	3,296	–
2003	263	4,000	546,200	65	193,685	33,580	13,194	2,043	14	2,955	–
2004	250	5,500	499,600	56	174,490	30,538	10,680	1,601	10	3,000	–
2005	260	4,000	420,400	50	163,955	34,644	17,759	1,929	3	3,050	–
2006	270	3,000	468,700	46	182,659	28,398	11,855	1,895	2	3,000	–
2007	280	7,900	458,700	49	179,012	38,313	17,775	1,673	2	3,750	–
2008	236	4,000	507,000	27	182,877	37,051	11,780	1,897	2	3,500	–
2009	270	5,000	553,500	24	229,370	45,041	20,615	2,350	2	3,000	–
2010	287	5,024	556,200	35	226,686	58,048	20,523	2,363	264	3,187	–
2011	310	4,900	591,000	32	235,298	62,705	19,081	2,723	234	3,438	–
2012	–	–	–	35	220,000	65,000	22,000	2,821	299	3,500	–

Source: Food and Agriculture Organization of the United Nations Database (FAO) (2014).

must provide feedback on the potential opportunities for increased intra-regional agricultural and food trade. Ultimately, the information should serve to enhance awareness among producers and traders of market opportunities in neighbouring countries, and encourage support for commodity development programs where similar export commodities are produced by other intra-regional countries. Moreover, improved statistical information on agricultural trade flows could also serve as a prerequisite to monitor the impact of market integration on the evolution of intra-regional trade flows compared to extra-regional flows. Improved trade statistics are also crucial to a fair and acceptable division of customs duties in a customs union (Mathews 2003).

8.4.3 Regional Energy Cooperation

Most CARICOM countries have very high energy import bills, except Suriname, Belize, and Trinidad and Tobago. Energy and energy services are viewed as central to the region's economic development plans. In recent times, CARICOM's dependence on fossil fuels has grown considerably to the extent

Table 8.11 CARICOM countries' production of sweet potato, yams and cassava, tonnes, 1993–2011

		1993	1995	2000	2005	2006	2007	2008	2009	2010	2011
Sweet Potato	Barbados	2,251	5,167	2,700	2,084	2,201	1,335	884	888	1,176	507
	Belize	659	189	261	75	64	23	63	32	33	36
	Guyana	–	–	2,933	1,500	1,732	1,510	1,541	1,522	1,566	1,730
	Jamaica	21,054	17,447	15,371	13,224	17,711	18,519	14,991	13,995	18,490	20,533
	St Kitts & Nevis	180	225	151	155	200	193	199	230	198	216
	St Lucia	900	507	836	204	498	529	604	397	362	306
	Suriname	5,000	7,000	3,041	4,150	4,120	3,948	2,894	3,931	4,243	3,334
	Trinidad & Tobago	140	500	171	265	290	128	155	271	1,315	1,238
Yams	Barbados	1,927	2,570	1,150	818	794	647	280	824	807	243
	Belize	715	123	11	124	97	111	91	65	55	49
	Guyana	–	–	3,804	1,500	1,300	1,250	1,246	1,381	1,752	1,553
	Jamaica	221,928	240,371	147,709	107,295	123,005	113,124	102,284	124,516	136,785	134,620
	St Kitts & Nevis	250	125	5	5	14	15	19	18	27	37
	St Lucia	4,200	4,317	412	456	429	471	504	508	584	534
	Suriname	–	–	–	–	–	–	–	–	–	–
	Trinidad & Tobago	255	147	12	16	16	17	18	25	19	18
Cassava	Barbados	693	818	500	199	375	448	466	691	400	308
	Belize	791	685	907	180	239	327	304	328	331	337
	Guyana	30,100	35,100	44,854	20,050	23,145	20,184	4,127	7,100	10,092	3,768
	Jamaica	21,054	17,447	15,371	13,224	17,711	18,519	14,991	13,995	18,490	20,533
	St Kitts & Nevis	–	–	–	–	–	–	–	–	–	–
	St Lucia	831	1,237	1,116	1,184	1,021	1,030	1,100	898	1,151	1,251
	Suriname	5,000	7,000	3,041	4,150	4,120	3,948	2,894	3,931	4,243	3,334
	Trinidad & Tobago	954	696	801	1,050	1,100	2,190	2,788	2,479	2,311	3,057

Source: FAO database, 2014.

that petroleum products account for an estimated 97 per cent of the region's energy consumption (Martin et al. 2013). There are few petroleum producing countries within the region; however, Trinidad and Tobago is the only net exporter of petroleum, petroleum-related products and natural gas. Suriname, Barbados and Belize produce crude oil for domestic use and are net importers, while Barbados produces natural gas for sale on the domestic market. The remaining countries are non-producers of hydrocarbons and are net importers (CARICOM Energy Policy 2013).

Efforts are now being undertaken towards the creation of a new energy portfolio for the region, characterized by a mix of renewable sources such as solar, wind and thermal as well as bio energy and fossil fuels. Further, affordable energy services have been recognized as being crucial for accelerating the region's economic growth, development and industrialization, by enabling the private sector to generate employment and raise incomes (CARICOM Secretariat 2013). In this regard, the COTED, at a special meeting in March 2013 approved a comprehensive regional energy policy for CARICOM. The goal of CARICOM's energy policy is

> Fundamental transformation of the energy sectors of the Member States of the Community through the provision of secure and sustainable supplies of energy in a manner which minimizes energy waste in all sectors, to ensure that all CARICOM citizens have access to modern, clean and reliable energy supplies at affordable and stable prices, and to facilitate the growth of internationally competitive Regional industries towards achieving sustainable development of the Community. (CARICOM Energy Policy 2013, 2)

Another important priority of the CARICOM Heads of Government is that of renewable and sustainable energy sources. In addition, reducing the region's dependence on fossil fuels; achieving greater efficiency and conservation of energy, within the context of energy security; and pursuing a low-carbon approach to development are also articulated regional policy priorities.

In accord with the achievement of these energy priorities, several member states have initiated national projects. Perhaps the most noteworthy initiative is Guyana's low-carbon development strategy. This strategy is aimed at protecting and sustaining Guyana's forests to reduce global carbon emissions. In addition, Guyana is exploring the use of hydro-electric power, wind and biofuels. Suriname is also exploring alternate energy sources; in the main, these include the utilization of mineral oil, hydro power, biomass and solar energy. Barbados has also made use of solar energy in the form of solar water heaters in homes and proposes to increase its use of renewable energy from 14 per cent to 30 per cent. Similarly, Jamaica has successfully implemented the use of solar water heaters in government buildings and has been exploring wind and biofuels as other sources of energy. Furthermore, St Lucia and Dominica have both been pursing energy efficient strategies with Dominica in particular, harnessing hydropower (McLean 2014).

Under the umbrella of creating a new energy portfolio, the CARICOM's regional AfT strategy has highlighted several strategic interventions which are deemed as priority projects including:

1. Formulation and implementation of a regional bio-energy strategy;
2. Completion of an assessment of renewable energy resources in areas with potential for wind and solar energy;
3. Establishment of a mechanism for financing small and micro renewable energy efficiency projects for micro, small and medium enterprises;

4. Implementing a harmonized approach or a mechanism for feeding renewable energy sources to grid;

5. Establishment of a regulatory framework to support cross-border trade in electricity and natural gas;

6. Assessment of the impact of energy costs as an input to production of goods for exports from CARICOM countries with special reference to natural gas and its relative competitiveness as a fuel source. (McLean 2014)

Suriname, Belize and Guyana are new energy producing economies. There is definite scope in the region for greater cooperation in energy services. Indeed, informally Trinidad and Tobago's energy service providers have already crossed the border over into Guyana and Suriname. Trinidad and Tobago has a world class energy service sector. The energy pipeline from Trinidad and Tobago to the Eastern Caribbean (dubbed the Eastern Caribbean Gas Pipeline Project) is an undertaking which would allow Trinidad and Tobago to supply natural gas to economies like Barbados, Guadeloupe, Martinique and St Lucia.

The major benefit of energy cooperation in the region is low cost electricity and reduced fuel prices. Cooperation can result in better supply logistics that will reduce the cost of fuel, which by extension can reduce the price of electricity and food in manufacturing countries. In places like St Vincent and the Grenadines where fuel prices are EC$15 per gallon, transport cost is very high and the price of manufactured goods are relatively uncompetitive. Regional cooperation can reduce the price of energy, and by extension, electricity, transportation and food production would become less costly and the region will enjoy a better standard of living and energy sustainability.

In furthering the integration process by strengthening regional energy cooperation, policymakers should embrace existing institutional initiatives. For example, the UNDP's South-South Hydrocarbon Capacity Development Program and the Extractive Industries Transparency Initiative (EITI). The benefit of using existing initiatives in this regard, whether in part or not, is that existing initiatives would have systems by which the processes can be monitored and evaluated over time, a factor which is critical to success. Such initiatives also provide best practices to drive the process. Moreover, through regional energy cooperation, regional debates can be facilitated and stimulated within the framework of existing institutional initiatives relating to the management of the extractive sector in the region. In addition, a key benefit of an integrated energy market for regional economic integration is the ability for review of the energy systems of individual countries and the translation of its implications for the region.

Energy production predictability is undermined by the high costs of internal transport networks, weaknesses in telecommunications and energy infrastructure. This can result in disruptions of supply linkages along the value chain. Mineral resources differ across CARICOM countries with some member states having a large mining component, while fuels are dominant in other countries. Collaboration via regional cooperation minimizes costs and facilitates production fragmentation. Certainly, an integrated regional energy market can aid in unlocking the region's full potential by filling intra-regional gaps and needs, as well as linking the region to an integrated global market for energy (Santi et al. 2012). In utilizing the resource strengths of one country to compensate for another's resource deficiencies, regional integration, creates conditions for CARICOM countries to better protect and exploit their shared wealth in mineral resources.

Notes

1. Eric Williams served as the premier of Trinidad and Tobago from 1959 to 1962. He later served as the first prime minister of Trinidad and Tobago from 1962 until his death in 1981.
2. This led to a movement within Jamaica for national independence from Britain. Jamaican referendum was the instigator, not the definitive cause of the federation's collapse. On 19 September 1961, some 54 per cent of the Jamaican electorate voted to end their participation. It was the lowest popular vote in any Jamaican election, but the government accepted the decision and initiated the plans to request complete independence for the state.
3. Norman Manley was Jamaica's prime minister at this time.
4. See CARICOM Secretariat: http://www.caricom.org/jsp/secretariat/legal_instruments/agreement _dickensonbay.jsp?menu=secretariat.
5. The Caribbean's "oils and fats agreement" operated from 1959 to 1970 when it was integrated into the CARIFTA agreement on farm produce. The purpose of the agreement was to protect local output against foreign competition by means of import restrictions and the regulating of trade with extra-regional countries. The agreement was mainly concerned with the production and trade of copra and coconut oil (Morton and Tulloch 1977).
6. http://www.discoverjamaica.com.
7. http://www.caricom.org/jsp/communications/publications/treaty_caricom_annex_art3.jsp?menu =communications.
8. Cumulative FDI inflows to China and India for the period 2000–2012 amounted to US$1952.12 billion, while the Caribbean amassed a mere US$36.2 billion.
9. In 1980, Guyana's agricultural research expenditure amounted to US$2.4 million. Agricultural research as a percentage of agriculture GDP amounted to 1.85 per cent (Janvry and Dethier 1985).
10. In 1974, the ACP countries signed the first Lomé Convention with EC member countries.
11. Standard International Trade Classification (SITC).
12. Lewis (1950) provided a framework for Caribbean industrial development. In particular, he proposed a strategy of import-substituting industrialization (ISI). However, the ISI strategy pursued by Caribbean countries was not according to Lewis's model, which placed emphasis on export promotion. Instead, the strategy implemented focused on domestic production to reduce import dependency and to generate employment. In this regard, tax holidays, tariff protection for local industries and industrial estates were provided. ECLAC (2001) noted that ISI in the Caribbean has not met its initial objectives and although in some countries such as Trinidad and Tobago, Jamaica, and Barbados, fledging manufacturing sectors were developed, it has failed to meet the expectations of employment, import replacement and contribution to GDP growth.
13. See https://www.wto.org/english/tratop_e/region_e/region_e.htm.

14. See Bhagwati and Panagariya (1996) for a systematic critique of the volume of trade and the geographic criteria.

15. Shakur and Nees (2011) assessed the level of trade complementarity between the Association of Southeast Asian Nations (ASEAN) and the Australia and New Zealand Free Trade Area (AANZFTA) and determined that New Zealand and the ASEAN 5 are moderate natural trading partners based on a trade complementarity index. See Pitigala (2005) for similar study on South Asian countries.

16. This model builds on the work of Schiff (1997).

17. The ROW is larger than the HC and the PC.

18. This section only reviews the first case. The interested reader is referred to Schiff (2001).

19. The PC's export supply curve begins its upward slope at various locations in the FTA environment. In particular, the PC's export supply curve can begin its upward slope between K and L (say) at point U (as illustrated in the figure 3.7); at point L or to the right of L, it can also begin its upward slope to intersect the horizontal segment FK to the left of point K. Where the PC's export supply curve begins its upward slope is determined by its export capacity.

20. The higher price in the HC's market following integration is what motivates the PC exporters to switch their exports from the ROW's market to the HC's market. Therefore, the PC exporters will shift all their exports to the HC's market for prices in the HC greater than or equal to P_w following integration.

21. The net loss or net gain depends on where X_B is located ($M_3 < X_B < M_4$), Schiff suggested that the closer it is located to L the more the HC gains and vice versa (figure 3.7).

22. The WTO replaced the GATT in 1994 but kept most of its rules in place.

23. The European Union in February 2001 brought the EBA regulation into force. The EBA provides duty-free access of goods from the least less developed countries (LLDCs) in the ACP bloc to the EU market. These goods will also be exempt from quota restriction. The provisions of the EBA have been incorporated as part of the European Union's GSP scheme. The purpose of this EBA thrust is to enhance the exports of these LLDCs so as to improve the potential for economic growth in these economies. One substantive feature of the EBA is that preferences granted to LLDCs extend for an indefinite period of time and are not subjected to periodic review. This in turn should provide a greater extent of certainty to producers and exporters from those LLDCs. It is hoped that this reduction in uncertainty may help to improve the production of goods targeted at the EU market.

24. The main difference between the GSP and Cotonou is in terms of market access. This is reflected in the utilization rate of both schemes. Another important difference between the two schemes relates to rules of origin. Rules of origin outline the various criteria a commodity must meet in order to be classified as originating from a particular country. Rules of origin are typically engineered to prevent the redirection of trade from non-participating economies through participating economies. Rules of origin are particularly relevant where various aspects of a product are processed, by non-participating economies. In recent times, where the global economy has witnessed a greater fragmentation of the production process, rules of origin have been increasingly called into play.

25. The Caribbean Forum of ACP states (CARIFORUM) represents fifteen nations, namely, Antigua and Barbuda, Bahamas, Barbados, Belize, Dominica, Dominican Republic, Grenada, Guyana, Haiti, Jamaica, St Lucia, St Vincent and the Grenadines, St Kitts and Nevis, Suriname, and Trinidad and Tobago. Negotiations for the CARIFORUM–EU EPA were launched on 16 April 2004 in Kingston, Jamaica. The plan and schedule for CARIFORUM–EC negotiation of an economic partnership agreement highlights the following broad objectives:

1. Attainment of economic development that is socially and environmentally sustainable;

2. Enhancement of the ability of small Caribbean states to play a more meaningful role in the international community consistent with their political and economic aspirations for self-determination;

3. Facilitation of Caribbean structural transformation which would allow for the reduction of that region's acute economic vulnerability and the emergence of new expressions of development; and

4. Adjustment of Caribbean economies in a manner and at a pace that is conducive to overall economic and social development.

26. The Armington principle of product differentiation is based on a world, which consists of m countries and n goods. A good is usually classified by "type" or "kind" and differentiated by its country of origin.

27. The type of detailed production data required to estimate a general equilibrium model is not readily available for CARICOM economies and so is not considered here.

28. It is likely that given the geographic distance of the European Union from CARIFORUM economies in general that the homogenous goods emanating from say the European Union or the United States will have different prices in the CARIFORUM sphere because of transportation costs.

29. This represents the efficiency gain as within the pre-EPA environment resources are realized from inefficient production into (assumingly) more efficient production.

30. Although manifesting as trade creation, this is really an increase in consumption.

31. The trade, revenue and welfare effects computed here are based on the assumption that an EPA is formed between the European Union and CARICOM countries in either 1998 or in 2008 so that tariffs on imports originating from the European Union are eliminated.

32. Percentage decline is computed as the change in imports from non-EU-ROW divided by initial imports from non-EU-ROW.

33. See, for example, Alturki et al. (2009), Chang and Mendy (2012), Kamau (2010), Igberaese and Diania (2012), Atoyebi et al. (2012), Yeboah et al. (2012), Arora and Vamvakidis (2011), Dabla-Norris et al. (2012) and Feldkircher and Korhonen (2012).

34. The real GDP for the CARICOM region and four EU countries (France, The Netherlands, Spain and United Kingdom) were summed before calculating the growth rate (see, for example, Dabla-Norris et al. 2012).

35. In July 2014, an agreement was signed to establish the BRICS Development Bank (now referred to as the New Development Bank [NDB]).

36. The G6 represents the six largest economies in the world. The present G6 members are France, Germany, Italy, Japan, United Kingdom and the United States.

37. The international harmonized commodity description and coding system six-digit level is utilized.

38. "Deep integration is important largely because of potential links to productivity gains that go beyond standard analysis of comparative advantage. There is evidence in some countries of beneficial synergy between increased trade, deep integration, increases in productivity and growth" (Evans et al. 2006, 87).

39. Davis (1995) demonstrated that IIT can occur from the combination of the two latter frameworks.

40. The H-O model is sometimes referred to as the Heckscher-Ohlin-Samuelson (H-O-S) model on account of the notable contributions made by Paul Samuelson to extend the traditional theory, including the Stolper–Samuelson theorem.

41. Falvey added that for this analysis, an industry is best defined by the range of commodities that a particular type of capital equipment can produce (see also Elkan 1972; Lancaster 1980).

42. Venables (1984) and Lawrence and Spiller (1983) developed extensions to this model while Greenaway and Milner (1986) documented several shortcomings of the neo-Chamberlinian models which derive from their structure.

43. If there are only two varieties of a particular commodity available, say, C_1 and C_2 but the consumer's ideal variety is C_3, he cannot combine and purchase varying quantities of C_1 and C_2 to obtain C_3 (Greenaway and Milner 1986).

44. Refers to the beliefs that one firm has about the way its competitor(s) may react if it varies its output (or price). The firm forms a conjecture about the variation in the other firm's output that will accompany any change in its own output.

45. Firms may find it easier to alter prices rather than output in the short run following trade liberalization or a demand shock. If we assume that at least in the short run, the production process is fixed due to limited capacity, employment contracts or large production runs, the firm is therefore prevented from increasing or decreasing its output in reply to another firm's behaviour, but it does allow the firm to alter its product prices.

46. This means that when contemplating a price cut, each firm makes the Bertrand assumption that the other firm's price will remain unchanged. Considering a price increase, on the other hand, the firm assumes that its competitor will react by reducing its price. The overall equilibrium achieved from the interaction of these two assumptions is described as a "semi-reactive Bertrand equilibrium".

47. See Graham (1996, 186–91) for all criticisms of the OLI paradigm.

48. Data is unavailable prior to 2000 and results reflect each country's trade with the world rather than bilaterally.

49. Due to size constraints, all data tables could not be included in this chapter. All data can be obtained from the authors upon request.

50. Pascal Lamy, the WTO director general emphasized this point by taking a wand to the opening session of the Hong Kong ministerial conference, 13 December 2005.

51. Legal texts: The WTO agreements: http://www.wto.org (2011).

52. Limão (2006) and Karacaovali and Limão (2008) have argued that preferential trade as a form of aid violates the fundamental principle of non-discrimination and creates incentives to impede MFN liberalization. Thus, in 1997 the WTO leveled the playing field among all its members in the international banana market. In this regard, the decision (by the WTO) to shift from preferential "trade as aid" toward more efficient and effective instruments to support developing countries could improve development outcomes and help strengthen the multilateral trading system (Hoekman 2007).

53. This term has been around for several decades and is sometimes linked to Raul Prebisch, the founding father of UNCTAD. Prebisch recognized very early that the Overseas Development Assistance was not realizing its intended objectives and what was really needed was trade and not aid.

54. The WTO website notes that the declaration of the fourth ministerial conference held in November 2001 in Doha, outlines the directive for negotiations to take place on a range of issues which includes the implementation of present agreements, analysis and monitoring. http://www.wto.org/english/tratop_e/dda_e/dohaexplained_e.htm (accessed December 2010).

55. The Integrated Framework is an international initiative through which the IMF, ITC, UNCTAD, UNDP, the World Bank and WTO combine their efforts with those of LDCs and donors to respond to the trade-development needs of LDCs. The Integrated Framework has two main objectives: to mainstream trade into national development plans and to facilitate the coordinated delivery of trade-related assistance (EU Aid for Trade Strategy 2007).

56. Dee et al. (2008) define trade facilitation as covering all the measures that affect the movement of goods, between buyers and sellers along the entire international supply chain.

57. Fredrick Bastint writing over a century ago noted that "between Paris and Brussels obstacles of many kinds exist. First of all, there is distance, which entails a loss of time, and we must either submit to this ourselves, or pay another to submit to it. Then came rivers, marshes, accidents, bad roads, which are so many difficulties to be surmounted. We succeed in building bridges, in forming roads, and making them smoother by pavements, iron railings etc. . . . They are called Custom House officers and they act in precisely the same way as ruts and bad roads" (Ikenson 2007, 6).

58. Other important border agencies are the immigration, border guards, and plant, food, and animal inspectors.

59. At the Uruguay Round that took place in 1993, countries agreed to reduce their tariffs by an average of more than one third. The advanced countries agreed to reduce tariffs on industrial imports by 64 per cent while the developing countries agreed to 33 per cent and the transitional economies agreed to 75 per cent of their industrial imports.

60. Non-tariff barriers adversely affect trade capacity in many developing economies. Custom and administrative procedures are definitely necessary, but they have the capacity to "thicken" the borders between economies and can in so doing restrict trade.

61. Another major source of development funds for the region comes from the tenth European Development Fund.

62. The Caribbean Media Corporation (2009) reports that the governor general Sir Carlyle Glean indicated that legislation to establish a national export council is being developed with assistance from the legal department and that the National Export Council will be responsible for the management and implementation of the national export strategy in all sectors, including ministries.

63. Gross national savings is computed by subtracting final consumption expenditure (household and government) from gross national disposable income. It consists of personal, business and government savings. The values are presented as a per cent of GDP where a negative value implies that the economy is spending more income than it generates, thereby drawing down national wealth (dissaving).

64. The Environmental Vulnerability Index (EVI) was developed by the South Pacific Applied Geoscience Commission (SOPAC), the United Nations Environment Programme and their partners. It is a standardized measure that characterizes vulnerability in an aggregate sense and identifies issues that may need to be addressed within each of the three pillars of sustainability: environmental, economic and social.

65. Improved forecasts for the population of the various CARICOM member states are now available and should be considered in making further planning decisions.

66. See http://www.travelinghaiti.com/history.asp.

67. These psychological goods include the following: (1) greater individual freedom to participate in choosing a government without fear or favour; (2) access to quality primary education; (3) access to quality primary health care, and other basic services; and (4) reasonable opportunity to obtain an equitable part of natural output.

68. The West Indian Commission (1992, 29) noted that a lot of talk and little action characterized the Caribbean sphere, and what should be established is, "community machinery, which will enable important decisions to be readily taken, and when taken, implemented without delay or dilution".

69. Significantly, these types of issues emerge if we form a regional strategy for sugar, education and tourism.

70. See http://ec.europa.eu/europeaid/documents/case-studies/trinidad-and-tobago_agriculture_sugar-industry_en.pdf

71. See https://www.caribbean360.com/business/st-kitts-sugar-factory-receives-last-cane.

72. The Caribbean is defined in this study as the OECS bloc of economies, the Bahamas, Belize, Barbados, Dominican Republic, Guyana, Haiti, Jamaica, Suriname, and Trinidad and Tobago.

73. It is important to note that while Caribbean merchandise trade requires margins of preference to subsist, services have grown without protection.

74. The Linder Mills Group was established in 1975 in England. The group's main focus is to conduct research and provide advice on environment, economic development and management issues in developed and developing countries. The group has conducted more than seven hundred projects in over 150 countries around the world to date.

75. The executive board of the IMF approved a four-year extended fund facility arrangement for Jamaica on 1 May 2013 worth US$932 million. The purpose of the programme is to improve the fiscal and public debt positions in Jamaica and improve the economy's competitiveness ("Ex-Minister: Jamaica Losing $15b to CARICOM Imports", *Trinidad Guardian*, 9 October 2013).

76. These are university graduates, media workers, artistes, musicians, sportspersons, nurses, teachers, artisans, persons who are holders of associate degrees or equivalent, and household domestics who are holders of Caribbean Vocational Qualifications.

77. http://www.oecs.org.

78. Twelve CARICOM countries are members of Petrocaribe. They include Antigua and Barbuda, the Bahamas, Belize, Dominica, Grenada, Guyana, Haiti, Jamaica, St Lucia, St Kitts and Nevis, St Vincent and the Grenadines, and Suriname.

79. Available at http://www.cepr.net.

80. http://www.normangirvan.info.

81. These include berthing facilities, facilities for handling transhipment cargo, port connectivity and services, equipment (e.g., gantry cranes), storage facilities, navigational aids, and so on.

82. See http://www.ialcsh.org/fileadmin/templates/iniciativa/content/pdf/gt2025/2013/Regional_Initiatives _and_plans_in_fns_-_En.pdf

83. As described using the concept of sustainable agricultural production.

84. The role of the regional food and nutrition security action plan is to implement the CARICOM Regional Food and Nutrition Security Policy and the first plan covers the fifteen-year period from 2012 to 2026. The action plan contributes to four of the eight millennium development goals: eradicating extreme poverty and hunger; promoting gender equality and empowering women; reducing child and maternal mortality; and ensuring environmental sustainability (CARICOM Secretariat 2011).

85. See http://www.zerohungerchallengelac.org/ab/doc/FoodNutritionSecurityPolicyAG.pdf.

References

Aggarwal, R. 2009. "The Private Sector: Important Partners in Aid for Trade". *International Trade Forum*. http://www.tradeforum.org/The-Private-Sector-Important-Partners-in-Aid-for-Trade/.

Alaba, Olumuyiwa B. 2006. "EU-ECOWAS EPA: Regional Integration, Trade Facilitation and Development in West Africa". A Draft Paper for presentation at the GTAP conference, United Nations Economic Commission for Africa (UNECA), Addis Ababa, Ethiopia, May.

Almeida P. 2009. "The BRIC's Role in the Global Economy". *Trade and International Negotiations for Journalists*, 146–54.

Alturki, F, J. Espinosa-Bowen, and N. Ilahi. 2009. "How Russia Affects the Neighborhood: Trade, Financial, and Remittance Channels". Working Paper 09/277, International Monetary Fund, Washington, DC.

Andreatta, S. 1998. "Transformation of the Agro Food Sector: Lessons from the Caribbean". *Human Organization* 57 (4): 414–29.

APEC (Asia Pacific Economic Co-operation). 1999. *Assessing APEC Trade Liberalization and Facilitation: 1999 Update, Economic Committee*, September. APEC: Singapore.

———. 2002. *Principles on Trade Facilitation*. http://www.apec.org/Meeting-Papers/Ministerial-Statements/Trade/2001_trade/annex_b.aspx.

Armington, P. 1969. "A Theory of Demand for Products Distinguished by Place of Production". *IMF Staff Papers*. 16: 159–78.

Arora, V., and A. Vamvakidis. 2011. "China's Economic Growth: International Spillovers". *China and World Economy* 19 (5): 31–46.

Arvis, J., M.A. Mustra, J. Panzer, L. Ojala, and T. Naula. 2008. "Connecting to Compete: Trade Logistics in the Global Economy". In *The Global Enabling Trade Report 2008*, 53–65. Geneva: World Economic Forum. http://www.weforum.org/pdf/GETR08/Chap%201.4_Connecting%20to%20Compete.pdf.

Atoyebi, K.O., F.O. Adekunjo, E. Olufemi, and K.I. Kayode. 2012. "Foreign Trade and Economic Growth in Nigeria: An Empirical Analysis". *Journal of Humanities and Social Science* 2 (1): 73–80.

Azhar, A., and R. J.R. Elliott. 2003. "On the Measurement of Trade-Induced Adjustment". *Weltwirtschaftliches Archiv* 139 (3): 419–39.

Balassa, B. 1966. "Tariff Reductions and Trade in Manufactures among the Industrialized Countries". *American Economic Review* 56 (3): 466–73.

Balassa, B., and L. Bauwens. 1987. "Intra-industry Specialisation in a Multi-Country and Multi-Industry Framework". *Economic Journal* 97 (388): 923–39.

Batra, G., D. Kaufmann, and A.H.W. Stone. 2003. "The Firms Speak: What the World Business Environment Survey Tells Us about Constraints on Private Sector Development". http://papers.ssrn.com/sol3/papers.cfm?abstract_id=541388.

Baugh, K. 2011. Statement made at the *Third Global Review on Aid for Trade*, Geneva, 18–19 July.

Bell, H. 2011. "Status of the 'BRICS': An Analysis of Growth Factors". *International Research Journal of Finance and Economics* 69: 19–25.

Bernal, R. 2010. "The Dragon in the Caribbean: China-CARICOM Economic Relations". *Round Table* 99 (408): 281–302.

Bernhofen, D.M. 2002. "Intra-industry Trade in Homogeneous Products". In *Frontiers of Research in Intra-industry Trade*, edited by Grubel, Lloyd and Lee, 49–66. New York: Palgrave Macmillan.

Bhagwati, J. 1991. *The World Trading System at Risk*. Princeton, NJ: Princeton University Press.

———. 1993. "Regionalism and Multilateralism: An Overview". In *New Dimensions in Regional Integration*, edited by Jaime de Melo and Arvind Panagariya, 22–51. Cambridge: Cambridge University Press.

Bhagwati, J., and A. Panagariya. 1996. "Preferential Trading Areas and Multilateralism: Strangers, Friends or Foes?" In *The Economics of Preferential Trade Agreements*, edited by Jagdish N. Bhagwati and Arvind Panagariya, 1–78. Maryland: AEI Press and Center for International Economics, University of Maryland.

Bishop, M., N. Girvan, T. Shaw, M. Solange, R. Kirton, M. Scobie, D. Mohammed and A. Marlon. 2011. Caribbean Regional Integration. A Report by the UWI Institute of International Relations (IIR). St Augustine, Trinidad, Institute of International Relations (IIR)/UK Department of International Development (DFID).

Bishop, M.L., and A. Payne. 2010. "Caribbean Regional Governance and the Sovereignty/Statehood Problem". Centre for International Governance Innovation (CIGI) Caribbean Paper No. 8, Waterloo, Ontario, Canada. http://www.cigionline.org/publications/2010/1/caribbean-regional-governance-and-sovereigntystatehood-problem.

Bonnick G. 2000. "Toward a Caribbean Vision 2020: A Regional Perspective on Development Challenges, Opportunities and Strategies for the Next Decade". World Bank – Caribbean Group for Cooperation in Economic Development, Washington, DC.

Boodram, K. 2013. "13 Jamaicans Claim Unjust Deportation". *Trinidad Express*. http://www.trinidadexpress.com/news/13-Jamaicans-claim-unjust-deportation-232934221.html.

Bourne, C. 1988. *Caribbean Development to the Year 2000: Challenges, Prospects and Policies*. London: Commonwealth Secretariat.

Brander, J.A. 1981. "Intra-industry Trade in Identical Commodities". *Journal of International Economics* 11 (1): 1–14.

Brander, J., and P. Krugman. 1983. "A Reciprocal Dumping Model of International Trade". *Journal of International Economics* 15 (3–4): 313–21.

Brewster, H.R., T. Dolan, and T. Stewart. 2002. *Implementation of the CARICOM Single Market and Economy: Work in Progress*. Caribbean Group for Cooperation in Economic Development (CGCED). Washington: World Bank, Caribbean Country Management Unit, Latin America and the Caribbean Region. June. http://ctrc.sice.oas.org/geograph/caribbean/brewster.pdf.

Brewster, H., N. Girvan, and V. Lewis. 2010. "Renegotiate the CARIFORUM EPA". *Trade Negotiations Insights* 7 (3): 8–10.

Brewster, H., and C. Thomas. 1967. *The Dynamics of West Indian Economic Integration*. Mona: Institute of Social and Economic Research.

Briguglio, L. 1995. "Small Island Developing States and Their Economic Vulnerabilities". *World Development* 23 (9): 1615–32.

Brown, J. 2000. *Small States in the European Institutions*. Turku: Jean Monnet Centre of Excellence.

Brulhart, M. 1994. "Marginal Intra-industry Trade: Measurement and Relevance for the Pattern of Industrial Adjustment". *Weltwirtschaftliches Archiv* 130 (3): 600–613.

———. 2002. "Marginal Intra-industry Trade: Towards a Measure of Non-Disruptive Trade Expansion". In *Frontiers of Research in Intra-industry Trade*, edited by P.J. Lloyd and H.H. Lee. Palgrave: Macmillan.

Brulhart, M., and R.J.R. Elliott. 1998. "Adjustment to the European Single Market: Inferences from Intra-industry Trade Patterns". *Journal of Economic Studies* 25 (3): 225–47.

Brulhart, M., and R.C. Hine. eds. 1999. *Intra-industry Trade and Adjustment: The European Experience*. London: Macmillan.

Busse, M., and S. Luehje. 2007. "Should the Caribbean Countries Sign an Economic Partnership Agreement with the EU? Challenges and Strategic Options". *Journal of Economic Integration* 22 (3): 598–618.

Busse, M., A. Borrmann, and H. Grobmann. 2004. "The Impact of ACP/EU Economic Partnership Agreements on ECOWAS Countries: An Empirical Analysis of the Trade and Budget Effects", Final Report, Hamburg Institute of International Economics, Hamburg, Germany.

Byun, J., and S. Lee. 2005. "Horizontal and Vertical Intra-industry Trade: New Evidence from Korea, 1991–1999". *Global Economy Journal* 5 (1): 1–29.

Cali, M., and D. Willem te Velde. 2009. "Aid for Trade in Small and Vulnerable Economies". *The Commonwealth Secretariat*, May.

CFNI (Caribbean Food and Nutrition Institute). 2007. "Overview of Vulnerability and Food and Nutrition Security in the Caribbean". Report prepared by the Caribbean Food and Nutrition Institute in Collaboration with the Food and Agriculture Organization and Funded by The Italian Cooperation, Government of Italy. http://www.euacpcommodities.eu/files/17_Vulnerability.pdf.

CARICOM Energy Policy Report. 2013. "Caribbean Community Energy Policy". Approved by the Forty-First Special Meeting of the COTED on ENERGY held 1 March 2013, in Trinidad and Tobago. http://www.caricom.org/jsp/community_organs/energy_programme/CARICOM_energy_policy_march_2013.pdf.

CARICOM Secretariat. 2011. "Regional Food and Nutrition Security Action Plan". http://www.fao.org/fileadmin/templates/righttofood/documents/project_m/caricom/CARICOMRegionalFoodandNutritionSecurityActionPlan-Oct2011.pdf.

2012. "CARICOM Studies Show the CSME Operating at About 64% Level of Compliance". Press release. http://www.caricom.org/jsp/pressreleases/press_releases_2012/pres22_12.jsp.

———. 2013. *Caribbean Community Regional Aid for Trade Strategy 2013–2015"*. Georgetown, Guyana: CARICOM Secretariat. http://www.caricom.org/Caribbean_Community_AfT_Strategy_final.pdf.

Cassiolato, J.E., and B.A. Lundvall. 2006. "The BRICS Project: First Draft of Position Paper". http://globelics.org/downloads/Other/BRICS+position+paper+051115.pdf.

Caves, R.E. 1981. "Intra-industry Trade and Market Structure in the Industrial Countries". *Oxford Economic Papers* 33 (2): 203–23.

Cernat, L. 2003. "Assessing South-South Regional Integration: Same Issues, Many Metrics". Policy Issues in International Trade and Commodities, Study Series no. 21.

Chan, A. 2003. "A Race to the Bottom: Globalisation and China's Labour Standards". *China Perspectives* 46: 41–49.

Chang, C., and M. Mendy. 2012. "Economic Growth and Openness in Africa: What is the Empirical Relationship?" *Applied Economics Letters* 19 (18): 1903–7.

Chernick, S.E. 1978. *The Commonwealth Caribbean: The Integration Experience*. (Report of a mission sent to the Commonwealth Caribbean by the World Bank.) Baltimore: Johns Hopkins University Press and the World Bank.

Clegg, P. 2005. "Banana Splits and Policy Challenges: The ACP Caribbean and the Fragmentation of Interest Coalitions". *Revista Europea de Estudios Latinoamericanos y del Caribe* 79: 27–45.

Cooper C., and B. Massell. 1965. "A New Look at Customs Union Theory". *Economic Journal* 75: 742–47.

Cotonou Agreement. 2010. *Partnership Agreement Between the Members of the African, Caribbean and Pacific Group of States of the One Part, and the European Community and Its Member States of the Other Part*. Signed in Cotonou on 23 June 2000. http://ec.europa.eu/world/agreements/prepareCreateTreatiesWorkspace/treatiesGeneralData.do?step=0&redirect=true&treatyId=376.

Cournot, A. 1838. *Researches into the Mathematical Principles of the Theory of Wealth*. New York: Macmillan.

Crespo, N., and M.P. Fontoura. 2004. "Intra-industry Trade by Types: What Can We Learn from Portuguese Data?" *Welwirtschaftliches Archiv* 140 (1): 52–79.

CTAG (Caribbean Trade and Adjustment Group). 2001. "Improving Competitiveness for Caribbean Development". Report for the Caribbean Trade and Adjustment Group prepared at the request of the CRNM and the CARICOM Secretariat (CRNM/CTAG/Final report/Rev2/08/01), Christ Church, Barbados.

CTO (Caribbean Tourism Organization). 2007. *Competing with the Best: Good Practices in Community-Based Tourism in the Caribbean*. Bridgetown, Barbados: Caribbean Tourism Organization.

——. 2012. "Caribbean Tourism Organization Latest Statistics 2012". http://www.onecaribbean.org/content/files/OCT30Lattab2012.pdf.

——. 2014. "Caribbean Tourism Organization Latest Statistics 2014". http://www.onecaribbean.org/statistics/latest-tourism-statistics-tables/.

Da Silva, O.M., R.R. Drumond, and F.M. de Almeida. 2011. "Similarity and Income Content at the International Trade: The Case of BRICS during the Period 2000/09". In *Institute of Agricultural Development (IAMO) Forum 2011: Will the "BRICS Decade" Continue?–Prospects for Trade and Growth*, 23–24 June 2011. Germany: Leibniz IAMO Halle (Saale).

Davis, D.R. 1995. "Intra-industry Trade: A Heckscher-Ohlin-Ricardo Approach". *Journal of International Economics* 39 (3–4): 201–26.

De Janvry, Alain, and Jean-Jacques Dethier. 1985. *Technological Innovation in Agriculture: The Political Economy of Its Rate and Bias*. CGIAR Study Paper no. 1. Washington, DC: World Bank. http://www.fao.org/docs/eims/upload/166907/dejanvry,dethier,CGsec.pdf.

De Schutter, O. 2010. "Food Commodities Speculation and Food Price Crises: Regulation to Reduce the Risks of Price Volatility". UN Special Rapporteur on the Right to Food. http://www2.ohchr.org/english/issues/food/docs/Briefing_Note_02_September_2010_EN.pdf.

Deardorff, A.V., and R.M. Stern. 1994. "Multilateral Trade Negotiations and Preferential Trading Arrangements". In *Analytical and Negotiating Issues in the Global Trading System*, edited by A.V. Deardorff and R.M. Stern. Ann Arbor: University of Michigan Press.

Dee, P., C. Findlay, and R. Pomfret. 2008. "Trade facilitation: What, Why, How, Where and When?" In *Infrastructure and Trade in Asia*, edited by D.H. Brooks and J. Menon, 28–53. Cheltenham, UK: Edward Elgar.

Demas, W. 1965. *The Economics of Development in Small Countries: With Special Reference to the Caribbean*. Montreal: McGill-Queen's University Press.

Dickey, David A., and Wayne A. Fuller. 1979. "Distribution of the Estimators for Autoregressive Time Series with a Unit Root". *Journal of the American Statistical Association* 74 (366): 427–31.

Dixit, A.K., and V. Norman. 1980. *Theory of International Trade: A Dual, General Equilibrium Approach*. Cambridge: Cambridge University Press.

Dixit, A.K., and J.E. Stiglitz. 1977. "Monopolistic Competition and Optimum Product Diversity". *The American Economic Review* 67 (3): 297–308.

Dollar, D., M. Hallward-Driemeier and T. Mengistae. 2004. "Investment Climate and International Integration". Policy Research Working Paper 3323, World Bank, Washington, DC.

Downes, A. 2009. "Global Economic Crisis and Caribbean States: Impact and Response". Presented at Commonwealth Secretariat Conference on the Global Economic Crisis and Small States, London, 6–7 July.

Drabek, Z., and M. Bachetta. 2004. "Tracing the Effects of WTO Accession on Policy-making in Sovereign States: Preliminary Lessons from the Recent Experience of Transition Countries". *World Economy* 27 (7): 1110.

Driver, T. 2008. "The Genesis of the Point Lisas Industrial Estate". Trinidad and Tobago: Ministry of Energy.

Duan, Y. 2010. "FDI in BRICS: A Sector Level Analysis". *International Journal of Business and Management* 5 (1): 46–52.

Dunning, J.H. 1981. "Explaining the International Direct Investment Position of Countries: Towards a Dynamic or Developmental Approach". *Weltwirtschajtliches Archiv* 117 (1): 30–64.

Eaton, J., and H. Kierzkowski. 1984. "Oligopolistic Competition, Product Variety, and International Trade". In *Monopolistic Competition and International Trade*, edited by H. Kierzkowski. Oxford: Oxford University Press.

ECLAC (United Nations Economic Commission for Latin America and the Caribbean). 1996. "Readiness of Small Countries to Participate in the Free Trade Area of the Americas (FTAA)". http://repositorio.cepal .org/bitstream/handle/11362/25083/S9630177_en.pdf?sequence=1.

———. 2001. "The Efficacy of Caribbean Industrial Policy in the New Era of Globalisation". Issue Brief No. 5. http://www.cepal.org/portofspain/noticias/paginas/2/9792/eclacib5.pdf.

———. 2002. "The Effects of Globalization on CARICOM Caribbean Economies". Chapter 11 in *Globalization and Development*. http://repositorio.cepal.org/bitstream/handle/11362/2726/S2002903.pdf?sequence=2.

———. 2005. "The Cotonou Agreement Selected Issues, Effects and Implications for Caribbean Economies". http://www.eclac.cl/publicaciones/xml/1/23581/L.66.pdf.

———. 2007. "Report of the Rio Group Technical Meeting on the Treatment of Asymmetries in the Context of Regional Cooperation". http://repositorio.cepal.org/bitstream/handle/11362/36749/LCCARL126_en .pdf?sequence=1.

———. 2010. "Analysis of Extreme Events in the Caribbean 1990–2008". http://www.eclac.org/publicaciones /xml/3/39533/LCARL.254.pdf.

———. 2011. "Study on the Vulnerability and Resilience of Caribbean Small Island Developing States (SIDS)". http://www.eclac.cl/publicaciones/xml/4/45364/LCARL.354.pdf.

———. 2012. *The International Financial Crisis and Its Implications for Latin America and the Caribbean*. http://www.eclac.org/pses34/noticias/documentosdetrabajo/2/47752/2012-666-SES-34-DDR-2.pdf.

The Economist Intelligence Unit. 2013. "Democracy Index 2012: Democracy at a Standstill". A Report from the Economist Intelligence Unit. https://portoncv.gov.cv/dhub/porton.por_global.open_file?p_doc_id=1034.

Eichengreen, B., and D. Irwin. 1998. "The Role of History in Bilateral Trade Flows". In *The Regionalization of the World Economy*, edited by J. Frankel, 33–62. Chicago: University of Chicago Press.

El-Agraa, A.M. 1999. *Regional Integration: Experience, Theory, and Measurement*. London: Macmillan.

———. 2002. "The UTR versus CU Formation Analysis and Article XXIV". *Applied Economics Letters* 9 (9): 621–24.

El Comercio. 2010. "Chinese Citizen Fell When Was Going to Kill His Fourth Victim". http://elcomercio.pe /lima/498842/ noticia-ciudadano-chino-cayo-cuando-iba-matar-su-cuarta-victima_1.

Elkan, P.G. 1972. Industrial Protection in New Zealand 1952–1967. NZ Institute of Economic Research *Technical Memorandum No. 15*.

Ellis, E.R. 2012. "Chinese Organized Crime in Latin America". *PRISM* 4 (1): 65–77.

EU Strategy on Aid for Trade. 2007. "Adoption of an EU Strategy on Aid for Trade: Enhancing EU Support for Trade Related Needs in Developing Countries". http://register.consilium.europa.eu/doc/srv?l =EN&f=ST%2013070%202007%20INIT.

Euromonitor International. 2011. *Emerging Outbound Markets: Looking Ahead in Uncertain Times*. http:// www.euromonitor.com/emerging-outbound-markets-looking-ahead-in-uncertain-times/report.

Evans, D., M. Gasiorek, A. Ghoneim, M. Haynes-Prempeh, P. Holmes, L. Iacovone, K. Jackson, T. Iwanow, S. Robinson, and J. Rollo. 2006. "Assessing Regional Trade Agreements with Developing Countries: Shallow and Deep Integration, Trade, Productivity, and Economic Performance". University of Sussex. Dfid Project Number 04 5881. https://www.sussex.ac.uk/webteam/gateway/file.php?name=dfif-rta-report.pdf& site=261.

Falvey, R.E. 1981. "Commercial Policy and Intra-industry Trade". *Journal of International Economics* 11 (4): 495–511.

Falvey, R., and H. Kierzkowski. 1987. "Product Quality, Intra-industry Trade, Imperfect Competition". In *Protection and Competition in International Trade. Essays in Honour of W. M.Corden*, edited by H. Kierzkowki, 143–61. Oxford: Basil Blackwell.

Fanai, V., V. Jandhyala, and S. Joy. 2011. "Caribbean Community (CARICOM): A study of India's Trade and Investment Potential". *Occasional Paper*, No. 144, Export-Import Bank of India.

FAO. 2003. *Trade Reforms and Food Security: Conceptualizing the Linkages*. Food and Agriculture Organization of the United Nations, Rome 2003. ftp://ftp.fao.org/docrep/fao/005/y4671e/y4671e00.pdf.

FAO/WTO. 2002. *Assuring Food Safety and Quality: Guidelines for Strengthening National Food Control Systems*. Joint Food and Agriculture Organization of the United Nations and World Health Organization Publication. http://www.who.int/foodsafety/publications/capacity/en/Englsih_Guidelines_Food_control.pdf.

Faustino, H., and J.R. Silva. 2002. "The Intra-industry Trade between Portugal and Spain in the 90s: The Competitive Cluster". *European Review of Economics and Finance* 1 (2): 43–74.

Feldkircher, M., and I. Korhonen. 2012. "The Rise of China and Its Implications for Emerging Markets: Evidence from a GVAR Model". *Bank of Finland Discussion Papers* 20, Finland.

Fieser, E. 2011. "Why Is China Spending Billions in the Caribbean?" http://www.globalpost.com/dispatch/news/regions/americas/110325/china-caribbean-investment-tourism.

Flores, M. 2013. "Initiatives and Plans in Food and Nutrition Security in Integration Organizations in Latin America and the Caribbean 2013". Working Group Meeting 2025 Guatemala. http://www.ialcsh.org/file admin/templates/iniciativa/content/pdf/gt2025/2013/Regional_Initiatives_and_plans_in_fns_-_En.pdf.

Fontagné, L., and M. Freudenberg. 1997. "Intra-industry Trade: Methodological Issues Reconsidered". *CEPII Working Paper* 97/02, Centre D'Etudes Prospectives et D'Informationales, Paris.

Fontagne, L., D. Laborde, and C. Mitaritonna. 2011. "An Impact Study of the EU-ACP Economic Partnership Agreements (EPAs) in the Six ACP Regions". *Journal of African Economies* 20 (2): 179–216.

Fox, A., J. Francois, and P. Londono-Kent. 2003. "Measuring Border Crossing Costs and their Impact on Trade Flows: The United States-Mexican Trucking Case". GTAP resource No 1282. https://www.gtap.agecon.purdue.edu/resources/res_display.asp?RecordID=1282.

Francois, F.J., and M. Manchin. 2007. "Institutions, Infrastructure and Trade". Working Paper No. 224, Centro Studi Luca d'Agliano Development Studies. http://papers.ssrn.com/sol3/papers.cfm?abstract_id=964209.

Frankel, J., and A. Rose. 1997. "Is EMU More Justifiable Ex Post Than Ex Ante?" *European Economic Review* 41 (3–5): 753–760.

Frankel, J.A., E. Stein, and S.J. Wei. 1996. "Regional Trading Arrangements: Natural or Supernatural?" *American Economic Review* 86 (2): 52–56.

Freeman, R.B. 2008. "The New Global Labour Market". *Focus* 26 (1): 1–6. http://www.irp.wisc.edu/publications/focus/pdfs/foc261a.pdf.

Freund, C., and N. Rocha. 2010. "What Constrains Africa's Exports?" World Bank Policy Research Working Paper 5184. World Bank Economic Review. http://elibrary.worldbank.org/doi/pdf/10.1596/1813-9450-5184.

Fridell, G. 2010. "The Case against Cheap Bananas: Lessons from the EU Caribbean Banana Agreement". *Critical Sociology* 37 (3): 285–307.

Frundt, H.J. 2009. *Fair Bananas: Farmers, Workers, and Consumers Strive to Change an Industry*. Tucson: University of Arizona Press.

Fukao, K., H. Ishida, and K. Ito. 2003. "Vertical Intra-industry Trade and Foreign Direct Investment in East Asia". *Journal of the Japanese and International Economies* 17 (4): 468–506.

Gabszewicz, J.J., A. Shaked, J. Sutton, and J.F. Thisse. 1981. "International Trade in Differentiated Products". *International Economic Review* 22 (3): 527–534.

Garcia, S., and M. Smart. 2011. "The Regional Policy for Food and Nutrition Security". CARICOM View. http://www.caricom.org/jsp/communications/caricom_online_pubs/caricom_view_jul_2011.pdf.

Garrity, M., and L.A. Picard. 1996. *Policy Reform for Sustainable Development in the Caribbean*. Washington, DC: IOS Press.

Gasiorek, M., and L.A. Winters. 2004. "What Role for the EPAs for the Caribbean". *World Economy* 27 (9): 1336–62.

General Agreement on Tariffs and Trade (GATT). 1994. *The General Agreement on Tariffs and Trade, Part 1-Article I: General Most-Favoured-Nation Treatment*. World Trade Organization, Geneva. http://www.wto.org/english/docs_e/legal_e/gatt47_e.pdf.

Girvan, N. 2006. "Production Integration in the Caribbean: A Critical Perspective". In *Production Integration in Caricom*, edited by Denis Benn and Kenneth Hall. Kingston: Ian Randle.

———. 2009. "The CARICOM-Canada FTA: What's the Hurry?" http://www.normangirvan.info/wp-content/uploads/2009/03/the-caricom-canada-fta-whats-the-hurry.pdf.

———. 2010. "Caribbean Community: The Elusive Quest for Economic Integration". In *Growth and Development Strategies in the Caribbean. Barbados*, edited by F. Alleyne, D. Lewis-Bynoe and X. Archibald, 199–218 Bridgetown, Barbados: Caribbean Development Bank.

———. 2013a. "On the Left: CSME Based on Faulty Concept". http://www.nationnews.com/print/237244/.

———. 2013b. "Reinventing the CSME". Address to the Caribbean Association of Judicial Officers Third Biennial Conference Accra Beach Hotel, Bridgetown, Barbados. http://www.normangirvan.info/wp-content/uploads/2013/09/CAJO-ADDRESS-By-Girvan.pdf.

Glasgow, R. 2011. "Brazil and Caribbean Relations – What of Integration?" *Trinidad and Tobago Newsday*. http://newsday.co.tt/commentary/0,142889.html.

Glewwe, P., and G. Hall. 1998. "Are Some Groups More Vulnerable to Macroeconomic Shocks Than Others?" *Journal of Development Economics* 56 (1): 181–206.

Gomes, L. 2003. *The Economics and Ideology of Free Trade: A Historical Review*. Northampton, MA: Edward Elgar.

Goodison, P. 2007. "The ACP Experience of Preference Erosion in the Banana and Sugar Sectors and Possible Policy Responses to Assist in Adjusting to Trade Changes". Agricultural Trade and Sustainable Development Programme, International Centre for Trade and Sustainable Development. February.

Government of Antigua and Barbuda. 2012. "A Food and Nutrition Security Policy for Antigua and Barbuda", Report Prepared by The Government of Antigua And Barbuda with Technical Support from the Caribbean Food and Nutrition Institute (CFNI/PAHO/Who) The Food And Agriculture Organization (FAO). The Government of Antigua and Barbuda. http://www.zerohungerchallengelac.org/ab/doc/FoodNutritionSecurityPolicyAG.pdf.

Graham, E.M. 1996. "The (Not Wholly Satisfactory) State of the Theory of Foreign Direct Investment and the Multinational Enterprise". *Journal of International and Comparative Economics* 20 (2/3): 183–206.

Grant, R.J., M.C. Papadakis, and D.J. Richardson. 1993. "Global Trade Flows: Old Structures, New Issues, Empirical Evidence". In *Pacific Dynamism and the International Economic System*, edited by C.F. Bergsten, and M. Noland. Washington, DC: Institute for International Economics.

Gray, P., and Martin, P.J. 1980. "The Meaning and Measurement of Product Differentiation in International Trade". *Weltwirschaftliches Archiv* 116 (2): 322–29.

Greenaway, D. 1982. "Identifying the Gains from Pure Intra-industry Exchange". *Journal of Economic Studies* 9 (3): 40–54.

Greenaway, D., and C. Milner. 1984. "A Cross Section Analysis of Intra-industry Trade in the UK". *European Economic Review* 25 (3): 319–44.

———. 1986. *The Economics of Intra-industry Trade*. Oxford: Blackwell.

———. 2003. "A Grim REPA?" University of Nottingham Internationalization of Economic Policy Research Paper 3 (30).

———. 2006. "EU Preferential Trading Arrangements with the Caribbean: A Grim Regional Economic Partnership Agreements?" *Journal of Economic Integration* 21 (4): 657–80.

Grimwade, N. 2000. *International Trade: New Patterns of Trade, Production and Investment*. 2nd ed. London: Routledge.

Grubel, H.G., and P.J. Lloyd. 1975. *Intra-industry Trade: The Theory and Measurement of International Trade in Differentiated Products*. New York: Macmillan.

Guillaumont, P. 1999. "On the Economic Vulnerability of Low Income Countries". Typescript. CERDI-CNRS, Université d'Auvergne.

Gyimah-Brempong, K. 1991. "Export Instability and Economic Growth in Sub-Saharan Africa". *Economic Development and Cultural Change* 39 (4): 815–28.

Haiti Crime and Safety Report. 2012. *Haiti 2012 Crime and Safety Report*. https://www.osac.gov/pages/Content ReportPDF.aspx?cid=12152.

Haiti Crime and Safety Report. 2013. *Haiti 2013 Crime and Safety Report*. https://www.osac.gov/pages/Content ReportPDF.aspx?cid=14000.

Hale, D. 2006. *In the Balance: China's Unprecedented Growth and Implications for the Asia-Pacific*. Canberra: Australian Strategic Policy Institute.

Hall, K., and M. Chuck-A-Sang. 2012. *Regional Integration: Key to Caribbean Survival and Prosperity*. N.p.: Trafford.

Hamilton, A. 1791. "Report on Manufactures". In *The Papers of Alexander Hamilton*, edited by Harold C. Syrett et al., vol. 26, 1916–79. New York and London: Columbia University Press.

Hamilton, C., and P. Kniest. 1991. "Trade Liberalisation, Structural Adjustment and Intra-industry Trade: A Note". *Weltwirtschaftliches Archiv* 127 (2): 356–67.

Hausman, W.H., L.H. Lee, and U. Subramanian. 2013. "The Impact of Logistics Performance on Trade". *Production and Operations Management* 22 (2): 236–52.

Head, K. 2000. "The Gravity for Beginners". Material presented at Rethinking the Line: The Canada–US Border Conference, Vancouver, Canada.

Helpman, E. 1981. "International Trade in the Presence of Product Differentiation, Economies of Scale, and Monopolistic Competition". *Journal of International Economics* 11 (3): 305–40.

Helpman, E., and P.R. Krugman. 1985. *Market Structure and Foreign Trade*. Cambridge, MA: MIT Press.

Hirsch, S. 1976. "An International Trade and Investment Theory of the Firm". *Oxford Economic Papers* 28 (2): 258–70.

Hirschman, A. 1958. The *Strategy of Economic Development*. New Haven: Yale University Press.

Hoda, A. 2002. *Tariff Negotiations and Re-negotiations under the GATT and the WTO: Procedures and Practices*. Cambridge University Press.

Hoekman, B. 2007. "Doha, Development and Discrimination". *Pacific Economic Review* 12 (3): 267–92.

Holland, M. 2003. "20/20 Vision? The EU's Cotonou Partnership Agreement". *The Brown Journal of World Affairs* 9 (2): 161–75.

Hornbeck, F.J. 2008. *CARICOM: Challenges and Opportunities for Caribbean Economic Integration*. CRS Report for Congress. Washington, DC: Congressional Research Service. http://www.sice.oas.org/TPD /CAR_EU/Studies/CRSCARICOM_Challenges_e.pdf.

Horta, L. 2008. *Indian Investors Enter the Caribbean*, Yale Global. http://yaleglobal.yale.edu/content/indian -investors-enter-caribbean.

Hosein, R. 2008. "CARIFORUM-EU Economic Partnership Agreement: The Welfare Impact and Implications for Policy in Trinidad and Tobago". *Journal of Business, Finance and Economics in Emerging Economies* 3 (1): 217–48.

Hosein, R., M. Franklin, and S.C. Joseph. 2010. "The Caribbean Diaspora: An Untapped Resource for Impacting Economic Development through Investments in the Caribbean". Paper presented at the Eleventh Annual SALISE Conference, "Turmoil and Turbulence in Small Developing States: Going Beyond Survival". http://sta.uwi.edu/conferences/09/salises/documents/M%20Franklin.pdf.

Human Development Report (HDR). 2001. *Making New Technologies Work for Human Development*. United Nations Development Programme. New York: Oxford University Press. http://hdr.undp.org/sites/default /files/reports/262/hdr_2001_en.pdf.

Hummels, D. 2001. "Time as a Trade Barrier". Typescript, Purdue University. http://www.krannert.purdue .edu/faculty/hummelsd/research/time3b.pdf.

Hymer, S. 1976. *The International Operations of National Firms: A Study of Direct Foreign Investment*. Cambridge: MIT Press.

Igberaese, F.I., and E. Ndidi Diania. 2012. "Trade Openness (Globalization) and Economic Growth Question in Nigeria: An Empirical Evaluation". *The Business and Management Review* 3 (1): 138–44.

Ikenson, D. 2007. "While Doha Sleeps: Securing Economic Growth through Trade Facilitation". Centre for Trade Policy and Studies, Executive Summary.

Imani Development. 2005. "Capacity Building in Support of Preparation of Economic Partnership Agreement: Trinidad and Tobago". Final Report Prepared for Government of Trinidad and Tobago. Caribbean Knowledge Management Centre.

International Monetary Fund (IMF). 2011. "New Growth Drivers for Low-Income Countries: The Role of BRICS". Washington, DC: International Monetary Fund.

Iwanow, T., and C. Kirkpatrick. 2008. "Trade Facilitation and Manufactured Exports: Is Africa Different?" *World Development* 37 (6): 1039–50.

Jaumotte, F. 2004. "Labour Force Participation of Women: Empirical Evidence on the Role of Policy and Other Determinants in OECD Countries". OECD Economic Studies, No. 37. http://www.oecd.org/social /labour/34562935.pdf.

Jenkins, R., and E.D. Peters. 2006. "The Impact of China on Latin America and the Caribbean". Paper prepared with the support of DFID China Office.

Jhinkoo, J. 2013. "Highlighting the China-Caribbean Relationship". *Caribbean Centre for Money and Finance, Newsletter* 6 (10).

Johnston, J. 2013. "The Multilateral Debt Trap in Jamaica". Brief, Center for Economic and Policy Research. Washington, DC. http://www.cepr.net/documents/publications/jamaica-debt-2013-06.pdf.

Kaiteur News. 2012. "13 Chinese Found Working Illegally at Imbaimadai". http://www.kaieteurnewsonline. com/2012/07/19/13-chinese-found-working-illegally-at-imbaimadai/.

Kaly, U., and C. Pratt. 2000. "Environmental Vulnerability Index: Development and Provisional Indices and Profiles for Fiji, Samoa, Tuvalu and Vanuatu". Phase II report for NZODA. SOPAC Technical Report 306: 89.

Kamau, L.N. 2010. "The Impact of Regional Integration on Economic Growth: Empirical Evidence from COMESA, EAC and SADC Trade Blocs". *American Journal of Social and Management Sciences* 1 (2): 150–63.

Kaplinsky, R., A. Terheggen, and J.P. Tijaja. 2010. "What Happens When the Market Shifts to China? The Gabon Timber and the Thai Cassava Value Chains". *World Bank Policy Research* Working Paper No. 5206. Washington, DC: World Bank.

Karacaovali, B., and N. Limão. 2008. "The Clash of Liberalizations: Preferential vs. Multilateral Trade Liberalization in the European Union". *Journal of International Economics* 74 (2): 299–327.

Karingi, S., R. Lang, N. Oulmane, R. Perez, M.S. Jallab, and H.B. Hammouda. 2005. "Economic and Welfare Impacts of the EU-Africa Economic Partnership Agreements". ATCP Work in Progress No. 10.

Kendall, P. 2008. "Globalization, Trade Liberalization and the CSME: A Draft". Staff paper prepared for the CARIBANK. http://www.caribank.org/uploads/publications-reports/staff-papers/Globalisation%20and %20the%20CSMEA.pdf.

Keohane, D. 2011. "Wooing the Bric Tourist". http://blogs.ft.com/beyond-BRICS/2011/10/07/wooing-the-bric -tourist.

Kim, S., H. Lee, and I. Park. 2004. "Measuring the Impact of APEC Trade Facilitation: A Gravity Analysis". Paper presented in the Reunion of the Economic Committee of the APEC, Santiago, Chili, 30 September.

Kipe, S. 2003. "Everything But Arms, Declining Agricultural Exports from Least Developed Countries". USDA Foreign Agricultural Service, Global Agricultural Information Network Report No. E23149.

Kirichenko, K. 2011. "The Potential of the Russian Market for the Philippines". Tourism Marketing and Intelligence.

Krishna, P. 2003. "Are Regional Trading Partners 'Natural'?" *Journal of Political Economy* 111 (1): 202–26.

Krueger, A. 1999. "Free Trade Agreements as Protectionist Devices: Rules of Origin". In *Trade, Theory and Econometrics: Essays in Honor of John C. Chipman*, edited by J. Melvin, J. Moore, R. Riezmond, 91–102. London: Routledge.

Krugman, P. 1979. "Increasing Returns, Monopolistic Competition and International Trade". *Journal of International Economics* 9 (4): 469–479.

———. 1980. "Scale Economies, Product Differentiation, and the Pattern of Trade". *American Economic Review* 70 (5): 950–59.

———. 1984. "Import Protection as Export Promotion: International Competition in the Presence of Oligopoly and Economies of Scale". In *Monopolistic Competition and Product Differentiation and International Trade*, edited by H. Kierzkowski, 180–93. Oxford: Oxford University Press.

———. 1991 "The Move Toward Free Trade Zones". In *Policy Implications of Trade and Currency Zones, Proceedings of a Federal Reserve Bank of Kansas City symposium*, 7–41.

——— P. 1993. "Regionalism versus Multilateralism: Analytical Notes". In *New Dimension in Regional Integration*, edited by J. De Melo and A. Panagariya, 58–78. Cambridge: Cambridge University Press.

———, P. 1995. "Growing World Trade: Causes and Consequences". *Brooking Papers on Economic Activity* 1: 327–62.

Kwiatkowski, D., P.C.B. Phillips, P. Schmidt, and Y. Shin. 1992. "Testing the Null Hypothesis of Stationarity against the Alternative of a Unit Root: How Sure are We that Economic Time Series Have a Unit Root?" *Journal of Econometrics* 54 (1–3): 159–78.

Lall, S., and J. Weiss. 2005. "People's Republic of China's Competitive Threat to Latin America: An Analysis for 1990–2002". *Oxford Development Studies* 33 (2): 163–94.

Lancaster, K. 1966. "A New Approach to Consumer Theory". *Journal of Political Economy* 74 (2): 132–57.

———. 1979. *Variety, Equity, and Efficiency*. New York: Columbia University Press.

———. 1980. "Intra-industry Trade under Perfect Monopolistic Competition". *Journal of International Economics* 10 (2): 151–71.

LaRocque, I. 2013. "On the status of the Regional Integration Process and Vision for the Future of CARICOM". Distinguished Lecture, Port of Spain, Trinidad and Tobago. http://sta.uwi.edu/uwiToday/pdfs/AmbassadorIrwinLaRocque.pdf.

Lawrence, R.Z. 1996. *Regionalism, Multilateralism, and Deeper Integration*. Washington, DC: The Brookings Institution.

Lawrence, C., and P.T. Spiller. 1983. "Product Diversity, Economies of Scale and International Trade". *Quarterly Journal of Economics* 98 (1): 63–83.

Lewis, F.B. 2008. "Marginal Intra-industry Trade: The Case of Jamaica's Trade with CARICOM". *The International Trade Journal* 22 (4): 415–56.

Lewis, G.K. 1968. *The Growth of the Modern West Indies*. London: MacGibbon and Kee.

Lewis, V. 2008. "The Federation of the West Indies: Its Life and End – A Comment". Panel Discussion Sponsored by the Barbados Historical and Archaeological Society. Errol Barrow Centre, University of the West Indies, Cave Hill, Barbados.

Lewis, W.A. 1950. "The Industrialisation of the British West Indies". *Caribbean Economic Review* 2 (1): 1–61.

Limão, N. 2006. "Preferential Trade Agreements as Stumbling Blocks for Multilateral Trade Liberalization: Evidence for the US". *American Economic Review* 96 (3): 896–914.

Linder S.B., ed. 1961. *An Essay in Trade and Transformation*. New York: John Wiley and Sons Ltd.

Lipsey, R. 1960. "The Theory of Customs Unions: A General Survey". *Economic Journal* 70: 498–513.

Liu, T. 2006. "Empirical Study on the Impact of Regional Trade Agreements on Strengthening China's FDI". Refereed paper presented at the ACESA 2006 Emerging China: Internal Challenges and Global Implications, Victoria University, Melbourne. https://www.researchgate.net/publication/255579363_Empirical _study_on_the_impact_of_regional_trade_agreements_on_strengthening_China's_FDI.

Loertscher, R., and F. Wolter. 1980. "Determinants of Intra-industry Trade among Countries and across Industries". *Review of World Economics* 116: 280–93.

Logan, S. 2009. "Ecuador: China's Human Trafficking Backdoor to the USA". *ISN Security Watch*, February 2, 2009.

Lora, E. 2005. "Should Latin America Fear China?" RES Working Papers 4409, Inter-American Development Bank Research Department, Washington, DC.

Lord, D. 2011. *Regional Seminar: Economic Relations between the US and the Countries of Latin America and the Caribbean in the First Two Years of the Obama Administration: Assessment and Perspectives*. Venezuela: Caracas.

Lowe, D. 2002. *Dictionary of Transport and Logistics*. London, GBR: Kogan Page.

Lucas, R. 1988. "On the Mechanics of Economic Development". *Journal of Monetary Economics* 22 (1): 3–42.

Magee, C. 2004. "Trade Creation, Trade Diversion, and Endogenous Regionalism". Mimeo.

Majewski, J. 1987. "Third World Development: Foreign Aid or Free Trade?" http://www.fee.org/the_freeman /detail/third-world-development-foreign-aid-or-free-trade.

Mamoon, D., S. Paracha, H. Mughal, and A. Ayesha. 2011. "Pakistan's Trade Competitiveness and Complementarities in South Asia". Working paper, Pakistan Institute of Trade and Development.

Manchin, M. 2006. "Preference Utilisation and Tariff Reduction in EU Imports from ACP Countries". *World Economy* 29 (9): 1243–66.

Markin, T. 2006. "China's Growing Trade Surplus: Causes, Consequences and Policy Implications". Refereed paper presented at the ACESA2006 Emerging China: Internal Challenges and Global Implications, Victoria University, Melbourne, 13–14 July.

Markusen, J.R. 1995. "The Boundaries of Multinational Enterprises and the Theory of International Trade". *Journal of Economic Perspectives* 9 (2): 169–89.

Marrakesh Declaration. 2002. *Towards an Information Society for All*. http://www.itu.int/itunews/issue/2002 /09/marrakesh.html.

Martin, R., C. Gomes, A. Alleyne, and W. Phillips. 2013. "An Assessment of the Economic and Social Impacts of Climate Change on the Energy Sector in the Caribbean". Economic Commission for Latin America and the Caribbean. http://www.eclac.cl/portofspain/noticias/documentosdetrabajo/8/49708/Energy.pdf.

Mathews, A. 2003. "Regional Integration and Food Security in Developing Countries". Food and Agriculture Organization of the United Nations Rome. http://www.fao.org/docrep/004/y4793e/y4793e00.htm #Contents.

———. 2010. "Economic Partnership Agreements and Food Security". Institute for International Integration Studies. http://www.tcd.ie/iiis/documents/discussion/pdfs/iiisdp319.pdf.

McIntyre, A. 1971. "Caribbean Economic Community". In *Readings in the Political Economy of the Caribbean*, edited by Norman Girvan and Owen Jefferson. Kingston: New World Group.

McKay, A., C. Milner, and O. Morrissey. 2000. "The Trade and Welfare Effects of a Regional Economic Partnership Agreement". CREDIT Research Paper 00/08, University of Nottingham.

McLean, S. 2014. "CARICOM Regional Integration: A Critical Assessment and Recommendations for the Way Forward". Working Paper, United Nations Economic Commission for Latin America and the Caribbean, Port of Spain, Trinidad.

Menon, J., and P.B. Dixon. 1997. "Intra-industry versus Inter-industry Trade: Relevance for Adjustment Costs". *Weltwirtschaftliches Archiv* 133 (1): 164–9.

Millennium Development Goals. 2013. *Millennium Development Goals Report: We Can End Poverty 2015.* New York: United Nations. http://www.un.org/millenniumgoals/pdf/report-2013/mdg-report-2013-english .pdf.

Min-Hua, C. 2011. "China's Outbound Tourist". *EAI Background Brief No. 663.*

Ministry of Energy and Energy Affairs. 2014. http://www.energy.gov.tt/our-business/oil-and-gas-industry/. Ministry of Energy and Energy Affairs, Trinidad and Tobago.

Ministry of Planning and Sustainable Development. 2012. "Building Competitive Advantage-Strategic Business Clusters and Enablers". Ministry of Planning and Sustainable Development, Trinidad and Tobago. http://www.planning.gov.tt/sites/default/files/content/mediacentre/documents/Building-Competi tive-Advantage.pdf.

Mishra, P. 2006. "Emigration and Brain Drain: Evidence from the Caribbean". IMF Working Papers 06/25, International Monetary Fund, Washington, DC.

Mlachila, M. and M. Takebe. 2011. "FDI from BRICS to LICs". IMF Working Paper, International Monetary Fund, Washington, DC.

Mlachila, M., P. Cashin, and C. Haines. 2010. "Caribbean Bananas: The Macroeconomic Impact of Trade Preference Erosion" IMF Working Paper WP/10/59, International Monetary Fund, Washington, DC.

Mohan, P., and E. Strobl. 2012. "The Economic Impact of Hurricanes on Caribbean Agricultural Exports". Paper presented at the Fourteenth Annual Conference of the European Trade Study Group 2012, KU Leuven. http://www.etsg.org/ETSG2012/Programme/Papers/98.pdf.

Moïsé, E., S. Sorescu, D. Hummels and P. Minor. 2013. "Trade Facilitation Indicators: The Potential Impact of Trade Facilitation on Developing Countries' Trade". OECD Trade Policy Paper no. 144. http://www .oecd.org/officialdocuments/publicdisplaydocumentpdf/?cote=TAD/TC/WP%282012%2924/FINAL& docLanguage=En.

Montoute, A. 2011. "Emerging Players in the Caribbean: What Implications for the Caribbean, Their Relations with the EU and the ACP?" European Centre for Development and Policy Management, discussion paper no. 116.

Mordecai, J. 1968. *Federation of the West Indies*. Evanston: Northwestern University Press.

———. 1968. *The West Indies: The Federal Negotiations*. London: George Allen and Unwin.

Morton, K., and P. Tulloch. 1977. *Trade and Developing Countries*. Overseas Development Institute. London: Crook Helm.

Myers, G. 2004. *Banana Wars: The Price of Free Trade*. London: Zed Books.

Nadav, H., and E. Kleiman. 2008. "Middle East Integration and the Barcelona Process". *Agora Without Frontiers* 13 (4): 394–413.

Naudé, W.A., and M. Matthee. 2007. "The Significance of Transport in Africa". Policy brief published by WIDER, no. 5. http://i.unu.edu/media/unu.edu/publication/755/pb05-07-the-significance-of-transport -costs-in-africa-.pdf.

Nelson, R., and E. Phelps. 1966. "Investment in Humans, Technological Diffusion, and Economic Growth". *American Economic Review* 51 (2): 69–75.

Neven, D.J., and L. Phlips. 1985. "Discriminating Oligopolists and Common Markets". *Journal of Industrial Economics* 34 (2): 133–49.

Njinkeu, D., J.S. Wilson, B. Powo Fosso. 2008. "Expanding Trade within Africa: The Impact of Trade Facilitation". Policy Research Working Paper no. 4790. World Bank, Washington, DC. https://openknowledge .worldbank.org/bitstream/handle/10986/6297/WPS4790.pdf?sequence=1.

Norman, G., and J.H. Dunning. 1984. "Intra-industry Foreign Direct Investment: Its Rational and Trade Effects". *Review of World Economics* 120 (3): 522–40.

O'Neill, J., S. Lawson, and R. Purushothaman. 2004. "The BRICS and Global Markets: Crude, Cars and Capital". *CEO Confidential*, October.

OECD (Organisation for Economic Co-operation and Development). 2001. *Business Benefits of Trade Facilitation*. TD/TC/WP(2001)21 FINAL. Paris: OECD.

———. 2003. "Quantitative Assessment of the Benefits of Trade Facilitation". TD/TC/WP(2003)31/FINAL, unclassified. http://vi.unctad.org/files/studytour/strussia10/files/12%20April/Hoffmann%20UNCTAD/OECD_Quantitative%20Assessement%20TF%20benefits.pdf.

———. 2007. "Aid for Trade: Making it Effective". In *Development Co-operation Report 2006: Efforts and Policies of the Members of the Development Assistance Committee*. OECD Publishing. http://dx.doi.org/10.1787/dcr-2006-3-en.

OECD/WTO. 2009. "Aid for Trade at a Glance 2009: Maintaining Momentum". http://www.wto.org/english/res_e/booksp_e/aid4trade09_e.pdf.

Okaru-Bisant, V. 2009. "The Seven Deadly Sins of Aid". *African Business* 355: 46–48.

Orbie, J. 2007. "The European Union and the Commodity Debate: From Trade to Aid". *Review of African Political Economy* 34 (112): 297–311.

Palit, A. 2008. "India's Trade Deficit: Increasing Fast but Still Manageable". *Institute of South Asian Studies*, 7 July.

Palmer, C. 2011. "Eric Williams and the Challenge of Caribbean Leadership". Feature Presentation at the Dr. Eric Williams Memorial Lecture, Central Bank Auditorium, St Vincent and Street, Port of Spain. http://www.central-bank.org.tt/sites/default/files/Dr%20Colin%20Palmer%27s%20Presentation%20at%20the%20Eric%20Williams%20Memorial%20Lecture%20June%2020112.pdf.

Panagariya, A. 1999. "The Regionalism Debate: An Overview". *World Economy* 22 (4): 477–512.

Parimal, J. 2006. "Rethinking Policy Options for Export Earnings". *South Centre Research Papers* 5. http://www.southcentre.int/wp-content/uploads/2013/05/RP5_Rethinking-Policy-Options_EN.pdf.

Park, J.H. 1995. "The New Regionalism and Third World Development". *Journal of Developing Societies* 11 (1): 21–35.

Park, W.G., and D.C. Lippoldt. 2007. "Technology Transfer and the Economic Implications of the Strengthening of Intellectual Property Rights in Developing Countries". Working Paper 62, OECD Trade Policy.

Parsan, E. 2006. "Aid for Trade: A Caribbean Perspective". Caribbean Regional Negotiating Machinery.

Pemberton, C.M.S., A.L. Stewart, and P.K. Watson. 2005. "Improving the Effectiveness of the Market for Bonds in the CARICOM Sub Region". *Social and Economic Studies* 54 (4): 166–201.

Perera, M. 2000. "The Impact of Structural Adjustments on Women Workers in the Formal Textile and Garment Sector in Sri Lanka". In *Structural Adjustment, Gender and Employment: The Sri Lankan Experience*. Geneva: ILO.

Phillips, P.C.B., and P. Perron. 1988. "Testing for a Unit Root in Time Series Regression". *Biometrika* 75 (2): 335–46.

Pitigala, N. 2005. "What Does Regional Trade in South Asia Reveal about Future Trade Integration? Some Empirical Evidence". World Bank Policy Research Working Paper 3497, February.

Portugal-Perez, A., and J.S. Wilson. 2010. "Export Performance and Trade Facilitation Reform: Hard and Soft Infrastructure". Policy Research Working Paper No. 5261, World Bank. https://openknowledge.worldbank.org/bitstream/handle/10986/3748/WPS5261.pdf?sequence=1.

———. 2012. "Export Performance and Trade Facilitation Reform: Hard and Soft Infrastructure". *World Development* 40 (7): 1295–307.

Powell. A. 2013. "Rethinking Reforms: How Latin America and the Caribbean Can Escape Suppressed World Growth". Latin American and Caribbean Macroeconomic Report 2013, Inter-American Development Bank.

Rao, S. 2008. "The Rise of the BRICS: What Does It Mean for Canada?" Conference Board of Canada. http://www.conferenceboard.ca/e-library/abstract.aspx?did=2372.

Raynolds, L. 2003. "The Global Banana Trade". In *Banana Wars: Power, Production, and History in the Americas*, edited by S. Striffler and M. Moberg. Durham: Duke University Press.

Rippel, B. 2011. "Why Trade Facilitation Is Important for Africa". Africa Trade Policy Notes, Note #27 World Bank. http://siteresources.worldbank.org/INTAFRREGTOPTRADE/Resources/trade_facilitation_note_nov11.pdf.

Rittgers, R., and J. La Gra. 1991. *Profiles of Farmer Organizations in St Vincent and the Grenadines*. Kingstown, St Vincent: IICA Office in St Vincent and the Grenadines.

Rodrigue, J.P., and T. Notteboom. 2011. "The Panama Canal Expansion: Business as Usual or Game Changer?" Port Technology International, No. 51.

Romer, P.M. 1986. Increasing Returns and Long-Run Growth. *Journal of Political Economy* 94 (5): 1002–37.

Romer, P.M. 1990. "Endogenous Technological Change". *Journal of Political Economy* 98 (5): 71–102.

Salvatore, D. 1995. *International Economics*. 6th ed. Englewood Cliffs, NJ: Prentice-Hall.

Sánchez, R.J, G. Perez, S.S. Faundez, and G. Wilmsmeier. 2009. "Pricing in the Market of Waterborne Transport: The Dry Bulk Case". Working paper, IDB/World Bank, Washington, DC.

Sanders, R. 2008. "Settling the China Question: A Caribbean Challenge". http://www.bbc.co.uk/caribbean/news/story/2008/05/printable/080502_sanders0505.shtml.

———. 2011. "China's Presence in Dominica". http://www.caribbean360.com/index.php/opinion/389630.html#axzz1L32altQl.

———. 2013. "The Commonwealth and China: Upholding Values, Containing the Dragon?" *The Round Table: The Commonwealth Journal of International Affairs* 102 (3): 223–34.

Santi, E., S.B. Romdhane, and W. Shaw (eds.). 2012. *Unlocking North Africa's Potential through Regional Integration: Challenges and Opportunities*. Tunisia: The African Development Bank (AfDB) Group.

Sauvant, K.P. 2005. "New Sources of FDI: The BRICS, Outward FDI from Brazil, Russia, India and China". *Journal of World Investment and Trade* 6: 39–709.

Scherer, F.M. 1979. "The Welfare Economics of Product Variety: An Application to the Ready-to-Eat Cereals Industry". *Journal of Industrial Economics* 28 (2): 113–34.

Schiff, M. 1997. "Small is Beautiful: Preferential Trade Agreements and the Impact of Country Size, Market Share, and Smuggling". *Journal of Economic Integration* 12 (3): 359–87.

———. 2001. "Will the Real 'Natural Trading Partner' Please Stand Up?" *Journal of Economic Integration* 16 (2): 245–61.

Schott, J.J. 2001. *Prospects for Free Trade in the Americas*. Washington, DC: Institute for International Economics.

SELA. 2013. "Latin American and Caribbean relations with Russia, India, China and South Africa". IPEA. Regional meeting on Latin American and Caribbean economic relations with emerging countries (BRICS), Brasilia, Brazil.

Shaked, A., and J. Sutton. 1982. "'Relaxing Price Competition through Product Differentiation". *Review of Economic Studies* 49 (1): 3–14.

———. 1983. "Natural Oligopolies". *Econometrica* 51 (5): 1469–83.

———. 1984. "Natural Oligopolies and International Trade". In *Monopolistic Competition and International Trade*, edited by H. Kierzkowski. Oxford: Oxford University Press.

Shakur, S., and C. Nees. 2011. "An Application of the Natural Trading Partner Hypothesis to New Zealand-ASEAN Trade". *Economics Bulletin* 31 (4): 3077–88.

Sharma, K. 2004. "Horizontal and Vertical Intra-industry Trade in Australian Manufacturing: Does Liberalization Have Any Impact?" *Applied Economics* 36 (15): 1723–30.

Simpson, M.C., D. Scott, M. Harrison, N. Silver, E. O'Keeffe, S. Harrison, M. Taylor et al. 2010. *Quantification and Magnitude of Losses and Damages Resulting from the Impacts of Climate Change: Modelling the Transformational Impacts and Costs of Sea Level Rise in the Caribbean.* Barbados: United Nations Development Programme.

Smith, A. 1776. *An Inquiry into the Nature and Causes of the Wealth of Nations.* London: Methuen and Company.

Somma, E. 1994. "Intra-industry Trade in the European Computers Industry". *Weltwirtschaftliches Archiv* 130 (4): 784–99.

South Centre. 2006. *Elements for the Architecture of Aid for Trade.* Geneva: South Centre.

Spence, M. 1976. "Product Selection, Fixed Costs, and Monopolistic Competition". *Review of Economic Studies* 43 (2): 217–35.

Stoeckel, A., and B. Borrell. 2001. "Preferential Trade and Developing Countries: Bad Aid, Bad Trade". Rural Industries Research and Development Corporation (RIRDC), Publication No. 01/116, Canberra.

Stone, J.A., and H.H. Lee. 1995. "Determinants of Intra-industry Trade: A Longitudinal, Cross-Country Analysis". *Weltwirtschaftliches Archiv* 131 (1): 67–85.

Stoneman, R., J. Duke Pollard, and H. Inniss. 2012. "Turning Around CARICOM: Proposals to Restructure the Secretariat". Report prepared and submitted by Landell Mills Ltd to the CARICOM Secretariat. http://www.caricom.org/Restructuring%20the%20Secretariat%20-%20Landell%20Mills%20Final%20 Report.pdf.

Summers, L. 1991. "Regionalism and the World Trading System". Symposium sponsored by the Federal Reserve Bank of Kansas City, Policy Implications of Trade and Currency Zones.

Svensson, J. 2003. "Why Conditional Aid Does Not Work and What Can Be Done About It?" *Journal of Development Economics* 70 (2): 381–402.

Te Velde, D.W., and D. Bezemer. 2006. "Regional Integration and Foreign Direct Investment in Developing Countries". *Transnational Corporations* 15 (2): 41–70.

Te Velde, D.W., and S. Nair. 2006. "Foreign Direct Investment, Services Trade Negotiations and Development: The Case of Tourism in the Caribbean". *Development Policy Review* 24 (4): 437–54.

Thangavelu, S.M., and C. Findlay. 2011. "The Impact of Free Trade Agreements on Foreign Direct Investment in the Asia-Pasific Region". In *ASEAN+1 FTAs and Global Value Chains in East Asia*, edited by C. Findlay, 112–31. ERIA Research Project Report 2010–29. Jakarta: ERIA.

Thorpe, M., and Zhang, Z. 2005. "Study of the Measurement and Determinants of Intra-industry Trade in East Asia". *Asian Economic Journal* 19 (2): 231–47.

Tourism Intelligence International. 2011. "Prospects for the Emerging Travel Markets 2012". http://www .tourism-intelligence.com/pdf/NL%20Nov%202011%20(11).pdf.

Tsikata, M.V., P.E. Moreira, and P.C. Hamilton. 2009. *Accelerating Trade and Integration in the Caribbean: Policy Options for Sustained Growth, Job Creation, and Poverty Reduction.* Washington, DC:World Bank.

UN (United Nations). 2006. *Trade Facilitation Handbook Part II Technical Notes on Essential Trade Facilitation Measures.* New York and Geneva: United Nations. http://www.unctad.org/en/docs.

UNCTAD (United Nations Conference on Trade and Development). 2001. *E-Commerce and Development Report.* UNCTAD: Geneva.

———. 2013. "UNCTAD on Emerging Markets FDI Trends". http://cfi.co/africa/2013/03/unctad-on-emerging-markets-fdi-trends/.

UNECE (United Nations Economic Commission for Europe). 2002. "Trade Facilitation in a Global Trade Environment". Forum on Trade Facilitation, Committee for Trade, Industry and Enterprise Development, TRADE/2002/21, para. 43, p. 15. 21 March.

———. 2008. *Guidebook on Promoting Good Governance in Public-Private Partnership.* New York: United Nations.

UNIDO (United Nations Industrial Development Organization). 2012. "Structural Change, Poverty Reduction and Industrial Policy in the BRICS". Vienna. http://www10.iadb.org/intal/intalcdi/PE/2013/10846 .pdf.

UNWTO (World Tourism Organization). 2011. *UNWTO Tourism Highlights.* http://mkt.unwto.org/sites/all /files/docpdf/unwtohighlights11enhr.pdf.

———. 2013. "A Solid Performance during the Northern Summer Peak Season". *UNWTO World Tourism Barometer* 11 (October). http://dtxtq4w60xqpw.cloudfront.net/sites/all/files/pdf/unwto_barom13_05 _oct_excerpt_0.pdf.

Van Genderen-Naar, J. 2012. "The CARIFORUM-EU EPA: Five Years Later". A Presentation to the ACP-EU Joint Parliamentary Assembly Paramaribo, Suriname.

Veeramani, C. 2001. "India's Intra-industry Trade Under Economic Liberalization: Trends and Country Specific Factors". Centre for Development Studies, Trivendrum Working Papers 313, Centre for Development Studies, Trivendrum, India.

Venables, A.J. 1984. *International Trade in Identical Commodities: Cournot Equilibrium with Free Entry.* London: Centre for Economic Policy Research, CEPR Discussion Papers, No. 9.

Viet, C.N. 2015. "The Impact of Trade Facilitation on Poverty and Inequality: Evidence from Low- and Middle-Income Countries". *Journal of International Trade and Economic Development: An International and Comparative Review* 24 (3): 315–40.1–26.

Viner, J. 1950. *The Customs Union Issue.* New York: Carnegie Endowment for International Peace.

Viswanathan, R. 2007. *Caribbean: A Place in the Sun for Indian Business.* http://www.thehindubusinessline. com/todays-paper/tp-opinion/caribbean-a-place-in-the-sun-for-indian-business/article1656150.ece.

Warner, B. 2012. "Caribbean Integration: Lessons for the Pacific?" Development Policy Centre, Australian National University. http://devpolicy.anu.edu.au/pdf/papers/DP-25-Caribbean-integration-lessons-for -the-Pacific.pdf.

Watkins, E. 2011. "GDF Suez, CIC Agree on €2.9 Billion E&P Deal". http://www.ogj.com/articles.

Wharton, C. 2009. "The Future of CARICOM Trade Relations with the United States and Canada: A Review of CBI and CARIBCAN and Prospects for Future Trade Agreements". Report prepared for the Caribbean Policy Development Centre Workshop on Canada-CARICOM Free Trade Negotiations. http://www .normangirvan.info/wp-content/uploads/2009/01/carlos-wharton-canada-fta.pdf.

Welo, T. 2011. "Assessing the Chinese Competitive Threat to the Industrials Sector". Leadership Series, Market Research, Pyramis Global Advisors.

West Indian Commission. 1992. *Time for Action: The Report of the West Indian Commission, West Indian Commission, Black Rock.* Barbados: Caribbean Development Bank.

Williams, E. 1946. *Education in the British West Indies.* Port of Spain: Guardian Commercial Printery.

———. 1966. *Capitalism and Slavery.* New York: Capricorn.

Williams, O.H., and R. Darius. 1999. "Bananas, The WTO and Adjustment Initiatives in the Eastern Caribbean Central Bank Area". ECCB.

Wilson, D., and R. Dragusanu. 2008. "The Expanding Middle: The Exploding World Middle Class and Falling Global Inequality". *Global Economics Paper,* 170, Goldman Sachs, New York.

Wilson, D., and R. Purushothaman. 2003. "Dreaming with BRICS: The Path to 2050". *Global Economics Paper No. 99.* New York: Goldman Sachs.

Wilson, J.S., C.L. Mann, and T. Otsuki. 2003. "Trade Facilitation and Economic Development: Measuring the Impact". World Bank Working Paper 2988, Washington, DC.

———. 2004. "Assessing the Potential Benefit of Trade Facilitation: A Global Perspective". World Bank Working Paper 3224, Washington, DC.

Wilson, S.J., C. Mann, P.Y. Woo, N. Assanie, and I. Choi. 2002. "Trade Facilitation: A Development Perspective in the Asia Pacific Region". http://siteresources.worldbank.org/INTRES/Resources/20929_APEC_TF _Report_Final.pdf.

Wilson, J.S., and T. Otsuki. 2007. "Regional Integration in South Asia: What Role for Trade Facilitation?" Policy Research Working Paper no. 4423. World Bank, Washington, DC. http://www-wds.worldbank .org/servlet/WDSContentServer/WDSP/IB/2007/12/03/000158349_20071203151741/Rendered/PDF /wps4423.pdf.

Wonnacott, P., and M. Lutz. 1989. "Is There a Case for Free Trade Areas?" In *Free Trade Areas and US Trade Policy*, edited by J. Schott, 59–84. Washington, DC: Institute for International Economics.

World Bank. 2005. "A Time to Choose: Caribbean Development in the 21st Century". Caribbean Country Management Unit, Poverty Reduction and Economic Management Unit, Latin America and the Caribbean Region, Washington, DC.

———. 2010. *Doing Business 2011: Making a Difference for Entrepreneurs*. Washington, DC: World Bank.

———. 2013. "In Grenada, Nutmeg Heads Up an Economic Revolution". http://www.worldbank.org/en/news /feature/2013/12/02/grenada-oecs-caribbean-smallholder-farmers-economy-agriculture.

WTO. 2001. Ministerial Declaration, Doha 4th Ministerial, WT/MIN(01)/DEC/1, 20 November, World Trade Organization. http://www.wto.org/english/thewto_e/minist_e/min01_e/mindecl_e.htm.

———. 2006. "Aid for Trade Task Force: Recommendations of the Task Force on Aid for Trade". WT/AFT/, 27 July, World Trade Organization. http://aric.adb.org/aid-for-trade-asia/pdf/WT%20AFT%201.pdf.

WTO Secretariat. 2011. *Market Access Division*. Geneva: World Trade Organization. http://www.wto.org /english/thewto_e/secre_e/div_e.htm.

Yeboah, O., C. Naanwaab, S. Shaik, and A.S. Akuffo. 2012. "Effects of Trade Openness on Economic Growth: The Case of African Countries". Paper presented at the *Annual Meeting of Southern Agricultural Economics Association*, Birmingham, AL, 4–7 February.

Yildiz, T. 2014. *Business Logistics: Theoretical and Practical Perspectives with Analyses*. Create Space Independent Publishing Platform.

Yoshino, Y. 2008. "Domestic Constraints, Firm Characteristics, and Geographical Diversification of Firm-Level Manufacturing Exports in Africa". Policy Research Working Paper No. 4575, World Bank. March.

Zaki, C. 2010. "Towards an Explicit Modeling of Trade Facilitation in CGE Models: Evidence from Egypt". ERF Working Paper 515. April.

Zouhon-Bi, S.G., and L. Nielsen. 2007. "ECOWAS: Fiscal Revenue Implications of the Prospective Economic Partnership Agreement with the EU". Africa Region Working Paper Series Number 103, World Bank.

Zsolt, D. 2012. "Real Effective Exchange Rates for 178 Countries: A New Database". Working Paper 2010/06, Bruegel; Discussion Paper 2012/10, Research Centre for Economic and Regional Studies, Hungarian Academy of Sciences, Working Paper 2012–01. Department of Mathematical Economics and Economic Analysis, Corvinus University of Budapest.

Websites

Caribbean Community Secretariat: http://www.caricom.org/

Caribbean Hurricane Network (2011): http://stormcarib.com/climatology

Caribbean Media Corporation (2009): http://www.cmccaribbean.com/

CARICOM (2011): http://www.fao.org/fileadmin/templates/righttofood/documents/project_m/caricom /CARICOMRegionalFoodandNutritionSecurityActionPlan-Oct2011.pdf

Central Statistical Office: www.cso.gov.tt/

CXC Headquarters (2013): http://www.cxc.org/

FAOstat (2013), FAO Statistical Yearbook (2013): http://faostat.fao.org/default.aspx

Food and Agriculture Organization of the United Nations Database (FAO) (2014): http://www.fao.org/statis tics/en/

Food Security Portal (2013): http://www.foodsecurityportal.org/

International Financial Statistics Database (IFS) (2014): http://elibrary-data.imf.org/FindDataReports.aspx?d=33061&e=169393

International Monetary Fund (IMF) (2014): http://www.imf.org/external/data.htm

National Oceanic and Atmospheric Administration (2014): http://www.nhc.noaa.gov

Trade Map (2014): http://www.trademap.org/

UNCTAD (2013): http://unctad.org/en/pages/DIAE/World%20Investment%20Report/WIR-Series.aspx

United Nations Commodity Trade Database (UNCOMTRADE) (2014): http://comtrade.un.org/db/dq/QuickQuery.aspx

United Nations Conference on Trade and Development (UNCTAD) (2014): http://unctadstat.unctad.org/ReportFolders/reportFolders.aspx

United Nations Economic Commission for Latin America and the Caribbean (ECLAC) (2014): http://estadisticas.cepal.org/cepalstat/WEB_CEPALSTAT/estadisticasIndicadores.asp?idioma=i

World Development Indicators (2014): http://data.worldbank.org/indicator/all

World Integrated Trade Solution (WITS) (2014): https://wits.worldbank.org/WITS/WITS/Restricted/Login.aspx

World Trade Organization Legal Texts: http://www.wto.org/english/docs_e/legal_e/final_e.htm

Index